GREAT
SCOTTISH LIVES

Published by Times Books
An imprint of HarperCollins Publishers
Westerhill Road, Bishopbriggs,
Glasgow. G64 2QT
www.harpercollins.co.uk
times.books@harpercollins.co.uk

First published 2017

ISBN 978-0-00-822895-8

10 9 8 7 6 5 4 3 2 1

The Times is a registered trademark of Times Newspapers Ltd

The contents of this publication are believed correct at the time of printing.
Nevertheless the publisher can accept no responsibility for errors or omissions,
changes in the detail given or for any expense or loss thereby caused.

HarperCollins does not warrant that any website mentioned in this title will
be provided uninterrupted, that any website will be error free, that defects will be
corrected, or that the website or the server that makes it available are free of
viruses or bugs. For full terms and conditions please refer to the site terms
provided on the website.

A catalogue record for this book is available from the British Library

Printed and bound by CPI Group (UK) Ltd, Croydon, CR0 4YY

Cover Image: Sir Alexander Fleming
© Prisma/UIG/Getty Images

MIX
Paper from
responsible sources
FSC™ C007454

This book is produced from independently certified FSC™ paper
to ensure responsible forest management.

For more information visit: www.harpercollins.co.uk/green

THE TIMES

GREAT SCOTTISH LIVES

OBITUARIES OF SCOTLAND'S FINEST

EDITED BY MAGNUS LINKLATER

Magnus Linklater is the former Scotland editor of *The Times* and
former editor of *The Scotsman.* He is the author of several books
on current affairs and Scottish history.

TIMES BOOKS

CONTENTS

Introduction 6

INTRODUCTION

Magnus Linklater

FROM SIR WALTER SCOTT in the nineteenth century to Tam Dalyell in the twenty-first, this collection of obituaries from *The Times* is a 200-year chronicle of great lives that have left their mark on the history and character of the Scottish nation. Politicians, artists, inventors, explorers, soldiers, academics, philosophers and troublemakers – these are men and women who have, in their different ways, broken the mould of their time, challenged its conventions and occasionally outraged them.

They cover a period that ranges from the age of the Enlightenment to the post devolution era – the building of empire, the industrial revolution, through two world wars and the economic chaos between them – culminating in the creation of a new Scottish Parliament and the legacy it has fashioned. Through all of these, Scots were often at the centre of great events, and their obituaries are, to an extent, a commentary on the times in which they lived.

This volume should not be read as a coherent history, nor is it necessarily a carefully balanced selection. These are lives judged, not from the vantage point of our time, but from the standpoint of their own time. That is its merit, and occasionally its idiosyncrasy. Great figures who seem to us now to loom large are sometimes dismissed with little more than a footnote; others are accorded page upon page of eulogy, which may seem, in the modern era, excessive. It is striking, for instance, that the Scottish colourists – artists like Peploe, Cadell or Fergusson, to say nothing of the designer and architect Charles Rennie Mackintosh, whose work is so valued today – were viewed by *The Times*, on their deaths, as worthy of only a few sketchy paragraphs. That may reflect a London perspective, but more likely the fact that their reputations have grown more in the last 50 years than during their own lifetimes. Statesmen and prime ministers, on the other hand, are chronicled with a depth of detail that amount almost to a political history of the age in which they lived.

There has had to be some editing. The death of the writer and philosopher Thomas Carlyle, for instance, prompted an obituary in *The Times* of more than 9,000 words, amounting almost to a full-scale critical biography. Those were the days when long columns of small print, uninterrupted by pictures, were routine. Running Carlyle's obituary at full length – to say nothing of others which frequently amounted to 5,000 words or more – would have required a volume three times the size of this one. Instead I have tried to keep the flavour of the tributes paid, rather than including every last paragraph.

There has had to be selection, of course, and I am open to criticism for the lives that have been omitted. Legitimate questions will be asked about why there is no mention here of the writer Lewis Grassic Gibbon, whose *Sunset Song* is on every respectable reading list; Walter Elliot, who created the modern Scottish Office; Sir William Lithgow, last of the great shipbuilders; the debonair Hollywood actor David Niven; Ewan MacColl, pioneering folksinger; the ballet director Kenneth Macmillan; the iconoclast journalist Sir John Junor – the list goes on.

There are two explanations. The first is that this is not, and was never intended as, a definitive collection; great Scottish lives have been well documented elsewhere in encyclopedias and biographies, researched, brought up to date, and accorded their proper place in history; a collection of contemporary obituaries makes no claim to replace them. The second is that, where there is a judgment to be made, I have favoured the well-written and the colourful over the dutiful and the worthy. Thus the Marquis of Queensberry – "a man of strong character, but unfortunately also of ill-balanced mind" – is included, not just because he formulated the Queensberry rules of boxing, but because the obituary itself is an entertaining account of an eccentric character, and, to an extent, a commentary on the society of his day. The life of Sir Colin Campbell – he of the "thin red line" at Balaclava – is a remarkable narrative of military exploits, but is also invested with an eloquence which is very much of its time. Thus: "he did not conceal his ill opinion of the Indian army, and considered the Sepoys as the mere bamboo of the lance, which was valueless unless it were tipped with the steel of British infantry."

The remarkable pioneer of nursing medicine Dr Elsie Inglis is lovingly described: "Her splendid organising capacity, her skill, and her absolute disregard of her own comfort ... drew forth the love and admiration of the whole Serbian people, which they were not slow to express."

I favoured the Labour rebel James Maxton, "tall, spare, pale, and almost cadaverous-looking, with piercing eyes and long black hair, a lock of which fell at emotional moments over the right ear ..." as well as Bill Shankly, the football manager, an "old-fashioned half-back [who] was said to have run with his palms turned out like a sailing ship striving for extra help from the wind."

No one could argue that the Russian-Scottish writer Eugenie Fraser changed history, but who, on the other hand, could resist an obituary that begins: "Ninety-six years ago, a baby girl, half Scottish, half Russian, wrapped in furs against the bitter cold of an Archangel winter, was taken by sledge across the River Dvina to the house of a very old lady [who] had lived long enough to remember seeing Napoleon's troops fleeing down the roads of Smolensk and to have had a son killed in the Crimean War."

There are too few women here, again a reflection of the age in which these obituaries were compiled; but those who are included are memorable: Katharine, Duchess of Atholl, the "red" duchess, and one of the first women to hold ministerial office: a "tiny, upright, hawk-like figure ... poised with an innate dignity that was reinforced by the greatness of her moral stature." Mary Somerville, the first woman controller at the BBC, of whom her obituarist wrote: "When troubles arose, no staff were ever better defended in public, though in private they were often told pretty frankly where their work had fallen short." Or Margo MacDonald, the SNP's "blonde bombshell," who once said: "I don't choose my enemies; they choose me."

Times obituaries have always been anonymous – and remain so today – an important tradition which allows judgment to be made about a subject's character without the accusation that the writer's personal prejudices are being deployed. Whoever it was who wrote of Sir Henry Campbell-Bannerman that "it is impossible for the impartial historian not to blame [him] both for the unwisdom of his initial policy [on South Africa], and for the costly injudiciousness of some of his phrases" was able to do so without risking a lengthy correspondence on the objectivity of the writer – or lack of it. Behind each obituary lies the opinion of *The Times* rather than the individual.

Overall, however, the impression that emerges from this pantheon of Scottish characters is one of the rich contribution they made to human society. Those who wished to undermine it are greatly outnumbered by those who reinforced it – the bridge-builders, the architects of civic programmes, the great military commanders, the explorers and the inventors, many of whom made robust comments on the world in which they lived. Alexander Graham Bell, for instance, was scathing about government interference in the commercial exploitation of the telephone which he had invented: "I am afraid that the comparatively low state of efficiency in this country [the UK] as compared with our system in the United States must be attributed to Government ownership. Government ownership aims at cheapness, and cheapness does not necessarily mean efficiency." His comments are as relevant today as they were then.

Here then is a cross-section of history, told by those who are offering a contemporary view of its most significant characters. However far in advance of their demise these accounts may have been composed, there is a frankness of view which rarely emerges from more considered opinions; and where that view is warmly admiring, then the expression of it comes across with an immediacy which is refreshing.

The death of Sir Walter Scott, the first name to appear here, provoked an outburst of affection which comes down to us across the years, its spontaneity undiminished by time:

"Of a man so universally known and admired, of a writer, who by works of imagination, both in prose and verse, has added so much to the stores of intellectual instruction and delight – of an author who, in his own time, has compelled, by the force of his genius, and the extent of his literary benefactions, a unanimity of grateful applause which generally only death (the destroyer of envy) can ensure – it would be superfluous, and perhaps impertinent in us, to speak ..."

It is often said that journalism is the first draft of history. If that is the case, then surely the obituary is the first sketch of those who shaped it.

SIR WALTER SCOTT

'The greatest genius and most popular writer of his age'

25 SEPTEMBER 1832

SIR WALTER SCOTT, the greatest genius and most popular writer of his nation and his age, expired at Abbotsford on Friday last – a man, not more admired or admirable for the inventive powers of his mind than beloved and respected for the kindness of his disposition and the manly simplicity of his character. After an absence of some months in Italy and other parts of the continent, which, it was fondly but vainly imagined by his friends, might restore his health – broken down by excess of mental labour – he returned about Midsummer last, with an instinct of patriotism, to lay his bones in his native land. On his way home, in descending the Rhine to embark for England, he suffered at Nimeguen, in Holland, a third time, a paralytic attack, which, but for the surgical skill and promptitude of his servant, must have been instantly fatal – and from which he never recovered sufficiently to be sensible of that zealous admiration with which a grateful country was desirous of honouring his name, and paying homage to his setting star.

It is almost needless to say, that though the death of this illustrious man has been long expected, no loss could be more deeply felt over the whole republic of letters, and none could excite more general or unmixed regret. His name and works are not only British but European – not only European but universal; for wherever there is a reading public – a literature – or a printing press, in any part of the world, Sir Walter must be regarded as a familiar household word, and gratefully admitted as a contributor to intellectual enjoyment.

Of a man so universally known and admired – of a writer, who by works of imagination, both in prose and verse, has added so much to the stores of intellectual instruction and delight – of an author who, in his own time, has compelled, by the force of his genius, and the extent of his literary benefactions, a unanimity of grateful applause which generally only death (the destroyer of envy) can ensure – it would be superfluous, and perhaps impertinent in us, to speak in this short announcement, as critics, or biographers. The illustrious author of *Waverley*, and twenty other historical romances displaying the spirit of *Waverley*, of *The Lay of the Last Minstrel*, and six other greater lays than ever ancient minstrel sung – has latterly been exempted from the proverbial injustice inflicted on contemporary genius; and has been able to realise the most ample visions of posthumous celebrity. He does not, therefore, require any vindication of his fame, or any display of his literary merits, at our hands.

Our object in alluding to his death and character is of a higher land than that of literary criticism. Our object is to speak of him as a tolerant, candid, and kind-hearted member of that great republic of letters, of which he would willingly have been elected President had that republic acquired a settled organisation – to recommend his personal simplicity of character and total absence of literary affectation, to the imitation of those who, though they cannot pretend to his genius, think themselves exempted – on the ground of their inferior powers – from the common restraints and customs of society, to which he always submitted – and to bestow its due need of praise on that noble and manly spirit of independence which led him to the immense labours of the last years of his life, that he might disengage himself from debts and difficulties under which a less resolute mind must have sunk, or from which a less honest one would have sought relief by leaning on those friends and patrons who would have been proud to have offered their aid. The republication of his novels, with notes and illustrations, was perhaps one of the greatest literary enterprises known in this country; and the success of the work, if it has not enabled him to leave much to his children, has at least satisfied the demands of his creditors. His indifference to the attacks of envy and malignity with which he was assailed in the earlier part of his career was as remarkable as his candid appreciation of the merits, and his zealous desire to promote the fame, of his friends. The garland which he threw on the grave of Byron, and the zeal with which be defended his personal character, when it evinced some courage to rebut the charges brought against his memory, will never be forgotten by the admirers of misguided genius.

Though Sir Walter Scott was an unflinching Tory all his life, his politics never degenerated into faction, nor did they ever interfere with his literary candour or his private friendships. Indeed, his party principles seemed to have been rather formed from his early connexions or his poetical predilections, than adopted for ambitious objects or even selected after mature examination.

But one distinguishing characteristic of this great author's mind and feelings deserves, even in the shortest allusion to his memory, to be mentioned as having given a colour to all his works – we mean his love of country – his devoted attachment to the land of his birth, and the scenes of his youth – his warm sympathy in every thing that interested his nation, and the unceasing application of his industry and imagination to illustrate its history or to celebrate its exploits. From the *Lay of the Last Minstrel*, or the border ballads, to the last lines which he wrote, he showed a complete and entire devotion to his country. His works, both of poetry and prose, are impregnated with this feeling, and are marked by the celebration of successive portions of its wild scenery, or of separate periods of its romantic annals. Hence his friends could often trace his residence, or the course of his reading, for periods anterior to the publication of his most popular works, in the pages of his glowing narrative or graphic description. Hence the *Lady of the Lake* sent crowds of visitors to the mountains of Scotland, who would never have thought of such a pilgrimage unless led by the desire to compare the scenery with the poem. No poet or author since the days of Homer was ever so completely a domestic observer, or a national writer, and probably none has ever conferred more lasting celebrity on the scenes which he describes. The border wars – the lawless violence of the Highland clans – the romantic superstitions of the dark ages, with their lingering remains in Scotland, the state of manners at every period of his country's annals, the scene of any remarkable event are all to be found in his pages, and scarcely a mountain or promontory "rears its head unsung" from Tweed to John o'Groat's.

The patriotism of Sir Walter Scott, though sometimes tinged with party, was always as warm as such poetical feelings could render it. Hence two or three of the most spirited of his lyrical pieces were written on the threatened invasion by Napoleon, and we need not cite his enthusiastic sympathy in the fame of his country, evinced in *Waterloo* and *Don Roderick*. His mind disdained that pretended enlargement, but real narrowness of spirit, which affects to consider all lands as alike, and would be ashamed to show any predilections for home.

But, as our object is not either criticism or biography, we must conclude these hasty remarks by referring for an account of Sir Walter Scott's publications to the short article which we have extracted from the *Globe*. He had abandoned for nearly 20 years the cultivation of poetry, in which he was first distinguished, for the composition of his historical novels: he had left thus a most respectable property on Parnassus to descend into a more fertile spot below. Thence he has given to the world twenty works which will communicate delight, and extend his fame to all ages. The enchanter's wand is now broken, and his "magic garment plucked off," but the spirits which this *Prospero* of romance has "called up," and placed in these noble productions, will last as long as the language in which they express themselves.

THOMAS TELFORD

Engineer whose roads, bridges and canals opened up the Highlands

4 September 1834

WE ANNOUNCE WITH feelings of deep regret, the death of this eminent and excellent individual, which took place at 5 o'clock yesterday afternoon at his house in Abingdon street.

Mr. Telford was in the 79th year of his age. The immediate cause of his death was a repetition of severe bilious attacks to which he had for some years been subject. He was a native of Langholm, in Dumfriesshire, which he left at an early age. His gradual rise from the stonemasons' and builders' yard to the top of his profession in his own country, or, believe we may say, in the world, is to be ascribed not more to his genius, his consummate ability, and persevering industry, than to his plain, honest, straightforward dealing, and the integrity and candour which marked his character throughout life.

Mr. Telford had been for some time past by degree retiring from professional business, to enable him the better to "adjust his mantle." He has of late chiefly employed his time writing a detailed account of the principal works which he planned, and lived to see executed; and it is a singular and fortunate circumstance that the corrected manuscript of his work was only completed by his clerk, under his direction, two or three days ago. His works are so numerous all over the island, that there is hardly a county in England, Wales, or Scotland, in which they may not be pointed out. The Menai and Conway bridges, the Caledonian canal, the St. Katherine Docks, the Holyhead roads and bridges, the Highland roads and bridges, the Chirke and Pont-y-ciallte Aqueducts, the canals in Salop, and great works in that county, of which he was surveyor for more than half a century, are some of the traits of his genius which occur to us and which will immortalise the name of Thomas Telford.

We have access to know that he was inclined to set a higher value on the success which has attended his exertions for improving the great communication from London to Holyhead, the alterations of the line of the road, its smoothness, and the excellence of the bridges than on the success of any other work he executed; but it seems difficult to draw a line of distinction with anything like nicety of discrimination as to the degree of credit to which an engineer is entitled for ingenuity to plan, and the ability to execute magnificent and puzzling improvements on the public communications of a great country. The Menai bridge will probably be regarded by the public as the imperishable monument of Mr. Telford's fame. This bridge over the Bangor ferry, connecting the counties of Carnarvon and Anglesea, partly of stone and partly of iron, on the suspension principle, consists of seven stone arches, exceeding in magnitude every work of the kind in the world. They connect the land with the two main piers, which rise 53 feet above the level of the road, over the top of which the chains are suspended, each chain being 1,714 feet from the fastenings in the rock. The first three-masted vessel passed under the bridge in 1826. Her topmasts were nearly as high as a frigate but they cleared 12 feet and a half below the centre of the roadway. The suspending power of the chains was calculated at 2,016 tons; the total weight of each chain, 12½ tons.

The Caledonian canal is another of Mr. Telford's splendid work in constructing every part of which, though prodigious difficulties were to be surmounted, he was successful. But the individuals in high station now travelling in the most remote part of the island, from Inverness to Dunrobin Castle or from thence to Thurso, the most distant town in the north of Scotland, will there if we are not mistaken, find proofs of the exertion of Mr. Telford's professional talent equal to any that appear in any other quarter of Britain. The road from Inverness to the county of Sutherland, and through Caithness, made, not only so far as respects its construction, but its direction under Mr. Telford's orders, is superior in point of line and smoothness to any part of the road of equal continuous length between London and Inverness. This is a remarkable fact, which, from the great difficulties he had to overcome in passing through a rugged, hilly and mountainous district, incontrovertibly establishes his great skill in the engineering department, as well as in the construction of great public communications.

These great and useful works do not, however, more entitle the name of Telford to gratitude of his country, than his sterling worth in private life. His easiness of access and the playfulness of his disposition, even to the close of life, endear his memory to his many private friends.

* * *

SIR JOHN SINCLAIR, BART.

Agricultural reformer whose 'Statistical Account' collected details of every parish in North Britain

6 JANUARY 1836

SIR JOHN SINCLAIR was born at Thurso Castle, in the county of Caithness, on the 10th of May, 1754. He received the rudiments of a classical education at the High School of Edinburgh, and having carried on his studies at the Universities of Edinburgh and Glasgow, he completed them at Oxford. At Glasgow he was a favourite pupil of the celebrated Adam Smith, who admitted him to familiar intercourse, and from whose conversation, as well as lectures, he imbibed a taste for political inquiries.

On the two first occasions which called forth his talents as a writer, his object was to rouse the sinking energies of the country in times of great disaster and embarrassment. At the close of the American war, the suspicion rapidly gained ground, under the influence of Dr. Price and Lord Stair, that the finances of the country were embarrassed beyond recovery, and that a national bankruptcy was inevitable. In reply to this dangerous assertion Sir John wrote a tract entitled *Thoughts on the State of our Finances*, which essentially contributed to restore the credit of

Great Britain on the Continent. It "deserved letters of gold," was the strong language of the British Minister at the Hague, to express his sense of its importance. In 1780 Sir John wrote his vindication of the British navy. No great victories had for a long period been gained at sea, and so general was the panic spread by the expected junction of the French and Spanish Beets, that even Lord Mulgrave, though a Lord of the Admiralty, was understood to have been carried away by the torrent of despondency. In a pamphlet entitled *Thoughts on the Naval Strength of the British Empire*, Sir John Sinclair so effectually revived the public confidence, that Lord Mulgrave himself returned him thanks for a defence of our naval service so powerful and so well timed.

It was in the same year, 1780, that Sir John was first chosen to represent his native county; and, with the exception of a short interval, he continued in the House of Commons till the year 1811, a period of above 30 years.

During a visit to the continent in 1785-6, Sir John's activity and perseverance enabled him to obtain information upon several points of great national utility; in particular on the art of coinage and on the manufacture of earthenware and of gunpowder. He described the last of these improvements to his friend Bishop Watson, Professor of Chemistry at Cambridge, before communicating it to the Board of Ordnance; and so important was the service rendered to the public, that the bishop in his memoirs represents his subordinate share in the transaction amongst his strongest claims to public gratitude.

Among the earliest and most laborious of Sir John Sinclair's literary undertakings was his *History of the Public Revenue, from the Remotest Eras to the Peace of Amiens* – a work which supplied the necessary data for effecting various improvements in our financial system, and especially for the introduction of the income-tax, without which the war could never have been brought to a successful issue.

It was on Sir John Sinclair's suggestion, that in 1793 Mr. Pitt proposed in Parliament the issue of Exchequer-bills for the relief of the commercial interest, then labouring under great distress. How soon and how effectually credit was restored by that politic measure, all merchants old enough to recollect the crisis must willingly, and many of them gratefully, acknowledge. Nor was Sir John's diligence in executing his plan inferior to his sagacity in devising it; much depended upon a large sum of money reaching Glasgow before a certain day; by applying every stimulus to all the agents he was enabled to accomplish this important object, contrary to the expectations of his most sanguine friends. Meeting the Prime Minister the same evening in the House of Commons, he began explaining to him his success, when Mr. Pitt interrupted him – "No, no, you are too late for Glasgow; the money cannot go for two days." – "It is already gone," was Sir John's triumphant reply; "it went by the mail this afternoon."

The gratitude of the Minister was in proportion to the magnitude of the service. He desired Sir John to specify some favour to be conferred upon him by the Crown. He requested the support of Government to his intended proposition for the establishment of "a Board of Agriculture."

A spirit of enterprise and of invention was excited among the farming classes, and a dignity attached to agriculture which it never had before acquired. Agricultural associations suddenly sprung up on every side; reports were published, in 50 volumes octavo, describing accurately every county in the United Kingdom, and the substance of the information thus accumulated was digested, by Sir John himself, into his *Code of Agriculture*, a work which has now reached the fifth edition.

Among the labours undertaken by Sir John Sinclair, the most arduous, and perhaps the most successful, was *The Statistical Account of Scotland*. So little had the subject been at that time attended to, that the very term "statistics" was of his invention (see *Walker's Dictionary*). The work was first commenced in 1790; it was prosecuted uninterruptedly for seven years, during which a correspondence was carried on with all the clergy of the church of Scotland, amounting nearly to 1,000; and it was brought successfully to completion by the gradual publication of 21 thick octavo volumes, in which a separate account is given of every parish in North Britain. Sir John made no attempt to derive even a partial compensation by the sale of his performance, for the immense expenditure he had incurred, but generously made over the whole work to the above mentioned body. A new edition, under their direction, is now in progress.

Along with his agricultural and statistical inquiries Sir John Sinclair from time to time exerted himself for the extension of the British fisheries. Having reason to believe that large quantities of herrings annually resorted to the coast of Caithness, he advanced a sum of money towards enabling certain enterprising individuals to decide the question. Their report was so favourable, that he prevailed upon the British Fishing Society to form a settlement in that county. The fishery thus established and encouraged has ever since continued rising in importance. It employs, on the coast of Caithness alone, about 14,000 individuals; it produces annually above 150,000 barrels of herrings; and being since extended to the neighbouring counties, has become the most productive fishery in Europe.

A tall athletic figure, in a military garb, his pretension to that costume was grounded on an important benefit to the public – that of raising, in 1794, a regiment of fencibles. Sir John's first battalion, consisting of 600 men, served in England; and the second, 1,000 strong, in Ireland. The latter corps furnished above 200 volunteers for the expedition to Egypt.

Among the measures recommended by Sir John Sinclair in Parliament, he always himself attached peculiar value to the grant for forming bridges, roads, and harbours throughout Scotland. To his other public services may be added that he originated and long presided over the Society for the Improvement of British Wool, and introduced, at his own risk, into the north of Scotland, the Cheviot breed of sheep, of which so many millions have, in consequence, pastured on our Highland hills; lastly, that he suggested in the House of Commons the appointment of a committee on the famines in the Highlands, and by prevailing on them to wave the want of precedent, and grant relief without delay, he was the means of saving thousands from starvation.

The value of the various services above enumerated has been acknowledged from all quarters by the most competent judges. King George III honoured him with friendly notice and correspondence conferred upon him the dignity of a privy councillor, and is understood to have intended for him further marks of Royal favour. Various agricultural associations presented him with pieces of plate. Out of 33 counties in Scotland no less than 25 voted him their thanks. The magistrates of Thurso, the town adjoining his own residence, publicly and gratefully acknowledged "that amidst other pursuits of a more extensive tendency, the improvement of his native county had been the peculiar object of his care and attention;" and the freeholders of Caithness passed resolutions thanking him for having brought to a completion measures "which laid a solid foundation for the future prosperity of the county."

His funeral took place within the chapel of Holyrood Palace, on the 30th of December, and although it was the wish of the family that the ceremony should be strictly private, yet the Lord Provost, magistrates, and Town Council, in their robes, and a deputation from the Highland Society of Scotland, of which Sir John was a distinguished member, solicited permission to join the procession on its entering the precincts of the palace, an unexpected tribute of respect which the friends of the deceased, we believe, did not decline, and which strongly marks the feeling which his loss has occasioned in the metropolis of Scotland. Sir John is succeeded in his title and estates by Sir George Sinclair, the present member for Caithness.

LIEUTENANT-GENERAL
SIR CHARLES NAPIER, G.C.B.

*'Few officers have seen more service or suffered more
from the casualties of war'*

30 AUGUST 1853

WE REGRET TO ANNOUNCE the death of this distinguished soldier, whose services, spread over a period of half a century, have shed no small lustre on the British arms. The melancholy event took place at his seat at Oaklands, near Portsmouth, yesterday morning, at 10 o'clock. We understand he had been suffering severely from illness for some time past, and death was therefore not unexpected by his friends.

Few officers have seen more hard service, or suffered more from the casualties of war, than Sir Charles Napier. He was literally covered with wounds, and his hairbreadth escapes amid dangers from which he never shrunk would require a volume to enumerate. Sir Charles entered the army as an ensign in January, 1794, and was a lieutenant in May of the same year. In 1803 he became captain, and in 1806 acquired the rank of major; was a lieutenant-colonel in 1811, colonel in 1825, a major-general in 1837, and a lieutenant-general in 1846. He was also colonel of the 221 Regiment of Foot. The following is a brief list of the more important services in which he was engaged: –

In 1798 he was engaged in the suppression of the Irish rebellion, and again in putting down the insurrection of 1803. In the Peninsula he commanded the 50th throughout the campaign, terminating with the battle of Corunna, and was made prisoner after receiving no fewer than five wounds, *viz*, leg broken by a musket shot, a sabre cut to the head, wound in the back with a bayonet, ribs broken by a cannon shot, and several severe contusions from the buttend of a musket.

In the latter end of 1809 he returned to the Peninsula, where he remained till 1811, and was present at the action of the Coa, where he had two horses shot under him; at Busaco, where he was shot through the face, and had his jaw broken and eye injured; at the battle of Fuentes d'Onor, at the second siege of Badajos, and a great number of skirmishes. In 1813 he served in a floating expedition on the coast of the United States of America, and landed a great number of times at Craney Island and other places. He served in the campaign of 1815, and was present at the storming of Cambray. Sir Charles, as is well known, commanded the force employed in Scinde, and, on the 17th of February, 1843, with only 2,800 British troops, attacked and defeated, after a desperate action of three hours duration, 22,000 of the enemy strongly posted at Meeanee. On the 21st of February Hydrabad surrendered to him; and on the 24th of March, with 5,000 men, he attacked and signally defeated 20,000 of the enemy posted in a very strong and difficult position at Dabba, near Hydrabad, thus completing the entire subjugation of Scinde. Early in 1845, with a force consisting of about 5,000 men of all arms, he took the field against the mountain and desert tribes situated on the right bank of the Indus to the north of Shikarpore, and, after an arduous campaign, effected the total destruction of these robber tribes.

In 1849 Sir Charles was appointed Commander-in-Chief of the Forces in India, but this position he did not long retain. For his services at the Corunna he received the gold medal, and also the silver war medal, with two clasps, for Busaco and Fuentes d'Onor. Long and arduous as his military services had been, he found time for the more peaceful pursuits of literature, and was the author of works on the colonies, on colonisation, and military law, &c. Sir Charles was born in 1782, and consequently was 71 years of age.

FIELD MARSHAL SIR COLIN
CAMPBELL – LORD CLYDE

Distinguished soldier who held the 'thin red line' at Balaclava

15 AUGUST 1863

ON THE 20TH OF OCTOBER, 1792, there was born in Glasgow a child in whose veins the gentle blood of the Highland lady commingled with that of the Lowland mechanic. No ray of hope or fortune illuminated his humble cradle; but by his own right hand, and by the exhibition of qualities which have raised nameless lads to fortune before now, that child came to fill a place among the foremost soldiers and highest dignitaries of the day. At a very early age Colin Campbell was taken from Scotland and put to school abroad and in England, and for many years he never revisited his native land.

As Ensign in the East Norfolk Regiment, he was taken to a military outfitter's – a pigtail was attached to the back of his head, a tight-fitting, epauletted, short-waisted, red coat covered with lace, a pair of leather knee-breeches, and betasseled Hessian boots were also duly provided for him, and he was sent off the same evening to Canterbury to join the 9th Regiment of Foot, which may be said to have commenced its military career. He had no time to enjoy the pleasure of his fine uniform, for the regiment marched the next day to embark for the Peninsula; in later years he was wont to recall the miseries of his first march to Margate in his leather tights and Hessians, and to declare that he endured more pain in that unaccustomed, and unsuitable, attire than he ever knew in his long afterlife of march-making.

For three weeks from the time when he had quitted the schoolboy's desk at Gosport he saw the French infantry cresting the hillsides of Vimiera, and took part in the opening actions of that series of campaigns which, after many checks and some reverses, led to the liberation of thankless Spain from the yoke of Bonaparte. Scarce landed from the transport which carried him from the shores of Spain, he was ordered off to participate in the shame, suffering, and disasters of the Walcheren expedition in 1809. The fever struck into his body so keenly that, until he went to China 30 years afterwards, "Walcheren," as he said, "was with me every season." From Walcheren he returned to Spain in 1810, where, with better fortune and guidance, he shared in the battle of Barossa in March, 1811, and the defence of Tarifa in January 5, 1812; and in 1812 he was transferred to a corps of the Spanish army, with which he was actively employed against the French in a long series of harassing skirmishes and operations. He was particularly struck with the Spaniards' powers of marching, their great sobriety and frugality. In 1813 he joined the Duke of Wellington's army again, and plunged into the thickest of the hard fighting which took place in that memorable year. He passed unscathed through Vittoria, the greatest of our victories after Waterloo, but in the desperate encounter at St. Sebastian he received two wounds. On the 9th of November, 1813, he became a Captain by brevet, and in that position had added to his wounds a bullet path through the thigh, received at the passage of the Bidassoa, which remained for 12 years. By the time he left France and proceeded to America, to serve against the Federal Government in 1814, he bore as many marks as the body of the saint who gave the name to the fortress where Sir Colin's wounds spoke for and returned themselves against his will; for an actual sabre slice, a thorough bayonet stab, and an ingoing bullet put all modesty to shame and insisted on mention in the despatches.

He had now been transferred to the 60th Rifles, and when the brief war was over in which we drove the President out of Washington after the "Races of Bladensburg," and were beaten at New Orleans, Colin Campbell was left on the same rung of the ladder of promotion, and he sturdily but not contentedly hung on it till he was 33 years of age – a Captain still. In 1823 he served as Brigade-Major, then obtained a sum to purchase his Lieutenant-Colonelcy.

When the interests of commerce and civilisation made it necessary for Great Britain to declare war against China in 1812, Colin Campbell went out in command of the 98th, and for 11 months his regiment was packed aboard a man-of-war, with a neglect of all consideration for health and comfort, which cruelly avenged itself upon officers and men. From China to India is a common step, though it is not attended with benefit to the constitution. Colonel Campbell had a short repose in Hindostan, but it was broken by the outbreak of the Sikh war. In virtue of his seniority he was appointed to the command of the Third Division of the army of the Punjab, and he soon flamed out on the field with more than the old Peninsular fire, and led his men with such skill that in all the great battles in which we stood foot to foot with the sternest foe we ever met or are likely to meet in India, his soldiers appeared in the very crisis of the fight. However, his critics were not disposed to be more favourable to him because he did not conceal his ill opinion of the Indian army, and considered the Sepoys as the mere bamboo of the lance, which was valueless unless it were tipped with the steel of British infantry. He was not regarded with favour by the Indian authorities, and his command on the frontier was terminated.

Colin Campbell was now, however, on the upward path. The ship of the State drifted into the Russian war, and from her decks, in 1834, marched the Glasgow boy at the head of three kilted and plumed regiments, which, fortunate in their chief and in their place, won much honour with little loss at the Alma, and almost as much reputation, in so far as one of them was concerned, with no loss at all on the famous day of Balaclava, when the thin red line of the 93rd was opposed to the Russian cavalry. Lord Raglan, to whom Sir Colin Campbell was not much known except by report, knew, however, that he was one whose eye never closed and whose hand never relaxed, and therefore he covered up the right flank of his army with the Highland Brigade, and gave their General the charge of Balaclava and all its works. There he had, indeed, little of the glory of battle, but much wearying anxiety and incessant vigilance. He was overlooked for promotion, until he returned to the Crimea to take a command which would no doubt have worthily employed him had not peace abruptly prevented the campaign. He had been gazetted a Major-General in 1854. In the October of the same year he was appointed to the colonelcy of the 67th Regiment. On the 4th of June, 1856, he was made

Lieutenant-General, and in that rank he fairly settled down, almost surprised at his late honours, if not quite satisfied with the part he had played in the great war wherein they were bestowed.

But his *opus magnum* was yet to be accomplished. When we were startled by the Indian mutiny, it was not a favourite in high places or a *dilettante* soldier who was selected to save our tottering empire. There was a sigh of satisfaction and content throughout the country when we were told that Sir Colin Campbell had at a moment's notice, and with alacrity, taken command of the forces engaged in putting down that which history will call the Great Mutiny. From the time that Sir Colin Campbell took the field and set his columns in motion, rebellion, the offspring of mutiny, withered and died.

When his labours in the field were over, and he had returned home to receive the acknowledgments of the whole country, the thanks of Parliament, the approbation of his Sovereign, and the honours he so valued as a soldier, he was not permitted to rest quietly on the laurels he had gathered. At the review of the Volunteers at Brighton he took the command at the request of the higher powers; but after it was over he said it was his last day in the field, and he shaved off his moustache as a sign that he had retired from active service. A few months ago he had a severe illness, in which the lungs and heart were implicated, but the old shot-and-steel-rent body resisted the attack of the great enemy, and to the delight of his friends he seemed to become nearly as well as ever he had been of latter years, and no one was more firm and vigorous for his years. Appointed Colonel of the Coldstream Guards in 1860, Field Marshal in 1862, Colin Campbell, Lord Clyde, had attained heights far beyond the flights of his highest ambition. At last came the illness of which he died, not perhaps as in his young days he would have desired, but as in his old age he would have surely sought to pass away – amid the tender cares and subdued sorrow of those who loved him well, and not the less that he had been the comrade of the soldier whose family stood by his pillow.

In person Lord Clyde was well knit, symmetrical, and graceful; but of late years his shoulders became somewhat bowed, though he lost little of the activity which was remarkable in so old a man. To the last his teeth remained full and firm in the great square jaws, and his eye pierced the distance with all the force of his youthful vision. His crisp, grey locks still stood close and thick, curling over the head and above the wrinkled brow, and there were few external signs of the decay of nature which was, no doubt, going on within, accelerated by so many wounds, such fevers, such relentless, exacting service. When he so willed it, he could throw into his manner and conversation such a wondrous charm of simplicity and vivacity as fascinated those over whom it was exerted, and women admired and men were delighted with the courteous, polished, gallant old soldier.

* * *

SIR DAVID LIVINGSTONE

Missionary and explorer, whose search for the real source of the Nile led to his death – 'fallen in the cause of civilisation and progress'

1 MAY 1873

THE FOLLOWING TELEGRAM, dated Aden, the 27th inst., has been received at the Foreign Office from Her Majesty's Acting Consul-General at Zanzibar:–

'The report of Livingstone's death is confirmed by letters received from Cameron, dated Unyanyembe, October 20. He died of dysentery after a fortnight's illness, shortly after leaving Lake Bemba for eastward. He had attempted to cross the lake from the north, and failing in this had doubled back and rounded the lake, crossing the Chambize and the other rivers down from it; had then crossed the Luapuia, and died in Lobisa, after having crossed a marshy country with the water for three hours at a time above the waist; ten of his men had died, and the remainder, consisting of 79 men, were marching to Unyanyembe. They had disembowelled the body and had filled it with salt, and had put brandy into the mouth to preserve it. His servant Chumas went on ahead to procure provisions, as the party was destitute, and gave intelligence to Cameron, who expected the body in a few days. Cameron and his party had suffered greatly from fever and ophthalmia, but hoped to push on to Ujiji. Livingstone's body may be expected at Zanzibar in February. Please telegraph orders as to disposal. No leaden shells procurable here.'

A plain Scottish missionary, and the son of poor parents, David Livingstone yet came of gentle extraction. Considering that his father and himself were strong Protestants, it is singular that his grandfather fell at Culloden fighting in the Cause of the Stuarts, and that the family were Roman Catholics down to about a century ago. More recently the Livingstones were settled in the little island of Ulva, on the coast of Argyleshire not far from the celebrated island of Iona.

Dr. Livingstone's father, Neill Livingstone, kept a small tea dealer's shop in the neighbourhood of Hamilton, in Lanarkshire, and was a 'deacon' in an independent chapel in Hamilton. The family motto was 'Be honest.' His son was born at East Kilbride, in Lanarkshire, in or about the year 1816. His early youth was spent in employment as a 'hand' in the cotton-mills in the neighbourhood of Glasgow; during the winter he pursued his religious studies with a view to following the profession of a missionary in foreign parts.

While working at the Blantyre mills, young Livingstone was able to attend an evening school, where he imbibed an early taste for classical literature. His religious feelings, however, warmed towards a missionary life; he felt an intense longing to become 'a pioneer of Christianity in China,' and hoped that by so doing he might 'lead to the material benefit of some portions of that immense empire.'

We next find him, at the age of 19, attending the medical and Greek classes in Glasgow in the winter, and the divinity lectures of Dr. Wardlaw in the summer. His reading while at work in the factory was carried on by 'placing his book on the spinning-jenny,' so that he could 'catch sentence after sentence while he went on with his labour.' In 1838 he resolved to offer his services to the London Missionary Society as a candidate for the ministry in foreign parts. The opium war, which then was raging, combined with other circumstances to divert his thoughts from China to Africa. Having been ordained to the pastoral office, he left these shores in 1840 for Southern Africa, and after a voyage of nearly three months reached Cape-Town. His first destination was Port Natal, where he became personally acquainted with his fellow countryman, the still surviving Rev. Robert Moffat, whose daughter subsequently became his wife and the faithful and zealous sharer of his toils and travels, and accompanied him in his arduous journey to Lake Ngami.

It was not until 1849 that he made his first essay as an explorer, strictly so called, as distinct from a missionary; in that year he made his first journey in search of Lake Ngami. In 1852 he commenced, in company with his wife, the 'great journey,' as he calls it, to Lake Ngami, dedicating his account of it to Sir Roderick Murchison, as 'a token of gratitude for the kind interest he has always taken in the author's pursuits and welfare.' The outline of this 'great journey' is so familiar to all readers of modern books of travel and enterprise that we need not repeat it here. It is enough to say that in the ten years previous to 1855 Livingstone led several independent expeditions, into the interior of Southern Africa, during which he made himself acquainted with the languages, habits, and religious notions of several savage tribes that were previously unknown to Englishmen, and twice crossed the entire African continent, a little south of the tropic of Capricorn, from the shores of the Indian Ocean to those of the Atlantic.

In 1855 the Victoria gold medal of the Geographical Society was awarded to Livingstone in recognition of his services to science. In the whole of these African explorations it was calculated at the time that Livingstone must have passed over no less than 11,000 miles of land, for the most part untrodden and untraversed by any European, and up to that time believed to be inaccessible.

Back in England, he was hailed as 'the pioneer of sound knowledge, [whose] scientific precision ... left his mark upon so many important stations in regions hitherto blank upon our maps.'

Early in the spring of 1858 Livingstone returned to Africa for the purpose of prosecuting further researches and pushing forward the advantages which his former enterprise had to some extent secured. Before setting out he was publicly entertained at a banquet at the London Tavern, and honoured by the Queen with a private audience, at which Her Majesty expressed, on behalf of herself and the Prince Consort, her deep interest in Dr. Livingstone's new expedition.

Within a very few months from the time of leaving England, Dr. Livingstone and his expedition reached that part of the eastern coast of Africa at which the Zambesi falls into the ocean; her two small steamers were placed at their disposal, and they resolved to ascend the river and thence make their way into the interior. In these journeys Livingstone and his companions discovered the lakes Nyassa and Shirwa, two of the minor inland meres of Africa, and explored the regions to the west and north-west of Lake Nyassa for a distance of 300 miles – districts hitherto unknown to Europeans, and which lead to the head waters of the north-eastern branch of the Zambesi and of several of that river's tributaries.

It is no slight thing to be able to boast, as Dr. Livingstone could boast, that by means of the Zambesi a pathway has been opened towards Central Highlands, where Europeans, with their accustomed energy and enterprise, may easily form a healthy and permanent settlement. This leads us to the third and last great journey of Dr. Livingstone, the one from which such great results have been expected, and in which he has twice or thrice previous to the last sad news been reported to have lost his life. Leaving England at the close of 1865, or early in the following year, he was despatched once more to Central Africa, under the auspices of the Geographical Society, in order to prosecute still further researches which would throw a light on that mystery of more than 2,000 years' standing – the real sources of the Nile. Of his explorations since that date the public were for several years in possession of only scanty and fragmentary details, for it must be remembered that Dr. Livingstone was accredited in this last expedition as Her Britannic Majesty's Consul to the various native chiefs of the unknown interior. One result was that his home despatches have been of necessity addressed, not to the Geographical Society, but to the Foreign Office. It was known, however, that he spent many months in the central district between 10 deg. and 15 deg. south of the Equator, and Dr. Beke – no mean authority upon such a subject – considers that he has solved the mystery of the true source of the Nile among the high tablelands and vast forests which lie around the lake with which his name will for ever be associated.

We are bound to record the fact that Dr. Livingstone claims to have found that 'the chief sources of the Nile arise between 11 deg. and 12 deg. of south latitude, or nearly in the position assigned to them by Ptolemy.' This may or may not be the case; for time alone will show us whether this mystery has been actually solved. During the last year or two our news of Dr. Livingstone has been but scanty, though from time to time communications – some alarming and others, again, reassuring – have reached us from himself or from other African Consuls, officially through the Foreign Office and privately through Sir Roderick Murchison. An account of his death at the hands of a band of Matites was discounted by Sir Roderick, who, with a keen insight which almost amounted to intuition, refused to believe the evidence on which the tale was based and gradually the world came round and followed suit.

In July, 1869, Dr. Livingstone resolved to strike westwards from his headquarters at Ujiji, on the Tanganyika Lake, in order to trace out a series of lakes which lay in that direction, and which, he hoped, would turn out eventually to be the sources of the Nile. If that, however, should prove not to be the case, it would be something, he felt, to ascertain for certain that they were the head waters of the Congo; and, in the latter case, he would probably have followed the course of the Congo, and have turned up, sooner or later, on the Western Coast of Africa. But this idea he appears to have abandoned. At all events, in the winter of 1870–71, he was found by Mr. Stanley, once more in the neighbourhood of his old haunts, still bent on the discovery of certain 'fountains on the hills,' which he trusted to be able to prove to be the veritable springs of the Nile.

During the last two years or so, if we except the sudden light thrown upon his career by the episode of Mr. Stanley's successful search after him, we have been kept rather in the dark as to the actual movements of Dr. Livingstone. Mr. Stanley's narrative of his discovery of the Doctor in the neighbourhood of Ujiji is in the hands of every well-informed Englishman, and his journey in company with him round the northern shores of Lake Tanganyika was recorded in the address delivered by Sir Henry Rawlinson, the President of the Geographical Society, last summer, who ended by predicting that 'he will continue his journey along the Congo, and emerge from the interior on the Western Coast.'

We fear that these forecastings have been falsified by the event, and that we must now add the name of David Livingstone to the roll of those who have fallen in the cause of civilisation and progress. After his death on 1 May 1873 from dysentery in what is now Zambia, his body, accompanied as far as Zanzibar by his two most faithful servants, was brought back to Britain for burial in Westminster Abbey. His posthumous reputation was fostered by Henry Morton Stanley.

It is impossible not to mourn the loss of a missionary so liberal in his views, so large-hearted, so enlightened. By his labours it has come to pass that throughout the protected tribes of Southern Africa Queen Victoria is generally acknowledged as 'the Queen of the people who love the black man.' Livingstone had his faults and his failings; but the self-will and obstinacy he possibly at times displayed were very near akin to the qualities which secured his triumphant success, and much allowance must be made for a man for whom his early education had done so little, and who was forced, by circumstances around him, to act with a decision which must have sometimes offended his fellow-workers. Above all, his success depended, from first to last, in an eminent degree upon the great power which he possessed of entering into the feelings, wishes, and desires of the African tribes and engaging their hearty sympathy.

THOMAS CARLYLE

'A great man of letters, quite as heroic as any of those whom he depicted'

THOMAS CARLYLE DIED at half-past 8 on Saturday morning at his house in Cheyne-row, Chelsea. He had been for some years in feeble health, and more than once his recovery seemed doubtful. Of late even his friends saw little of him, and growing weakness and pain had compelled him to give up his old habit of taking long walks every day. The announcement of his death opens a chasm between the present and the past of our literature, a whole world of associations disappears. A great man of letters, quite as heroic as any of those whom he depicted, has passed away amid universal regret.

About eight months before Robert Burns died, and within but a few miles of Dumfries, the scene of his death, was born the most penetrating and sympathetic interpreter of his genius. Carlyle's birth-place was Ecclefechan, an insignificant Dumfriesshire village, in the parish of Hoddam, known by name, at least, to readers of Burns, and memorable for an alehouse which was loved only too well by the poet. There Carlyle was born on the 4th of December, 1795. He was the eldest son of a family of eight children; his brothers were all men of character and ability; one of them, Dr. John Carlyle, was destined to make a name in literature as the translator of Dante. Mr. Carlyle's father, James Carlyle, was the son of Thomas Carlyle, tenant of Brown-Knowes, a small farm in Annandale, and of Margaret Aitken. At the time of his eldest son's birth James Carlyle was a stone mason, and resided in Ecclefechan; but he became afterwards tenant of Scotsberg, a farm of two or three hundred acres, which is now occupied by Mr. Carlyle's youngest and only surviving brother. Of James Carlyle, his son once said, 'I never heard tell of any clever man that came of entirely stupid people,' and his own lineage might well have suggested this saying. Carlyle never spoke of his father and mother except with veneration and affection. All extant testimony goes to show that Mr. Carlyle's father and mother were of the finest type of Scotch country folk – simple, upright, and with family traditions of honest worth.

Carlyle learnt to read and write in the parish school of Hoddam, where he remained until his ninth year. The parish minister, his father's friend, taught him the elements of Latin. From the parish school he passed to the Burgh School of Annan, six miles distant, where he saw Edward Irving, 'his first friend,' as he once called him, who was some years his senior. Carlyle was barely 14 when he entered the University of Edinburgh. It was then in its glory. Some of its professors possessed a European reputation. The eloquent and acute Dr. Thomas Brown lectured on moral philosophy; Playfair held the chair of natural philosophy; the ingenious and quarrelsome Sir John Leslie taught mathematics; and Dunbar was professor of Greek. However, the only professor for whom Carlyle seems to have had much regard was Sir John Leslie, who had some points of affinity to his pupil; and the feeling was returned. Carlyle made few friends at the University. He was lonely and contemplative in his habits. He took no part in the proceedings, and his name is not to be found on the list of members of the Speculative Society, which every clever student was then expected to join. In after years he laid it down that 'the true University of these days is a collection of books,' and on this principle he acted. Not content with ransacking the College Library, he read all that was readable in various circulating libraries – among others, one founded by Allan Ramsay – and acquired knowledge which extended far beyond the bounds of the University course. He left the University with no regret.

Carlyle had been intended for the church, but could not bring himself to embrace the doctrines of his father's kirk, and turned his hand instead to work by which he could earn his bread. For a year or two he taught mathematics in the burgh school of Annan, and remained there only two years; at their close he was appointed teacher of mathematics and classics in the burgh school of Kirkcaldy. Teaching Fifeshire boys however was not Carlyle's vocation. After staying about two years in Kirkcaldy he quitted it, leaving behind him the reputation of a too stern disciplinarian to begin in Edinburgh the task his life as a writer of books.

Carlyle tried his 'prentice hand in Brewster's *Edinburgh Encyclopaedia*, to which he contributed many articles on geographical and biographical subjects; among others, articles on Sir John Moore, Dr. Moore, Nelson, the elder and younger Pitt, Montaigne, and Montesquieu. They give but faint, uncertain promise of the author's genius and of those gifts which made his later works as individual as a picture by Albert Dürer or Rembrandt. But they indicate patient industry and research and minute attention to details. At the instance of Sir David Brewster he translated Legendre's *Geometry and Trigonometry*, prefixing to the treatise a short and modest introduction on Proportion. Carlyle about this time mastered German; his brother was studying in Germany, and the letters from Dr. Carlyle heightened his interest in its language and its literature, which was then in full blossom. The first fruits of this knowledge was an article contributed to the *New Edinburgh* on *Faust*, a subject to which he was so often to return.

About this period of Carlyle's life the once famous John Scott was editing *The London Magazine* and had gathered round him a group of clever writers; Hazlitt, Lamb, Croly, Cary, and Allan Cunningham amongst them. Carlyle joined them. Here appeared, in 1823, the first part of the *Life of Schiller*. No name was attached to it. Those who knew that it was Carlyle's work predicted great things from a writer who, in youth, exhibited noble simplicity and maturity of style, and who had conceptions of criticism very rare in those times. In the following year he published, again anonymously, a translation of *Wilhelm Meister's Lehrjahre*. Goethe was then no prophet out of his own country. He was known to no Englishman but De Quincey, Coleridge and a few students of German literature. The novel was sneered at, and the savage, elaborate invectives which De Quincey hurled at Goethe did not spare the translator. Undeterred by sneers and remonstrances, Carlyle published in 1827 several volumes entitled *German Romance*, containing translations from the chief writers of the romantic school.

In 1827 he married Miss Jane Welsh, the only daughter of Dr. Welsh, of Haddington, a descendant of John Knox. She had inherited a farm lying remote and high up among the hills of Dumfriesshire; and there Carlyle found the Patmos which his perturbed spirit needed. To the farmhouse of Craigenputtock – a plain, gaunt two-story dwelling, with its face blankly looking towards the hill, some 15 miles from town or market – came Carlyle and his bride in 1828. Here for six years he lived with this one friend and companion – a companion worthy of him, a talker scarcely inferior to himself, a woman, as he himself termed her, of 'bright invincibility of spirit.'

Carlyle toiled hard in this temple of industrious peace. In these obscure youthful years, he wrote, read, and planned much, and made incursions into many domains of knowledge. In a bare, scantily furnished room of the farmhouse, now shown with pride to visitors, he pursued this plan and wrote essay after essay and did much of his best work. Here were composed his essays on Burns, Goethe and Johnson, Richter, Heyne, Novalis, Voltaire and Diderot. *Sartor Resartus* was composed here; the manuscript to be laid aside until some other time. Carlyle contributed to the *Edinburgh Review*, which was still under the management of Jeffrey. The relationship was not perfectly smooth or entirely satisfactory to either editor or writer. It was difficult to adjust the boundaries of the respective provinces, Carlyle being apt to take offence at the ruthless hacking and hewing of his work in which Jeffrey indulged, and the latter being cut to the quick by the eccentricities of style displayed by his contributor, and surprised that Carlyle was not grateful for efforts to impart trim grace and polish to his articles. With Professor Napier, on the other hand, Carlyle's dealings were much to his satisfaction. *Sartor Resartus,* that unique collection of meditations and confessions, passionate invective, solemn reflection, and romantic episodes from his own life, was composed at Craigenputtock in 1831. It is not a little astonishing that this book, every page of which is stamped with genius of the highest order, failed at first to find admirers or appreciators. Even John Stuart Mill who afterwards delighted in the book, admitted that when he saw it in manuscript he thought little of it. Not for seven years after its composition did *Sartor* appear as a volume.

It 'had at last,' says its author, 'to clip itself in pieces, and be content to struggle out, bit by bit, in some courageous magazine that offered.'

Strengthening and helpful and rich in fruit were these years in his Nithsdale hermitage. But the time came for him to leave Craigenputtock. A historian, a critic, a biographer must needs have libraries within his reach. Some ties which bound Carlyle to Dumfriesshire had been severed. His father had passed away full of years, and it became fit, and even necessary, that Carlyle should leave his mountain seclusion and betake himself to London. He settled in Cheyne-row, in a small three-storied house, which he never afterwards quitted.

Carlyle was a man of mature years when he removed to London. The first years after his coming to the city were the most fruitful of his literary life. Essays, histories, lectures, biographies poured from his brain with surprising rapidity. No book-hack could have surpassed the regularity and industry with which he worked, late and early, in his small attic. A walk before breakfast was part of the day's duties. At 10 o'clock in the morning, whether the spirit moved him or not, he took up his pen and laboured hard until 3 o'clock; nothing, not even the opening of the morning letters, was allowed to distract him. Then came walking, answering letters, and seeing friends. One of his favourite relaxations was riding, in an omnibus. In the evening he read and prepared for the work of the morrow.

His best books were by no means instantaneously successful. Even *The French Revolution*, with all its brilliancy and captivating élan, had to wait for a publisher. He found his first warmest admirers on the other side of the Atlantic. Before fame in its common form had come to him, men whose private opinions were to be future public opinion had conceived the highest notion of his powers and the future before him; and the little parlour in Cheyne-row had become the gathering place, the favourite haunt of many literary men. At different times between 1837 and 1840, Mr. Carlyle delivered at Willis's Rooms and Portmansquare courses of lectures on some of his favourite subjects – *German Literature, The History of Literature, The Revolutions of Modern Europe,* and *Heroes and Hero-Worship*. Each of these lectures was a considerable event in literature. People of all shades and schools were amazed. Crabbe Robinson, who attended the whole of one course, says of a certain lecture, 'It gave great satisfaction, for it had uncommon thoughts, and was delivered with unusual animation.' 'As for Carlyle's Lectures,' writes Bunsen, 'they are very striking, rugged thoughts, not ready made up for any political or religious system; thrown at people's heads, by which most of his audience are sadly startled.'

The French Revolution, the first work to which Mr. Carlyle put his name, appeared in 1837. It would have been published sooner but for the famous disaster which befell the manuscript of the first volume. The author had lent it to Mr. John Stuart Mill; the latter handed it to Mrs. Taylor, his future wife. What became of it was never exactly known. Mrs. Taylor left the manuscript for some days on her writing table: when wanted it could nowhere be found; and the most probable explanation of its disappearance was the suggestion that a servant had used the manuscript to light the fire. Carlyle at once set to work to reproduce from his notes the lost volume; he swiftly finished his task, but he always thought that the first draft was the best.

There followed Carlyle's political period, when he produced pamphlet after pamphlet, abhorring the Chartists and their movement. Carlyle pronounced them one and all vain and unprofitable. His criticisms were often grotesque caricatures. They abounded in contradictions, and it was always pretty clear that Mr. Carlyle found it much easier to rail at large than to suggest any working substitutes for the systems which he despised. De Quincey was unanswerable when he said to Carlyle, 'You've shown or you've made another hole in the tin kettle of society; how do you propose to tinker it?'

In 1845 he published *Oliver Cromwell's Letters and Speeches, with Elucidations.* The work was well received. It passed rapidly through several editions. In a petition addressed in 1839 to the House of Commons on the subject of the Copyright Bill, Mr. Carlyle had said of his literary labours that they had 'found hitherto, in money or money's worth, small recompense or none,' and he was by no means sure of ever getting any. Between 1858 and 1865 appeared the ten volumes of Mr. Carlyle's laborious *History of Frederick the Great*. On this work Mr. Carlyle spent more time and trouble than on any of his other books. It is a marvel of industry. Every accessible memoir and book bearing on the subject was read and collated. And yet the ten volumes are painful to read. Peculiarities of diction, embarrassing in others of Mr. Carlyle's books, have grown to be wearisome and vexatious; little tricks and contortions of manner are repeated without mercy; miserable petty details are pushed into the foreground; whole pages are written in a species of crabbed shorthand; the speech of ordinary mortals is abandoned; and sometimes we can detect in the writer a sense of weariness and a desire to tumble out in any fashion the multitude of somewhat dreary facts which he had collected.

Since his *Frederick* was published Mr. Carlyle had undertaken no large work. But he had not been altogether silent. During the American War was published his half-contemptuous, we had almost said, truculent, account of the issues in his *Ilias in Nuce*, enunciating his old predilection for the peculiar institution. In 1865 he was elected Rector of Edinburgh University. Those who remember the old man's appearance, as he talked to the lads before him with amiable gravity of manner, his courageous, hopeful words, did not expect that in a few hours exceeding sorrow would befall him. During his absence from London his wife died. Her death was quite unlooked for; while she was driving in the Park she suddenly expired. When the coachman stopped he found his mistress lifeless. Carlyle might well say that 'the light of his life had quite gone out;' and the letters which he wrote to his friends are full of exceeding sorrow, and were at times the voice of one for whom existence has nothing left.

Mr. Carlyle has shunned many literary honours which were always within his reach. He did not accept the Grand Cross of the Bath, and on the death of Manzoni, in 1875, he was presented with the Prussian Order 'for Merit' – an honour given by the Knights of the Order and confirmed by the Sovereign, and limited to 30 German and as many foreign Knights.

Those who remember him best do so through his talks. One who heard them often describes them thus: 'His talk is still an amazement and splendour scarcely to be faced with steady eyes. He does not converse only harangues. Carlyle allows no one a chance, but bears down all opposition, not only by his wit and onset of words, resistless in their sharpness as so many bayonets, but by actual physical superiority, raising his voice and rushing on his opponent with a torrent of sound ... He sings rather than talks. He pours upon you a kind of satirical, heroical, critical Poem with regular cadences and generally catching up near the beginning some singular epithet which serves as a refrain when his song is full ... He puts out his chin till it looks like the beak of a bird of prey, and his eyes flash bright instinctive meanings like Jove's bird.'

This is not the fit time to try to measure Mr. Carlyle's services or the worth of his works. Wherever, in truth, men have turned their minds for the last quarter of a century to the deep relations of things his spirit has been present to rebuke frivolity, to awaken courage and hope. No other writer of this generation ever cast so potent a spell on the youth of England. To many he was always a teacher. He brought ardour and vehemence congenial to their young hearts, and into them he shot fiery arrows which could never be withdrawn. What Hazlitt said of Coleridge was true of him – he cast a great stone into the pool of contemporary thought, and the circles have grown wider and wider.

DR. JOHN RAE

Arctic explorer who uncovered the fate of the Franklin expedition

26 JULY 1893

BY THE DEATH OF Dr. John Rae we have lost one of the most striking personalities in the history of Arctic exploration and one of the few remaining men connected with the stirring episode of the search for Franklin. Though born in the Orkneys 80 years ago, until his last illness no more vigorous-looking or active man walked the streets of London. The hardships he endured during his many years' work in the Arctic regions seemed to have made no impression upon his frame; his robust health, indeed, made him somewhat intolerant of others not gifted with his iron constitution. Dr. Rae was a man of a disposition at once generous and sensitive. Probably he was somewhat unjustly dealt with by the Admiralty, who in some editions of their Polar charts gave others the credit for what Rae had done. But Rae's work as an Arctic explorer is too well known to be affected by any mistake of this kind. When he returned to England in 1854, bringing with him many relics of the Franklin expedition in the Erebus and Terror, and conclusively proving that the worst fate had overtaken its members, he received the reward of £10,000 which had been offered by Government. The Royal Geographical Society showed its estimate of what Rae had accomplished by awarding him its gold medal (1852).

When Rae was a youth of 16 he went to Edinburgh to study medicine. In 1833, having obtained his surgeon's diploma, he was appointed surgeon to the Hudson's Bay Company's ship which annually visited Moose Factory, on the shores of Hudson's Bay. His interest in the Arctic regions and in Arctic exploration was soon aroused. His first expedition was undertaken in 1846, when he succeeded in laying down 700 miles of now coast on the northern mainland of America, uniting the surveys of Ross on Boothia with Parry's in Fury and Hecla Strait. In 1848, in company with Sir John Richardson, Rae undertook one of the earliest expeditions sent out to search for the missing Franklin expedition. In that and the following year all the coast between the Mackenzie and the Coppermine rivers was searched in vain. In 1850 Rae was sent out in command of another search expedition, and between that and 1854 he examined the whole of Wollaston Land, all the coast east of the Coppermine river; Victoria Land, and Victoria Strait. In this time Rae travelled in all some 5,300 miles, a considerable proportion of it being new country, and much of the travelling being done on foot. In 1853 Rae was once more in the Arctic at the head of an expedition which connected the surveys of Ross with that of Dease and Simpson and proved King William's Land to be an island. It was on the last journey that Rae was able to collect evidence which showed that not only were the Erebus and Terror lost, but that in all probability every member of the Franklin expedition had perished. Though Lady Franklin continued the search for some years longer, Government took no further part in a search which most people were convinced would be in vain. During the nine or ten years' work of Dr. Rae he was able to lay down some 1,500, if not 1,800, miles of previously unexplored ground. Even if the deductions which some of his enemies would make were allowed, it is evident that Rae did original work enough to entitle his name to occupy a high and permanent place in the history of Arctic exploration.

In 1860 Rae took part in surveying for a cable from England, by the Faeroes, Iceland, and Greenland, to America; and in 1864 he conducted a difficult telegraph survey from Winnipeg, across the Rocky Mountains. For the last 15 years Dr. Rae's tall, lithe, muscular figure has been prominent at the meetings of the Geographical and other societies. He was a Fellow of the Royal Society and had been honoured by foreign scientific bodies. Dr. Rae was an ardent Volunteer, even in his later days, and an excellent shot. In 1850 he published a "Narrative of an Expedition to the Shores of the Arctic Sea in 1846 and 1847." The accounts of the other work done by Rae will be found in the publications of the Royal Geographical Society and in official reports.

ROBERT LOUIS STEVENSON

Novelist, poet and travel writer: 'Even when he brooded over the physical and metaphysical nightmares ... the vagaries of his inspirations were invariably kept in check by exquisite taste and sound literary judgment'

18 December 1894

ROBERT LOUIS BALFOUR STEVENSON was born in Edinburgh on November 13, 1850, and was the son of Thomas Stevenson, Secretary to the Commissioners of Northern Lights, and the greatest practical authority on lighthouses of his generation. It was he who built the lighthouse at Skerryvore. Louis Stevenson, as he was familiarly called, was educated at private schools and the University of Edinburgh, and had been brought up for the law. We believe he served his apprenticeship to a Writer to the Signet and he was subsequently called to the Bar. But he never cared to tread the *salle des pas perdus* in the old Scottish Parliament House, and he wrote feelingly in his 'Picturesque Edinburgh' of that dreary purgatory of the gossiping unbriefed. The roving spirit and an hereditary tendency to literature were too strong for him. Nor can we conceive Mr. Stevenson submitting himself to the drudgery of legal routine, and bending his neck to the yoke of exacting Scottish observances. For he was always unconventional – in his costume, in the very cut of his hair, and, above all, in the brilliancy of his conversation and in his unrivalled talent as a raconteur.

For example, the friends whom he fascinated have often heard him tell the story of *the Bottle of Rousillon*, which appears as a chapter in *The Wrecker*, and he never told it exactly in the same way, but always with new and more piquant embellishments. He went abroad for his health and it was borne in upon him to narrate his experiences. Whether he wrote of California or the Cevennes, the charm of the polished narrative was irresistible. Yet he never realised his veritable vocation, till he floated into fame, in 1883, after the cruise to his *Treasure Island*.

His first books had rather a *succès d'estime*, although they had

44

commended themselves to the appreciation of the most capable critics. It is very much to say of him that he subsequently made himself popular, without degenerating from that refined literary standard. It was no longer a question of settling to the practice of law in Edinburgh. He exchanged Scotland for the French Bohemia and became for a time a denizen of the Quartier Latin, while he was always the *bienvenu* in the artist colony at Barbizon. It seems strange, by the way, but the only reminiscences of those pleasant Fontainebleau visits are to be found in one of his latest novels, *The Wrecker*.

We need not catalogue his works in chronological order. His health had always been feeble. He gratefully dedicated the *Child's Garden of Verses* to the good old lady who had lovingly nursed him into boyhood. Too soon again his strength showed signs of failing and it was delicacy of the chest which first sent him abroad. But he had always sufficient command of money, and latterly, at least, his malady and anxieties were alleviated by an ample and increasing income. English editors and publishers treated him handsomely; as for the Americans, their passion for him made them forget their usual sharp practice with unfortunate English authors; and their flattery took the agreeable form of substantial cheques. The descendant of sea-faring Norsemen was free to indulge his love for the sea, and when living on shore he could choose his places of residence at such sunny marine resorts as Bournemouth or Torquay.

As for his native Edinburgh, much as he admired it, he wisely avoided what he has denounced as the vilest climate in the world. Finally, the man who paints himself in the *New Arabian Nights* as the misanthrope of the Fiji Sandhills, had sought a home in the South Seas where he was destined to die. But to the last he never lost touch with his countrymen, nor interest in that new world where he was naturalised; and the magician of the realms of romance was still the hardheaded Scotchman, as has been proved by his exhaustive communications to us on the troubled politics of Samoa.

The death leaves a melancholy blank in the literary world. We regret Mr. Stevenson selfishly as well as sincerely, because in the crowd of successful and rising writers there is no one left who can even approximately fill his place. He had the instincts and susceptibilities of a born man of letters, and it is noteworthy that his earliest productions were not the least finished of his works. His most marked characteristics were distinctly his own, which is only another way of saying that he had rare and special genius. Though he had innumerable admirers in his own craft animated by laudable ambition, and stimulated by no dishonourable envy, no one has rivalled, or even approached, him in his special lines.

To begin with, he had the charming and exquisitely graceful style which seems to have come naturally to him, and within certain wide though well-defined limits his versatility was as remarkable as his brilliancy. His tact and self-knowledge assured him against attempting anything where he was likely to fail. Yet no one could be less monotonous in the manner of his workmanship or the selection of his subjects. Few would have predicted that the vivacious author of the uneventful *Inland Voyage* and the *Travels with a Donkey*, would have cast irresistible spells on the devourers of sensational fiction as the author of *Treasure Island* or *Dr. Jekyll and Mr. Hyde.* Yet there is evidence of the same dramatic power in all these books; although in the former the dramatic element is toned down to the sober key in which the thoughtful travels are narrated.

But whether Stevenson indulged in fond and picturesque recollections of the scenes and circumstances of his childhood and youth; whether he threw off his spirited, or pathetic verses or wrote fairy tales to please childish fancies; whether he gave free rein to a wonderfully vivid imagination in his wild romances of the Scottish Highlands and the South Seas or in almost grotesque extravaganzas of superstition and crime; even when he brooded over the physical and metaphysical nightmares which shaped themselves under the master's touch into terribly impressive possibilities, the vagaries of his inspirations were invariably kept in check by exquisite taste and sound literary judgment.

That his genius had a morbid tinge there is no denying, and, indeed, it is to that we are indebted for his most marvellous *tours d'esprit.* We fancy we can trace through the varied series of his writings the sad story of failing health, of broken nights, and the sowing of the seeds of pulmonary disease. He had his moods of inspired depression and pessimism, even while the vigorous intellectual powers were still unimpaired. *The Suicide Club,* with its forbidding title, *The Dynamiter,* and the *Dr. Jekyll* may suffice to show that. But even in his middle life when memory revived early recollections, what can be fresher or more healthy?

Even as a youth he had learned to shudder at the fogs and winds and gray skies of his birthplace. Yet 'the romantic town' of 'Marmion' was a 'meet nurse' for such a poetic child. He revelled in the beauties of the scene and the wild romance of the associations, from the castle on its hill, down the High-street and gloomy Canongate to the Palace of Holyrood; from *the Heart of Midlothian* to the *Queensferry of The Antiquary.*

In fact he was sitting at the feet of Scott, whom he worshipped. Like Scott he was the best of companions and the soul of good fellowship, as is shown in the dedication to one of his novelettes, when he fondly recalls the debates in the Speculative Society and the subsequent adjournments to some favourite convivial haunt. But there is far more of Sterne than Scott in the narratives of his early wanderings. He models himself on the author of *The Sentimental Journey,* though in more masculine vein. *The Inland Voyage* was the travel of a romancist who consciously made mountains of molehills and who succeeded in extending the hallucination to his readers. Always original, he struck sympathetically into a vein the riches of which had for long been left unworked; and we can almost fancy that the title of *With a Donkey in the Cevennes* was ironically meant as an aggressive challenge to critical innocence. But the reviewers took the writer pleasantly and seriously, and he might well have been proud of the eulogies of hyper-critical connoisseurs.

The stories of his philosophical wanderings and ponderings, his poetry, his essays, and his 'familiar studies' might each have entitled him to a high place in literature, but it is as the popular novelist that he will be most widely remembered. Dramatic imagination comes to the aid of a realism which vividly reflects the scenes as his fancy paints them. We are haunted with the Highland outlaws and join in the revels of the pirates. Incident succeeds swiftly to incident, and each striking situation has its direct relation to the steady development of the ingenious plot. The interest never flags, and the curiosity is perpetually being stimulated. In the incidents there is almost invariably characteristic originality, and the situations, although often unexpected, are never unnatural.

Most sensational writers devote themselves to developing the stage action and are either indifferent to the interpretation of character or incapable of it. Mr. Stevenson, on the contrary, is always suggesting studies in strange individualities, or human problems which excite the curiosity of the reader. He analyzes those individualities with subtle skill, or leaves them to analyze themselves in their conduct. Not unfrequently conflicting appreciations have left a difficult problem unsolved. For example, the most competent critics differ widely in their estimates of the meaning and artistic merit of the Master of Ballantrae. Are the inconsistencies in that commanding personality conceivable? Are the redeeming touches true to nature?

We fancy that Mr. Stevenson has idealised a veritable personage, with his habitual tendency towards exaggeration and eccentricity of colour. So it is with that other most impressive personage, John Silver, the smooth-spoken tavern-keeper and cook of 'Treasure Island,' who for cold-blooded truculence and diabolical astuteness might have been the favourite *élève* of Satan himself. The greatest immortals in fiction, such as Scott or George Eliot, were in the habit of painting from people they had known, though they combined the results of their studies and observations. Stevenson, although always on his guard against absurdities, seems to carry romancing into his most powerful delineations. The practice is the more effective, from the sensational point of view, that elsewhere sobriety of drawing and colouring is more closely observed.

Nor are the Scotch stories less graphic. *Kidnapped* is as full of sensation as *Treasure Island*, with greater variety of more probable incident. When

Alan is run down in the Western Seas, when he is fighting for dear life in the deck-house, when the fugitives, exhausted by thirst, heat, and hunger, are being hunted through mountains and moorland by the soldiers, and when David is cast away on the reefs off Mull, there is as much of poetry as of prose in the epic.

It was in *The Black Arrow* that Stevenson came nearest to the limits of the ground on which he prudently hesitated to venture. For necessarily even his bright imagination almost ceased to be realistic in conjuring up the dim days of the 'Wars of the Roses,' and consequently he has failed in vividly presenting what he but faintly saw himself. The simple repetition of the expression 'shrew' shows how much he was at a loss in mediæval language.

One of his charms is that he is never prolix, and his tales in the *Arabian Nights* are marvels of sensational condensation. Take, for example, *The Pavilion on the Links,* in which the absconding banker is tracked to his doom by the gentlemanly carbonari he has been foolish enough to swindle. Scarcely less thrilling is *A Lodging for the Night,* of which that most disreputable of all the Bohemian poets, Villon, is the hero.

The handling of the horrible and grotesque culminated in the *Dr. Jekyll and Mr. Hyde,* where the possible discoveries of the practical chemist are pressed into the service of the supernatural. We have spoken of the little volume as the expression of a nightmare, and indeed we happen to know that it was born of a dream. It has all the effect of having been dashed off in a prolonged trance of unhealthy inspiration, and for the touches which heighten the terrors of the unholy transformation we are indebted to a not very enviable phase of genius.

Very different is the impression left on us by Mr. Stevenson's poems. It is delightful to see in the *Garden of Verses* how happily the man can identify himself with the child; how he rises in estimation and reputation when he seems to stoop. The secret is that there is nothing of effort in the little book; that the many-sided man of the world could be a child when it pleased him, and that fancy lives freshly again in the past as it followed memory back to the nursery. It is enough merely to name Mr. Stevenson's latest books, which are fresh in the public memory. By far the most remarkable is the volume which, after appearing in Atalanta under the title of *David Balfour,* was published in volume form, in 1892, with the name *Catriona.* It has the double charm of continuing the fascinating history of David and of Alan Breck, and of being Mr. Stevenson's only love story. Later came *The Ebb-Tide,* a story of Tahiti, written, like *The Wrecker,* in collaboration with Mr. Lloyd Osbourne, the author's stepson. Stevenson had met in America, some ten or twelve years ago, Mrs. Osbourne, a widow with two children, and had married her; and it was with her help that he wrote *The Dynamiter.* Lastly, we may mention the elaborate and beautiful *Edinburgh* edition of Mr. Stevenson's collected works, which is now being issued under the superintendence of his intimate friend Mr. Sidney Colvin. By a sad coincidence the second volume of this edition appeared on the very day of the announcement of the author's death.

Stevenson died of a cerebral hemorrhage at Valima, the house he had built himself on the Samoan island of Upolo, on 3 December 1894. He was 44. As this obituary emphasises, he was a restless and chronically sick man who found physical relief, satisfaction and inspiration in travel. The obituary does not mention his most taxing, but ultimately rewarding, journey. In France in 1876 he fell in love with a married American woman, Fanny Vandegrift Osbourne. When she returned to California, Stevenson resolved to follow her, travelling steerage to New York on board the *Devonian* and then taking the transcontinental railroad. At Monterey he collapsed and was nursed back to health by ranchers. He finally reached San Francisco in December 1879 and married the by-then divorced Fanny in May 1880. She was ten years his senior, and was to prove both a vivid companion and a devoted nurse.

THE MARQUIS OF
QUEENSBERRY

'A man of strong character, but unfortunately also of ill-balanced mind'

THE DEATH OF LORD QUEENSBERRY, which occurred last night in London, removes a curious figure from the social world. The late peer represented a type of aristocracy which is less common in our time than it was a century ago – the type which is associated in the public mind with a life of idleness and indulgence rather than with the useful aims which such a man as the late Duke of Westminster set steadfastly before him. The eighth Marquis of Queensberry was in many ways a man of strong character, but unfortunately also of ill-balanced mind, and he never turned to any account either his talents or the powers which his position gave him. For his failure to do so he was perhaps not altogether to blame. The title he bore still has associations clinging to it from the days of the fourth Duke of Queensberry, whose personality is preserved to us in the memoirs of the 18th and early 19th centuries. For more than half a century "Old Q.," as he was called, was notorious for his follies and wildness. He began to be noted for his escapades before he left school. At 70 he was still a "polished, sin-worn fragment," and the picture of him that lives in the mind of posterity is that of a worn-out *roué*,

"Ogling and hobbling down St. James's-street."

Thackeray, of course, drew a portrait of him in his younger days, when he was Lord March, in *The Virginians*.

It cannot be said that the eighth marquis, his kinsman, did anything to bring the title into better repute. Born in 1844, he succeeded his father at the age of 14. The seventh marquis was killed by an accidental discharge of his gun while he was shooting, and by a sad coincidence the same manner of death befell the late peer's heir, Lord Drumlanrig, a popular young nobleman, who had been a Lord-in-Waiting to the Queen and had acted as assistant private secretary to Lord Rosebery when he was Foreign Secretary in Mr. Gladstone's 1892 Ministry. Shortly before his death, Lord Drumlanrig had been created, for purposes of official convenience, Lord Kelhead, so that he was able to sit in the House of Lords with his chief. A curious feature of the situation thus brought about was that the son became a peer of the United Kingdom with a seat in the Upper House, while the father was only a Scottish peer and had no seat. He had sat from 1872 until 1880 as a representative peer for Scotland, but in the latter year he was not re-elected. Lord Kelhead died in October, 1894, at the age of 27, and his brother, Lord Douglas, became heir to the title.

Lord Queensberry was an undoubted authority on one thing, and that one thing was boxing. The Queensberry rules, which govern the contests of the prize-ring, will keep his fame alive at any rate amongst pugilists and amateurs of the "noble art." Of his career there is little to be said. He served in the Navy for a time, and he held a commission in the Dumfriesshire Volunteers. Except in these capacities he came little before the public, save when his eccentricities were subjects of nine-day wonder for all the gossips of the town. As an instance may be mentioned his demonstration at a performance of Tennyson's drama, *The Promise of May*, at the Globe Theatre in 1882. At a certain point in the play Lord Queensberry rose in the stalls and protested, in the name of Free Thought, against the manner in which the poet had drawn the character of a freethinker, denouncing it as "an abominable caricature." He was at this time a strong supporter of Mr. Bradlaugh and other militant apostles of Atheism. Lord Queensberry's intervention in a scandalous case which disturbed society some years ago will probably be within most people's recollection. The action he then took was dictated by the fact that the name of his son, Lord Alfred Douglas, was connected with the proceedings, which eventually brought the affair into a criminal Court.

Lord Queensberry married in 1866 Sibyl, daughter of Mr. Alfred Montgomery and granddaughter of the first Lord Leconfield. By her he was divorced in 1887. He married again in 1893, but in the following year the second marriage was also annulled.

Lord Douglas of Hawick, who now becomes marquis, was born in 1868. He is married to a daughter of the Rev. Thomas Walters, vicar of Boyton, Launceston, and has two sons and a daughter. Besides the sons of the late marquis already mentioned, there is Lord Sholto Douglas, who gained a curious reputation in America some years ago. There is also one daughter, who was married last year to Mr. St. George Lane Fox-Pitt.

* * *

LORD KELVIN

Scientist and inventor: 'He may be said to have taken all physical science to be his province'

17 DECEMBER 1907

WE DEEPLY REGRET to announce the death of the most distinguished British man of science, Lord Kelvin, which took place last night, at his Scottish residence, Netherhall, Largs. Lord Kelvin had not been well for over three weeks. He caught a chill on November 23, and his condition became serious some days ago.

William Thomson, Baron Kelvin of Largs, was born in Belfast on June 24, 1824. The second son of James Thomson, a remarkable man who, though he started with very slender advantages of education, died in 1849 Professor of Mathematics in the University of Glasgow, he began to attend the classes at Glasgow at the age of 11, and in the year he attained his majority graduated from Peterhouse, Cambridge, as Second Wrangler and first Smith's Prizeman. His success immediately earned him a Fellowship at his college, and in the following year, after spending a short time in Regnault's Laboratory in Paris, he returned to succeed Dr. Meikleham in the Chair of Natural Philosophy at Glasgow.

It is not often that a father and son simultaneously hold professorships at an important University; but even that does not exhaust the academic record of the Thomson family. Lord Kelvin's elder brother James was Professor of Engineering in the University from 1873 to 1889, so that three professors at Glasgow were provided by two generations of the descendants of a small farmer in the north of Ireland. The rest of Lord Kelvin's life is chiefly a record of strenuous and successful scientific work which obtained early recognition.

The Royal Society made him one of their number in 1851, and, after conferring on him successively a Royal and a Copley medal, accorded him in 1890 the highest honour at their disposal by choosing him to be their president. At the British Association, of which he acted as president at Edinburgh in 1871, he was an assiduous attendant. Much of his work was first published as communications or reports to that body, and it was only at its last meeting that he delivered a long address on the constitution of matters and the electronic theory. Honorary degrees he received in abundance, among them being D. C. L. from Oxford and LL. D. from Cambridge, Dublin, and Edinburgh, together with many foreign academical distinctions.

In 1896 he was knighted for the part he took in the laying of the Atlantic cable, and when, in 1892, Lord Salisbury created him a peer he borrowed his title from the stream that flows below the University in which his scientific life had been spent. He received the Order of Merit on its institution in 1902 – he was already a member of the Prussian Order 'Pour le Mérite' – and in the same year became a Privy Councillor. But perhaps the crowning occasion of his life was the celebration of his jubilee as professor at Glasgow in 1896, when a unique gathering assembled to do him honour, and congratulations from scientific men in all quarters of the globe testified to the universal admiration with which his genius was regarded.

Three years later, after 53 years' service, he resigned his Glasgow professorship. But his retirement by no means meant the cessation of active work. While still maintaining his connexion with the University, of which in 1904 he was unanimously chosen Chancellor in succession to the Earl of Stair, he continued to contribute to the proceedings of various scientific societies, and much of his time was devoted to the rewriting and revision of his Baltimore lectures on molecular dynamics and the wave theory of light.

These lectures were delivered at Johns Hopkins University in 1884, and the printing of them, begun in 1885, was only brought to a conclusion in 1904. He chose the wave-theory as his subject with the deliberate intention of accentuating its failures, but in his preface to the volume published in 1904 he was able to express his satisfaction that it contained a dynamical explanation of every one of the difficulties which had been encountered in the lectures 20 years before. Lord Kelvin was also a director of several manufacturing companies, and his name formed part of the style of the Glasgow firm which manufactures his compass and measuring instruments. He was president of the institution of Electrical Engineers for the present year, though he did not live to deliver his inaugural address.

Within the limits of a short article it is impossible to give a full account of Lord Kelvin's achievements in the realms of scientific thought and discovery. Generally recognised at the time of his death as the foremost living physicist, he was not less remarkable for the profundity of his researches than for the range and variety of his attainments. Not confining himself to a single more or less specialised department of learning, he may be said to have taken all physical science to be his province; for there were few branches of physical inquiry that he did not touch, and all that he touched he adorned. Perhaps this many sidedness of his intellectual interests may be connected with the deep conviction he cherished of the unity of all Science, and his impatience of conclusions which, drawn from a limited field of study, were in opposition to the well-ascertained facts of wider generalisations.

On one occasion, when accused of being 'hard on the geologists,' he repudiated the suggestion with the remark that he did not believe in one science for the mathematician, another for the chemist, another for the physicist, and another for the geologist. All science, he said, is one science, and any part of science that places itself outside the pale of the other sciences ceases for the time being to be a science.

Some idea may be obtained of the amount of his scientific work from the fact that, according to the Royal Society's Catalogue of Scientific Papers, down to the year 1883 he had published 262 memoirs under his name, not including papers published jointly with other men; while his republished mathematical papers – not yet completed – already fill three substantial volumes. Nor must his contributions to the increase of natural knowledge – to use one of his favourite expressions – be reckoned merely by the sum of the results at which he was personally able to arrive.

Hundreds of men are proud to recognise him as their master, and in all parts of the world scientific workers may be found who have not only profited by his advice and been stimulated by his enthusiasm, but owe to him in many cases the very subjects of research upon which they are engaged – either as his direct suggestions or as problems opened out by his prior investigations.

To solve the puzzle of the ultimate constitution of matter may be regarded as the goal of the pure physicist's ambition. The problem afforded Lord Kelvin a congenial field of speculation, and he succeeded in propounding an hypothesis as to the nature of atoms which, according to Clerk Maxwell, satisfied more of the conditions than any hitherto imagined. Starting from a number of mathematical theorems established by Helmholtz respecting the motion of a perfect, incompressible fluid, he suggested that the universe may be filled with such a primitive fluid of which in itself we can know nothing, but of which portions become apparent to our perceptions as matter when converted by a particular mode of motion into vortex-rings. These vortex-rings (of which a fair imitation is given by smoke rings in air) are the atoms or molecules that compose all material substances. They are indivisible not because of their hardness and solidity, but because they are permanent both in volume and in strength. Lord Kelvin's work on the atomic theory, though perhaps his most striking contribution to mathematical physics, is only a small part of the whole. Light, electricity, and magnetism, to mention a few wide departments, all engaged his attention, to what extent may be judged from the fact that his papers on electrostatics and magnetism alone up to 1872 filled a volume of 600 pages.

Some of the earliest and not least important of Lord Kelvin's work was in connection with the theory of heat: indeed he is to be looked upon as one of the founders of the modern science of thermodynamics. In 1824 Sadi Carnot published his book on the motive power of heat, setting forth the conditions under which heat is available in a heat-engine for the production of mechanical work, but it attracted little or no attention until Lord Kelvin about the middle of the century drew the notice of the scientific world to its value and importance.

A direct and immediate result of Lord Kelvin's study of Carnot's work was his definition of the 'Absolute scale of temperature' – that is, a scale which, unlike the graduations of an ordinary thermometer that are based on the observed alterations in volume produced in a particular material by heat or cold, is independent of the physical properties of any specific substance. A second addition to science soon followed in the principle of the dissipation of energy, enunciated in 1852. A further general inference is that this earth, as now constituted, has been within a finite time, and within a finite time will again become unfit for human habitation.

In a paper communicated to the Royal Society of Edinburgh in 1862 he declared that for 18 years it had been pressed on his mind that much current geological speculation was at variance with essential principles of thermodynamics, and proceeded to show from considerations founded on the conduction of heat that the earth must within a limited time have been too hot for the existence of life. Six years later, in an address on 'Geological Time' which provoked a lively controversy with Huxley, he brought some other physical considerations to bear on the question.

Since the tides exercise a retarding influence on the rotation of the earth, it must in the past have been revolving more quickly than it does now, and calculations of its deceleration indicate that within the periods of time required by some geologists it must have been going at such a speed that it could not have solidified into its present shape. But Lord Kelvin did not think the amount of centrifugal force existing 100 million years ago incompatible with its present form. Again he pointed out that the sun cannot be regarded as a permanent and eternal factor in the universe.

It is only fair, however, to say that his arguments have not been universally endorsed even among physicists; and it has been urged that there are other assumptions – in regard, for instance, to the conductivity of the earth's interior – not less admissible than those adopted by him, which lead to results much more favourable to the geological and biological demand for more time. Radium, too, has been invoked to explain the maintenance of the sun's heat.

Great as were Lord Kelvin's achievements in the domains of scientific speculation, his services to applied science were even greater. A prolific and successful inventor, he had nothing in common with that frequent class of patentees who are brimming over with ideas, all crude, most worthless, and only in occasional instances capable of being worked up into something valuable by men combining the requisite mechanical skill with an adequate knowledge of scientific first principles. Invention with him was not a mere blind groping in the dark, but a reasoned process leading to a definitely conceived end.

Of the scores of patents he took out few have not been found of practical and commercial value. It was in connection with submarine telegraphy that some of his most valuable inventions were produced in this department, indeed, his work was of capital importance and of itself sufficient to establish his title to lasting fame. Lord Kelvin was a firm believer in the practicability of transoceanic telegraphy and did not hesitate to show by acts the faith that was in him. He became a director of the Atlantic Telegraph Company, which hazarded large sums in the enterprise of making and laying a cable, and he took an active and personal part in the operations which culminated in the successful laying of the short-lived cable of 1853.

As is well known, the system broke down completely after it had been in use for a very short time, and there is little reason to doubt that the reason of its untimely end was the inability of its insulation to stand the potentials to which it was exposed. Lord Kelvin, who believed that but for this treatment the cable would have worked satisfactorily, declared that feeble currents ought to be employed together with very sensitive receiving instruments, and, characteristically, was ready, not only with a theoretical prescription, but with the working instrument, his mirror galvanometer, that enabled it to be carried into effect.

Some of his finest work is to be found in his electric measuring instruments, a subject in which his knowledge and authority were unrivalled. More especially was this the case in regard to electrostatic measurements – perhaps the most difficult of all. When the need for accurate instruments in his studies on atmospheric electricity caused him to take up the matter, the electrometers in existence were little more than electroscopes – capable of indicating a difference of electric potential, but not of measuring it; but in his quadrant, portable, and absolute electrometers his skill and ingenuity put at the disposal of electricians three beautiful instruments of exact research.

Measurement he regarded as the beginning of science and as the origin of many of the grandest discoveries. Hence he was always ready to do anything by which it could be facilitated, whether in matters of daily life or abstruse scientific inquiry. Thus on the one hand the metric system found in him a strong supporter, and he rarely missed a chance of bestowing a word or two of half-humorous disparagement upon the unhappy English inch or 'that most meaningless of modern measures, the British statute mile.'

A keen amateur yachtsman, he developed navigational aids for ships, a steady compass that could still work accurately when a ship rolls at sea, and a sounding mechanism to measure depth at regular intervals.

As a lecturer Lord Kelvin was rather prone to let his subject run away with him. When this happened, limits of time became of small account, and his audience, understanding but little of what he was saying, were fain to content themselves with admiring the restless vivacity of his manner (which was rather emphasised than otherwise by the slight lameness from which he suffered) and the keen zest with which he revelled in the intricacies of the matter in hand. Similarly, the intelligence and patience of his Glasgow classes were not always equal to the mental strain entailed by his expositions, and, though they were thoroughly proud of him and his attainments, their orderliness was not of the strictest kind, and they were not above varying the proceedings with an occasional practical joke. But he was quick to express his approval of a piece of good work, or his delight at a new result or well-planned experiment; and no one could come in contact with him without feeling the charm of his kindly, lovable nature, and falling under the spell of the enthusiasm and untiring energy with which he devoted himself to the advancement of knowledge.

Lord Kelvin was twice married; first, to Margaret, daughter of Mr. Walter Crum, of Thornliebank; and, secondly to Frances Anna, daughter of Mr. Charles R. Blundy, of Madeira. There was no issue of either marriage.

A devout Christian, Kelvin believed that his theory of heat-death and his calculations of the age of the earth exposed flaws in Charles Darwin's idea of evolution. To some Victorians, however, the implications of his ideas about the finite habitability of the earth seemed to offer a doom-laden vision of an icy end to all things rather than a fiery one.

SIR HENRY
CAMPBELL-BANNERMAN

*Prime Minister who showed 'a shrewd sense of what
the public wanted at the moment'*

23 APRIL 1908

IN THE OPINION OF his followers, Sir Henry Campbell-Bannerman has been a successful Prime Minister; but few would be found to say that his life offers a specially interesting subject of study to the biographer. In his case the interest was not that of genius, of versatility, of obstacles unexpectedly overcome, of high intellectual variety, of impassioned eloquence, or of mordant wit. It was just the interest which in a lesser degree attaches to the career of any very successful business man. A line of action early and definitely adopted; strong party consistency rigorously observed; a shrewd sense of what the public wanted at the moment; a firm will, a temper never ruffled except with intention, a gift of speech just adequate to its purpose and no more; a pleasant humour, a ready tact in dealing with friends and opponents, and behind it all the valuable background of ample wealth – these were the endowments of Sir Henry Campbell-Bannerman, and they made him Prime Minister.

By origin he belonged to the middle-class, being by birth a member of an outlying branch of the clan Campbell, and no known relation to the Bannermans who hold the baronetcy. He was born in 1836, the second son of James Campbell, who after making a considerable fortune in business in Glasgow became Lord Provost of that city, and was knighted. Sir Henry's elder brother, who lives at the family place of Stracathro in Forfarshire, and whose own serious illness was an added sorrow to the closing months of his brother's life, is a strong Conservative in politics, and as such represented Glasgow and Aberdeen Universities till 1906, when he retired, and was succeeded by Sir Henry Craik. Sir James

Campbell married Janet, daughter of Henry Bannerman, a Scotsman settled in Manchester, who became very rich and whose son Henry, dying in 1872, left all his property to the young Henry Campbell on condition that he added the name Bannerman to his own.

It was in this way that be became possessed of Castle Belmont, near Meigle, where so much of his later life was spent. Henry Campbell's early education was received partly near home, partly abroad, where he became a good French scholar; then, after passing through Glasgow University, he went to Trinity College, Cambridge, where he took his B.A. degree in 1858 and his M.A. in 1861. In 1860 he married Charlotte, daughter of General Sir Charles Bruce, K.C.B. a lady who, till her death in 1906, was, in spite of the ill-health which incapacitated her for many years, the close associate of all his thoughts and plans. They had no children, but this only threw them closer together, and the long holidays which they spent in each other's company, in Scotland or on the Continent of Europe, are said by those who knew them to have been ideal episodes in the "marriage of true minds."

In 1868 Henry Campbell had his first chance of entering Parliament, and in the May of that year he was brought forward by the advanced Liberals of Stirling to contest the burghs at a by-election. The new voters under the Reform Act of 1867 had not yet taken their place on the register, so that on a poll of 1,059 votes the young "advanced" candidate suffered defeat at the hands of Mr. Ramsey, a Liberal of more Whiggish colour, by a majority of 71. Then came the dissolution, and at the end of the year, on a poll which had grown to 3,883, Henry Campbell secured a majority of 519. He thus entered on that flood tide of Liberal opinion which made Mr. Gladstone Premier and gave him what was thought in those days to be an overwhelming majority.

In Gladstone's third session the sensible, steady-going, impeccable Scotch member, who had married a general's daughter and was about to inherit a great fortune, was chosen to be Financial Secretary of the War Office. From 1874 to 1880 Disraeli and the Tories were in power; when Gladstone returned, Campbell-Bannerman was moved, in 1884, to what was at that time the most conspicuous and difficult post in the

Ministry, that of Chief Secretary for Ireland, in which he succeeded Sir George Trevelyan.

It was a fortunate appointment. Of the three former occupants of the post one had been driven to resign by the intrigues of his own party, one had been murdered, the third, Sir George Trevelyan, had, after two short years, come back prematurely aged. Campbell-Bannerman was immediately called, by his opponents, "our chief antagonist and our hapless target ... and a very dull man." But it was not many days before they began to have an inkling they had made some mistake. Before the end of the year the story went round that his critics were describing him as "the only possible Chief Secretary, with the hide of a rhinoceros and the heart of an iceberg." This, of course, was only a pleasant way of saying that Campbell-Bannerman went on quietly administering the law and that he was the very last man in the world to take the Irish members at their own valuation.

Up to the time when Campbell-Bannerman, with the rest of the Gladstonian Cabinet, went out of office, in the summer of 1885, there seemed no reason to doubt the sincerity of the Chief Secretary's Unionist principles. During the election campaign in October and November, 1885, he not only repudiated the notion of yielding to what he called "the Separatist faction," but argued forcibly that the law should be specially and permanently amended to strengthen the arm of justice against intimidation and boycotting, and to secure that Irish jurymen should not be allowed to combine to create impunity for terrorist violence and menaces.

A very few weeks later, when Lord Salisbury's Government was thrown out on the Address and Gladstone once more came into office prepared to solve the Irish question by a deal with Parnell, Campbell-Bannerman blossomed out at once as an undisguised Home Ruler. In spite of the brave words of his election address and his campaign speeches, he went with his leader in the full adoption of the policy of Parnell and Davitt. Indeed he declared to a colleague, in a phrase of which he was the inventor and which had much success at the time, that he had "found salvation long ago, though he had kept his secret well."

But he did not return to Ireland; the Chief Secretaryship was given to Mr. Morley, who was no new convert, and the member for the Stirling Burghs went back as Secretary of State to the scene of his earlier labours.

He remained at the War Office during the short Government of 1886, and returned again during Gladstone's second Home Rule Government of 1892-93. Of his first tenure of this high post there is little to record, except that within the office itself and in Parliament he made a good impression.

His tenure of the War Office was brought to an end in June, 1895, by a chance vote on the insufficiency of small-arm ammunition. He, of course, was blamed as Secretary for War; but it must be added in fairness that Mr. Balfour, speaking at Manchester in the following January, at a very anxious moment in our history, paid a handsome tribute to the "additions to the fighting power of the Army" which had been made by the Home Rule Government between 1892 and 1895.

The cordite vote, in fact, was only a pretext to get rid of a Government of which the country was tired, and which ought, in the opinion of most people, to have resigned or dissolved after the defeat of the Home Rule Bill by the House of Lords.

Campbell-Bannerman was made a G.C.B; but for some years afterwards he remained one of the least prominent of the Liberal leaders. But all this time the internal of the party continued; and on December 14 the world was taken by surprise when Sir William Harcourt announced his withdrawal from the leadership of the Opposition in the House of Commons. The party deliberated in private, and, at a meeting on February 6, 1899, at the National Liberal Club, the names of Mr. Asquith and Sir Henry Fowler having been withdrawn, unanimously voted that Sir Henry Campbell-Bannerman should lead the party in the House of Commons. This position Sir Henry filled till the end of 1905, if not with overmastering ability, at least with sufficient success to make his choice as Prime Minister almost inevitable when the time came for a change of Government.

For a long time one question, and one question only, filled the public mind – our relations with South Africa, and the war which broke out in

October. With regard to this crisis in our history, it is impossible for the impartial historian not to blame Sir Henry Campbell-Bannerman both for the unwisdom of his initial policy and for the costly injudiciousness of some of his phrases. Speaking at Ilford, soon after the Bloemfontein Conference, he used a sentence which he liked so well that he repeated it in the City of London on June 30, thus proclaiming it as the deliberate policy of his party; it was "I can see nothing whatever in all that has occurred to justify either warlike action or military preparations." Of course the Boers took this to mean that, whatever they did, we should not proceed to extremities. The Liberal leader was also accused of attacking British soldiers when he spoke of the destruction of farms and the policy of the concentration camps as "methods of barbarism." It was in vain that he subsequently explained: "I have always borne public testimony to the humane conduct of the officers and men of the Army, and absolved them from all blame." But the word went round among the Boers that public opinion in England was bitterly divided, and that they had only to hold out.

Meantime the party itself was by no means a happy family, and Lord Rosebery opened a split, when he came out of retirement to propose the abandonment of Home Rule, and went on to found the Liberal (Imperialist) League, with himself as president and Sir Edward Grey, Sir Henry Fowler, Mr. Asquith, and Mr. Haldane as vice-presidents, all of them men destined within a few years to enter a Campbell-Bannerman Cabinet; but with their titular chief he himself had henceforth no political relations.

Very little need be said of Sir Henry Campbell-Bannerman's conduct of his party during the last four sessions of Unionist rule. It was sound and competent, and, as the subsequent general election showed, was efficient in keeping the party together and in educating the country, but it was not marked by any unexpected qualities.

On December 4 Mr. Balfour resigned, and Sir Henry Campbell-Bannerman was sent for. For a moment it seemed uncertain whether Sir Edward Grey and the other vice-presidents of the Liberal League would accept office; but the difficulties were quickly removed; and by

December 10 Sir Henry had completed a strong Cabinet, containing, on the one hand, Mr. Asquith, Mr. Haldane, and Sir Edward Grey, and on the other Mr. Lloyd-George and Mr. John Burns.

In January, 1906, came the general election. The rout of the late Government was complete. The Unionists, who had numbered 369, came back 157; while the Liberals, who, with a few Labour members, had been 218 all told, now comprised 379 faithful followers of the Government, and – the most astonishing feature of all – no fewer than 51 Labour members who, on most questions, could be depended on for votes. Such a majority had never been seen in any Parliament since that following the first Reform Bill; and, though both sides had expected that the new House of Commons would be strongly in favour of the new Government, none of the party prophets anticipated anything like what really happened.

It may suffice to say that, as regards domestic legislation, a great deal was achieved; but the fate of several of the most important measures of the Government shows that even the strongest Minister, with a vast and obedient majority behind him, cannot in this country expect to have everything his own way. Sir Henry Campbell-Bannerman was not conspicuous either in the statement of policies or in the conduct of Ministerial measures in the House of Commons; but, on the whole, he proved himself an adroit tactician and especially skilful in holding together a party composed of incongruous and often unruly elements. The determination he displayed to push his measures through and to obtain the full advantage of his party's numerical strength at whatever cost to the traditions of free debate and the rights of minorities produced continual friction.

During the debate on the Address, a year later, he went out of his way to give an indirect answer to Lord Rosebery's challenge on the Irish question. The Prime Minister asserted with deliberate emphasis, "The Irish people should have what every self-governing colony in the Empire has – the power of managing its own affairs. That is the larger policy I have spoken of."

The principal measure of 1906 was the Education Bill; it was so much amended in the Lords that the Government took offence and refused to proceed with it. Another important measure was Mr. Harcourt's Plural Voting Bill; but this the Lords refused to pass until they had before them a complete scheme of electoral reform. In the following Session a Scotch Land Bill, the effect of which would have been to assimilate the Scotch land system, not to that of England, but to that of Ireland, was postponed by the Lords until they could compare it with the Government's Small Holdings Bill for England – another cause of deep offence, for which the House of Lords was threatened with condign punishment.

The House of Lords, however, have not been cowed upon this point by the menaces of the Prime Minister and his colleagues, and they have again refused to yield to the demand that the Scotch Lowlands should be turned into another Ireland. Gradually the threats against the Upper House have lost their shrill tones, and the Prime Minister's effort to whip up the agitation once again last autumn was so conspicuous a failure that, at the beginning of 1908, he practically withdrew from it and exonerated the Peers from anything like deliberate obstruction. Nevertheless, he proposed, early in February, a verbose and lengthy resolution, to the effect that the Scotch Bills passed by the House of Commons and rejected by the House of Lords should be sent up again without delay and by the most stringent use of the closure. But after the repeated Liberal defeats since the close of the autumn there ceased to be any probability that a renewed effort would be made to precipitate an agitation originally intended to end in an early dissolution or a complete victory.

His impaired health prevented Sir Henry Campbell-Bannerman from taking any share in the recent discussions of Licensing and Education, and Mr. Asquith discharged the duties of leader of the House of Commons practically since the opening of the Session. Grave trouble of a personal nature fell upon him during the years of his Ministry. The health of his wife, with whom, as we have said, he had lived for six and forty years in the most perfect union, had been for some time seriously affected; and on August 30, 1906 she died at Marienbad. He himself was physically not so strong as he looked, and this heavy blow affected him deeply. In the autumn of 1907, after he had helped to entertain the German Emperor at the Guildhall, he had to attend the Colston banquet at Bristol where he made a speech. The effort was too much for him; he had a serious heart attack, and for some hours his life was in danger.

He recovered, but not entirely; and was compelled to spend all December and the first three weeks of January at Biarritz. A few days after the opening of the Session he caught influenza, suffered from a recurrence of some of the former symptoms, and was soon found to be unfit either to attend Cabinet Councils or to be present in his place in Parliament, except for two or three days, when he unfortunately overtasked his powers in the delivery of an important and exhausting speech on February 13. Two days after he had again to withdraw from his place in the House of Commons and to leave his duties to Mr. Asquith, who it was well known was to succeed to the Premiership when a vacancy was created. His condition, grave from the outset, rapidly grew worse. For a time it was hoped that he might still continue to retain his office, at least temporarily, but increasing weakness compelled a prompt decision. On the 5th of April the King received at Biarritz a letter from Sir Henry Campbell-Bannerman tendering his resignation in compliance with the urgent recommendations of his medical advisers. This was graciously accepted, and Mr. Asquith was summoned.

Sir Henry Campbell-Bannerman's loss to his party is almost irreparable at a crisis when electoral difficulties are multiplying when there are ominous signs of disintegration and division which he, more than any of his colleagues, had the gift of smoothing over, if not removing.

KEIR HARDIE

Founder of the Labour Party who led a stormy political career

27 SEPTEMBER 1915

MR. J. KEIR HARDIE, LABOUR M.P. for Merthyr Tydvil, died from pneumonia after a long period of ill-health in a Glasgow nursing home yesterday. Born in Scotland in 1856, he was engaged in mining work from the age of seven to that of 24. He was elected secretary of the Lanarkshire Miners Union in 1880, and at once threw himself with great zeal and little discretion into the work of a trade unionist and political agitator. He attempted to secure election to Parliament as a Labour candidate for Mid-Lanark in 1888, but was badly beaten. At the General Election four years later, however, he was elected for South-West Ham, and made his first appearance at St. Stephen's in circumstances which necessitated the interference of the police. He was defeated in West Ham in 1895, but at the General Election of 1900 was elected for Merthyr Tydvil, which remained faithful to him until his death. He was for many years chairman, and throughout his political career the obvious leader, of the Socialist body known as the Independent Labour Party. When the Labour Party became a distinct group in the House of Commons in 1906 he was elected its first chairman, and held the position for two Sessions.

For over 20 years Mr. Keir Hardie was regarded as the most extreme of British politicians. The hard and narrow environment of his youth predisposed him to take a gloomy view of the state of society, and sympathy for suffering humanity, he was one of those men who spend their lives in expressing the views of a minority. He certainly spent his public life in advocating unpopular causes. He did not hide his republican opinions; he was one of the strongest opponents of the South African War; he made speeches during a tour in India in 1907 which, in view of the unrest prevailing at the time, could only be branded as mischievous; and he was the most pronounced of all the pacifists before the outbreak of the European War. He was probably the most abused politician of his time, though held in something like veneration by uncompromising Socialists, and no speaker has had more meetings broken up in more continents than he.

Although showing courage in some of his earlier adventures in the House of Commons, when he constituted a Socialist party of one, he never caught the ear of that Assembly, and was an ineffective leader of the independent group which owed its existence in great measure to his unflagging energy. He did much good and unselfish work for Labour causes, but did not at any time gain the complete confidence of the working class. The Labour Party disappointed his hopes. He was out of tune with the more moderate views of the trade unionist majority for a considerable time, and his views ceased to have any influence in the councils of the party with the coming of the war. His health was declining and his voice has been hardly heard since the collapse of International Socialism in August, 1914. He seems to have accepted the war with resignation, and the bitter passions which he aroused in his life were in great measure forgotten before his death.

DR. ELSIE INGLIS

*Founder of the Scottish Women's Hospitals, whose work
in Serbia made her a legendary character*

28 NOVEMBER 1917

WE REGRET TO ANNOUNCE the death of Dr. Elsie Inglis, M.B., C.M., Commissioner of the London Units of the Scottish Women's Hospitals, which took place at Newcastle-upon-Tyne on Monday. She had just returned from Russia.

Miss Inglis, to whom belonged the honour of originating the Scottish Women's Hospitals, was pre-eminently a Scottish woman. As a medical woman she specialised in surgery, and for many years held the post of joint surgeon to the Edinburgh Hospital and Dispensary for Women and Children, and was also Lecturer on Systematic Gynæcology in the Royal Colleges School of Medicine, Edinburgh. She had a large practice in Edinburgh, and took an important part in connection with the medical education of women in Scotland.

On the outbreak of war Dr. Inglis felt that the medical services of women should be given to the country. She conceived and carried out with marked success the idea of forming the Scottish Women's Hospitals, staffed entirely by women. Unfortunately the British War Office refused to consider hospitals staffed entirely by women, and Dr. Inglis and her committee offered their services to the Allies, and they were at once accepted.

In April, 1915, Dr. Inglis left for Serbia to act as Commissioner to the Scottish Women's Hospitals established there. The typhus scourge was at its worst. She took with her a splendid group of colleagues of the Scottish Women's Hospitals. Her splendid organizing capacity, her skill, and her absolute disregard of her own comfort, month after month, drew forth the love and admiration of the whole Serbian people, which they were not slow to express. The typhus epidemic carried off one-third of the Serbian Army Medical Corps, and the situation was desperate. About that time, Lady Paget was struggling against fearful odds in Skopje, in the south of Serbia. Dr. Elsie Inglis set to work in the more central districts of Serbia, organizing four big hospital units where the need was greatest. Her grasp of detail was wonderful, and she had indomitable resolution. Yet she was above all a woman. Never will the Serbians forget her cheerful and kindly greetings and her complete composure in the very worst circumstances. Never can they forget that most characteristic remark of hers which was heard so often at the Serbian Medical Headquarters Staff: – "Tell me, please, where is the greatest need for hospitals, without respect to difficulties, and we shall do our best to help Serbia and her valiant soldiers." Among the Serbian peasants, in the very heart of the Shumadija, the stories gathering round her name assume almost a legendary character.

Thanks to the devotion and sacrifices of a band of British and French and American relief workers, the typhus epidemic was mastered. But tragedy deepened when the united hordes of Germans, Austrians, Hungarians, and Bulgarians assaulted an already shattered nation. Perhaps it was then that Dr. Inglis's most heroic work was done. At Lazarevatz her hospital was overcrowded. Later, by Kragujevatz, the same state of things existed; wounded soldiers were lying in the streets. She gave up her own beds and rugs, and she and her colleagues passed whole nights in alleviating the sufferings of the men. Next, she was found at Kraljevo, where, declining to leave her Serbian wounded, she was captured with her staff at Krushevatz by the enemy. After enduring many discomforts as prisoners of war, she and her staff were finally released and sent home. She at once volunteered with a Scottish Women's unit for service in Mesopotamia, but again War Office obstruction frustrated her plan. Giving herself no rest, she worked on for Serbia in this country, and took a leading part in the organisation of the Kossovo Day celebrations, in June, 1916. The equipping of a Southern Slav Volunteer Corps for the Dobrudja front was the occasion of yet another act of sacrifice on her part. She set out for the Dobrudja, and was attached, at her own request to the Southern Slav Division that fought alongside the Russian troops. She went through the Rumanian retreat with the Southern Slav Division, and remained with it till her recent return from Russia. The insanitary Dobrudja came after a long period of strain. Her work, however, was still as spirited and enthusiastic as ever, and she returned to England with new plans for service. For the splendid service which she rendered to Serbia the Crown Prince conferred on her the Order of the White Eagle. She is the only woman on whom such an honour has been conferred.

Apart from her war activities, Dr. Inglis was known throughout Scotland as one of the keenest supporters of all forms of women's work, and her interest in the advancement of women was untiring. All who came in contact with her carried away with them the impression of energy, courage, indomitable pluck, and a most capable and striking personality.

The following tribute is paid to Dr. Inglis by a fellow-worker of the Scottish Women's Hospitals: –

"Every one will hear with the deepest regret the death of Dr. Elsie Inglis, that splendidly brave woman, to whom belongs the honour of originating the Scottish Women's Hospitals. She had not been well for several months, but she would not give in, and worked to the very end. After landing in England from Russia she had a collapse and passed quietly away."

She was the second daughter of John Forbes David Inglis, of the Indian Civil Service, Chief Commissioner at Lucknow. She was born in India, and for some years lived in Australia. She was educated in Edinburgh and Paris, and received her medical training in Edinburgh, but she walked a hospital in Ireland.

The funeral will be at St. Giles Cathedral, Edinburgh, on Thursday next, at 2. The date of a memorial service in London will be announced later.

ANDREW CARNEGIE

Steel magnate who became one of the greatest of all philanthropists

11 AUGUST 1918

MR. ANDREW CARNEGIE DIED AT 7.30 this morning at Lenox, Massachusetts. The cause of death is given as bronchial pneumonia. Mr. Carnegie had been living at his summer home at Lenox ever since the wedding of his daughter.

Andrew Carnegie was born in the ancient Royal Burgh of Dunfermline, in the county of Fife, Scotland. He himself gave the date of his birth as November 25, 1837, but local authority gives 1835 as the correct year.

The chief industry of his native town was then the hand-loom weaving of fine linen. The weavers were highly intelligent and disputatious, and Dunfermline was a centre of Chartist agitation and passionate Dissent. Carnegie's father owned four hand-looms and employed apprentices. He was a revolutionary politician, a street orator, and an agitator against the industrial conditions which, by a singular irony, the son was destined to turn to such enormous profit. His mother, to whom he was devotedly attached until her death at the age of 80, was the daughter of Thomas Morrison, a man of mark in Dunfermline as an orator, lay preacher, reformer, and agitator.

The introduction of the power-loom ruined the business of Carnegie, senior, and was the cause of the emigration of the whole family to America when Andrew was about 12 years old. He had been taught by his mother and had been to a day school, but that was all the education he had until at the age of 30 he took courses of study in New York.

On their arrival in America in 1848 the Carnegie family settled in Alleghany, opposite Pittsburg, on the other side of the Ohio river. There they all found work at once, Andrew as a bobbin boy at 4s. 10d. a week in the cotton mill in which his father worked at the loom. Their next-door neighbour was a shoemaker named Phipps, who had a son a little younger than Andrew. This was Henry Phipps, afterwards second partner in the Carnegie steel and iron companies, the oldest of Carnegie's early associates; and the only one who remained with him till the end, but even they quarrelled after 50 years of friendship.

From the cotton mill Andrew passed to a small factory where he fed the furnace in the cellar and tended the engine. That was all the manual work he ever did, for he was soon taken into the office. Next, by the patronage of a Dunfermline man who knew his father, he became a telegraph messenger under the Ohio Telegraph Company. He mastered the code, risked taking a message against rules, and was rewarded by being made operator at £60 a year. Then by the help of Colonel T. A. Scott he passed to the telegraphic service of the Pennsylvania Railroad, with another rise of salary.

He remained for 11 years in the employ of the railway company and got together a small capital by engaging in modest commercial enterprises more or less connected with the railway and under the benevolent advice of Colonel Scott, to whom he became private secretary. The whole region was humming with activity. There were oil companies, manufacturing enterprises, railways, and banks, and Carnegie, who was put in charge of important works during the Civil War, and became superintendent of the line in 1863, acquired friends and business experience, as well as money.

Carnegie thus was ready for the vast expansion of the iron and steel production which began about 1864. The protective tariff of 1861 was the general background; the local factors were the development of the Pennsylvania coalfields near Pittsburg, the substitution of coal and coke for charcoal in producing pig iron, the opening up of the Lake Superior iron ore deposits, the development of transport by rail and water, and the introduction of the Bessemer steel process.

Carnegie was responsible for none of these, but took advantage of all of them. He was neither inventor nor creator, like Krupp or Armstrong or Westinghouse, but a manipulator with a quick eye for opportunities and a rare sagacity in utilizing men. He used men of all sorts, raw youths or those of standing and influence, to their advantage when it served his purpose. He made many millionaires, but there is no record of those that he exploited and cast adrift.

In 1864 Carnegie bought his first interest in iron works, forming with his younger brother, old companions of his boyhood, and a German named Kloman, who had technical knowledge, the Union Iron Mills Company. Soon afterwards he secured the backing of the president and vice-president of the Pennsylvania Railroad, the greatest local magnates, for a new venture the Keystone Bridge Company. He resigned his railway appointment and devoted himself entirely to his private interests.

The Union Mills Company was not very successful, but Carnegie showed tenacity in holding on, and astuteness in buying out his senior partner when things were at their worst. His own part was to run about and get orders while the partners ran the works and the local business. He maintained this division of labour throughout his career, in all the successive enterprises being the travelling and publicity manager, but insisting on constant reports and keeping a firm grip on the actual works.

In 1873 he went into the steel business, employing as capital £50,000 which he had earned as commissions from Colonel Scott for placing the stock of a new railway on the European market. This was his share in the new company of Carnegie, McCandless, and Co., the total capital of which was £140,000. There were 11 partners. Twenty-six year later, when the business was sold for over £90,000,000, all Carnegie's partners save one had died or gone out, and Carnegie's personal share was more than one-half of the colossal total.

The story of the fortunes of the company is long and tortuous. It involved many commercial transactions of a mysterious nature. But the amassing of this portentous wealth is a most remarkable achievement. He went through no long-drawn struggle against adversity, nor is his story one of incessant toil and application. He escaped the daily grind and left it to others. The secret of his success in great measure lay in his withdrawal from the daily worries that beset the men on the spot and his consequent leisure to see the large movement of affairs and steer his course accordingly.

But he was a thorn in the flesh to his partners and the working officials, continually goading them to further efforts, playing off the output of one furnace or mill against that of another. He was insatiable. Even when in 1889 the profits rose to £4,000,000 the effect on him was determination to have them doubled next year. But this was not greed, but a love of winning the game, a game in which the measure of success was money.

Carnegie's naturally kind and generous disposition and the memories and traditions of his Dunfermline proletariat days came into conflict with his consuming ambition. The business side always won. He would pay large wages because that paid him, but otherwise he was a relentless and unthinking employer. Notwithstanding the views in his book, *Triumphant Labour*, he fought strikes with bitterness, and in the great Homestead strike of 1892, the cause of which was the determination of the masters to force a return to the killing double shift, he was entirely against the Amalgamated Association of Iron and Steel Workers.

Encouraged by Carnegie's benevolent theories, the association had come to interfere more and more with the management of the works. Carnegie insisted, even against his partner, Mr. Frick, on making it a fight to a finish. After the most sanguinary of all labour conflicts, amounting to civil war on a small scale, in which in one day 10 men were killed and over 60 wounded, Carnegie won. He fought, however, from the safe distance of Atlantic City, leaving to his partners and managers the dangers of the battle.

In his "Gospel of Wealth" Mr. Carnegie stated his opinion that "surplus wealth was a sacred trust which its possessor was bound to administer in his lifetime for the good of the community". How far he succeeded in divesting himself is not yet known, but the total amount of his benefactions is prodigious. In 1908 it was estimated that he had given over £57,000,000 in America, over £7,000,000 in Great Britain, and £1,000,000 in Europe. Education, public libraries, organs, peace movements, and the Hero Funds were the best known of his objects. The two conspicuous omissions from a set of objects thought out with much care were hospitals and churches.

There has been much difference of opinion as to the utility of his beneficence. His endowment of the Scottish universities, in particular, has been singled out for adverse comment. But it is to be remembered that the introduction of the system of options and several other important changes, such as the reflex effect of the endowments on secondary schools, were the work of the Carnegie Trustees and their advisers, rather than of Carnegie.

From boyhood Carnegie was a reader, and in middle age he developed an inclination to write. His first two books, *An American Four-in-Hand in Great Britain* and *Round the World*, were very obvious descriptions of luxurious travel. *Triumphant Democracy,* published in 1886, was an echo of political ideas imbibed in boyhood and a scream of eulogy of American democratic institutions, to the disparagement of his native country. *Wealth,* published in 1886, and *The Empire of Business,* which appeared in 1902, contained *naïve* but rather engaging egotism mingled with his philanthropic aspirations. *Problems of To-day,* published in 1908, is his best book. It consists of nine social-economic essays on wealth and labour, informed with his own experience and written from an anti-Socialistic point of view.

Carnegie's private life was simple, wholesome, and unostentatious. He had no vices and eschewed luxury and display. He was a bachelor until he was 50, when he married Miss Whitfield, of New York. Thereafter he never wearied of extolling domestic life. He has one child, a daughter, whose recent marriage was one of the great events of American life.

His principal amusements were entertaining, fishing, and golf. There were few distinguished persons whose acquaintance he did not make, and no one could come in contact with him without being impressed by the strong and shrewd character underlying a superficial but real good nature.

In later life he lived chiefly at Skibo Castle in Sutherlandshire, and his early detestation of British institutions could not be maintained when he voluntarily made his residence there. One of his dreams was the union of Great Britain and the United States. The other great dream, the abolition of war, received a great shock in 1914. During the conflict he relapsed into complete silence and seclusion.

* * *

ALEXANDER GRAHAM BELL

Inventor of the telephone, whose interest was the mechanism of speech

3 AUGUST 1922

THE WHOLE WORLD OWES a great debt to Dr. Alexander Graham Bell, whose death is announced on another page, for his invention of the telephone as it exists to-day. He will assuredly be remembered among the great inventors whose pioneer work has profoundly affected the daily life of all civilised peoples.

The telephone is an electrical instrument, but Bell was not an electrician nor primarily even a physicist, but rather a physiologist whose interest centred on speech and the mechanism of speech. This interest offers a remarkable example of heredity, for his father, Alexander Melville Bell, was an authority on physiological phonetics, and his grandfather, Alexander Bell, one on phonetics and defective speech. Both of them were Scotsmen, and he himself was born in Edinburgh, on March 3, 1847, and was educated at the High School and University of that city. When quite a young man he removed across the Atlantic with his father, and he was only twenty-five when he was appointed professor of vocal physiology in Boston University. The germ of the great invention with which his name is associated came to life white he was at Brantford, in Canada, and his first instrument was made at Boston, though it was descended, perhaps a little irregularly, from observations he had made when he was a pupil teacher in Elgin, Scotland.

At Brantford, in the middle of 1874, he was working on a tuned system of multiple telegraphy, and had attained the conception of an undulatory current, realizing that speech could be transmitted if an armature could be moved as the air is moved during the passage of a sound. At the same time he was studying, by means of a dead man's ear, the movements of the air during the utterance of a sound, and it struck him that as the small membrane that forms the ear drum can move the comparatively heavy chain of bones in the ear, a larger membrane ought to be able to move an iron armature. By the linking up of these two branches of inquiry the telephone was evolved.

Bell made his first rough speaking telephone in 1875, and the first long-distance transmission of speech dates from August, 1876, when the Dominion Telegraph Company lent him their wires for experiments, the transmitting apparatus being in Paris, Ontario, and the receiver in Brantford, eight miles away. At first transmission was in one direction only, but a few months later, after his return to Boston, reciprocal conversations were carried on between two persons at a distance from each other.

To begin with, the invention was received with a certain amount of incredulity, which on some occasions was perhaps not entirely unjustified. There is a story that when Sir William Preece, at the Royal Institution, was exhibiting some of the earliest specimens brought to this country, he arranged for a wire to Southampton, where he stationed a man with a cornet, who was to play during the lecture. Members of the audience in London were invited to listen to the strains from Southampton, and a little doubtfully admitted that they heard them, but it was afterwards found that the cornet-player had mistaken the day. Even when it was beyond doubt that the apparatus would work, there were shrewd financiers who missed fortunes through regarding it as a mere toy, and Bell told how, in the early days of the commercial exploitation of the telephone, he "created a great smile" by outlining the central exchange system which exists to-day.

Bell was also the inventor of the photo-phone and the graphophone, and he made some experiments in artificial flight. He served as president of the American Association to Promote Teaching of Speech to the Deaf, and was the author of a memoir on the formation of a deaf variety in the human race, and of the census report on the deaf of the United States, 1906. He held various honorary degrees, and was the recipient of the Albert Medal of the Royal Society of Arts in 1902, and of the Hughes Medal of the Royal Society in 1918. The freedom of his native city was conferred on him during a visit he paid to this country at the end of 1920.

It was during that visit also that he gave to *The Times* an interesting account of the romance of the telephone, which appeared on November 25 in that year. He then made the following comment when asked what he thought of the British telephone system: –

I do not want to say too much about it. I think you do very well, but you do not compare well with the United States, and I think recent history in the United States reveals the cause. We had the best system of telephony in the world before the war in the United States. Then we came into the war, the telephone was taken out of the hands of private companies and run by the Government. Immediately the efficiency of the service fell. Now the control has been returned to the companies, and I hope the efficiency will improve. The decrease in efficiency in consequence of Government ownership is found elsewhere. I visited Australia some years ago, and the telephone system, which was in the hands of the Government, could not be compared to ours in America. I am afraid that the comparatively low state of efficiency in this country as compared with our system in the United States must be attributed to Government ownership. Government ownership aims at cheapness, and cheapness does not necessarily mean efficiency.

Our experience in the United States, now that the control has been returned to the private companies, will form a good test of the value of private ownership. We have hardly a house without the telephone, but in Scotland a few days ago, looking through the telephone lists in our large cities, I was struck by the small number of private individuals with telephones. The telephone certainly has not gone into the homes here as it has in the United States. We do not mind paying for a good service, but we certainly object to pay a big price for a poor service.

Bell married in 1877 Mabel Gardiner, daughter of D. D. Hubbard, by whom he had two daughters.

* * *

ANDREW BONAR LAW

'One of the best-loved figures in our parliamentary history'

31 OCTOBER 1923

THE DEATH OF MR. BONAR LAW removes from the political stage, if not one of the greatest, certainly one of the best-loved figures in our Parliamentary history. As Prime Minister, he held office for only a few months, but the House of Commons has had few more successful leaders, and he will be remembered not so much for his brief career as Prime Minister as for the important part he played as a member of the Cabinet during and after the Great War. He was the first Prime Minister, as Mr. Baldwin was the second, who had the qualification of a career in business.

His active life may be divided into three unequal periods. The first is that of the forty-two years which separated his birth, in New Brunswick, Canada, in 1858, from his entry into Parliament in 1900. The second was spent in the House of Commons as a follower and then a colleague of Mr. Balfour in his Ministry, and subsequently in Opposition. The third dates from November 13, 1911, when on the retirement of Mr. Balfour he was unanimously elected leader of the Unionist Party in the House of Commons; and was concluded by his resignation of the Premiership on May 21, 1923.

Andrew Bonar Law was not born to hereditary wealth, like so many of our Prime Ministers, nor was he, like all of them before Disraeli, brought up in contact with the great political world, and in full view of its activities and ambitions. He had neither family connexions nor Eton friendships nor Oxford distinctions to smooth his path to political success. Nor had he the literary and social genius which made Disraeli well known when he was little more than a boy.

Young Law, the son of a Presbyterian minister and a Glasgow mother, spent his earliest years in Canada, but was soon sent to the High School in Glasgow, and, when school-days were over, placed in business with a Glasgow firm of iron merchants, who were of a family related to his own. He had a marked success as a man of business, and, if that had been his ambition, he might no doubt have become one of the magnates of the industries of the Clyde.

Like Joseph Chamberlain, with whom he was soon to be so closely connected, he decided, comparatively early in life, that he had made as much money as he needed, and that it was time to gratify the political ambitions which he had entertained from boyhood. The result was that in 1900 he retired from business and entered Parliament as Conservative member for the Blackfriars Division of Glasgow.

Few men have made their mark more quickly. His first speech, a reply to an attack by Mr. Lloyd George on the conduct of the South African War, attracted attention, not only by its argumentative power, but by its exhibition of his extraordinary gift, conspicuous throughout his career, for dealing with a complicated series of facts and arguments without the assistance of a single note. This speech won for him the warm congratulations of his leaders and the admiration of the House. But the Press Gallery was not equally complimentary; and in later years he would tell the story of his disappointment when, conscious of his success, he looked to see what the newspapers would say of him, and got no better reward for his trouble than the remark that "the debate was continued with characteristic dullness by Mr. Bonar Law." To the very end his great qualities were far more clearly perceived and appreciated by members of Parliament than they were by the world outside.

He became Parliamentary Secretary of the Board of Trade in 1902, and when, during the following year, Chamberlain proposed the policy of Tariff Reform and resigned in order to preach it, Bonar Law was perhaps his most active, convinced, and convincing supporter.

The country, however, did not respond to the appeals either of Chamberlain or of Bonar Law. Mr. Balfour, who struck an uncertain note, resigned, and the Unionist Party was routed at the General Election which followed in January, 1906. Bonar Law lost his seat, but soon returned to Parliament as member for Dulwich. The failure of Chamberlain's health increased Bonar Law's importance among Tariff Reformers, who saw in him the ablest exponent of their views.

At the second General Election of 1910, Bonar Law, abandoning his safe seat, came near to victory in a gallant fight in North-West Manchester. Meanwhile, the Conservative Party grew more and more dissatisfied with Mr. Balfour's leadership, and he resigned in the autumn of 1911. The Conservative members of Parliament seemed almost equally divided between the claims of Mr. Long and Mr. Austen Chamberlain to the succession. All but those who were very much behind the scenes were surprised when the difficulty was solved by the retirement of both in favour of Mr. Bonar Law, who had returned to the House as member for Bootle. One of the reasons in his favour was, no doubt, that, though at least as convinced a Tariff Reformer as Mr. Austen Chamberlain, he had a name less alarming to those who did not love that policy. The rest was done by his ability in debate, and by the general liking which his unpretentious kindliness, simplicity, and common sense had won from his party, and, indeed, from the House as a whole.

Bonar Law held the Leadership for over nine years, and the first three and a half of these were spent in Opposition. Naturally enough, having come in to make good what was considered Mr. Balfour's weakness, he was more tempted to exhibit the opposite fault. No leader of Opposition has ever taken up a more uncompromising attitude than

Bonar Law assumed as against all the policies of the Asquith Ministry. No doubt he was fortified by the probably well-founded conviction that not one of these policies would have been ratified by the electorate if it could have been submitted as a single issue. It was with this feeling that he declared that a meaner Bill, or one brought forward by meaner methods, than the Welsh Disestablishment Bill had never been introduced into Parliament.

On the Irish question, no prominent Conservative, except Sir Edward Carson, went further than the Leader of the party in uncompromising resistance to the proposals of the Ministry. He went over to Belfast, and at a great demonstration of Ulstermen advised them to trust to themselves, prophesying that if they did so they would save themselves by their exertions and save the Empire by their example. And in July, 1912, he said, in a speech at Blenheim, that he could imagine no lengths of resistance to which the Ulstermen might go in which he would not be prepared to support them, subsequently declaring in Parliament that these words were deliberate and had been written down beforehand.

There is this at least to be said with confidence about his Irish attitude. He fixed his attention on what the history of the next ten years proved to have been the real point, though Mr. Asquith's Government attempted to ignore it till their blindness had led the country to the verge of civil war. The World War prevented the possibility of the Irish war, but when the question again became alive it had become clear to all that Bonar Law had been right in always regarding the problem of Ulster as the vital one.

The moment it became obvious that the risk of war was acute and immediate, Bonar Law gave an assurance of Opposition support to Mr. Asquith. And the promise was more than fulfilled. All that a leader of Opposition could do to encourage the King's Government and strengthen its hands was done by Bonar Law from the eve of the declaration of war.

Ten months later, he and his friends were invited by Mr. Asquith to share the responsibilities of office. The post which Bonar Law took was that of Colonial Secretary but his most important work as a Minister was not departmental. He showed admirable loyalty to the Prime Minister, as Mr. Asquith frequently testified,

But he became gradually dissatisfied with a certain lack of vigour in the conduct of the war, and in December, 1916, he supported Mr. Lloyd George in his demand that it should be entirely entrusted to a Committee of four, of whom the Prime Minister was not one. The strangest thing about this strange proposal is that Mr. Asquith considered accepting a slight modification of it. It was made on December 1. By the 5th Mr. Asquith had definitely rejected it, and first Mr. Lloyd George and then Mr. Asquith resigned.

The King naturally invited Mr. Bonar Law to form a Ministry, but Mr. Lloyd George was plainly the man of the moment, and he became Prime Minister on December 7. He formed a War Cabinet of five, of whom, of course, one was Bonar Law, who, taking the lead of the House of Commons, was not expected to attend the Cabinet as regularly as the other four, but was effectively Leader of the House of Commons, Chancellor of the Exchequer, and a member of the War Cabinet.

In this third capacity he played a less conspicuous part; but he knew what he wanted and meant to get it. "We are fighting for peace now," he told the Pacifists, "and for security for peace in the time to come; you cannot get that by treaty. There can be no peace till the Germans are beaten and know that they are beaten."

The Ministry decided to appeal to the country directly after the Armistice, and to make their appeal as a Coalition, though most of the Labour Ministers resigned and the Labour Party had their separate election programme. Bonar Law, who was himself returned for Central Glasgow, a seat which he held till his death, joined with the Prime Minister in issuing a manifesto to the electors which was completely successful in winning the election, but had disastrous results when it was won.

There can be little doubt that its general suggestion of a new heaven and earth after the war came rather from the somewhat shallow optimism, or from the electioneering instincts, of Mr. Lloyd George than from the Scottish caution and common sense of Bonar Law. It is likely that Bonar Law was more pleased with the overwhelming victory which the manifesto produced than alarmed at the unrealisable expectations which it was certain to arouse.

The principal business of the new Ministry, in which Bonar Law ceased to be Chancellor of the Exchequer but remained Leader of the House of Commons, was the making of the Peace. But with that Bonar Law, though appointed one of the Plenipotentiaries, had little to do, as his duties in Parliament seldom allowed him to attend the Paris Conference. He had, indeed, enough to do at home. On the whole, Bonar Law and his colleagues, inspired by Mr. Lloyd George, may be said to have met the difficulties, for which they were partly responsible, with a mixture of sympathy and firmness which gave time for illusions to wear themselves out, and for economic realities to assert themselves in the minds of all parties.

In March 1921, Bonar Law was suddenly taken ill, and at once resigned and went abroad. He returned in time to support the so-called Treaty of December, 1921, constituting the Irish Free State. For that Agreement Bonar Law had no responsibility, but he returned to his place in the House of Commons to give it his support and urge Ulster to accept it, insisting that England would never allow her to be invaded or coerced by the rest of Ireland.

Bonar Law had a great reception in the House on his reappearance. But he at once resumed the retirement which his weak health continued to make necessary. However, he was now watching events more closely, and, as even the speech on the agreement showed, with more detachment. The position, amounting to something like a dictatorship, which Mr. Lloyd George had assumed was regarded with more and more dislike by a large number of Conservatives, and Bonar Law, no longer in daily touch with the wand of the magician, gradually became critical of it. Matters came to a crisis in the autumn and, finally, on October 19, 1922, a meeting of Conservative members of the House of Commons was held at the Carlton Club, at which a motion was carried declaring that the Conservative Party should fight the election "as an independent party with its own leader and its own programme." This motion Bonar Law had, the day before, been persuaded to come and support. The result was that Mr. Lloyd George resigned and Bonar Law became Prime Minister on October 23.

The election campaign almost immediately followed, and the new Prime Minister's speeches sharply marked his departure from the Lloyd George system and atmosphere. He declared for a policy of tranquillity and economy, reduction of our commitments, so far as our obligations allowed, both abroad and at home, and abandonment of the practice of constant personal intervention by the Prime Minister in the work of the Departments. Never was an election a greater contrast to its predecessor. Instead of a flood of promises, there were no promises at all. But the electors were tired of them, and in 1922 Bonar Law, with his simplicity and tranquillity, was as much the man of the moment as Lloyd George had been in 1918 with his magniloquent promises and programmes. The elections resulted in the return of 344 Conservatives, giving the new Ministry a sufficient majority even if all sections of the Opposition combined against them.

Mr. Bonar Law's Premiership was one of the shortest on record. It was with many fears that he had gone to the Carlton Club meeting, but he had been given reason to hope that he might be able to bear the strain of office for at least a year. He bore it only for about six months, when his voice failed and he had to go away for a complete rest. When he returned, on May 20, 1923, he was too ill to do anything but resign.

In so short a Premiership, interrupted by a General Election, he had obviously little opportunity to leave any great mark on public affairs. The chief problems with which he had to deal were unemployment at home and Franco-German relations abroad. His refusal to receive a deputation of the unemployed, whom he referred to the Minister of Labour, was a courageous illustration of his determination to leave each Department to do its own business, and, after some agitation, was vindicated by success. For the rest Bonar Law maintained his old popularity in the House of Commons, of which his qualities both of mind and of temper made him a born leader. Indeed, he held the affections of his colleagues and of members of Parliament as very few leaders have. When his daughter married almost every member of the House subscribed to a present for her; and the same kind of feeling was shown when he finally retired in such tributes as that of his successor, Mr. Baldwin: "Of Mr. Bonar Law I cannot trust myself to speak: I love the man."

No man could have played the part which he played during the five most strenuous years of English history without being possessed of very rare qualities. "Character, character, character," said one of those who had known him longest. That, and his modesty and simplicity, his life of duty and austerity, his complete indifference to pomps and vanities and privileges of power, combined to give him a place in hearts of his friends and in the confidence of the nation which men of more dazzling genius have been able to win.

Mr. Bonar Law married in 1891 Annie Pitcairn, daughter of Harrington Robley, of Glasgow. She died in 1909, leaving several children. Two of the sons were killed in the war; one of the daughters is the wife of Major-General Sir Frederick Sykes.

DOUGLAS HAIG

'The greatest soldier that the empire possessed.'
His qualities were industry, coolness, and tenacity

31 JANUARY 1928

THE GREATEST SOLDIER that the Empire possessed has passed away suddenly, while still in the fullness of his powers. Lord Haig not only shouldered the heaviest military burden that any Briton has ever borne, but, when the War was over, and with the same foresight that distinguished him in his campaigns, he took up a task which probably no other could have accomplished, and devoted all his time and energy to the service of his old comrades in the field.

Haig's great characteristic was thoroughness. From his boyhood he seemed almost to foresee what destiny had in store for him and was constantly preparing himself for it. Among his contemporaries none could rival him in the knowledge of his profession. He had worked up through every grade of the Staff and had commanded every unit, so that, when he reached the position of Commander-in-Chief of the greatest Army that the Empire had ever put in the field, he was known to all his subordinates as being a master of every detail.

As a young man in South Africa, and in 1914, when he commanded the I Corps, Haig showed that he was able to manœuvre troops in a war of movement. By the time he became an Army commander the front in France had become stabilised, and he then showed his ability to adapt himself to the changed conditions of trench warfare. It was he who was responsible for planning the operations that were to be undertaken at Neuve Chapelle, and so well did he foresee the character of the new struggle that his dispositions and orders for that battle became in their essential details the model of all future British attacks during the War, except in regard to the length of the preliminary bombardment.

To thoroughness he added coolness, optimism, and an intense tenacity of purpose. In the darkest days of the First Battle of Ypres and of the March offensive he never became ruffled, but continued to carry on his duties as though he were at manœuvres. His judgment was sound; he never failed to appreciate the difficulties of his situation; but at the same time he saw those of his adversary, and was always able to distinguish the factors favourable to himself. His bulldog tenacity was remarkable. Once he had taken a decision nothing would move him from it, and, though at times he was severely criticised for persisting in operations long after their advantages had passed, he held strongly to the opinion, expressed in his celebrated order of April 11, 1918, that "Victory will belong to the side which holds out the longest ... There is no other course open to us but to fight it out. Every position must be held to the last man; there must be no retirement. With our backs to the wall, and believing in the justice of our cause, each one of us must fight on to the end."

In spite of this tenacity he was always willing to listen to his allies and to cooperate with them. One of the most striking features of the First Battle of Ypres was the manner in which he worked with the French – with Dubois, who commanded the IX Corps, and with D'Urbal, the commander of the Eighth Army. Later on, too, when he was Commander-in-Chief, he was in the closest cooperation with both Foch and Petain. He resisted, however, to the utmost all attempts to commit him to enterprises which he considered dangerous, and where he considered that the public good required it he was always willing to subordinate his own interests. He gave a notable example of this characteristic at Doullens, for it was due to him more than to anyone else that Foch was appointed without opposition and without friction to the supreme command. It was he, too, who, after Lord Milner had proposed that Foch should be appointed to co-ordinate the action of the Allied Armies on the Amiens Front, urged the inadequacy of this step, and had Foch's authority extended to cover the whole of the Western Front.

Douglas Haig was born in Edinburgh, June 19, 1861, the youngest of the sons of John Haig, of Cameron Bridge, Fife, sixth in descent from Robert Haig, who was the second son of the 17th laird of Bemersyde, Roxburghshire. He was educated at Clifton Bank School, St. Andrews,

Clifton College, where he played Rugby football, and Brasenose College, Oxford, whence, as University candidate, as was the custom then, he passed not direct into the Army but into the R.M.C., Sandhurst. There he exhibited altogether exceptional zeal for a cadet, not only listening to the instruction but writing out notes of it each day. Commissioned into the 7th Hussars in 1885, he went out to India, and soon became known as a polo player and breaker of polo ponies. But sport did not interfere with his duties, and in the course of time he was appointed adjutant of his regiment. His first step on the ladder was his selection to be A.D.C. to the Inspector-General of Cavalry in India.

With his eye on the Staff College, Haig had begun to resume military study seriously. He qualified at the entrance examination for the College in 1894 and was given a nomination by the Duke of Cambridge in the following year. Thus he entered Camberley in the same class as Field-Marshal Lord Allenby and with Captain (Sir Herbert) Lawrence, his future Chief of General Staff, in the class above him. During the second year Colonel G. F. R. Henderson, the historian, then one of the instructors, said one evening to a group of students, "There is a fellow in your batch who will be Commander-in-Chief one of these days," and then, without hesitation, said "Haig."

On the conclusion of the course in December, 1897, Captain Haig was attached to the Egyptian Army and took part in the Omdurman Campaign, receiving a brevet majority. Returning home at its close, he was appointed Brigade Major of the Aldershot Cavalry Brigade. In September, 1899, he was sent out to Natal and took part as Staff Officer of Sir John French in the Natal operations, just escaping from being shut up in Ladysmith. As Chief Staff Officer of the Cavalry Division during the advance he added greatly to his reputation. He was given a brevet lieutenant-colonelcy and appointed to the command of the 17th Lancers, which, however, he did not take up until the end of the war. From October, 1903, to August, 1906, he was Inspector-General of Cavalry in India, being promoted major-general in May, 1904, and marrying the Hon. Dorothy Vivian, daughter of the third Lord Vivian, during a visit home in 1905.

By the outset of the Great War, he was General Officer Commanding the Aldershot Command with the First and Second Divisions under him. He commanded these formations as a corps at the Army Manœuvres in 1912 and 1913, being created K.C.B. in the latter year.

In August, 1914, he went with the B.E.F. to France. After the First Battle of Ypres Sir Douglas Haig was promoted full general for distinguished service, and in December, on the formation of armies, was selected to be the commander of the First Army, then newly formed. In that command, under the orders of Sir John French, he fought Neuve Chapelle, Aubers Ridge, Festubert, and Loos.

When, on December 22, 1915, Sir Douglas Haig took over the command of the British Armies in France, on the removal of Sir John French, he had many great problems to face. His first efforts were directed towards the reorganisation, training, and reinforcement of the British forces in the France and Flanders theatre of war. Nothing from without – political, military, or popular – diverted his purpose from the prosecution of direct war while he remained the commander. He could be dismissed, but that was the affair of higher authority. His duty was for the day and the days to come.

His powers were set to a test at an early date. The Germans, ever alive to vital points in war, began an intensive attack on Verdun, a citadel recognised as of primary importance in the War on the Western Front. In the defence of that place the French had to exert the greatest military effort they made in the War. That effort was great in every sense of the word, but it was not sufficient to avert disaster to the Allies if it was to be fought alone. A support for the French in that defence was obviously necessary, and that support was promptly given by Sir Douglas Haig.

In cooperation with Joffre, with whom he was always in the closest sympathy, he began his preparations for the great series of the battles of the Somme. The sector of attack was selected with a high degree of military wisdom that relief might be given to Verdun, that the Allies in other theatres of war might be assisted, and that the German strength in front – never slight in the face of British troops – might be worn down. His former skill as a Staff officer was displayed in his direction of the very complicated preparations for battle. With a full knowledge of the great issues, he gave his firm support to those engaged in matters which those outside might consider to be minor detail, and yet are in themselves the seed of victory. There were then no solutions for the apparent deadlock of siege warfare, save, possibly, direct attack. The method of direct attack was chosen, accompanied by an artillery support previously unknown in the annals of war.

The great effort failed in many ways, but its failure was in the main due to climatic conditions. Yet the effort was in one important sense not a failure – it served to save Verdun, and it broke the spirit of the German Army, which entered the battle at the zenith of its efficiency and enthusiasm. It was a great venture, and it cost many lives – a cost which humanity is apt to remember without admitting the profit. In the judgment of history it may be that the country will recognise the wisdom and discount the cost. The Somme over, there was a disposition on the part of those who did not understand its effect on the enemy to criticise the Commander-in-Chief. He was accused of being reckless of life; and he was blamed for his supposedly premature use of the tanks on September 15.

Immediately after the Somme, Haig began his preparations for a new offensive. He still believed that a "break-through" was possible. The Arras offensive, designed for the early spring in that year, was modified into a relatively minor attack over a front of 15 miles from Vimy Ridge southwards to Croisilles. The same attention to initial preparations was made, and the same early success was attained. The weather again took its share in the decision, and an early burst of success ended in a dreary series of days of heavy bombardment, in which the vast losses outweighed the territory gained.

Arras over, the long-contemplated attack on Messines was undertaken. It was admittedly a perfect battle of its kind, and the Commander-in-Chief deserves his share of credit in an enterprise which needed the support of his authority at a time when his popular reputation was declining. Success – complete success – attended the effort, and there was a general revival of spirit throughout the armies in France.

Yet at this moment of success a period of gloom was beginning for the Allies. Certain French troops, dissatisfied with their leaders, failed, whole divisions refusing to go to the front and to obey the orders of their officers. It was an ugly episode, but it was overcome by tact and decision. In the task of maintaining the line and keeping the Germans engaged, Haig and the British troops took a great part. In June, 1917, prompt preparations were made for the series of operations now known as the Battles of Ypres, 1917. Here, again, there was a minor degree of tactical success attended by very great loss. Miles of territory were nibbled away in nearly three months of action, but the German reserves were sent to the Dutch frontier to meet the expected arrival of the British from that direction. The weather again played its deadly part, the ground became a quagmire, and the mechanical weapons on which, properly, so much store was set failed in their task.

In March, 1918, came the great test of the War. The Germans, aided by climatic conditions – the weather, it seemed, never failed them in the operations of war – overran large sectors of the British front. At each point the Allied troops fell back, and there was consternation among the general public. On the other hand, there was definite confidence at General Headquarters. It was known that in so swift an advance the Germans must overreach themselves, and that ultimately, after two or three such offensives, victory must be in the hands of the Allies. To ensure complete cooperation of the Allies, at Haig's suggestion Foch was now given supreme command. At the darkest hour, on April 12, in the second German offensive, on the Lys, against Kemmel, Sir Douglas issued his "backs to the wall" order.

Thenceforward the tale is no less complicated, but it deals with victory. Haig had his plans, and, after due consideration, in almost every case Foch adopted them in preference to his own. There was a mass of heavy fighting, but in each stage it was inspired, so far as the British troops were concerned, by Haig. There were no mistakes, and future generations may turn to the military record of that year with pride, not only in the British troops, but in their commander, who had borne without complaint the stress of the years that had passed. There will be credit for Lord Haig in the earlier years of his effort, but in military achievement in the field his reputation may well rest on his share in the history of the last months of the War, when the fate of nations was in the balance, and when he never lost heart.

When Haig came home after the War was over he might have claimed any appointment in the gift of his fellow-countrymen. But he had marked out the course he meant to pursue – namely, to devote himself to the interests of ex-Service officers and men. He began a determined, and in the end successful, attempt to group together all ex-Service men into a single organisation, which should be non-political and non-sectarian, and in which officers and men should find a common opportunity of serving the country in peace as they had served her together in war.

The British Legion is essentially the work of one man, Haig. It is a work carried through in the face of no little doubt and suspicion in its early days, but the fact that the work of demobilisation, and after that the yet vaster work of absorption of the discharged millions of the Army, went through without active civil commotion is very largely due to the work that Haig did in 1919 and 1920 in giving the ex-Service men an object to work for; and thereafter, when the Legion had been formed, in directing its activities into right and worthy channels.

Sir Douglas Haig's return with his Army commanders after the War, in December, 1918, was celebrated with great public rejoicings. In March, 1919, he was appointed to be Field-Marshal Commanding-in-Chief the Forces of Great Britain, a post which was abolished in 1920. Many honours were conferred on him. Twelve Universities gave him honorary degrees, including Oxford, where his old college, Brasenose, had already made him an honorary Fellow. He was installed as Rector of St. Andrews, and was later elected Chancellor. Many cities and boroughs conferred on him their honorary freedom. He had been made a Knight of the Thistle in 1917, the year of his promotion to field marshal, and in June, 1919, he received the honour of the Order of Merit, while all the

Allies conferred on him high decorations. From France he received the *Médaille Militaire*, the greatest distinction available for a foreign general.

On August 6, 1919, a vote, including £100,000 to Sir Douglas Haig, was moved in the House of Commons by Mr. Lloyd George, then Prime Minister. In 1921 Bemersyde House and fishings, on the River Tweed, were presented to Lord Haig by his fellow-countrymen in the Empire in recognition of his services in the War, and he thus became 29th Laird of Bemersyde.

Lord Haig is survived by his widow and four children. He is succeeded by his only son, Viscount Dawick, who was born in March, 1918. His daughters are Lady Alexandra Henrietta Louise, for whom Queen Alexandra was sponsor, Lady Victoria Doris Rachel, for whom Princess Victoria was sponsor, and Lady Irene Violet Janet Haig.

* * *

RICHARD BURDON, LORD HALDANE

Lawyer, philosopher, and one of the greatest of all war ministers

20 AUGUST 1928

LORD HALDANE, WHOSE DEATH we announce this morning, possessed one of the most powerful, subtle, and encyclopædic intellects ever devoted to the public service of this country. He was a lawyer whose profound learning broadened instead of narrowing his sympathies, a philosopher of distinction, an apostle of education, and an administrator of equal courage and efficiency. The work for which, as Secretary of State for War, he was chiefly responsible is among the most important in the annals of the War Office, and his service on the

Woolsack, which he occupied for two periods, gives him high rank among the long and distinguished roll of the Lord Chancellors of England.

Because his visit to Germany in 1912 did not lead him to anticipate the War of 1914, he was at the outbreak of hostilities, at the very moment when his work of Army organisation was bearing its most brilliant fruit, violently attacked, and his own sayings were distorted to give colour to the accusations. Extravagantly unjust though this campaign against him was, it did not fail of effect, and he became extremely unpopular. Some of those colleagues who shared with him responsibility for the advice offered to the nation and the conduct of its affairs between 1912 and 1914 failed to give him, when he most needed it, the support which he had every right to expect of them, and when the First Coalition was formed, with Mr. Asquith as Prime Minister, in 1915, Lord Haldane was not included in the Government. He did not return to power for eight years, emerging at last as the first Labour Lord Chancellor. His adherence was, at the outset, of considerable value to a party without administrative experience and his advice was continually sought, but his new associates were not bound to him by such strong ties of temperament, manner, or opinion as make for enduring confidence.

That he was, at more than one stage of his career, unfortunate in his friends, few will deny; that he was subjected, during the early stages of the War, to ignorant or malicious abuse, is clear to all who are able to distinguish between disloyalty and misjudgment. But he suffered more than most men would have suffered in the same circumstances, for he had a manner in his own defence which was the worst of weapons against the calumnies of the market-place, and did little to conciliate his more reasoning critics. This appearance of aloof tactlessness was due, in part, to his voice, which was not well suited to eloquence, but even more to something within himself which, while it raised him in intellect far above most of his contemporaries, made him almost a stranger to the workings of the general mind of England. He was a subtle thinker who found it hard to understand – and unfortunately allowed his audience to become aware of his difficulty in understanding – why others did not think as subtly as he.

By nature a metaphysician and by profession a lawyer, he had an exact and an exacting mind, and, though he was in private a kindly and generous man who was neither unduly puffed up by success nor soured by misfortune, he was, in public, singularly without those qualities, good and bad – qualities of ease and warmth and humour on the one hand, of flattery and smooth persuasion on the other – which endear a politician to the masses and, perhaps, to more exalted audiences as well. He had, in short, a seeming tendency, when engaged in controversy, to treat the world as a class-room which made it at once intolerant of his mistakes and less grateful than it might otherwise have been for his high administrative and intellectual services.

Richard Burdon Haldane was born on July 30, 1856, of Scottish and Northumbrian stock. His father, Robert Haldane, belonged to an old Scottish family, and was a Writer to the Signet in Edinburgh. His mother, who died on May 21, 1925, in her 101st year, was a daughter of Richard Burdon-Sanderson, a country gentleman with property in Northumberland, and a great-niece of Lords Stowell and Eldon. Haldane was educated at Edinburgh and Gottingen Universities, obtaining first-class honours in philosophy at Edinburgh, and the Gray and Ferguson scholarships open to the four Scottish Universities.

At the age of 23 he was called by Lincoln's Inn, having read with William Barber, who at that time had a large business as an equity junior and conveyancer. After he had been at the Bar some six years and was firmly established, he decided to attempt the House of Commons. He had always been an ardent Liberal, and in 1880 had been one of Albert Grey's most active lieutenants in founding the Eighty Club. Now, in 1885, he won Haddingtonshire from the Conservatives by a narrow majority, in spite of his firmly conscientious declarations that, as a Nonconformist, he was opposed to Church Establishment, a course which was expected to lose him a considerable number of votes. His majority was increased at almost every election during the 25 years in which he represented the original or reconstituted constituency, and his place in Parliament was safe. He was a constant attendant in the

House, but his increasing practice made it more and more difficult for him to combine his political activities with his work as a junior, and in 1889 he took silk.

In the Commons Haldane steadily added to his reputation as an earnest man and he went willingly to the War Office. He was not the creator of the General Staff, which had already been set up in the War Office on the recommendation of the Esher Committee in 1904; but he brought it into existence throughout the Army in 1906 and saw that it took its novel and important position, both there and in the War Office itself, as a thinking and training department relieved from the daily cares of administration.

The Infantry Militia, which had long been in every sense a wasting force, was converted into a Special Reserve to provide for the war wastage of the Expeditionary Force till such time as war enlistments should have produced further supplies of trained men. The Garrison Artillery Militia, useless as it stood, was converted to Field Artillery, trained in cadres formed from Regular batteries surplus to requirements, to fill the very large deficiency in the mobilisation needs of that arm, and by 1910 this had been fully made good. The Yeomanry and the Volunteers, whose numbers and arms of the Service had grown up anyhow, were similarly reshaped in 1908 into an organised Territorial Force of 14 Mounted Brigades and 14 Infantry Divisions, with Artillery and Engineers for coast defence besides.

When, in 1912 (having been created Viscount Haldane of Cloan in 1911), he left the War Office for the Woolsack, the success of his policy was already assured, and his military colleagues, some of whom had not unnaturally doubted at first whether the ideas of this gentleman from the Chancery Bar were of permanent military value, had come to appreciate him as the one and only true successor to Cardwell.

Haldane's first tenure of the Lord Chancellorship continued until 1915, in May of which year he received the Order of Merit. But when the first Coalition was formed he was excluded from it, and from that time onward gradually moved in sympathy farther and farther away from his old colleagues. He had long been in close touch with the Fabian Society, and it became known, even before the end of the War, that he had Labour leanings which were likely to prove decisive. It was not, however, until the elections of December, 1922, that he publicly declared his Labour sympathies. "I want," he said, "to see a strong Labour minority in the next Parliament."

There was, then, nothing open to him but a choice between isolation on the one hand and a qualified adherence to Labour on the other; He rejected isolation, not because he was personally ambitious, but because he felt that by adopting a new allegiance he could do service which would not be possible to him acting alone. In January, 1924, he therefore entered the Cabinet once more as Lord Chancellor. His position was one of peculiar difficulty. His colleagues were in many respects strange to him; the rank and file of his party were altogether unable to regard him as one of themselves; he was the only member of the Government with Cabinet experience; and in the House of Lords, where he was never popular, he was the only representative of his group who was at all formidable. Worse than all this, though his lips had to defend the Government's action, his mind was hedged about with reservations concerning it.

Concerning his attainments in his own profession there is no dispute. He was a counsel of the first rank and a Lord Chancellor of exceptional abilities. He raised the Judicial Committee of the Privy Council to a position in which it commanded increasing confidence in India and the Dominions. In this he accomplished a part only of his Imperial desires, for during his Lord Chancellorship he recommended that the representative aspect of the Judicial Committee should be developed – to some extent this was done – and he thought of what might be called a system of Imperial assize under which members of the Judicial Committee, as his Majesty's advisers, should visit India and the Dominion to hear appeals on the spot.

As a philosopher Lord Haldane cannot be classed among those few original thinkers who mould the philosophical conceptions of a future age. But his wide philosophic culture and his thorough mastery of early 19th century German philosophy, combined with a deep interest in the development of modern scientific thought, entitle him to an honourable place among the British "school" of Hegelians to which he belonged.

Haldane remained true to the Hegelian tradition to the last, and the development of the new realist schools of thought never caused him to modify the fundamental principles of his early idealism. This to a younger generation may give his thinking an old-fashioned air, but in philosophy, as elsewhere, fashions are liable to be transitory, and the rapid expansion and diversification of scientific theory stands in greater need than ever of that criticism of categories which was the central conception of his philosophical ideals.

Lord Haldane was created a Knight of the Thistle in 1913 and received the Order of Merit in 1915; but his other honours were entirely academic. He was Rector of Edinburgh University in 1905-8, Chancellor of the Universities of Bristol and St. Andrews, hon. D.C.L. of Oxford and Durham, LL.D. of Cambridge, Edinburgh, Manchester, Birmingham, Bristol, McGill, and the University of Wales, and hon. Ph.D. of Gottingen. He was elected F.R.S. in 1906, and was president of the Royal Economic Society and a member of the Committee of Council on Education in Scotland.

Lord Haldane was unmarried, and his peerage becomes extinct. He leaves two brothers, Dr. J. S. Haldane, F.R.S., Reader in Physiology at Oxford, and Sir W. S. Haldane, formerly Crown Agent for Scotland; and a sister, Miss Elizabeth Haldane, C.H., the translator of Hegel and biographer of Ferrier and Descartes, who is also known for her social work, especially in nursing.

SIR ROBERT LORIMER

*Influential architect who created the Scottish baronial style, and whose
masterpiece is the Scottish National War Memorial*

14 SEPTEMBER 1929

SIR ROBERT LORIMER, THE ARCHITECT of the Scottish National War
Memorial, whose death is announced on another page, must be
pronounced to have been one of the most original architects of our
time. The originality was all the more remarkable in that he worked
for the most part in traditional forms hallowed by associations. He
might almost be said to have evolved a style of his own, in which Gothic
and Renaissance elements were blended in a manner which bore no
resemblance to the mingling of motives which marked the transition
from one to the other, and everything he did bore the stamp of his
personality. Of no other contemporary architect can it be said that his
buildings are more immediately recognizable. To his originality in
design Lorimer added a passion for fine craftsmanship, and he was one
of the first of our architects to see the importance of "team-work," in
which – allowing for all the differences between ours and the Gothic
period – the architect, sculptor, painter and glazier, should once more
be closely associated.

Robert Stodart Lorimer, who was a younger son of the late Professor
Lorimer, of Edinburgh University and Kellie Castle, Fife, and brother
of the well-known painter, Mr. John Henry Lorimer, A.R.W.S. R.P., was
born on November 4, 1864. At the age of 21 he entered the office of
Sir Rowand Anderson, LL.D., in Edinburgh, remaining there for the
next 4½ years as pupil. After an interval of travelling in England, he
went as assistant to the late G. F. Bodley, R.A., whose excellent influence
could be traced in his handling of Gothic, with an emphasis upon plane
and mass rather than upon the linear character, which was a natural
consequence of medieval methods of construction. Lorimer was with
Bodley in London for only 18 months. He then returned to Edinburgh,

and, in 1893, set up in practice for himself. The greater part of his earlier work was connected with the restoration of and addition to old Scottish houses, a practice which gave him a profound understanding of the vernacular style with its methods and materials.

The first work that brought Lorimer into public notice was the new chapel for the Knights of the Thistle, St. Giles' Cathedral, Edinburgh, for which he was chosen by the trustees in 1909. In this work he made full employment of the elaborate carving which was to be a feature of most of his buildings, though his later work is simpler, with the decorative detail concentrated at particular points.

No doubt it was the success of the chapel which prompted his selection, in 1919, to design the Scottish National War Memorial on Edinburgh Castle Rock. The complete plan as originally proposed included the internal alteration of some of the existing buildings on the Rock to adapt them for museum purposes, but this part of the scheme was dropped, and in October, 1922, Lorimer submitted to the King and Queen, on their visit to Holyrood, a model showing his proposals and embodying the minor alterations suggested by the memorial committee after consultation with the Ancient Monuments Board for Scotland and the Office of Works. In a recent letter to *The Times*, on August 30, to be precise, apropos the controversy over the Haig Statue, Lorimer told us how his original design was received with "a tornado of abuse." It was characteristic of his masculinity that no attempt was made to amend the design. It was thrown on the scrap-heap and an entirely new scheme – suggested by a layman – was begun.

The Scottish National War Memorial was opened by the Prince of Wales in July, 1927, and was then fully described in *The Times*. As will be remembered, it takes the form of an addition to Edinburgh Castle, to the north of the existing barrack, in the form of a shrine approached through a hall of honour recording all the Scottish regiments that took part in the War. But not only are soldiers recorded, but in the decorations, of carved stone or stained glass, are commemorated the Navy, the Air Force, the Women's Services – even the animals and birds that were employed upon active service. The shrine is centred upon a natural outcrop of rock, upon which is placed the Golden Book containing the names of the Scottish men and women who died in the War. There can be no doubt about the popular admiration which the memorial has evoked. It is visited annually by great numbers, and the impression made upon them is unmistakable. Expert opinion may be divided as to its architectural merits, but it can be said that it actually improves the silhouette of the Castle Rock when seen from below, and that as an example of collaboration between different artists and craftsmen, and as a museum of commemorative symbolism in detail, it must be unique.

More recent works of Lorimer's were the new Department of Zoology of the University of Edinburgh, on Blackford Hill – an example of his severely-practical designing for contemporary needs – and the new Chapel at Stowe School, which was opened by Prince George so lately as last July. It was fully described and illustrated in *The Times* at the time, but attention may again be called to it as a peculiarly characteristic work of its author; showing his ingenuity in combining old and new, his blending of Gothic and Renaissance flavours, and his delight in symbolical ornament carried out in terms of fine craftsmanship. Possibly when all is said about his powers as a designer of buildings it is as an inspirer of "team-work" in others that Lorimer will be best remembered. Everybody who came in contact with him became infected with his enthusiasm, and his workmen worshipped him.

Among the Scottish buildings restored or added to by Lorimer are Dunrobin Castle, Sutherland, Balmanno Castle, Perthshire, Monzie Castle, Crieff, and The Glen, Innerleithen; and he was responsible for the present form of Arkinglas and Dunderave Castle, Argyllshire, Marchmont House, Berwickshire, Bracken-brough, Penrith, and Rowallan, Ayrshire. In England he restored Lympne Castle, Kent. A peculiarly charming example of his ecclesiastical work is the Roman Catholic Church of St. Peter, Morningside, Edinburgh.

Lorimer was a man of vigorous personality, interested in many sides of art, definite in his views and a keen controversialist. He contributed frequently to *The Times*, his letter of August 30, already mentioned, being his second on the subject of the Haig Statue. His principal recreation was foreign travel.

He was elected A.R.A. in 1920 and R.S.A. in 1921, was knighted in 1911, and created K.B.E. in 1928. He married in 1903 Violet, daughter of the late Mr. Edward Wyld, of The Tile House, Denham, Bucks, and had three sons and one daughter.

* * *

ARTHUR JAMES, LORD BALFOUR

Statesman and thinker, whose declaration led to the creation of a Jewish state

20 MARCH 1930

THE DEATH OF LORD BALFOUR deprives the country of one who had long been the most intellectually distinguished of its statesmen. The length of his political life is measured by the fact that he had led both the House and the Opposition with Gladstone facing him on the other side of the table, and had even sat in Parliament under the leadership of Disraeli. He had lived on to be himself Prime Minister, and, after resigning the leadership and apparently bringing his political career to an end, to resume office in the great crisis of the War, and during the seven years 1915-1922, which are perhaps the most critical in our history, to play a part which, on some matters of the highest importance, was second only to the Prime Minister's. It was not until last year, when he was 80, that he finally retired from office.

If the League of Nations increases in strength and authority as the years go by, he will, once more, be remembered as the man whose wisdom, courage, and personal charm did more than could be done by any other statesman to guide the League through the first three critical years of its life.

Arthur James Balfour was the eldest son of James Maitland Balfour, of Whittingehame, East Lothian, and of Lady Blanche, daughter of the second Marquess of Salisbury. He was born at Whittingehame on July 25, 1848, and was named Arthur after the great Duke of Wellington, who was an intimate friend of his grandmother, the second Marchioness of Salisbury. He went to Eton at 14 and did well enough, though he carried off no prizes, intellectual or physical. All through his life he suffered from an extremely poor verbal memory, as well as an inability to grasp the intricacies of English spelling.

In 1866 he went up to Trinity College, Cambridge, where he devoted himself chiefly to philosophy under Henry Sidgwick, who was to become his brother-in-law. At the General Election of 1874 he came forward for Hertford, practically a "pocket" borough, at the urgent wish of his uncle, Lord Salisbury, was elected unopposed, and so began a Parliamentary career which was to last for more than half a century. His first Parliament ended with the dissolution of 1880 and the fall of Disraeli. Balfour kept the seat by a majority of 164 (564 to 400), and in the Parliament of 1880-85 he began to make his name.

Lord Salisbury became Prime Minister in June, 1885, and at the General Election in November Balfour was returned for East Manchester, a purely working-class constituency, and held the seat for 21 years. The election was hardly over before it was known that Gladstone was going to declare for Home Rule. He did so when Parliament met, and resumed office with the help of the Irish vote. But he split his party in two, and the combination of Conservatives and Liberal-Unionists which defeated him a few months later (July, 1886) continued to govern the country for the next 20 years, with a brief interval during which they were almost as powerful in Opposition as they had been in office.

In the new Ministry Balfour became Secretary for Scotland with a seat in the Cabinet, and it was not till nine months later that he was offered and took the great opportunity of his life as Chief Secretary for

Ireland. He framed and passed probably the best, as it was the most drastic, of the long series of Irish Coercion measures, and with this in his hand he determined to show Ireland that Parliament was her master. His physical endurance through long nights of inflamed debate was only equaled by his unaffected indifference to the threats and attempts to take his life.

Perceiving that the poverty of Ireland and its bad land system were at the root of the trouble, he at once passed a Bill admitting leaseholders to the benefits of the Act of 1881, and another granting £5,000,000 more to the sums already in hand for land purchase. Finally, in 1891, he carried a Land Purchase Act of his own, which provided £23,000,000 for the same purpose.

He also undertook a tour with his sister and his private secretary, George Wyndham, in 1890 through the miserable and dangerous congested districts of the West. In Ireland the personal touch has often done what nothing else could do. The news that Balfour was fearlessly driving through the worst parts of Ireland in an open car was received with admiration and enthusiasm in England. But that was nothing to the demonstrative welcome he received from the peasants of Connaught. He had come to see their misery, and they saw in him their deliverer. This memorable Chief Secretaryship, the decisive event of Balfour's life as committing him irrevocably to politics, lasted a little over three years and a half. In October, 1891, Mr. W. H. Smith, the Leader of the House of Commons, died, and Balfour inevitably took his place. Perhaps this was the highest moment of Balfour's career, so far as personal success was concerned.

The new century saw three great events: the death of Queen Victoria in January, 1901; the Boer surrender which ended the war in May, 1902; and the retirement of Lord Salisbury in July of the same year. Balfour naturally succeeded him, with Chamberlain's full approval. Each had gifts which the other lacked; and Chamberlain's gifts were of a kind that counts more easily in politics than Balfour's. But Balfour's tact, charm, good temper, and dialectical skill had shown themselves to be of immense value in the House; and there was moreover the fact, decisive in itself, that he was the Conservative leader, and that it was his party, and not Chamberlain's, which provided the bulk of the Unionist combination, both in Parliament and in the country.

In spite of these advantages, however, Balfour's Prime Ministership cannot be said to have been a great personal success. It lasted a little more than three years, from July, 1902, to November, 1905; and throughout the whole period the Ministry was plainly losing ground. Balfour realised from the first that, just as Chamberlain had broken up the Liberal Party from which he had sprung, so now he was doing the same thing by the party to whom he had transferred a recent allegiance. As a trained economist Balfour shrank from the methods of his colleague and his cheap platform appeals.

With a Front Bench manned by so many Ministers of slight experience, moderate Parliamentary status, and slender debating ability, it was inevitable that they should be shepherded by their leader, their mistakes rectified, and their particular business forwarded when a difficult situation arose. Balfour rarely left the Bench; if he did so for a brief interval he was always within call. In this way the necessary business of the Government during the Session was accomplished, but at no small cost. At the end of 1905 it required all Balfour's tact, persuasion, and personal influence to bring the Government to an end by resignation before meeting Parliament. The Cabinet was sharply divided, but the truth was that the mandate of 1900 was exhausted, and such Parliamentary obligations as were really due were accomplished. The great defeat at the General Election of January, 1906, followed.

Balfour's position was now one of extreme difficulty. He had lost the seat at Manchester which he had held since 1885, and suffered under inevitable discredit from the great defeat. He was soon found a seat as member for the City of London, but at first the new majority assumed towards him an air of contemptuous indifference. It was not long, however, before he had taught them their mistake, and the hostile House of 1906-1910 learnt to regard him with the admiration, and even with a good deal of the affection, with which he had been regarded by its predecessors.

Thenceforward, till the outbreak of the War, Balfour naturally remained in comparative retirement, though he spoke with vigour and effect both in Parliament and in the country against the Home Rule and Welsh Disestablishment proposals of the Government, which were rejected by the Lords in 1912 and 1913. He also used his now leisure in giving many addresses on literary and philosophic subjects.

On the outbreak of war Balfour's services were immediately placed at his country's disposal, and they were immediately used. For he began at once, and before any other Conservatives took office, to be very closely associated with the Government, having retained his seat on the Committee of Imperial Defence, of which, as we have seen, he was the chief author. He was thus from the first, at least for war purposes, a kind of unofficial member of the Cabinet.

On the formation, in May, 1915, of the first Coalition Cabinet he became First Lord of the Admiralty. This post was pressed on him by Mr. Asquith, though he himself would have preferred an office of minor importance. He at once restored the harmony of the Board, which had been disturbed by Lord Fisher and Mr. Churchill, who had now both resigned.

Six months later Mr. Lloyd George superseded Mr. Asquith as Prime Minister, and since Lord Grey refused to remain at the Foreign Office, Balfour was the obvious man to take his place. Not only had he occasionally acted as Foreign Secretary years before, as a substitute for Lord Salisbury, but he had always taken an exceptional interest in foreign affairs, and his share of responsibility for the recent foreign policy of the country was as great as that of Lord Lansdowne, and not very much less than that of Lord Grey.

Balfour had hardly taken up his new duties when Germany instituted the unrestricted submarine campaign, which soon brought the United States into the war. The result of this was that he left England for America in April, 1917, as the head of a British Mission sent to arrange cooperation with that country. His quickness, his charm, his eloquence, and his complete appreciation of the highest American ideals made his visit a triumphant success; and he received the great compliment, never before paid to a British subject, of being asked to address the House of Representatives.

In other respects the fact that the War occupied the whole attention of the Government and was in the hands of a War Cabinet of four, of whom Balfour was not one, diminished the importance of his tenure of the Foreign Office. Indeed, Mr. Lloyd George as Prime Minister rapidly obtained a personal ascendancy in his Ministry which overshadowed all his colleagues. It was Balfour, however, who in November, 1917, made the famous declaration regarding the provision of a "national home" for the Jews in Palestine after the War.

The War ended in November, 1918, and the principal business of 1919 was the making of the Peace. Balfour was, as Foreign Secretary, the second British representative at the Conference which assembled at Paris in January and gave him many opportunities of exhibiting his powers of persuasion and of putting a case. But after a time, when the Prime Ministers began to take things almost entirely into their own hands, and to set aside rather lightly, and often with little knowledge, decisions which had been carefully arrived at by the Foreign Ministers and their staffs, Balfour undoubtedly took less trouble about work which so often seemed only done for the sake of being at once undone. The result was those rather frequent appearances in the tennis courts which suggested a physical vigour and an official leisure which equally astonished the world of the Conference.

A few months after the Peace of Versailles was signed Balfour left the Foreign Office, becoming Lord President of the Council in October, 1919. About the same time he was chosen Chancellor of the University of Cambridge in succession to his distinguished brother-in-law, Lord Rayleigh.

Balfour did not again hold any Cabinet office involving important administrative duties. But he continued active, and in February, 1920, he presided at the first meeting of the Council of the new League of Nations. Until he retired from office in October, 1922, he remained the chief British representative on the League. In this position his great gifts of intellect, character, and personal charm once more found an ideal field, and all who knew the work whether of the Council or of the Assembly knew that in each case the success attained was largely due to the admiring confidence universally inspired by Balfour.

He did not take office in the new Government formed by Mr. Bonar Law, and in March, 1922, he was first created a Knight of the Garter, and then, in the following May, was raised to the peerage as Earl of Balfour and Viscount Traprain of Whittingehame. He had received the Order of Merit in 1916.

In the spring of 1925 Lord Balfour paid a visit to Palestine to open the University of Jerusalem, and was received with enthusiasm by the Jewish population, while the Arabs showed no open hostility. He returned much impressed by the advance which Palestine had made in industries and agriculture, and convinced that the Arabs had also been benefited by the establishment of the Jewish colonies, and that the "novel experiment" would be a success. His last letter to *The Times*, which he signed with General Smuts and Mr. Lloyd George, urging the appointment of an authoritative Commission to investigate the whole working of the Mandate, appeared on December 20 last.

Immediately after his return Lord Balfour joined Mr. Baldwin's second Ministry as Lord President of the Council, in succession to the late Lord Curzon and took under his special charge the Civil Research Committee which was set up by the Cabinet. By this time he had become a national rather than a party figure. The second phase of his official career began when he was 67, and lasted till he had reached the age of 81, a wonderful record for a statesman who had retired on the grounds of ill-health at the age of 63. He held the office of Lord President from 1925 till the end of that Parliament, and attended a Council at Craigweil House on May 10, 1929, when he had his last audience of the King. But this was a final effort made after a long abstention, due to illness, from all public appearances.

Lord Balfour was unmarried, and his peerages descend by special remainder to his brother, the Right Hon. Gerald William Balfour, who married Lady Betty Lytton, and has a son, Robert Arthur Lytton Balfour, born in 1902. Failing that line, there are further remainders to the sons of Lord Balfour's late brother, Colonel Eustace Balfour.

* * *

SIR ARTHUR CONAN DOYLE

The creator of Sherlock Holmes, whose pamphlet on the causes of the Boer War won him a knighthood

8 JULY 1930

SIR ARTHUR CONAN DOYLE, novelist, patriot, and in his later years ardent spiritualist, whose death in his seventy-second year we announce this morning, came of a family well known in the world of art and humour. His grandfather was John Doyle, the portrait painter and lithographer, who, under the signature of "H. B.," produced the still well-remembered caricatures of the Duke of Wellington and other great men of his day. Of the sons of John Doyle one was the yet more famous Richard ("Dicky") Doyle, who designed "the best known picture in the world," the present cover of *Punch*, and worked much for that journal until his religious convictions – the family being Irish and Roman Catholic – compelled him to sever his connexion with a paper that attacked the Pope. Another son was Charles Doyle, also an artist, who settled in Edinburgh.

Arthur Conan Doyle was the eldest son, born on May 22, 1859, of this Charles Doyle. He received his education at Stonyhurst and at Edinburgh University, and adopted the profession of medicine, practising at Southsea from 1882 to 1890. Though it is not to medicine that he owed his fame, his knowledge and experience were of service to him in more than one way. He introduced the subject again and again into his novels, and not only into the specifically medical stories, such as *Round the Red Lamp*; and, always patriotic and keenly interested in the work and fortunes of the British Empire, he put himself at the disposal of his country during the South African War and served as senior physician to the field hospital equipped and maintained by Sir (then Mr.) John Langman.

One result of this experience was an important pamphlet (following a book on "The Great Boer War") entitled *The Cause and Conduct of the War*, which was translated into 12 European languages, and given away by thousands. The object of the pamphlet was to put the facts of the case fairly and temperately before the peoples of Europe, and to disabuse them of some, at least, of the erroneous ideas that had been industriously spread on the subject of our political morality and our methods of warfare. It was doubtless in recognition of these services, no less than of those he rendered in fiction, that in 1902 he received the honour of knighthood. His public career also included two unsuccessful contests for a seat in Parliament, the first for Central Edinburgh in the Liberal Unionist interest in 1900, the second for the Hawick Burghs as a Tariff Reformer in 1906.

It is, however, as a writer of fiction that Sir Arthur Conan Doyle was most widely known. The stories which his name brings instantaneously to the mind are those of which Sherlock Holmes is the central figure. The personality of the eccentric amateur detective – with his fiddle, his dressing-gown, his strong tobacco, his courage and resource, and his genius for the unravelling of mysteries which no mere professional detective could hope to possess – was well fitted to catch the popular imagination and his creator made use of him with an ingenuity which was none the less remarkable because he knew each secret to start with, and worked backwards from it. And it cannot have been wholly by luck or accident (though it may have been by inspiration) that the character of Holmes's friend, Dr. Watson, has become no less famous and even more beloved than Holmes himself. Besides this remarkable success in rejuvenating detective fiction – to the great advantage of his successors – Conan Doyle achieved sterling results in the long list of historical romances that sprang from his fertile brain, from 1887, when he published his first book, *A Study in Scarlet,* for some half a century onward. The tales of the Napoleonic era concerning Brigadier Gerard; *Micah Clarke, The White Company, Sir Nigel* – these and others are still popular, and deserve to be. But none of them, nothing else that Doyle ever wrote, equals *Rodney Stone,* which contains, incidentally, the best exposition of the author's passion for pugilism.

His work for the stage was less successful than his books. Only one of his plays achieved a great vogue: the little *Story of Waterloo,* which provided Sir Henry Irving with one of his favourite and most effective characters, that of the very old soldier, Corporal Gregory Brewster.

In his later years Sir Arthur Conan Doyle gave himself up more and more to the enthusiasms which his quick sympathies aroused in a generous nature. These included Home Rule for Ireland, prison reform, divorce, and especially spiritualism. Always fond of travelling, he visited Australia in 1921 and South Africa when he was 70, in the interests of the beliefs to which he had been converted from the sheer materialism of his early manhood. He wrote a history of spiritualism; and his views on the evidence for it and on evidence in general coloured much of his later fiction. Among his many exploits in defence of what he believed to be truth and justice was his long and finally successful struggle for the release of Oscar Slater. In this he showed himself as keen and generous a sportsman as he did in the hunting-field (it took a weight-carrier to bear the massive frame of him), on the cricket-field, on the golf links, and in all the relations of life.

Doyle was twice married, first to Miss Louisa Hawkins, of Minsterworth, Gloucestershire, who died in 1906; and secondly, to Jean, daughter of Mr. J. B. Leckie, of Crowborough.

Defries's *Geddes, the Interpreter* (Routledge, 1927) gives an appreciative account of one of the most remarkable men of our time.

The second feature in Geddes's genius was his uniquely elaborate schematic representation of all human activities. It was a notation, with nothing mystical about it, by which, like some ancient thinkers, he sought to give a graphic representation of all the possible ways of thinking and feeling and acting in regard to any problem of life. Beginning with very simple idea-diagrams, such as a triangle to represent the three biological categories – Organism, Functioning, Environment – or their sociological correspondents – Folk, Work, Place – the schemata became gradually more and more complex and comprehensive. Some indication of them will be found in the numbers of the *Sociological Review* for recent years, and to those who find such notations useful they appear as the most remarkable organa which the mind of man has devised for disclosing all the possible relations of any subject. Many thinkers see only one aspect, many see three, a few see nine, but there are far more than these to be discerned.

Patrick Geddes was one of Huxley's students about the same time as Lloyd Morgan, a veteran still happily with us; he had many great teachers, such as Lacaze-Duthièrs at the Sorbonne; he frequented zoological stations, notably at Roscoff and Naples; he travelled far and wide and made many influential friends; he was wont to ascribe to a period of eye trouble and darkness in Mexico the development of his reflectiveness, but that was doubtless in greater part inborn. For a number of years he served as assistant in the Botany Department in the University of Edinburgh, and during that time he delivered an extraordinarily brilliant extra-mural course of lectures on zoology and developed an enthusiasm for economics, statistics, and sociology, greatly influenced by minds so different as Auguste Comte and John Ruskin! Thereafter came a long period as Professor of Botany in University College, Dundee, a period which included strenuous educational efforts of many kinds, both at home and abroad. He took an active part in university extension work and was one of the originators of "Summer Meetings," now so popular. His intense patriotism in the best sense, along with a lifelong geographical interest, led to the "Outlook Tower" on the Castle hill in Edinburgh, a centre for regional surveys and for the display of his increasing store of historical charts and picturesque schemata, many of which were eventually sunk by the *Emden* while being transported for exhibition in India.

All through his life Geddes started or supported a succession of striking educational experiments, such as his university hostels in Edinburgh; and this enthusiasm was largely an expression of his generous conviction that the inequalities in intellectual power, of which many of us are somewhat oppressively aware, are mainly due to mis-education, not to any natural disability. Whether right or wrong in this equalitarianism Geddes earned the intense gratitude of many students whom he inspired. This inspiration came about mainly through personal contact and cooperation, for lecturing did not greatly appeal to him, and his output of books was cramped by a strange fastidiousness which led him, like many an artist, to throw away one brilliant sketch after another till the opportunity passed altogether, or else to over-elaborate the canvas till intelligibility was obscured. And yet, as many passages and short essays show, he had a remarkably felicitous style. He had a strong love of the visually beautiful, especially when brought into human service, as in great buildings or homely gardens. He liked his scenery with man at home in it, conquering not conquered.

Inheriting a very fine mental and moral, as well as physical, nature, Geddes disciplined himself in nobility. He was the most disinterested of men, thinking everything of a cause, next to nothing of himself. He enjoyed plain living and high thinking. His devotion to resolute thinking, which often began at half-past 4 in the morning, made one proud of the human race. Never far from seriousness, he was a good companion, at his best on a long walk and free from care. Though always struggling against material limitations, he had many Red Letter Days, for his greatest joy was in intellectual discovery, and he was always discovering.

Geddes was very happy in his family life until there came the sorrows of the War. His first wife, Miss Anna Morton, of Liverpool, bore him three children – a daughter Norah, married to an Edinburgh architect, Mr. F. C. Mears, a son Alistair, of great promise and singular attractiveness, killed on Air Service during the War, and a younger son, Arthur, at present a lecturer on geography in Edinburgh University. Mrs. Geddes died of fever in India during the War period, when her husband was acting as Professor of Sociology in Bombay. Some years ago Geddes married Miss Lilian Brown, of Paisley, a union that brought great happiness, smoothing and prolonging the Montpellier period, when, in spite of extraordinary virility and mental youthfulness, Geddes began to feel the taxes on a disinterested life, spent in the service of his day and generation. Lady Geddes helped him nobly. He was very rich in distinguished friends, yet richer still in a multitude of humble students who are mourning to-day with a great pride in their hearts.

* * *

KENNETH GRAHAME

Author of 'The Wind in the Willows,' who showed 'an intimacy with the child-mind'

7 JULY 1932

WE ANNOUNCE WITH MUCH REGRET that Mr. Kenneth Grahame, the author of *The Golden Age* and *The Wind in the Willows*, died suddenly yesterday at Pangbourne at the age of 73.

In the literature of his time Grahame seems sure of his place among the rare few, like Lewis Carroll, Edward Lear, Thackeray, Stevenson, and Barrie, who have revealed to grown up Olympians the tender hearts and wondering minds, the adventurous spirits, and the solemn absurdities of children. Like his fellows in that select company, Grahame was intensely original. He had his special intimacy with the child-mind; his dream-children are all his own in their quiddity and their astonishing realism.

Kenneth Grahame came of good Scottish stock. The son of Mr. J. C. Grahame, advocate, he was born in Edinburgh in 1859. He was educated at St. Edward's School, Oxford, and in 1878 entered the service of the Bank of England, where he held the responsible post of secretary from October, 1898 to July, 1908. He served in the London Scottish for seven years. An attempt was made on his life at the Bank on November 24, 1903, by a madman who fired about five shots from a revolver; but only one was aimed at Grahame direct, and even as to this there was some doubt, as the bullet penetrated the ceiling of the room. The assailant was overpowered with the aid of the fire hose, and was subsequently ordered to be detained during his Majesty's pleasure.

In 1890 Grahame's first published work appeared, a short satirical tale called *The Headswoman*. His earliest work to attract attention appeared in W. E. Henley's *National Observer*, and his *Pagan Papers* (1893) consisted of "middles" contributed to that journal. The essays that make up the book meander in leisurely, humorous fashion through much pleasant country. The chief charm of the little book, however, is that it contains six of the 18 sketches of childhood that make up *The Golden Age*, which was published two years later, in 1895. On its appearance Swinburne, an exacting critic, declared it to be "one of the few books which are well-nigh too praiseworthy for praise ... Immortality should be the reward ... Praise would be as superfluous as analysis would be impertinent." In the literature of childhood this book has not been surpassed in its combination of insight, humour, and pathos. It is curious to recall that the author of this unique series of studies of childhood, placed in the setting of the English countryside, was at the time it was written a bachelor, immersed in the routine of his duties in the City of London. It appeared in a list of the five best books about children at the recent Lewis Carroll exhibition.

The Golden Age was followed in 1898 by *Dream Days*, in which we renew acquaintance with "Edward," "Harold," and "the girls," but it never attained the popularity of its forerunner. It was 10 years before

Kenneth Grahame again published anything of importance; this time, in 1908, a book frankly for children (which the others were not), *The Wind in the Willows*. Though it was not well received by the critics, the adventures of "Mr. Badger," "Toad" (of Toad Hall), "Mole," "Water Rat," and the rest, have delighted innumerable readers of all ages. The latest edition, published for last Christmas, contained perfect illustrations by E. H. Shepard. There was even an industrial magnate who named his country cottage "Toad Hall," after the mansion which Badger, Rat, and Mole won back for the rightful owner who had lost it through his own folly. Mr. A. A. Milne's dramatic version, *Toad of Toad Hall*, was one of the successes of the Christmas seasons of 1930 and 1931. On his retirement from the Bank of England for reasons of health in 1908, Grahame settled with his family in the country. He married in 1899, Elspeth, daughter of the late Robert William Thomson, of Edinburgh and Stonehaven, sister of Sir Courtauld Thomson, and stepdaughter of the late Lord Moulton. His only child, a very promising son, died while an undergraduate at Christ Church.

The funeral will be at Pangbourne Church on Saturday at 3 o'clock.

PROFESSOR J. S. HALDANE

Philosopher and scientist, whose researches saved the lives of coal miners, deep-sea divers, and soldiers attacked by gas

16 MARCH 1936

PROFESSOR J. S. HALDANE, C.H., F.R.S., who was a great figure in both pure and applied science, died at his home at Oxford at midnight on Saturday at the age of 75. Not long ago he returned from visiting Persia and Iraq to study sunstroke cases among oil workers, and seemed in excellent health. But he caught a chill which developed into bronchial pneumonia, and last Tuesday was reported to be sinking. It was then that his son, Professor J. B. S. Haldane, suggested blood transfusion, which he gave himself, and the patient responded remarkably, but the improvement did not last.

As a physiologist Haldane revolutionised our ideas on respiration, and thereby opened up a new aspect of physiology. Philosophy had a great influence with him from the earliest days, and dissatisfaction with the teaching of physiology which he experienced as a medical student led him to think the more deeply about the true significance of biology. The trend of his thought was shown as early as 1883 in an essay contributed jointly by himself and his brother, Lord Haldane, to *Essays in Philosophical Criticism,* and the views that he then expressed formed the foundation of the philosophical arguments which later in life were the subject of many of his addresses and published books – *Mechanism, Life and Personality,* 1913, *The New Physiology,* 1919, *The Sciences and Philosophy,* 1928 (Gifford Lectures delivered at Glasgow), *The Philosophical Basis of Biology,* 1931 (Donnellan Lectures delivered at Dublin), and *Materialism,* 1932.

Haldane condemned the doctrine of "vital force" as vigorously as he did the mechanistic theory of life by which that doctrine was succeeded. To him physiology implied the nature of the life of the organism, and to understand this the organism must be studied as a whole. A year ago, in *The Philosophy of a Biologist,* Haldane published a concise summary of his pyramidal view of the universe as a universe of personality and the manifestation of God.

Almost the whole of his researches were made with man as his subject; he established the subject of human physiology on a true basis, showing how delicate methods of chemical and physical investigation can be used to elucidate normal function in an intact person. In applied science or industrial hygiene his work was not less valuable, for the solution of the problems which he took up has been of direct and lasting benefit to mankind. He was always opposed to the separation of theoretical from applied science; many of his own researches in pure physiology owed their origin to facts which he noticed in his work on mining problems, and, in turn, these investigations directly helped him in the solution of other problems in applied physiology. Though clear and concise as a writer, Haldane was an awkward and hesitating lecturer, unless he had fully prepared beforehand what he had to say, and yet what he said was always significant, for he had an extraordinary faculty for picking out what was important from the irrelevant. The research student could not have had a more inspiring guide or a kinder friend. Few men have done more to advance natural science.

John Scott Haldane was born in Edinburgh on May 2, 1860, the son of Robert Haldane, of Cloan, Auchterarder, and Mary Burdon Sanderson, and brother of Lord Haldane, Sir W. S. Haldane, and Miss Elizabeth Haldane. He was educated at Edinburgh Academy and Edinburgh University, and he also studied for a time at the University of Jena. After graduating in medicine at Edinburgh in 1884 he became demonstrator to Professor Carnelley at University College, Dundee, with whom he took part in an extensive investigation into the organic and inorganic impurities of the air of dwellings, schools, and sewers.

After spending a few months in Berlin studying physiological chemistry, Haldane was in 1887 invited by his uncle, Sir John Burdon Sanderson, Waynflete Professor of Physiology in the University of Oxford, to become one of his demonstrators. Soon after this he showed that the symptoms actually produced by exposure to black-damp and after-damp in mines were different from those given in the textbooks. This association with the mining profession was maintained throughout his career, and encouraged him to investigate in detail the composition of the atmosphere met with in different circumstances in mines and its effect on man. He introduced several simple tests by which small though dangerous quantities of this gas could be detected in the air, laying emphasis in particular on the fact that small animals, such as canaries or mice were affected far more quickly than man by carbon monoxide and could therefore be used to give warning of danger. In 1896 he investigated for the Home Office the cause of death in three colliery explosions, and his report, which was subsequently translated into several languages, was of fundamental importance in the development of means for combating the dangers arising from explosion in mines or from underground fires.

Between 1892 and 1900 Haldane introduced a number of new methods for investigating various aspects of the respiratory functions, publishing papers on methods for determining the respiratory exchange, the amount of haemoglobin in the blood, the quantity and tension of the gases of the blood, the volume of the blood, and the analysis of air. The apparatus which he designed for air analysis, described fully in his *Methods of Air Analysis,* published in 1912, and for blood gas analysis, is widely used at the present day.

The year 1905 saw the publication of what is undoubtedly the most important and fundamental of his physiological researches. In this paper, in which he was associated with Dr. Priestley, he showed that the regulation of the breathing is normally determined by the tension of carbon dioxide in the respiratory centre in the brain, and that this nervous centre is exquisitely sensitive to variations in the tension of carbon dioxide in the arterial blood which reaches it. Since carbon dioxide is one of the principal products of the metabolism of the tissues, an explanation was afforded of the automatic changes in the breathing which occur with alteration in bodily activity. Indeed, this paper afforded the first real insight into the astonishing delicacy with which the quantitative coordination of the natural activities of different parts of the body may be brought about by chemical means.

It was no doubt his work on gaseous exchange in the body and the function of the kidneys that prompted him to turn his attention to the physical chemistry of gases and liquids, and although his books *Gases and Liquids* (1928) and *The Theory of Heat Engines* (1930) met with much adverse criticism, they indicate how unsatisfactory he had found certain current hypotheses when applied to the results of his own investigations.

From 1896 onwards Haldane served on a number of Departmental Committees, which included inquiries into the ventilation of tunnels on the Metropolitan Railway, the health of Cornish miners, and the incidence of ankylostomiasis and miners phthisis, the ventilation of factories and workshops, and the manufacture and use of water gas, an appendix to the latter report giving an interesting account of his experimental researches on the natural air interchange in rooms.

It was due to his work as a member of a committee appointed by the Admiralty to investigate the problem of deep diving that the risks of caisson disease have now been practically abolished. He worked out what is now known as stage decompression by an elaborate experimental investigation in which he had the cooperation of Dr. Boycott and Lieutenant Damant, R.N., an investigation conducted in part in a steel pressure chamber at the Lister Institute and finally with actual divers in deep water lochs on the west coast of Scotland.

This method, by which the diver may be brought safely to the surface, has now been adopted practically universally, and has made it possible to conduct salvage operations successfully at great depths.

Some years before the War Haldane had served as a member of a committee appointed to inquire into the physiological effects of food, training, and clothing on the soldier, which resulted in a radical alteration in the scale of rations for active service.

When the use of poisonous gas was introduced by the Germans during the War Haldane was called in by the Secretary of State for War in an advisory capacity, and at once went out to the Front, where he was able to verify the type of gas used and the nature of the effects produced by it. On returning to England he made every effort to speed up the production of an emergency respirator capable of stopping chlorine, the gas in question, and to prevent the issue of inadequate respirators, some of which did, in fact, in the confusion of the moment, find their way oversea. At the same time he recognised that the emergency respirator was but an improvisation, and he pointed out that satisfactory protection could only be ensured by some form of box respirator.

In 1901 Haldane was elected a Fellow of New College, and in 1907 he was appointed Reader in Physiology at Oxford. He resigned his Readership in 1913 on the death of Gotch, who had succeeded Burdon Sanderson in the chair of Physiology. A year later the War broke out. He had been invited to deliver the Silliman lectures at Yale University in 1915, but owing to the War they had to be postponed till 1916. The publication of the full series of lectures was delayed till 1922. Under the title of *Respiration*, this volume gives an account of his researches in pure physiology and of many of his investigations in applied physiology, and it will remain as a lasting record of his genius.

In 1912 he was invited to become director of a research laboratory founded by the Doncaster coalowners. In 1921 this laboratory was transferred to Birmingham University, and he was shortly afterwards made an honorary Professor in that university. Under his direction this laboratory made a great number of investigations on matters connected with the safety and hygiene of coalmines, the bulk of this work being published in the *Transactions of the Institution of Mining Engineers.* Many risks have to be run by the miner, and the reduction of these risks and the preservation of a high standard of health in collieries were causes which Haldane always had at heart, and he spared himself neither time nor trouble when the welfare of the miner was at stake. The high value that the mining profession set on his work was shown by his election in 1924 to the presidency of the Institution of Mining Engineers, a signal honour for a physiologist, and this post he held for several years.

For many years Haldane served as one of the gas referees under the Board of Trade. He was elected a Fellow of the Royal Society in 1897, and was awarded a Royal Medal for his researches in respiration in

1916. He was also awarded gold medals by the Institution of Mining and Metallurgy, the Institution of Mining Engineers, and the Royal Society of Medicine, the Baly medal of the Royal College of Physicians, and the medal of the North of England Institute of Mining Engineers. He received honorary degrees from many universities – LL.D., Edinburgh and Birmingham, D.Sc. Oxford and Leeds, Sc.D. Cambridge and Dublin, and D.Sc. Engineering, Witwatersrand. He was created a Companion of Honour in 1928 in recognition of his scientific work on industrial disease, a distinction which had been already conferred on his sister, Miss Elizabeth Haldane.

Haldane married in 1891 Louisa Kathleen, daughter of Mr. Coutts Trotter, and he leaves a son, John Burdon Sanderson Haldane, F.R.S., who is Professor of Genetics in the University of London, and a daughter, Mrs. Naomi Margaret Mitchison, who is known as a novelist and writer of originality and distinction.

The funeral will be at Golders Green at 2 p.m. to-morrow, and at Gleneagles Chapel, Auchterarder, on Wednesday at 3.30. A memorial service will be held at New College, Oxford, the date to be announced later.

ROBERT CUNNINGHAME GRAHAM

A Scottish hidalgo – and the first man to say "damn"
in the Commons

23 MARCH 1936

MR. ROBERT BONTINE CUNNINGHAME GRAHAM, the news of whose death in Buenos Aires was published in the later editions of *The Times* on Saturday, was born in Scotland in 1852. He received the name of Cunninghame Graham collaterally with the representation of the Cunningham Earldom of Glencairn and the claim to the Menteith peerage, which, in view of the illegitimacy of the Stewart line, enabled him to claim a Kingship of Scotland by descent from Robert II. To antiquaries such as Andrew Lang he was always "the uncrowned King."

But to ancient lineage he added much else; he was the most picturesque Scot of his time. In him Spain and Scotland met, for, owing to his Spanish grandmother, he was brought up as a child of Cadiz, while his mother, a Fleeming of Cumbernauld House, a lady of great ability and charm, was as much a Scot as his father, Mr. Cunninghame Graham Bontine. After two years at Harrow in Montagu Butler's house, Robert went to South America at the age of 16. There he ranched in Argentina and enlisted in the Uruguayan Army. As a traveller he explored the vestiges of "the great Christian Commonwealth" left by the Jesuits in Paraguay. He saw the last Indians haunting the ruined missions, "mumbling their maimed rites," and he recalled "the flowers, the scents, the herds of horses, the ostriches, and the whole charm of the New World which those who saw it even a quarter of a century ago saw little altered from the remotest times." The eighties found him farming on the Mexican border, where at Horsehead Crossing he met Buffalo Bill making his first show. There sprang up a close friendship with Cody, whom he compared to the Spanish Conquistadores, and with whom he came to know "the buffalo, the Apaches, and tribes of the Rio Grande."

In 1879 he married a Chilean lady, Gabriela de la Balmondière, who shared her husband's interests and was a poet, water-colour painter, botanist, and mystic. She collaborated with him in his second book, *Father Archangel of Scotland*, published in 1896. She died in 1906.

In the early eighties he settled down on his ancestral domain of Gartmore and Ardoch in the hope of averting the sale which became inevitable in 1898. He contested N.W. Lanarkshire in 1882 and 1886, the second time successfully as a Liberal, but he soon developed in the House into a Socialist and became a devotee of William Morris and a comrade of [the Marxist Henry] Hyndman and [Labour activist John] Burns. At the end of the Session of 1887 he was suspended, being described as the first man who said "damn" in the Commons, and declaring: "I never withdraw." In November of the same year he stood by Burns in the Trafalgar Square riots and incurred a sword-cut on the head from a guardsman. His life was saved by Burns, who accompanied him to Pentonville Prison for six weeks, the appearance of M.P.s causing the greatest interest among the prisoners, who in after years used to hail him in the streets in ever-growing numbers. In 1892 he was again suspended for interrupting Mr. Asquith with the words, "I want to know about the swindling companies." His political aversions were directed against all forms of machinery and stock exchange. Capital he opposed as the enemy of romance. Though he adopted Socialism, he prophesied ironically of the time when "all shall sit, apparelled in one livery, at little tables, drinking some kind of not too diuretic table water, approved by the County Council, and reading expurgated Bibles."

His sympathies lay outside "the beefy pale of the Anglo-Saxon race," to whom, however, he introduced South America in a series of studies and biographies which led W. H. Hudson, a congenial South American wanderer, to describe him as "alone of European writers in rendering something of the vanishing colour of that remote life." He wrote *A Vanished Arcadia*, concerning Paraguay (1901), and accounts of

Hernando de Soto (1903), Bernal del Castillo (1915), and the Brazilian mystic, Antonio Conselheiro (1920).

Mogreb-el-Acksa, his most important travel book, described an attempted journey through Southern Morocco to Tarudant, disguised as a Turkish doctor named Sheikh Mohammed El Fasi (1897). Trying to pass beyond Atlas through the almost unknown province of Sus, which he described as "Arcadia grafted on Feudalism," he was arrested by the Cadi of Kintafi and only released after a painful captivity. His interest in Morocco led to the preface he wrote to M. Aflalo's indictment of the Anglo-French agreement, which developed into one of the frictional causes of the War. He was a master of the old-fashioned art of writing a preface, the decay of which he attributed to advertisements. His preface to Compton Rickett's *William Morris* contains a true sketch of the Master, and he added a generous epitaph to Martin Hume's posthumous studies. His own place in literature must be somewhere between Martin Hume and Borrow, for he was not far behind the one in Spanish scholarship, and exceeded the other in the scope of his Iberian adventures. He was never better portrayed than as a Don Quixote in Lavery's picture now at Glasgow. In contemporary letters Bernard Shaw used him as the type of Saranoff in *Arms and the Man,* "the Bulgarian braggadocio," in doubt whether he was "a chivalrous gentleman or a humbug." In *Captain Brassbound's Conversion* Shaw drew an even closer sketch of him as a melodramatic hero against the background of an imaginary Morocco taken from *Mogreb-el-Acksa.*

In his Scottish surroundings Cunninghame Graham could have sat for Stevenson's Master of Ballantrae or to Daudet for a Scottish version of Tartarin. His voyages, adventures, and hunting episodes lost little in the telling. We may instance his thrilling account of an ostrich hunt or of the jaguars he had seen killed on foot by men with forked sticks and bamboo spears. He was too much of a rolling stone to gather up many friendships, but he possessed stout comrades in strange parts of the tropical and Labour worlds. A few days in Ireland converted him to the Irish cause, and led to an economic tract describing the evolution of an Irish village. He owned but two Masters, Morris and Parnell; the latter he knew personally and followed to the grave, the only non-Irish member to do so. His economics were couched in the sarcastic rather than the statistical, and, though he had a great fund of ridicule, he cannot be said to have possessed real humour or charm. He did not write a book till he was 40. His *Guide to the Menteith District* has been called the best guide book in any language, and his translation of his wife's "St. Teresa" into Spanish remains the solitary Spanish classic written by an English author. In thought he claimed complete agnosticism.

During the War he was engaged in buying horses for the British Government in the markets of Argentina and cattle in Colombia, and writing a book on Cartagena between-whiles. His later books, dealing with horses and horsemanship, the exploits of the Conquistadores, Scottish history, and much else are written with a proud and passionate eloquence. The final crusade of this extraordinary man was on behalf of Scottish Home Rule. He was the first president of the National Party of Scotland, founded in 1928, and had been first chairman of the Scottish Parliamentary Labour Party. In the election for the Lord Rectorship of Glasgow University in 1928 he was defeated by Mr. Baldwin, then Prime Minister, by only 66 votes.

An aristocratic Socialist and a cowboy dandy, he would have been as much out of place with an ancient Scottish peerage as he was as a truculent Radical in the Commons. He was neither an essayist nor a historian, but he could marvellously catch the pathetic side of history from surroundings, whether it was the ruined missions of Paraguay or the Scotch College in Valladolid or Sir John Moore's grave in a garden by the sea. Whether he tilted at windmills in Trafalgar Square or rode a wild pony with lasso and Mexican saddle in Rotten Row, he was exuberantly unique.

The body of Mr. Cunninghame Graham will be put on board *the Almeda Star,* which will sail for England from Buenos Aires on March 26, states Reuter.

PHOEBE TRAQUAIR

Mural painter whose decorative art gave life to many public buildings

6 AUGUST 1936

ALTHOUGH IRISH BY BIRTH, Mrs. Phoebe Anna Traquair, who died in Edinburgh on Tuesday in her eighty-fifth year, had lived and worked so long in Edinburgh that people had come to think of her as a Scottish artist. To many her work and fame were unfamiliar. She did not paint pictures or model statuettes. Even the habitués of Scottish art exhibitions did not all know her name, though in 1920 she was elected an honorary member of the Royal Scottish Academy, an honour unduly belated but prized by her admirers, even more than by herself, as a recognition of the high merit and unusual character of her art.

Her gift was in many ways that of a decorator; but, unlike most modern decorative designers and painters, and like the great imaginative artists of the medieval and early Renaissance epochs, whose work she admired so whole-heartedly, she was first of all interested in what she had to say. The story she was telling, the symbols of worship or praise she used, the significance of the colour schemes she wove, were all real to her, and, while her natural bent towards decorative beauty and intricate pattern was marked, these spiritual qualities were the determining elements in her gift. At the same time, her instinct for charm of design and richness of colour gave the expression of her thought a peculiar and fascinating personal turn. So, if in technique she was in some respects an amateur, the lovely animation of her conceptions, whether grave or gay, and the richly varied decorative beauty she so often attained made amends for any deficiencies in professional skill.

It was as a mural painter that Mrs. Traquair did her most important and memorable work. Beginning with the decoration of the mortuary in the Sick Children's Hospital, Edinburgh, in 1884, she next painted a charming series of panels, illustrating the canticle "O all ye works of the Lord; praise Him and magnify Him forever," in the Song School of

St. Mary's Episcopal Cathedral. This decoration of the Song School was considerably advanced before she paid her first visit to Italy. But her art was already akin in many ways to that of the earlier Italian fresco-painters, and she returned from Florence with added knowledge of her craft and its possibilities and with her artistic nature enriched by direct contact with the work of the Primitives.

Some years later (1893) she began in the Catholic Apostolic Church, Edinburgh, what, everything considered, is not only her own greatest undertaking but one of the most striking and beautiful schemes of mural decoration executed in modern times in this country and, indeed, anywhere. The nave, with its great symbolic figures on each side of the chancel arch, the "Christ in Glory" amid the Heavenly choir, which fills the whole west gable, and the four-and-twenty scenes from the Old and New Testaments along the side walls below the clerestory, is a remarkable achievement; but it is in the side chapel and the northern aisle of the chancel, where the whole scheme has been completed and the effect is extraordinarily beautiful, figure panels and border decorations on walls and ceilings being wrought into one wonderful harmony, that her genius is most fully revealed. The better part of 10 years was given to this work, which was executed directly on the walls and entirely without assistance. Since then she decorated a church in Yorkshire and another in the New Forest, the latter for Lord Manners, with conspicuous success.

Mrs. Traquair, who was the third daughter of Dr. William Moss, a well-known Dublin physician, was brought up partly in County Wicklow and partly in the Irish capital, where she studied in the National Gallery and the School of Art in Merrion Square. But marriage with Dr. Ramsay Traquair, F.R.S., the Scottish zoologist, when he was appointed Keeper of the Natural History collections in the Royal Scottish Museum, brought her to Edinburgh and resulted in her abandoning the practice of art during the following nine or 10 years. When she took it up again, needlework, in which she subsequently executed some superbly decorative figure panels, was her first medium. From that, encouraged by Ruskin, she passed to illumination, and from that again, like many medieval artists, to mural painting. She had a turn for all sorts of art craftsmanship, however, and worked in beaten brass and tooled leather, and, above all, for in it she attained some of her loveliest results, in enamel.

A little woman and sparely built but overflowing with nervous energy, her artistic activities were remarkable both in extent and quality, and withal she had a fine social instinct and made many friends. Her interests were wide and varied and her conversation, flavoured by just a suspicion of Irish accent, was animated and persuasive and lightened by infective laughter and flashes of illuminative wit. To talk with her in her own home, surrounded by beautiful things of her own making and reproductions of the great things she loved, was an experience which those so privileged must remember with delight. Her husband died in 1913, and she is survived by a married daughter and two sons, the elder of whom became an oculist in Edinburgh and the younger is Professor of Architecture in McGill University, Montreal.

* * *

SIR J. M. BARRIE

Playwright who created Peter Pan and put Kirriemuir on the map

19 JUNE 1937

JAMES MATTHEW BARRIE, whose death is announced on another page, was born at Kirriemuir, Forfarshire, on May 9, 1860. He was one of the ten children of a hand-loom weaver in a town of hand-loom weavers; but during his boyhood hand-looms at Kirriemuir gave place to machines. "As quickly as two people may exchange seats, the daughter, till now but a knitter of stockings, became the breadwinner; he who had been the breadwinner sat down to the knitting of stockings." His mother, the daughter of a stonemason, was described by a Free Church minister as a "humble, tender, gracious, evangelical, prayerful soul." From her son's book about her, published in 1896, we know Margaret Ogilvy to have been all that, and also astute, humorous, wilful, and very ambitious for her son.

Like many humble Scottish families, the Barries – a clear-headed lot, as they were described – were intellectually disposed. While the father soaked himself in Gladstone, the mother's favourite reading was Carlyle, and both read much in the Bible. So James Matthew spent his boyhood in the atmosphere of religion, of thrift, of hard work, and of self-education.

He commenced as an author at a very early age, encouraged, he suspected, by his mother, who wanted both to see the small boy occupied and to save the pennies spent on magazines containing stories written by other people. At the Academy, Dumfries, where Barrie went to school, literary composition gave way to cricket and football; but during the year before he went to Edinburgh University (for in spite of forebodings his parents managed to give him a college education) he wrote a great part of a never-published three-volume novel. There was never a question in his own mind of his following any profession but that of author. "An author!" cried his friends. "And you an M.A.!" Even his mother's early disapproval could not deter him. Writing was "his hand-loom"; and, although he declared that all his writing, except his letters to his mother, was "honest craftsmanship, done to give her coal and food and softer pillows," if any man was a born author it was Barrie. How his mother's disapproval changed to championship, pride – and jealousy of other writers, especially of a fellow named Robert Louis Stevenson – forms a very touching and amusing part of the book of *Margaret Ogilvy*.

After writing for some time at home, he determined to court "that grisette of literature, who has a smile and a hand for all beginners," journalism. By answering an advertisement, he was engaged as leader-writer on the *Nottingham Daily Journal*. The grisette was easily won. His work on the paper included, besides leader-writing, a good deal of police-court reporting, in which he showed his power of making something out of what appeared to others to be nothing. He also wrote short sensational novels, which he sold for £5 apiece.

One who knew the ingenious author at this time has preserved a memory of him as shy, reserved, and lonely even for a Scot (the shyness and reserve of Scots were always a matter of mingled pride and regret to Barrie).

In Nottingham, also, he found time to write articles which he "shot" at Frederick Greenwood, then editor of the *St. James's Gazette*. When one or two had been accepted, he determined to face the trials of the capital. In London be stayed at old Furnival's Inn in Holborn, where every day he wrote an article for the *St. James's Gazette*. A very fair proportion of them was accepted. Among them was a series of papers on "How I built a Bridge over the Ganges." He had never been in India; he had never built a bridge. But on the out-door tray of a bookshop in Holywell Street there was a book on engineering. He did not buy it; he read it in snatches in the street. And so he built his bridge over the Ganges, and his bridge was seriously discussed by Indian officials in letters to the paper where alone he built it.

But by now he had discovered something even more valuable than the reach of his impudent imagination. He had discovered that literature could be made out of his own people, the people of Kirriemuir. He called the place Thrums and made it famous. Thereafter, thanks to Greenwood, "he never wanted a guinea." In 1888 a book of these collected sketches, called *Auld Licht Idylls,* and in 1889 another book, *A Window in Thrums,* put Barrie among the authors and Thrums among the places which reading folk knew better than their own homes.

In his first notable novel, *When a Man's Single* (1888), he combined what his shrewd eye had gleaned from Thrums and from Fleet Street, and in 1890 he published a book of humorous and sentimental sketches called *My Lady Nicotine*. It was much admired, and by others besides pipe-smokers. It seemed to prove the arrival of a pleasant, second-rate talent. No one was prepared, all those years ago, to anticipate the succession of surprises which this shy and singular mind was to reveal.

His earliest plays were all unsuccessful, but in 1895 *The Professor's Love Story* (written for Sir Henry Irving, who accepted it, but, finding himself unable to produce it, passed it on to Sir John Hare, who could not read it, because it was in Barrie's handwriting) was bought outright for £50 (the author bought it back afterwards), and in 1897 the play of *The Little Minister* established him as a wealthy man. He was getting on for 40, and had worked hard for his reward.

The publication, in 1896, of his next novel revealed an unsuspected possibility. In *Sentimental Tommy* there was a strong hint of cruelty. Critics will probably point out that this cruelty was not the callousness of the sentimentalist, but the savageness of self-criticism. To read it now is to see a sensitive and proud mind lashing itself for the weaknesses to which it knows itself prone.

Nearly all Barrie's energy was now devoted to the theatre. In 1902 he published the book, *The Little White Bird*; in 1906 *Peter Pan in Kensington Gardens*; in 1911 *Peter and Wendy*; the first of them the seed, the other two but branches, of a gigantic theatrical beanstalk. No one needs to be assured that to all the "Peter Pan" stories children have contributed their share. These stones had their origin in tales made up for and with some real children one summer in the pine woods round Barrie's house at Black Lake, near Farnham. With these "Peter Pan" volumes Barrie's work as writer of books is closed; but the Christmas story, *Farewell, Miss Julie Logan*, which he wrote for *The Times* in 1931, showed that his power of narrative was unimpaired.

In the theatre, where originality and variety are distrusted and feared, Barrie made his way by a series of surprises. The years before the War produced *Quality Street, The Admirable Crichton, Little Mary, Peter Pan, Alice Sit-by-the-Fire, Josephine, What Every Woman Knows,* and *Rosalind,* besides a number of shorter plays, like *The Twelve-Pound Look, The Will, Pantaloon, Punch, A Slice of Life.* The list is not complete but the names mentioned will be sufficient to remind playgoers of the very various and original qualities of Barrie's mature work.

In spite of all his success, however, Barrie did not find playwriting a primrose path, even after he had pursued it for some distance. He had his downright failures with the public, among them *Josephine* and *The Adored One,* which latter not even Sir John Hare and Mrs. Patrick Campbell could pull into success. *The Wedding Guest* was held up for several years before it had a hearing. Charles Frohman urged him not to insist on *What Every Woman Knows* being acted. And *Peter Pan* itself was refused at least once by Tree; and when staged at last without faith by Frohman was an utter failure for the first few days of its first run.

Barrie not only had ideas like no one else's: he had a way of playing with them which was the cause of constant surprise and delight. And that play leads to the consideration of the great crux in his psychology. He could play like a child; he could be as tender as a woman – he, the reserved and cautious Scot – more tender, indeed, than any woman would dare to be except in private; and he could be as hard as nails, as cruel as the grave, as cynical as the Fiend. The strain of cruelty that appeared first in *Sentimental Tommy* was far plainer in *What Every Woman Knows* and in other plays. To explain it the psychologists of the day will probably point to *Margaret Ogilvy* and talk of an unsatisfied "mother-complex."

In one sense Barrie, like his Peter Pan, never did grow up. But when he told a gathering of dramatic critics that he was not "whimsical," or "fantastic," or "elusive," but a realist, he meant it; and he spoke part of the truth. He looked very clearly and steadily at life; and much of what he saw hurt him. He told the truth as he saw it; and for relief to his sensitiveness he could go play, either with and for children, as in *Peter Pan,* or in ingenious nonsense, or by making toys of the very ideas which hurt him. The cruelty in him came of his intellectual vision; the tenderness came of his warm, trusting, but painfully sensitive heart.

During the War he set to work more steadily than any other dramatist to amuse and distract and heal people's stricken minds, and to raise money for War purposes, by writing plays for occasional performance. Personally, the War did not leave him unscathed. This great lover of children was himself childless (he had married, but had divorced his wife in 1909), and the children of his heart's adoption were the children with and for whom he had first made up the Peter Pan stories – the four sons of Mr. Llewelyn Davies and his wife, a daughter of George du Maurier. Of these one, George, was killed in the War; the death of Michael, a boy of exceptional promise, by drowning at Oxford after the War was another terrible blow to him.

But besides occasional war plays he produced during the War two of his most notable comedies: *A Kiss for Cinderella*, in which he played with childish fancies and with adult emotions and ideas more charmingly than ever before, and *Dear Brutus*, the play about second chances, which brought into harmony his contempt for ordinary folly and his faith in something indefeasible in human nature.

After the War, his chief plays were a characteristic piece of playful nonsense, *The Truth about the Russian Dancers*, and *Mary Rose*, a play that was almost passionately liked and disliked: a strange, creepy, harrowing, exquisitely painful play of the supernatural and the natural. He wrote also a first act, *Shall we join the Ladies?* which contained so good a mystery that Barrie himself shrank from resolving it by completing the play. His last dramatic production was the play, *The Boy David*, which he wrote for Miss Elisabeth Bergner and which was played by her in 1936.

In 1913 he was created a baronet. So great was the royal pleasure in his stories and his play about Peter Pan that Lord Esher was able to gain for him the privilege of a private key to Kensington Gardens and the right to enter them at any time. To Kensington Gardens he presented a statue (by Sir George Frampton) of Peter Pan, known and admired by many London children. In 1922 he was given the Order of Merit; and in the same year he was elected Rector of St. Andrews University. His inaugural address was a stirring appeal to the powers of youth to remake the world. In 1929 he made a peculiarly appropriate gift to the Hospital for Sick Children in Great Ormond Street, of which he was an old friend and a frequent visitor. This was the gift, which he had at first thought of making in his will, of all the rights in *Peter Pan*.

Of the outer life of this strange and appealing character there is little to be added, except his love of cricket, first acquired possibly at the Academy in Dumfries. He was not a good cricketer, but he loved the game, and loved getting up teams of his friends to play at Broadway, at Edwin Abbey's house at Fairford, and elsewhere. But of his private life, his personality, there is more to be said than can fitly be said in a newspaper. His wealth, his thrift, his pipe-smoking, his diminutive size and great brow, the Scottish accent which he never lost (he admitted that he used to think in broad Forfarshire), his gentle ways, his silences, his droll, shy, twinkling talk, the brilliance and audacity of his public speaking at its best – these and a hundred other fragments can only be fitted into a whole by those who knew him well, which few people were permitted to do. Few men so shy, so reserved as Barrie have been so well beloved as he in private. For he had the charm of a little child, as well as genius, and the wisdom, the quiet staunchness of a grown man.

* * *

JAMES RAMSAY MacDONALD

Four times Prime Minister, Labour and national leader,
who kept the country on course during the depression

9 NOVEMBER 1937

JAMES RAMSAY MACDONALD, whose sudden death at sea yesterday is announced on page 14, was born in humble circumstances on October 12, 1866, in the Highland seaside village of Lossiemouth. He rose to be more than any other individual, the architect of the fortunes of the Labour Party and Prime Minister of the first Labour Government in Great Britain.

His boyhood, though Spartan, was not sordid, and he had from the first good, though lowly placed friends. He attended the village school, where an appreciative master soon discerned his talents and made him a pupil teacher, thus saving him from the necessity of having to earn a living by manual labour. He used his opportunity to read widely, and by the time he was 18 years old he had amassed a large stock of miscellaneous knowledge, including at least the elementary principles of science, had formed an evolutionary conception of society, and was already as a democrat taking part in local politics and helping in a by-election.

He decided to seek his fortune in London with the idea of finding work on which to support himself while preparing to become a teacher of science. He faced and overcame many hardships; addressing envelopes was one of his first occupations, and he eventually obtained a clerkship in a City warehouse. Incessant private study and attendance at classes at Birkbeck College and other educational courses injured his health temporarily and he had perforce to abandon the idea of a Queen's scholarship at South Kensington. When he had recovered his health, however, he obtained through friends the position of private secretary to the late Thomas Lough, a well-known Radical, then embarking upon a political career. He remained with Lough for nearly four years, until in 1891 he felt strong enough to be independent.

His literary style was now formed, and he soon began to make his way as a journalist, writing for influential newspapers and working for Sir Sidney Lee on *The Dictionary of National Biography*. It was only natural that his next step should be to join the Independent Labour Party, then newly formed and under the chairmanship of Keir Hardie. He became a speaker for it, and very soon, in 1895, its Parliamentary candidate for Southampton. He polled only a handful of votes, but it was through his candidature that he met Margaret Ethel Gladstone, daughter of a well-known man of science, Dr. J. H. Gladstone, and a niece of Lord Kelvin. They had tastes and ideals in common; and they were married in November, 1896. The union was one of unalloyed happiness, and lasted for 15 years until Mrs. MacDonald's death in 1911. The couple travelled widely, visiting South Africa after the war. But before that, at the General Election of 1900, MacDonald had made his second attempt to enter Parliament. He stood for Leicester, but came out at the bottom of the poll. However, the fruits of his hard work and his organising power became patent to all the world at the General Election of 1906. Of

50 Labour candidates 29 were elected to Parliament, he himself finding a seat in the constituency he had vainly tried before, Leicester. He was just under 40 years of age when he set foot in Westminster.

His maiden speech brought him a message of congratulation from Joseph Chamberlain. However, when called upon to speak in the great debate which heralded the entry of this country into the War, he dismayed all but a handful of his friends by striking a note of suspicion of his own country's policy, disbelief in the existence of any moral obligation or material danger, and unequivocal adherence to a policy of neutrality. Unhappily, he thought it his duty to justify his attitude by repeated attacks upon the sincerity of those who were the custodians of his country's safety and honour, and when he attempted to join Dr. Munro's Ambulance Unit in Belgium later in the year, he was arrested and practically deported by the Belgian authorities. At the General Election of 1918 he was beaten at Leicester by 14,000 votes, and appeared to have been relegated to obscurity.

By the end of 1922 the wheel had gone its full circle. He was elected for Aberavon on the flood tide of the reaction against the Coalition, and on his return to the House of Commons he was chosen, on the initiative and through the votes of the contingent of Labour members from the Clyde, as chairman of the party. Since the election had returned more Labour than Liberal members he became also leader of the official Opposition.

In January, 1924, Mr. Baldwin was defeated, on a vote of no confidence moved by MacDonald, by the united votes of the Labour and Liberal Parties, and, although a Labour Administration could clearly only exist on Liberal sufferance, MacDonald never hesitated for a moment in accepting office.

The new Prime Minister had undoubtedly the good will of many who were not his political supporters when he moved into Downing Street. These were solid achievements in the field of foreign policy obtained by the Prime Minister in his capacity as leader of the nation; but he was not so happy as leader of his party. His life-long prejudice against the Liberals prevented him from treating with due consideration those upon whose good will the life of his Administration depended, and in addition he had now to face as a Minister of the Crown those impatient Socialists whose zeal was an electoral asset but a departmental embarrassment. On the issue of Soviet Russia, the Liberals were convinced they had no longer to deal with the Cabinet, but with forces which the Cabinet were unable to manage, and soon after the opening of the autumn session the Government were defeated. In the subsequent election, Mr MacDonald retained his seat at Aberavon by a reduced majority, but his party emerged from the election with a loss of some 40 seats.

The political solidarity of his party was shaken by the events of 1926, and he set himself to build it up again. In spite of a very severe illness contracted during a visit to the United States in 1927, at the end of the year his robust constitution had recovered sufficiently for him to draft a comprehensive programme, which, since it was not subjected to a time schedule, contained enough to appeal to all shades of opinion. There can be no doubt that his efforts contributed materially to the pronounced successes of his party, and to the almost complete failure of the special Liberal effort. He returned to Westminster at the head of a party 288 strong. For the first time Labour was the largest single party in the House of Commons; and, although the Liberals held the balance of power, it was clear that no other party could form a Government.

He started on his second administration supported by the high hopes of nearly 8,500,000 electors, and the ready sympathy of many others who did not belong to his party. The complexion of the new Government was Radical rather than Socialist. The extremist section of the party was practically excluded from office, and even the Trade Union element in the Cabinet was remarkably small. His first task was to renew the Naval Conference which had proved abortive in 1925. Preliminary conversations with the American Ambassador, General Dawes, were followed by a visit to President Hoover in the United States, during which the Prime Minister never forgot to speak and act as a national representative. When the Conference finally assembled in London in January, 1930, agreement was finally reached between Great

Britain, the United States, and Japan, which represented a sensible advance towards naval disarmament.

He was less fortunate at home. The domestic policy of the Government proved bitterly disappointing to his Socialist followers, and they were soon at their old tactics of attempting to put pressure upon their leaders. Internal divisions in the Labour Party were too acute to permit the Government to do anything effective, or even drastic, and they had the bad luck to hold office at a time when the world depression was rapidly deepening. It is useless to deny that during 1930 and the greater part of 1931 the Government presented an appearance of playing for time when in fact there was no time for which to play. Unemployment rose as rapidly as trade declined, and desperate efforts made to stimulate public works not only failed to stem the tide but helped to darken the shadow of impending financial disaster.

The sinister prospect of a series of enormous deficits was finally disclosed to the public by the Report of the May Committee, which showed the well-recognised signs of an unbalanced Budget. The result was a flight from the pound and something resembling panic, at least among foreign holders of British balances. MacDonald never ceased to press upon his colleagues the necessity of balancing the Budget by drastic and immediate economies. The proposal appalled some of them, particularly when it became evident that the required economies could not be obtained without some lessening of the cost of unemployment.

After many days of anxious and agitated dissension the deadlock was complete, and Mr. MacDonald was obliged to inform the King, who had returned specially to London, that he saw no prospect of agreement. From that critical interview there emerged the suggestion of forming a National Government. Next day the leaders of the Conservative and Liberal parties were summoned to the Palace, and within a few hours the Labour Government had resigned and MacDonald had formed a National Government instead.

He was under no misapprehension about the meaning of his decision. He knew that it would shatter the party which he had built

It soon became clear that a new mandate was required, and a General Election followed in November. With all his old courage, MacDonald insisted upon contesting Seaham again, and thus exposing himself on most unfavourable ground to the full blast of the vindictiveness of his opponents. The election was a triumph for the Government, and MacDonald's own courage was largely responsible for the survival, practically unimpaired, of the National Labour group; but the price was the personal defeat of himself and – an event which he felt much more keenly – of his son. In February, 1936, however, both were returned at by-elections, and MacDonald became one of the members for the Scottish Universities.

* * *

JOHN BUCHAN,
LORD TWEEDSMUIR

Author of 'The Thirty-Nine Steps,' 'Greenmantle' and 'Mr Standfast' –
as important a historian as he was a novelist

11 FEBRUARY 1940

LORD TWEEDSMUIR, GOVERNOR-GENERAL OF CANADA, whose death is announced on another page, was even better known as John Buchan, the author. Novelist, lawyer, publisher, historian, soldier, biographer, politician, and proconsul, he had a career as varied as it was distinguished, and his great talents were given to English letters and to the binding together of the peoples that speak the English language. His loss will be mourned equally in Scotland, of which he was a true and worthy son, and throughout England and the Dominions, in whose service his life was spent.

John Buchan was born on August 26, 1875, at Perth, where his father, the late Rev. John Buchan, was a minister. His mother, a daughter of a Peebles farmer, had been brought up in the Free Church, in the tradition of the Disruption, and was a strong churchwoman who proved the ideal wife to a minister of that Church in his several charges. Her husband, also a native of Peebles, had a strong love of literature, which he instilled into his children, whom he brought up on the ballads and folklore of the Border. It was in such an atmosphere that John Buchan and his brothers and sisters grew up. Of them, William, a brilliant young Indian Civil servant, died on his first leave; Alastair, a subaltern in The Royal Scots Fusiliers, was killed in action at Arras in 1917; a daughter, Anna, became well known as the novelist "O. Douglas"; and Walter, later Town Clerk of Peebles, edited, and partly wrote, *The History of Peeblesshire.*

In due course the family moved to Glasgow, where for some time John Buchan senior was minister, and the young John proceeded to Glasgow University. Every morning he would get up at six and walk the four miles through the South Side of Glasgow across the Clyde to the early class, pausing on the bridge to gaze at the river and the lights of the shipping at the Broomielaw. From Glasgow he went up to Brasenose College, Oxford, where he had a brilliant career. A hard worker, he applied his talents to literature and history, winning the Stanhope Essay Prize in 1897 and the Newdigate the next year. He graduated with a First in *Literae Humaniores* and was President of the Union in his last year. Thus to his earlier love of Scotland was added the love of Oxford, and the two influences remained strong in his character for the rest of his life. On going down he was called to the Bar by the Middle Temple in 1901, and soon afterwards went out to South Africa to join the other young men who had been collected round him by the High Commissioner, Lord Milner.

He returned home in 1903 to devote himself to literature. He had already won a reputation for himself by the publication, while still at the University, of three books in one year, *Sir Quixote, Musa Piscatrix,* and *Scholar-Gipsies,* which won immediate recognition and were a foretaste of the prolific output which he was always to maintain. He acted for a time as assistant to St. Loe Strachey, then editor of the *Spectator*. It was his adventure stories in the Stevenson tradition that first acquired a wide public. Buchan had a gift for conveying atmosphere and describing scenery which was equally vivid and accurate whether he wrote of what he had seen or not. He drew largely on Scotland, and in one of his earliest successes, *Prester John*, written in 1910, he made use of his African experience.

In a much later novel, *The Courts of the Morning*, with a setting in South America, the effect was the same although he had never visited the country. The description of military operations there was of a kind which led the authorities to prescribe it as one of the official texts to be read at the Staff College. During the years of the last War he produced what must be the greatest trilogy of spy-stories, *The Thirty-Nine Steps*, *Greenmantle*, and *Mr. Standfast*. Above all he possessed the great art of the writer of that kind of fiction, which is to make the reader feel that he himself is the hero.

The last War brought Buchan for a time to G.H.Q. in France in charge of news services. He was, however, soon transferred to England and was appointed Director of Information under the Prime Minister (Mr. Lloyd George) with the task of coordinating the various departments concerned with publicity and propaganda. All this did not interfere with his literary output. A member of the publishing firm of Nelson and Sons, he occupied such time as he could spare in the intervals from service at home and abroad in producing a popular history of the War which ran to 24 volumes in the Nelson Library series. Later his *History of the Great War*, a revised and rewritten version, appeared in four volumes.

Buchan's reputation as a historian stands at least as high as his reputation as a novelist. During the years from 1928 to 1940 he produced a number of biographies, the best known of which are perhaps his *Montrose, Oliver Cromwell* (a best seller), *Julius Caesar*, and *Augustus*. Most of those works were popular in character, but popular in the best sense. As with his novels, his insight into the motives of action, his capacity for making his readers believe in the characters of which he wrote, and the vivid narration of scene and atmosphere gave his works a wider public than that usually accorded to the historian. As a writer of Lowland Scottish verse, of which he published a volume in 1917, Buchan held firmly that Scots was not a "book tongue," and combated the view often advanced that all Scottish rhyme, from Burns downwards, was a mere antiquarian exercise.

In 1919 Buchan received recognition from his old university of Glasgow, when he received the degree of LL.D., and in 1930 he received a similar honour from St. Andrews. From 1921 to 1930 he was a Curator of the Oxford University Chest, while he was also a trustee of the National Library of Scotland and of the Pilgrim Trust.

Buchan's ambitions had always been political, but it was not until he was in his fifty-second year that he entered the House of Commons at the Scottish Universities by-election. He was elected with a majority of over 14,000, his Labour opponent forfeiting his deposit. Buchan was in every way a worthy University representative. Besides his own constituency, he took under his wing his other University, and his interests and activities at Oxford were many and varied. From his home at Elsfield overlooking the marshes, he kept a fatherly, and indeed companionly, eye on young Conservatism. During a time when Conservatism was not too flourishing among the young he earned unending gratitude by his zest and sympathy. He was made a Companion of Honour in 1932. In the following two years he was twice appointed Lord High Commissioner to the General Assembly of the Church of Scotland, of which, as an elder, he was himself a member. At the Palace of Holyroodhouse he was serving an apprenticeship to the higher dignity to which he was soon to be called. In the summer of 1934 he received his D.C.L. from Oxford.

In the next year he was appointed Governor-General of Canada. A peerage naturally followed, and he was created G.C.M.G. Lord Tweedsmuir soon proved that he was no ordinary Governor-General. He revealed a surprising knowledge of Canadian people and institutions, acquired during previous visits and through an extensive acquaintanceship among Canadians in England both during and after the last War, and he was himself familiar to the people of the Dominion through his writings. While maintaining the necessary ceremonial to the full, he preferred his personal contacts to be more informal, not only under his own roof but by indulging his old taste for travel. There were few parts of the Dominion which he did not visit, thus affording himself an opportunity of meeting all kinds and classes, and that in spite of recurrent ill-health which might have led a less energetic man to be content with a more sedentary life.

He paid an official visit to the President of the United States, and in 1937 he made a 10,000-mile expedition, following the trail of his fellow Scot, Sir Alexander Mackenzie, laid nearly a century and a half ago. He penetrated up the Mackenzie River into the Arctic Circle, and thence by air to northern British Columbia. He then struck south to the lake country of Tweedsmuir Park, the 5,400 square miles set aside and named in his honour by the Government of British Columbia to be a public park in perpetuity. In July, 1938, he came home on leave and was installed as Chancellor of Edinburgh University, thus, as was remarked in a leading article in *The Times*, adding a third university to his collection. Last summer he and Lady Tweedsmuir made a tour of Western Canada.

Last October he went to New York to consult certain physicians and it was hoped that his health would improve. He returned to Canada, and gave an inspiring speech to the Toronto Women's Canadian Club at the end of November in which he said: "Let us remember that in this fight we are God's chivalry." Many Canadians greatly wished Lord Tweedsmuir's term of office to be extended, but Mr. Mackenzie King (Prime Minister) announced with regret a month ago that the state of Lord Tweedsmuir's health prevented his accepting any extension. He was made a Privy Councillor in 1937, was an Hon. Fellow of B.N.C., an Hon. LL.D. of Edinburgh, McGill, Toronto, Queen's, Manitoba, Harvard, and Yale, and Hon. D.Litt. of Columbia.

He married in 1907 Susan Charlotte, daughter of the late Hon. Norman Grosvenor, and had three sons and a daughter. The Hon. John Norman Stuart Buchan, who succeeds as second baron, was educated at

Eton and at Brasenose College, Oxford, and was for a short time in the colonial administrative service in Africa, but later joined the service of the Hudson's Bay Company. His only daughter married in 1933 Captain Brian Ramsay-Fairfax-Lucy.

* * *

ARCHBISHOP LORD LANG

Scots prelate who became Archbishop of Canterbury and was in office during the abdication

6 DECEMBER 1945

ARCHBISHOP LORD LANG OF LAMBETH was Archbishop of York from 1909 to 1928, and Archbishop of Canterbury from 1928 to 1942, in which year he resigned and was created a baron.

The Most Rev. and Right Hon. William Cosmo Gordon Lang, P.C., G.C.V.O., D.D., D.C.L., LL.D., D.Litt., Baron Lang of Lambeth, of Lambeth, Surrey, was born on October 31, 1864, a son of the Very Rev. J. M. Lang, D.D., minister of Fyvie, and sometime Principal of Aberdeen University. He was christened "Cosmo Gordon" in compliment to a local laird. His first baptismal name of William he dropped in later years. He was educated privately and at Glasgow University. It was said of him that "nothing on earth can prevent that young man from becoming a bishop, if he goes to England."

To England the young man went, as an undergraduate at King's College, Cambridge. But towards the end of his first term he competed successfully for a history scholarship at Balliol College, Oxford. In one of his first letters home he expressed surprise to his mother that he appeared to be the only freshman who had read Hegel; and soon he became known there as "Father Cosmo," or "the Father Confessor," for his was the manner of a man born to give advice, with a dignity older than his years. He reached the chair of the Union Society. In 1885 he took a second class in Lit. Hum., and a year later a first class in the final school of Modern History.

He had already become a student of the Inner Temple, and after taking his degree at Oxford he read with Mr. W. S. Robson, subsequently Attorney-General and a Lord of Appeal in Ordinary, who thought Lang's talents for the law altogether exceptional. The legal studies, however, were varied by other occupations. To supplement a scanty income he gave Extension lectures. He was interested in Toynbee Hall and its social work. His knowledge of politics and powers as a speaker were utilised on election platforms.

In 1889 he was elected to a Fellowship at All Souls. Then came the striking change which converted the son of the manse and law student into an Anglican clergyman, later to occupy the throne of St. Augustine. Of the exterior forces which helped this decision the influence of Charles Gore and Edward Talbot was probably the strongest. Almost on the eve of his call to the Bar Lang withdrew his name, was confirmed by Bishop King of Lincoln, and quitted Mr. Robson's chambers for Cuddesdon Theological College. In 1890 he was ordained, and began his clerical career as one of the staff of Leeds Parish Church, where Dr. Talbot was vicar. Quickly he made his mark as an effective preacher and an indefatigable worker in the slum district put in his charge. He formed, for instance, a class of over 100 of the roughest lads, and soon had them completely under his control. To Oxford he returned in 1893, as Fellow and Dean of Divinity of Magdalen College, while the next year, when still but 30, he became vicar of St. Mary's, the University Church.

Then came another turning-point in Lang's career. In 1896 he was offered by the Crown the living of Portsea and accepted it. The decision astonished most of his friends in Oxford. Only two years had passed since his appointment to St. Mary's. There he seemed ideally placed, and the usefulness of his work to the University was evident. His detractors observed that Portsea was a recognised step towards high preferment, and that Lang always had a keen eye for people and places that would aid his advancement. But it was a real zeal for work among the poor that induced him to exchange his delightful post at Oxford for intense labour among the industrial multitudes of Portsea. Here, too, he had a fine opportunity for his powers both as a preacher and as an organiser. Each Sunday night St. Mary's, Portsea, a splendid church, was thronged by a congregation of 2,000 when the vicar was in the pulpit. At Portsea Lang had Randall Davidson as his Diocesan, and was appointed an Honorary Chaplain to Queen Victoria in 1899, preaching before her from time to time at Osborne. His father was already one of her Scottish Chaplains in Ordinary.

The death of Queen Victoria nearly synchronised with that of Mandell Creighton, Bishop of London. Dr. Winnington-Ingram was translated to that see, and the vacant post of Bishop-Suffragan of Stepney and Canon of St. Paul's was given to Cosmo Lang – after a little delay, for the Prime Minister (the third Marquess of Salisbury) characteristically addressed the offer to "the Rev. C. Langport." In the autumn of that year Archbishop Maclagan resigned, and Mr. Asquith had to make his first episcopal nomination. The names of various senior Bishops were put forward, but Mr. Asquith did not know them personally as he knew the Bishop of Stepney, and Lang, at the age of 45, became Archbishop of York without any previous experience as a Diocesan. A northerner himself, he was heartily welcomed in Yorkshire. Soon he was the valued friend of the principal landowners, and also a most effective speaker to industrial audiences in the great manufacturing towns.

On November 12, 1928, notice of the resignation of Randall Davidson, Archbishop of Canterbury, took effect. Cosmo Lang was clearly marked out to succeed him. On December 4, with ceremonial at once simple and stately, the new Primate of All England was enthroned in Canterbury Cathedral. Not long afterwards he was found, in fact, to be suffering from a duodenal ulcer – virtually the first illness he had ever experienced. It was not until the summer of 1929, after a voyage in the Mediterranean, that he was able to resume work, which now included the laborious task of preparing for the seventh Lambeth Conference.

This, duly held in 1930, proved successful in every way. Its programme was remarkable for its vision and boldness. The discussions, and the resolutions to which they led, had a lasting value. The Conference was attended by 308 Bishops, illustrating the striking growth of the Anglican communion. The strain of the Conference injured the Archbishop's health, and his doctors ordered three months' rest. In March, 1931, he went for another Mediterranean cruise and visited Palestine.

On his return Lang seemed completely to enjoy life. His genius as a public speaker became greater than ever. Perhaps his greatest triumph of speech was the five-minute sermon which he had preached many years before at the Coronation of King George V and Queen Mary. As a speaker, his great skill was perhaps never shown more convincingly than in the tributes he paid to the memory of King George V. The sorrow which the death of the king brought to Dr. Lang was intensified by the very different relationship in which he stood with Edward VIII. He felt that, as Primate of All England, he was bound to intervene when a crisis developed over the new King's projected marriage, but at such moments he lacked the profound sagacity of his predecessor, Randall Davidson. A broadcast he delivered soon after the abdication provoked wide criticism.

He was deeply interested in politics. His speeches in the House of Lords were apt to lose something of their effect by undue length, but always they showed uncommon abilities linked with deep moral earnestness. In spite of the very numerous claims upon him the Archbishop found time to serve on the Joint Committee on Indian Reforms, which sat for 18 laborious months. He worked hard to promote closer relationships between the English and Presbyterian Churches. For this he was peculiarly well equipped by reason of his descent and early upbringing.

His attempts to reach agreement on the church's adherence to the Book of Common Prayer were interrupted by the war. More successful were Lang's efforts to bring about a concordat between the Anglican and Free Churches on the thorny question of religious teaching in elementary schools. With consummate skill and patience he influenced rather than seemed openly to lead, negotiations carried on over a number of years. It is difficult to exaggerate the wisdom, skill, and perseverance by means of which Lang had enabled a measure of agreement to be reached.

The urgent demands made upon him by the 1939-45 war forbade his fulfilling the intention he had often expressed, to retire at the age of 75; but on January 21, 1942, Lang announced to the Canterbury Convocation that he had decided to resign his office of Archbishop. He felt that great tasks of reconstruction in Church as well as State must follow the war, and the Lambeth Conference – which normally would have assembled in 1940 – would then meet. For this work he felt a younger man was needed, for already he was in his seventy-eighth year. His resignation took effect on March 31. The tributes paid to him were enthusiastic and wholeheartedly sincere. Great as was the change brought to his manner of life, he was happy in his retirement. The gracious action of the King in placing the King's Cottage, Kew Green, at his disposal gave him a delightful residence, at the back of which Kew Gardens were open to him at any hour for the turning of a key. His peerage enabled him still to attend and to take part in the House of Lords debates, and, as he was no longer an official, he was made an elected trustee of the British Museum, which again enabled him to continue work in which he delighted. Whatever else ecclesiastical historians of the future may say about him, it will remain true that few men of greater all-round powers have ever filled the chair of St. Augustine.

JOHN LOGIE BAIRD

Inventor of television, who first demonstrated the transmission of the
living human face 'with light, shade and detail'

15 JUNE 1946

MR. J. L. BAIRD, THE TELEVISION PIONEER, died at his home at Bexhill
early yesterday morning at the age of 58, after an illness which began
in February. Until then he had been actively engaged in research in
his own company's laboratories. His company successfully showed the
Victory parade by television at the Savoy Hotel last Saturday, but he was
too ill to be present.

John Logie Baird was born in 1888 at Helensburgh, Scotland, son of
the minister of the West Parish Church. He was educated at Larchfield
and the Royal Technical College, Glasgow, where he won an associate
scholarship in electrical engineering. He was one of the outstanding
inventors of his time, and well deserved the ultimate success which
came to his experiments over so many years. As a young man he was
fascinated by the possibility of "seeing by wireless," and at the age of
18, when indifferent health caused him to give up London business
life, Baird went to Hastings, where he established a small laboratory and began his experiments. After some months his primitive
apparatus succeeded in reproducing objects in outline, and by 1926
he achieved true television and demonstrated before members of the
Royal Institution the transmission of living human faces with light,
shade, and detail. By this time Baird had moved his laboratory to an
attic in Soho to continue his research, and full reward came to him in
1929 when television was broadcast first by the German Post Office, and
two months later by the B.B.C. using his system. A year earlier Baird
had been the first man to demonstrate transatlantic television and
the transmission of images from this country to the *Berengaria* in
mid-Atlantic.

Another step forward in television was made in 1931 when the modulated arc was used as the source of light, and it resulted in a far more brilliant picture than had been possible with the neon tube or a device known as the "Kerr cell," the only two forms of illumination previously used. Experiments were also being made with the cathode-ray tube about this time, and eventually it was adopted by Baird as the most successful method of providing a well-defined and brilliant picture. In 1937 the B.B.C. was transmitting both by Marconi-E.M.I. and Baird methods, but following a report by the Television Advisory Committee, it was decided that only the Marconi system should be used. Just before the war Baird gave a demonstration of television in natural colour, using the cathode-ray tube and an arrangement of colour filters, which produced a satisfactory projection on a screen 2ft. 6in. by 2ft. He has also to his credit the invention of the "Noctovisor," an apparatus for seeing in the dark by invisible rays; and in April of this year Baird was reported to have completed his researches into a new phase of television which would enable audiences in special cinemas to see events as they occurred miles away. A bronze plaque in Queen's Avenue, Hastings, records that television was first demonstrated by John Logie Baird from experiments started there in 1924 – thus he had every claim to the title, "the father of television." Since 1941 Baird had been consulting technical adviser to Cable and Wireless, Limited.

He married Margaret Albu in 1931. There were one son and one daughter of the marriage.

JAMES MAXTON

Labour rebel and agitator who said his aim was
"to fan the flames of discontent"

24 JULY 1946

MR. JAMES MAXTON, M.P. for the Bridgeton Division of Glasgow, which he had represented as an I.L.P. member since 1922, died yesterday at Largs, Ayrshire, where he had been lying ill for some months.

For many years Maxton was an extremely prominent Parliamentary figure, and, in spite of his fierce denunciations of political opponents, was greatly liked by members of all parties. A speaker of fire, force, wit, and deep sincerity, he could raise popular audiences to great heights of enthusiasm, and at Westminster drew keen attention also, though he seldom commanded complete agreement even from his own side of the House. By nature an uncompromising rebel, he lacked constructive and administrative ability; and his impatience with gradualism and any kind of concession to expediency involved him in constant quarrels even with those most closely allied to him in political views. But his broad and disarming humanity never failed to protect his friendships.

A man of austere personal habits and an idealist, Maxton was also a person of great gentleness and understanding, with a genius for friendship. He was a philosopher too; and in his last phase he possibly realised that through gazing too fixedly at the stars his feet had been caught in many pitfalls and that as a political leader he had been rather a failure. But he was in no way soured or disappointed. He became a great House of Commons man, who could fill the House whenever he rose to speak; and the political rebel from Clydeside matured into a humanist whom his Parliamentary colleagues of all parties came to regard with a degree of affection rarely stirred in the turbulent world of politics.

Tall, spare, pale, and almost cadaverous-looking, with piercing eyes and long black hair, a lock of which fell at emotional moments over the

160

right ear, Maxton indeed looked the part of a revolutionary. He was one of the most compelling speakers these islands have lately produced. He would begin quietly, in almost a halting manner, gradually warming up until his periods flowed in heady spate. He was singularly consistent and single-minded, and the claims of expediency and strategy had no meaning for him. Much of the affection he inspired arose from a genuine and pretty wit; while, of course, his courage and complete probity were everywhere realised.

James Maxton, the son of a Glasgow teacher, was born on June 22, 1885. He went first to Grahamston School, Barrhead; then at 12, to Hutcheson's Grammar School, Glasgow, and at 15 to the Glasgow Pupil Teachers' Institute. He completed his education at Glasgow University, of which he was an M.A. As an undergraduate he was a noted half-miler and he belonged to the Conservative Club and to the University company of the First Lanark Volunteers. Becoming a teacher he taught in four schools in 10 years. But soon after his graduation he had embraced Socialism with all the ardour of a convert, and much of his leisure time was passed in speaking for the Independent Labour Party. He became chairman of its Scottish divisional council, and in 1914 he was appointed to the national administrative council as representative for Scotland.

During the 1914-18 war Maxton was a pacifist. In March, 1916, he sustained a conscientious objection to military service before the Barrhead tribunal; but while that body's decision was pending he was arrested for a seditious speech on Glasgow Green – the offence lying in the incitement of munition workers to strike. He was sentenced to 12 months imprisonment in Calton Jail, Edinburgh. After he was released in February, 1917, he worked as a labourer, a shipping clerk, and a political worker. Eventually he made a living as an I.L.P. organiser. In the 1918 general election he stood for the Bridgeton Division of Glasgow, but was defeated. The next year he was elected to the Glasgow education authority, and for three years studied local administration. The same period (1919-22) covered his first marriage, to Sissie Whitehead, a teacher, who died in the latter year soon after giving birth to a son.

Maxton was elected M.P. for Bridgeton in 1922 by a majority of nearly 8,000, and with a group of Labour members from Clydeside set out to "ginger up" the whole movement. His revolutionary views were expressed with such violence that he found himself on numerous occasions in trouble with the Chair. Though he and his friends had been largely responsible for placing Ramsay MacDonald at the head of the party he was not asked to take office in either of the Labour administrations. His avowed aim was "Socialism in our time," coupled with "expropriation without compensation"; he found the pace of the Labour Government too slow, failing to appreciate the difficulties caused through their lack of an absolute majority. He spoke with his usual ruthlessness on the General Strike. In his early days he had no reverence for Parliamentary institutions as such. "My function as an agitator," he once said, "is to fan the flames of discontent"; and this he did with enthusiasm, though with much abatement of violence as he passed middle life.

In 1926 Maxton was appointed chairman of the I.L.P. (at that time still regarded as the "spear-head" of the Labour movement). The next year he shocked his orthodox colleagues by issuing, with the late A. J. Cook, the famous "manifesto" which deprecated the Mond-Turner conversations on peace in industry, and urged a more radical directive to Labour policy on the lines of no compromise with capitalism. The same intransigent spirit led him to quarrel impatiently with the Labour Government in 1929, to invite expulsion from the League Against Imperialism in the same year, and eventually to destroy altogether the power and influence of the I.L.P. By 1933 that once vigorous body had become so attenuated that the Parliamentary group consisted of only three members, Maxton, Mr. George Buchanan, and Mr. McGovern. In one of time's revenges Maxton was himself reproved by its consultative committee when he congratulated Mr. Chamberlain on the agreement made with Hitler at Munich in 1938.

Maxton published a study of "Lenin," and a contribution to the series called "If I Were Dictator," and was himself the subject of a biographical study by Mr. Gilbert McAllister. Innumerable caricatures were made of him; Sir John Lavery painted him in oils, and Lady Kennet sculptured a portrait head. He married again in 1935, his second wife being Madeleine Glasier.

* * *

SIR HARRY LAUDER

*Self-confessed "minstrel," who became the most popular variety
artist of his time, and was 'a man writ large'*

27 FEBRUARY 1950

SIR HARRY LAUDER, THE SCOTTISH COMEDIAN, died last night. He had been lying ill at his home near Strathaven, Lanarkshire, since last summer.

The genius of this remarkable favourite of the British (not only the Scottish) public all over the world arose from a combination of nationality and personality, both of high degree. Behind his rich chuckle and sudden spurts of earnestness there lay immense power, and in his humour and his wisdom he was the absolute Lowland Scot, displaying for all the world to see the great strength and the small weaknesses of the type. The broods of stories circulated about his careful husbandry of the "bawbees" were not without foundation, and his realisation of their value as publicity was characteristic of one who owed so much of his success to the force of personality. For, though his early career was built upon the firm foundation of an accomplished stage technique assisted by a pleasing and expressive baritone voice, his later triumphs were due to the realisation by the public at large that here was a superlative minstrel (his own word) who was also a man writ large.

His father was an Edinburgh man, his mother a MacLennan of the Black Isle, and he was born at Portobello on August 4, 1870. He was but a boy when his father died, and his mother had little on which to keep her seven children. Harry worked at many an odd job, became a "half-timer" in a flax mill in Arbroath, later a pit-head boy at Hamilton, and then a miner. While in this last occupation he met and married in 1890, Annie, daughter of James Vallance, underground manager of the pit in which he worked. Already he had begun to sing, and was winning prizes at local competitions. From that he rose to touring with concert-parties; then to variety engagements. Belfast saw his first professional appearance, and he came to London in 1900 and was engaged as an "extra turn" at Gatti's-in-the-Road. His warm reception was quite unexpected but thereafter he soared to heights of popularity and remuneration which few, if any, variety artists have ever reached. London paid him royally; America and the colonies gave him unheard-of salaries. The newspapers reported his doings as if he were a famous statesman or a crowned-head. Processions escorted him on great occasions; public bodies sent him off at Liverpool and received him at New York or Sydney.

He not only sang to his audiences; he talked to them, and by means of shrewd informal chats, anecdotes and advice, he grew deeper into their intimacy than any other comedian of his kind. Even those who could see nothing in him but a sturdy, stocky little man wearing the kilt with all its appurtenances and carrying a huge curly walking-stick, a man with twinkling eyes, a wide smile, a juicy giggle and a resonant voice, could not be insensible to the hold he had over the affections as well as the admiration of his audience.

Jokes about Harry Lauder's wealth and his Scottish care of it were common. But they were friendly jokes. It was known that he could be very generous when he had a mind to be. During the war of 1914-18 he threw into his country's cause every ounce of his material and moral weight. By his example and influence he awoke and confirmed the spirit of patriotism, winning many recruits for military service before conscription came in. He raised large sums for public ends by giving concerts and variety performances, and was assiduous in going to the Western Front to entertain the fighting men. There was one moment in his career when the power of his personality blazed forth. During the war he produced an indifferent revue in a London theatre. The curtain of the first act fell upon a patriotic song sung by Harry Lauder, whose only son had recently been killed in action. The intensity of conviction with which he sang that song was tremendous. When the war was over his services were thought worthy of the knighthood with which he was honoured in 1919. He wrote his own songs and the music to them; and even all these years after his prime some of them – *I love a lassie, Stop yer tickling, Jock, Just a wee Deoch-an-Doris, Roamin' in the Gloamin', It's nice to get up in the morning* (but the list might be almost indefinitely increased) – are still familiar to thousands. In *Roamin' in the Gloamin',* one of his books of reminiscences, issued soon after his wife's death in 1927, he paid tribute to a partnership of the greatest happiness which had lasted for little short of 40 years.

Not long before his sixty-eighth birthday he fell and fractured a thigh, but made a complete recovery and when war broke out in 1939 he emulated the example he had himself set in 1914. Again he gave his rich talent to entertain the fighting men, giving his services free provided that the men of the forces did not have to pay to hear him. He gave several broadcasts in the special transmissions to the forces, and when the war ended, though in his seventy-fifth year, he continued to give occasional performances on the air, which evoked, at any rate from older listeners, nostalgic memories of the kind of music-hall in which Sir Harry Lauder had been so bright an ornament.

SIR ALEXANDER FLEMING

'No one was more aware than he of the indispensable part played by
other investigators in the development of penicillin'

12 MARCH 1955

SIR ALEXANDER FLEMING, D.Sc., M.B., F.R.C.P., F.R.C.S., F.R.S., the discoverer of penicillin, died suddenly yesterday at his home in London of a heart attack at the age of 73.

Alexander Fleming, the son of a farmer, was born at Lochfield, near Darvel, in Ayrshire, on August 6, 1881. He received his early education at the village school and at Kilmarnock Academy. At 13 years of age he was sent to live with his brother in London, where, for the next two or three years, he continued his education by attending the Polytechnic Institute in Regent Street. At that time he displayed no particular scientific ability nor felt any urge to be a doctor. For some years he worked in a shipping office in Leadenhall Street, but he found office routine deadly dull and after four years in the City a small legacy enabled him to escape. The brother with whom he was living had already taken his medical degree and he encouraged his younger brother to take up medicine. Thus at the age of 20 he became a student at St. Mary's Hospital Medical School, winning the senior entrance scholarship in natural science. He showed that he had found his true bent by winning almost every class prize and scholarship during his student career. He qualified in 1906 and at the M.B., B.S. examination of London University in 1908 he obtained honours and was awarded a gold medal.

In 1909 he became a Fellow of the Royal College of Surgeons. In 1906 he had begun to assist Sir Almroth Wright in the inoculation department at St. Mary's Hospital, and this association led to his taking up the study of bacteriology. Under the stimulating influence of Wright, who was at that time engaged in his researches on the opsonic theory, he acquired great experience and skill in bacteriological technique and in clinical pathology. For recreation he attended the drills and parades

166

of the London Scottish, which he had joined as a private in the year before he resigned from his post with the shipping company. For some years he went to the annual camp and, being a fair shot, to the meetings at Bisley. On the outbreak of war in 1914 he resigned from the London Scottish so that he could go to France as a captain in the R.A.M.C. He worked in Sir Almroth Wright's laboratory in the Casino at Boulogne and received a mention in dispatches. At the end of the war he returned to St. Mary's as assistant to Sir Almroth Wright and was also appointed lecturer in bacteriology in the medical school. He subsequently became director of the department of systematic bacteriology and assistant director of the inoculation department. For some years he acted as pathologist to the venereal disease department at St. Mary's and was also pathologist to the London Lock Hospital. In 1928 he was appointed Professor of Bacteriology in the University of London, the post being tenable at St. Mary's. He retired with the title emeritus in 1948, but continued at St. Mary's as head of the Wright-Fleming Institute of Micro-Biology. Though last year he formally handed over the reins to Professor R. Cruikshank, he continued his own research work there and only the day before yesterday was at the institute discussing plans for the lecture tour in the Middle East he had been asked to undertake by the British Council.

Fleming's first notable discovery, that of lysozyme, was made in 1922. He had for some time been interested in antiseptics and in naturally occurring antibacterial substances. In culturing nasal secretion from a patient with an acute cold he found a remarkable element that had the power of dissolving bacteria. This bacteriolyte element, which he also found in tears and other body fluids, he isolated and named lysozyme.

Penicillin was discovered in 1928 when Fleming was engaged in bacteriological researches on staphylococci. For examination purposes he had to remove the covers of his culture plates and a mould spore drifted on to a plate. After a time it revealed itself by developing into a colony about half an inch across. It was no new thing for a bacteriologist to find that a mould had grown on a culture plate which had lain on the bench for a week, but the strange thing in this particular case was that the bacterial colonies in the neighbourhood of the mould appeared to be fading away. What had a week before been vigorous staphylococcus colonies were now faint shadows of their former selves. Fleming might have merely discarded the contaminated culture plate but fortunately his previous research work on antiseptics and on naturally occurring antibacterial substances caused him to take special note of the apparent antibacterial action of the mould.

He made sub-cultures of the mould and investigated the properties of the antibacterial substance. He found that while the crude culture fluid in which the mould had grown was strongly antibacterial it was non-toxic to animals and human beings. The crude penicillin was, however, very unstable and was too weak and too crude for injection. Early attempts at concentration were not very successful, and after a few tentative trials its clinical use was not pursued, although it continued to be used in Fleming's laboratory for differential culture. The position in 1929 was that Fleming had discovered and named penicillin, had investigated its antibacterial power, and had suggested that it might be useful as an antiseptic applied to infected lesions. Attempts to produce a concentrated extract capable of clinical application were not successful and had been abandoned. In the light of later knowledge Fleming's original paper of 1929 was remarkable. It covered nearly the whole field, realised most of the problems and made considerable progress in solving them. The resuscitation of penicillin as a chemotherapeutic agent was due to the brilliant work of Sir Howard Florey and his colleagues at Oxford, notably Dr. E. B. Chain.

After the establishment of penicillin as a life-saving drug Fleming was overwhelmed with honours. He was knighted in 1944 and in the following year he shared the Nobel prize for medicine with Sir Howard Florey and Dr. E. B. Chain. He was William Julius Mickle Fellow of London University in 1942, and received an award of merit from the American Pharmaceutical Manufacturers Association in 1943. He was elected F.R.S. in 1943 and F.R.C.P. in 1944, under the special by-law. His other honours included the Moxon medal of the Royal College of Physicians (1945), the Charles Mickle Fellowship of Toronto University

(1944), the John Scott medal of the City Guild of Philadelphia (1944), the Cameron prize of Edinburgh University (1945), the Albert Gold Medal of the Royal Society of Arts (1946), the honorary Gold Medal of the Royal College of Surgeons (1946), the Actonian Prize of the Royal Institution, and the honorary Freedom of the Boroughs of Paddington, Darvel, and Chelsea. He had innumerable honorary degrees from British and foreign universities, and in 1951 was elected Rector of Edinburgh University. Only last weekend thieves stole property from his flat in Chelsea worth about £1,000 and later an appeal was made to them to return a gold seal of great sentimental value.

Fleming was president of the London Ayrshire Society and of the Pathological and Comparative Medicine Sections of the Royal Society of Medicine. Apart from the papers describing his great discoveries, he contributed to the Medical Research Council System of Bacteriology, to the official Medical History of the 1914-18 War, and to many other publications. He was a keen amateur painter, and he had many friends among artists. He was also very fond of motoring and of gardening. He remained quite unspoiled by the publicity and acclaim that came to him, and no one was more aware than he of the indispensable part played by other investigators in the development of penicillin. Animated by the spirit of the true scientist, he looked ever forward.

He was twice married, first to Sarah Marion, daughter of Mr. John McElroy. She died in 1949, leaving a son. In 1953 he married Dr. Amalia Criutsouris, of Athens, who had been a member of his staff at the Wright-Fleming Institute.

SIR WILLIAM BURRELL

Shipowner and art collector

13 MARCH 1958

SIR WILLIAM BURRELL DIED on Saturday at the age of 96. The son of William Burrell, the shipowner, he was born on July 9, 1861. He entered his father's business when he was 15 and began buying pictures about the same time to find later (as he himself said) that the principal value of these early purchases lay in the frames. The purchases of his maturity were somewhat shrewder. In 1944 he offered to Glasgow Corporation his collection of works of art valued at over £1m., with £450,000 towards the erection of a building to house it. This princely assemblage is as varied as it is large. One of its most important sections consists of Gothic tapestries of which the German examples of the fifteenth and sixteenth centuries are especially fine. The collection is also rich in stained glass, silver, medieval sculpture, early furniture, and English embroidered pictures of the seventeenth century.

No suitable building has yet been chosen for exhibiting the whole collection but it is partly on show at the Kelvingrove Art Galleries, Glasgow; the remainder is stored in different buildings in the Glasgow area.

A selection of Burrell's paintings was for a time on loan to the National Gallery of Scotland and was shown at the Tate Gallery in 1924. A large selection was also shown at the McLellan Galleries in Glasgow in 1949. This included some of his 22 pictures by Degas, two large and several small works by Daumier, examples of Cezanne, Renoir, Manet, and other nineteenth-century masters; and among the work of earlier painters pictures by Rembrandt, Velazquez, Hals, and Bellini.

In 1946 Burrell was awarded the Saint Mungo prize of £1,000, which is given to the man considered by a committee of representative citizens to have done the most for Glasgow in the previous three years.

He was knighted in 1927, and in 1944 the freedom of the City of Glasgow was conferred upon him.

EDWIN MUIR

Poet of serenity who translated Kafka

5 JANUARY 1959

MR. EDWIN MUIR, C.B.E., poet and critic, died in hospital at Cambridge on Saturday at the age of 71. The major landmarks of the world of writing are not those men who stand at its busy centres but those whose personal vision, integrity, and creative resource fit them rather for the calm and opportunity of comparative isolation. Edwin Muir was among these. His last years, spent in a beautiful Cambridgeshire village, serenely completed a life which had always been nearer to distinction than to celebrity. Here at Swaffham Prior, Muir's study looked out on a scene (a graveyard on a hill, a ruined church, a ruined tower) which might well have come from his own verse; and it was in this room that some of his best work was done. Indeed, he became at 70 perhaps the foremost poet in English to be writing actively week by week. Starting late in life as a poet, he died at an advanced age; but it was his prime. Old age and declining powers were things that he did not experience.

Muir's life began in a remote croft on the main island of Orkney, where he was born in 1887. Both his father's and his mother's family had been crofters for generations; but it was not a period in which crofting could flourish and in 1902 the Muirs moved to modest quarters in Glasgow. Then, in drab works and offices, Muir became to some extent the victim of that more brutal side of modernity which later he was so humanely and yet so searchingly to indict.

Already he was reading widely, thinking deeply, and beginning as a writer himself: contributing, under A. R. Orage, for example, to the *New Age*. But the true beginning of his literary career was his marriage in 1919 to Willa Anderson (in her turn a Shetlander), whose more emphatic personality, and also perhaps quicker practical sense, contributed profoundly to his life and in large measure made it possible for him to do what he did.

Muir began to write verse only in the 1920s. Even then his prose was at first more important. His early criticism (*Latitudes*, 1924; *Transition*, 1927) is remarkable for, among other things, almost the first wholly outspoken recognition of D. H. Lawrence as the major genius of his generation. *The Structure of the Novel* (1927) is a lucid and thoughtful book; it may owe a little to Stevenson but it reveals unmistakably the fresh mind of its author. Other and later critical pieces were published as *Essays on Literature and Society* (1949). Muir's social insight shows also in *Scottish Journey* (1936). Yet these works have been less influential than the translations from German fiction which he and Willa Muir, over a number of years, produced in collaboration. Of these *Jew Süss* may once have been the best known; but the most important in the end proved certainly to be those from Kafka (*The Castle*, 1930; *The Trial*, 1935, &c.). Before their appearance Kafka was almost unknown in Britain. The Muirs virtually created his literary reputation among us. Their translations are still standard and have recently been reissued.

It is not difficult to see how Kafka's intense yet sedate anxieties would have had their appeal for Muir; and the partial kinship of his mind with Kafka's sometimes appears in his verse. But the strongest influence on that verse is undoubtedly Muir's own life and his endeavour to come to terms with life. The remote and spacious islands where he was born have left their image throughout his work. Yet it is perhaps two things together, the archaic simplicities and enduring strength of his background, and also his interest in other literary models than the fashionable ones (his decisive tribute to Dante comes here to mind), which brought it about that his poetry was always a poetry more of things than of words, a poetry with little place for a rich language because what it sought was a plain reality.

The potentialities of his style, one assessed with difficulty through the critical ideas most current to-day, were not indeed fully apparent in his earlier volumes (for example, *First Poems*, 1926, or *Journeys and Places*, 1937), although here as always there is much to praise. Not until *The Voyage*, 1946, and *The Labyrinth*, 1948, was it apparent that his serene but subtle gravity of cadence and power to transmit in a naked minimum

Edwin Muir

of words a single poignant, insistent, inescapable image could produce work of altogether outstanding quality. Moreover, after the war he had returned to Prague as head of the British Institute, and the fall of Czechoslovakia to Communism had affected him deeply. Poems like *The Combat* or *Adam's Dream* now proved that he was not drawing on the good and evil in his early life merely in order to retreat into a private landscape. These pieces, with *Collected Poems*, 1952, *One Foot in Eden*, 1956, and later substantial poems (like *The Last War*), which were published in periodicals up to within a few months of his death, revealed him as now, of all living English poets, the one most immediately and profoundly concerned to confront, and surmount, the challenges of his time.

After Czechoslovakia and a short period of work in Rome, Muir returned to Scotland, became Warden of Newbattle Abbey College outside Edinburgh, and in 1955 was appointed Charles Eliot Norton Visiting Professor at Harvard. This, the award of literary prizes, the conferment of a C.B.E. in 1953, and the growing list of his honorary doctorates (Prague, 1947; Edinburgh, 1947; Rennes, 1949; Leeds, 1955; Cambridge, 1958) show that his achievement was being widely recognised. But those who knew him during his last years will recall more his ineradicable modesty than his growing fame. The latter did not disturb or even preoccupy his days. In the first place he lived for a world of poetry, and seemed, purely and easily, to know its essence where others knew only its decoction. But he was happy also in the simplicities of life, the quiet meal, the short stroll, the calm, relaxed conversation where he always showed a gentleness without weakness, and that charity of mind which comes from a deeper clarity. Ignorant, for a long time, of the slow-moving efforts being made in many quarters to secure him from financial anxiety, he worked on even into his last illness as a reviewer. What he found to praise was always what marked out the writer, never what merely tallied with the critic's yardstick. Young people who met him at this time (last year, for example, he was the first Churchill Professor at Bristol) instantly saw through his unassuming manner to the integrity and strength within; and when he chose that line of work he was a fine and ennobling teacher.

These are incidentals. His family and friends will remember him as a good and in some ways almost a saintly man. Others will remember him after them, for now he is among the English poets.

* * *

THE DUCHESS OF ATHOLL

A lifetime of service, and the first of two women
to become government ministers

22 OCTOBER 1960

HER GRACE KATHARINE MARJORY, Duchess of Atholl, D.B.E., Hon. D.C.L., Hon. LL.D., F.R.C.M., former Hon. Colonel of the Scottish Horse, and one of the first women to hold ministerial office in this country, died yesterday in Edinburgh. She was born in 1874.

Her busy life covered a remarkable span of public duty, from the time of her marriage in the reign of Queen Victoria until the present day. An author and scholar as well as a politician and a great aristocrat, she held honorary doctorates of the universities of Oxford, Glasgow, Manchester, Durham, Columbia, Leeds, and McGill. Completely sincere, grave and alert, her tiny, upright, hawk-like figure was poised with an innate dignity that was reinforced by the greatness of her moral stature. Always in earnest, she found it impossible to compromise in matters of principle, and was sometimes carried into extreme positions by the logic of her views. As a result she was often misunderstood, and her steadfast opposition to all forms of totalitarianism led her into paradoxical situations. Utterly unselfish, kind and good, she was the soul of honour and incapable of meanness. Politically a Tory, she was bred in the Whig tradition, and was a hard-working, tireless and thorough liberal humanist, whose life was devoted to the public interest. She leaves no children.

She was the widow of Brigadier-General the 8th Duke of Atholl, K.T., P.C., G.C.V.O., D.S.O., Lord Lieutenant of Perthshire, a former Lord Chamberlain, Lord High Commissioner to the General Assembly of the Church of Scotland and a Grand Master Mason of Scotland, one of the greatest highland figures of his time. Her own aristocratic roots in Perthshire also went very deep. Her father, Sir James Ramsay of Bamff, 10th Bart., LL.D., Litt.D., 25th Laird since 1232 in the unbroken male line, was a well-known historian, gained a double first at Oxford and was a continental mountaineer who celebrated his eightieth birthday by walking 25 miles across the Atholl hills.

Kitty Ramsay married the future Duke of Atholl in 1899. When her husband succeeded to the dukedom in 1917, she turned Blair Castle into an auxiliary hospital and served as its commandant. At its inception she had become president of the Perthshire Branch of the Red Cross. Before that war she served on the committee that investigated the medical and nursing services in the highlands and Isles. After the war she was elected chairman of the Scotties Board of Health's Consultative Council for the Highlands and Islands.

She entertained many distinguished visitors at Blair Castle, among them, in 1921, Lloyd George, then Prime Minister, who wanted talented women of all parties in the Commons and pressed the Duchess to stand for Parliament, while two years later, Lord Haldane hinted at Liberal and Labour support should she stand as a Unionist. Accordingly in 1923 she was elected Unionist M.P. for Kinross and West Perthshire. But she immediately wrote an article in the *Spectator* firmly opposing Mrs. Pankhurst's scheme for a "Women's Party" in Parliament. In 1924 she was appointed Parliamentary Secretary to the Board of Education: she and Margaret Bondfield being the first two women ever to become Ministers in a British Government.

During the financial cuts of 1927 her personal intervention with Mr. Baldwin saved the educational grants to local authorities from being merged in the general block-grant system. She took an active part in the Imperial Education Conference that year, and next year was responsible for the Atholl Report on examinations for part-time students. Although she ceased to be a Minister when the Conservative Government fell in 1929, she held her seat in the Commons.

In Opposition the Duchess joined an all-party committee to prevent enforced circumcision of Kikuyu girls, and represented them at an international conference on African children in Geneva. She was hotly opposed by native reactionaries, especially by Jomo Kenyatta, who strongly upheld this cruel custom. The Duchess wrote that "there was something very unsympathetic about him". From this time onwards her life was devoted to combating totalitarianism in al its forms.

When the war that she had foreseen broke out, the Duke and Duchess had already prepared hostels at Blair Castle and four Atholl shooting lodges to receive refugee children from Glasgow, while her brother-in-law, Lord James Murray, arranged for 400 more children to be sheltered in Mid-Atholl. After Dunkirk she became secretary of the local invasion committee to organise civil cooperation with the military. The remaining years of her life were tirelessly devoted to exposing and combating the Soviet menace, to supporting the cause of the unhappy Poles, Czechs, and Hungarians, also the Baltic and Balkan peoples abandoned to the Russian yoke, and to organizing practical assistance for refugees from communist tyranny. She who had made her curtsy to Queen Victoria, had known Kitchener and Baldwin and Madariaga, now befriended Kravchenko. It seems fitting that the last decoration she received was the Order of Polonia Restituta, conferred on the Duchess by the exiled President of Poland. In 1958 she published her autobiography, including the life of her husband and appropriately called *Working Partnership*.

DR. JOHN MacCORMICK

Dominant figure in the Scottish nationalist movement

14 OCTOBER 1961

DR. JOHN M. MacCORMICK, chairman of the Scottish Covenant Association and one of the leading personalities within the Scottish nationalist movement for more than 30 years, died in a Glasgow hospital yesterday at the age of 56. Perhaps even to speak of a "movement" in this context may be misleading, for there is much disagreement between the various groups who want Scotland to have greater control of her own affairs. But no man in the past quarter-century has done more to draw the issue to the attention of the general public on both sides of the Border.

A former Rector of Glasgow University and a Glasgow lawyer, it was he who launched the Scottish Covenant which secured more than two million signatures in the early 1950s. He was a small, spry figure with considerable charm who often made friends where he could not win allies.

John MacDonald MacCormick, the younger son of Captain Donald MacCormick, a sea captain who was a native of Mull, was born on November 20, 1904. He was educated at Woodside School, Glasgow, and at Glasgow University, where he became associated with Scottish nationalism. After a spell as secretary of the University Labour Club he founded the Nationalist Association of the University in 1927. The following year, while still a law student, he was one of the founders and the first chairman of the National Party of Scotland. When it subsequently merged with the more moderate Scottish Party, MacCormick became honorary secretary.

He held that position until the great division in the Scottish nationalist movement in 1942. The clash, which may have been exacerbated by differences of personality, was centred largely on whether the party should support the Government in the war. MacCormick believed that it should, and when he was outvoted he promptly resigned and founded the Scottish Convention, which was later to be the means of his greatest propaganda success.

MacCormick stood unsuccessfully for Parliament on a number of occasions. He contested the Camlachie division of Glasgow in 1929; Inverness-shire in 1931, 1935, and 1945; and Paisley in 1948, where he had both Liberal and Conservative support. Having found from bitter experience how fruitless it was to oppose the major parties at the poll, it was no doubt in search of an alternative means of gathering influence that he launched the Scottish Covenant in October, 1949. This document, guilefully phrased so as not to offend many supporters of the established parties – it sought only a federal Parliament for Scotland, with "adequate authority" in Scottish affairs – attracted eventually more than two million signatures.

That, however, was the peak of MacCormick's influence. The Covenant may have succeeded in provoking the appointment of a Royal Commission on Scottish Affairs, but it did not provide an effective springboard for further political action. Very possibly, as many of the critics suggested, it was regarded by many of its signatories as an emotional protest rather than a call for specific measures.

In 1950 he was elected Rector of Glasgow University. His installation address – when he was bombarded by flour, tomatoes, and other missiles from his audience – was a disgraceful scene. But this was no indication of his popularity with the students in general. So conscientiously did he take his duties that he soon won the respect and liking of many of those who had opposed his election. A ready speaker, who had toured the United States in 1930 with a student debating team from Glasgow, he was at home in the university atmosphere. He was made an honorary LL.D. of Glasgow in 1951.

His published works included *The Flag in the Wind*, a highly readable account of his career in Scottish nationalism; and *Catastrophe and Imagination*, a more ambitious but less successful venture into a wider literary field.

In 1938 he married Margaret Isobel Miller, by whom he had two sons and two daughters.

ADMIRAL OF THE FLEET, VISCOUNT CUNNINGHAM OF HYNDHOPE

Outstanding naval leader of the Second World War

13 JUNE 1963

ADMIRAL OF THE FLEET Viscount Cunningham of Hyndhope, G.C.B., O.M., D.S.O., the outstanding naval leader of the Second World War, died in London yesterday at the age of 80. In the early part of the war he held major command at sea as Commander-in-Chief of the Mediterranean Fleet and subsequently of the Anglo-American expedition to North Africa. Later, as First Sea Lord from 1943 to 1946, he shared responsibility for the central direction of the war.

Though his merits and abilities fully justified his selection for the high posts he held, actually he owed his tenure of them to a large extent to luck. After his promotion to Vice-Admiral in 1936 he was unemployed for a year, and in view of the state of the flag lists at that time he himself hardly expected to hold more than perhaps one more minor command before concluding his career by retirement. Within three years, however, owing to unexpected retirements or deaths of flag officers senior to him, he found himself, as Commander-in-Chief of the Mediterranean Fleet, holding one of the two greatest sea commands, with the acting rank of Admiral, and well in the succession for promotion to Admiral of the Fleet. He held the Mediterranean Command at the outbreak of war in 1939, and few could have been more suitable for it. Essentially a man of action rather than an administrator, it was the general feeling in the Mediterranean Fleet that their Commander-in-Chief was the man to seize every opportunity that might present itself of conducting the war with vigour; and so indeed it proved when, in 1940, Italy joined our enemies. Faced with a pronounced material superiority, he himself remarked that a vigorous offensive was the only possible policy.

Under his inspiring leadership, complete ascendancy over the Italian Fleet was quickly established, and maintained even when the loss of both north and south coasts of the Eastern Basin enabled strong German land-based air forces to dominate the narrow seas. After an interlude in Washington, Cunningham returned to the Mediterranean command in November, 1942, as Allied Naval Commander-in-Chief, when the Anglo-American recovery of North Africa redeemed the balance once more. The next year he had the satisfaction of receiving the surrender of the Italian Fleet; and when Sir Dudley Pound died in harness in 1943, there was by common consent but one officer to succeed him as First Sea Lord. A man of florid and smiling countenance, with the blue eyes of the born sailor and the genial manner of one whose naval career had been passed chiefly in small ships, Cunningham was never one to insist on rigid formalities or precedents, and though he would excuse no failure in courage or seamanship, he would ever turn a blind eye to faults arising from dash or excess of zeal.

Andrew Browne Cunningham was the son of Professor D. J. Cunningham, of Dublin and Edinburgh, and brother of General Sir Alan Cunningham. He was born on January 7, 1883, and educated first at Edinburgh Academy and later at Mr. Foster's School at Stubbington. He passed into the *Britannia* as a naval cadet in January, 1897.

His first command, which he held from May, 1908, to January, 1910, was torpedo boat No. 14 in the Home Fleet, one of the first oil-burning ships in the Navy, known to those serving in them as the "oily wads". There could be no better training for a young officer in seamanship, self-reliance and initiative than such a command. From there Cunningham graduated to a bigger ship, taking command of the destroyer *Vulture* in reserve for a year until, in January, 1911, he achieved the aim of every young destroyer officer of the day, a command in the "running flotilla", the destroyer *Scorpion*, of the 1st Flotilla, Home Fleet. Cunningham was still in command of her on the outbreak of war.

In the history of the Dardanelles campaign, the name of the *Scorpion* is constantly occurring – she was ever in the forefront. On October 30, 1914, she and the *Wolverine* opened the campaign against Turkey by running into the Gulf of Smyrna and sinking a Turkish minelayer which was lying alonside the pier at Vourlah. On March 4, 1915, she was part of the force supporting the landing on the south side of the straits, and it is on record that she ran right into the mouth of the river Mendere and silenced a battery which was holding up the advance of the Marines ashore. Time and again the *Scorpion* was in action, supporting the flank of the Army with her fire, assisting in the landing or evacuation of troops. On June 30, 1915, Cunningham was promoted to commander, remaining in command of the *Scorpion*, and on March 3, 1916, he was awarded the D.S.O. for his services off the peninsula.

In February, 1918, he transferred to the command of the *Ophelia* in the Dover Patrol, coming again under the command of Sir Roger Keyes, who had been Chief of Staff at the Dardanelles, and he transferred a month later to the *Termagant*. In her he took part in numerous engagements, including the Zeebrugge expedition, and after the Armistice he was awarded a Bar to his D.S.O. for his services. In February, 1919, he transferred to the *Seafire*, of the 5th Destroyer Flotilla, in which he again saw active service in the operations in the Baltic under the command of Rear-Admiral Sir Walter Cowan, commanding the 1st Light Cruiser Squadron; for this, in the next year, he was awarded a second Bar to his D.S.O. He was promoted to captain at the end of 1919, and on the conclusion of the Baltic operations returned to Rosyth with his flotilla.

In September, 1920, he was put in charge of Sub-Commission "C" of the Naval Inter-Allied Commission of Control, and in that capacity he supervised the demolition of the fortifications at Heligoland – an appointment in which his prolonged contact with German officers and officials gave him a knowledge of the people and language which was of great value to him in later years when he came to occupy a high position at the Admiralty. In 1929 he was selected for a course at the Imperial Defence College, on the conclusion of which he took command of the battleship *Rodney*, one of the most sought after of captains' commands.

In January, 1934, he was made C.B. and took command of the destroyer flotillas of the Mediterranean Fleet – Rear-Admiral (D) with his flag in the *Coventry* – which he held through the period of the Italo-Abyssinian War until March, 1936. Three months later he was promoted to Vice-Admiral, and the prospects of his further employment, except perhaps in a shore command at home, seemed remote. A year later, however, he was suddenly appointed Second-in-Command of the Mediterranean Fleet and Vice-Admiral Commanding Battle Cruiser Squadron, temporarily, in the vacancy caused by the illness of Vice-Admiral Sir Geoffrey Blake, and on that officer being invalided Cunningham's appointment was made permanent. After a series of promotions, he became an admiral in January, 1941.

On the outbreak of war in September, 1939, as Italy remained "non-belligerent", the Mediterranean seemed liable to prove a backwater, and practically all the Mediterranean Fleet was withdrawn for service in other seas. It was brought up to strength the following year, however, when it became clear that Mussolini was bent on war, only to be left in marked inferiority by the defection of its French contingent; on that melancholy occasion, Cunningham showed himself a skilled diplomatist as well as a war leader, and was able to secure the effective neutralisation of Admiral Godefroi's squadron – which had been part of the Allied Fleet under his command – without rancour or bloodshed. Within a few weeks of Mussolini's declaration of war, Cunningham, in the Battle of Calabria, had chased a superior Italian Fleet back into the shelter of its bases; a few months later the Fleet Air Arm attack at Taranto put half the Italian Navy out of action; and in March, 1941, in the brief night action known as the Battle of Cape Matapan, three of the largest Italian cruisers were destroyed in a few minutes. The arrival of the *Luftwaffe* on the shores of the Mediterranean at the end of 1941, and the loss of Cyrenaica, Greece, and Crete made it impossible for the British Fleet, lacking support in the air, to operate freely or to keep the sea route fully open. When Cunningham handed over the Mediterranean Command to Sir Henry Harwood in May, 1942, to go to Washington as the British representative with the Joint Chiefs of Staff, there was little left for it to do within the Mediterranean itself until the recovery of North Africa again gave it sea room.

Cunningham was away no more than six months. When the Anglo-American descent on French North Africa in "Operation Torch" of November, 1942, began the expulsion of the Axis from Africa, he returned there as Allied Naval Commander-in-Chief under General Eisenhower as Supreme Commander of the invading forces. Two months later he again took over, in addition, as Commander-in-Chief of the whole Mediterranean Fleet, and was promoted Admiral of the Fleet. He had the satisfaction of completely regaining control of the Mediterranean, and, in September, 1943, of receiving the surrender of the whole Italian Fleet. The death of the First Sea Lord, Admiral of the Fleet Sir Dudley Pound, in October brought him back to the Admiralty in his place. He was at the head of affairs for the rest of the war.

Cunningham, who retired in 1946, was created G.C.B. while holding the Mediterranan command in 1942, and baronet on relinquishing it. On the break-up of the coalition Government in 1945 he, together with his brother Chiefs of Staff, Field Marshal Sir Alan Brooke and Marshal of the R.A.F. Sir Charles Portal, was created a baron, taking the title of Lord Cunningham of Hyndhope, which he retained on promotion to a viscountcy in the New Year Honours of 1946. In the Birthday Honours that year he was made O.M.

In 1950 and again in 1952 he was Lord High Commissioner to the General Assembly of the Church of Scotland. His memoirs, *A Sailor's Odyssey*, were published in 1951.

His marriage to Nona Christine, daughter of Horace Byatt, of Midhurst, Sussex, took place in 1929.

MARY SOMERVILLE

First woman to reach Controller rank in the BBC

2 September 1963

MISS MARY SOMERVILLE, O.B.E., died yesterday at her home in Bath. She was 65. Although she made history as the first woman to reach the Controller rank in the B.B.C. – she was Assistant Controller of the Talks Division from 1947 to 1950, and Controller for the ensuing five years – it is for her work in school broadcasting that she will be remembered. A superb producer herself, she taught countless others. Indeed her influence over the whole range of radio production was great and went on through the regular appraisals of programmes the B.B.C. asked her to make after her retirement.

Mary Somerville was born in New Zealand in 1897, the daughter of the Rev. J. A. Somerville. She was educated at the Abbey School, Melrose, Selkirk High School, and Somerville College, Oxford, where she took a degree in English in 1925. Her professional life was bound up with the B.B.C., which she joined in 1925 and to which she devoted herself for 30 years, becoming successively Educational Assistant, Director of School Broadcasting, and Secretary of the Central Council on School Broadcasting, Assistant Controller Talks, and finally Controller Talks.

Mary Somerville did not initiate school broadcasting – the first broadcasts to schools went out in 1924 under the direction of the late T. C. Stobart – but it is rightly associated with her name, because it was she who built up School Broadcasting Department and worked out the close relationship between producer and consumer in which it was firmly grounded – now as then. She subscribed wholeheartedly to Professor Whitehead's view that "education must essentially be a setting in order of a ferment already stirring in the mind". Broadcasting, she thought, could help to start the ferment; the task of setting in order belonged to the teacher. She never forgot that education is a two-way process, and that it was vital for the B.B.C. to know what was happening to the children in the listening schools. This essential data was provided in 1926 by an investigation financed by the Carnegie Trustees in the county of Kent, which set the future pattern for school broadcasting and established a working partnership between the B.B.C. on the one hand, the Board of Education, the local education authorities, and the whole body of teachers on the other.

School broadcasting in sound and TV now employs a staff of over 60; its programmes go out to nearly thirty thousand schools; it is a source of training and advice for visitors from all parts of the world. In so far as such an achievement can ever be credited to one person, that person was Mary Somerville. She gave 18 years of life to school broadcasting (there were no half-measures in her zeal); she pondered, she pioneered, she fought authority and convinced sceptics; she triumphed.

Mary Somerville was happiest in a position where the hard work was still to be done; she had the courage of her convictions, and because she had both courage and convictions in good measure, her B.B.C. career was not without its stormy passages.

On issues of principle she was never afraid to say "That is *wrong*"; and she won the affection as well as the respect of her colleagues for her ability to stand firmly behind her decisions. When troubles arose, no staff were ever better defended in public, though in private they were often told pretty frankly where their work had fallen short.

Whatever her designation, she was always an educationist in the widest sense of the word. This did not mean that she believed in didactic broadcasting. On the contrary, she disliked it because it was bad radio, and because nothing that was bad radio could be good education. But she judged a broadcast, in whatever context, by the tests she had used in building up school broadcasting; the right relationship between speaker and hearer, and the right use of radio techniques, so that the end product – "what comes out of the box" she called it – was an experience and an extension for its hearers, and not simply an easy alternative to reading.

To the end of her life she had an exceptional capacity for learning new things, and she never lost the ability to revere and admire; her colleagues were often surprised by the catholicity of her respect for the views of the very varied people she talked to in her private and professional life, until it occurred to them that their own opinions were being treated in the same way.

Perhaps this receptivity to the impact of new experience was the real basis of her contribution to broadcasting. She did not want, in her own words, "to force what was thought good for the public down its throat", but she did believe in providing what was good. She herself had found in broadcasting a source of enrichment: she hoped to make it so for others.

She was appointed O.B.E. in 1935 and in 1943 Manchester University made her an honorary M.A.

She married Ralph Penton Brown in 1928 by whom she had a son. The marriage was dissolved by divorce in 1945. She married secondly in 1962 E. Rowan Davies.

* * *

WILLIAM GALLACHER

First Communist member of parliament, imprisoned four times
for his political activities

13 AUGUST 1965

MR. WILLIAM GALLACHER, from 1935 to 1950 Communist member of Parliament for West Fife, and president of the British Communist Party from 1956 to 1963, died yesterday. Until the general election of 1945 "Willie" Gallacher, as he was known to political friend and foe alike, was the only Communist M.P. Then he was joined for five years by "Phil" Piratin, who sat for Mile End, and Gallacher thus became leader of a party of two. Both lost their seats at the general election of 1950.

In spite of his extreme views, Gallacher made few enemies. He was ordered by the Speaker more than once to withdraw from the Commons for disorderly conduct and un-Parliamentary remarks, but he left little rancour behind. He was a consistent critic of the monarchy, and on the occasion of the marriage of the Queen spoke against the motion for a congratulatory address and protested against what he termed the "lavish expenditure" involved. He was imprisoned four times for his political activities.

For all the wildness of his oratory when he was on his feet there was much that was likeable about Willie Gallacher. He had a lively sense of humour and the fanatical communist in him was agreeably leavened by this ingredient. Sometimes it was difficult to believe that this amusing little Scotsman could be at the same time a dedicated communist, as he was. Even though he often got the House of Commons by the ears he was nearly always quickly forgiven. His experience at Westminster – where he sat through two Parliaments opposite Churchill – seemed to have mellowed even Gallacher. In the end he won quite a niche for himself in the esteem of the House of Commons.

The fourth of seven children, Gallacher was born on Christmas Day, 1881, of an Irish father and a Highland mother. He was educated at Paisley Elementary School but forsook his studies at the age of 12. He had done an early-morning milk round since he was 10, but his first full-time job was that of a grocer's delivery boy. While in this employment he made his first stand against unpaid overtime. Next he became an engineer's apprentice, signed on as a ship's steward during a spell of unemployment, and was shipwrecked on his first voyage.

Gallacher's introduction to politics was through the temperance movement, but he soon passed on to the Social Democratic Federation, which, in 1921, merged into the Communist Party. He became a member of the Communist International, as well as a member of the executive committee of the British Communist Party. In 1924, and again in 1935, he served on the executive committee of the Communist International.

During the First World War he was an ardent opponent of militarism, and was vociferous in his agitation against the "capitalists" in the "class struggle". After visiting the United States and Ireland he became the leader of the workers in the Glasgow Albion Motor Works. He was elected to the executive committee of the United Brass Founders' Association, and chairman of the Clyde Workers' Committee. He told the story of the activities of this committee and the story of the struggles on the Clyde during the 1914-18 War in his autobiography *Revolt on the Clyde*.

His first term of imprisonment was in 1917, when he was sentenced to 12 months for his political activities. He also served terms of three months' imprisonment in 1918, three months in 1921, and 12 months in 1925. On the latter occasion he was charged, with other leading communists, at the Old Bailey with sedition, and served his sentence in Wandsworth Gaol.

His contacts with Russia and the Soviet leaders were close and cordial. In 1920 he went, as a stowaway, to Moscow to attend the second congress of the Communist International. There he met Lenin. On his return he took part in the final negotiations for merging a number of left-wing organisations in the United Kingdom into the British Communist Party. In the 1930s he was a staunch supporter of the "hunger marchers", and paid visits to Spain in the Republican interest during the Spanish Civil War. But in the Second World War he was in some difficulty in trying to follow the vagaries of the "party line".

He was the unsuccessful communist candidate for West Fife at the general elections of 1929 and 1931, but won the seat in 1935, defeating the late "Wullie" Adamson, who had been Secretary of State for Scotland in the second Labour Government. He held the seat in 1945 with a majority of 2,056 in a three-cornered fight, but in 1950 he was at the bottom of the poll.

He was more than once refused a visa for the United States, but managed to go there in 1946. In the summer of 1963 an American visa issued for him to visit a sister who was ill in Chicago was withdrawn, but after public pressure both in the United States – the *Washington Post* was sharply critical of the State Department – and in Britain had been exerted the visa was restored. In 1948 he visited Prague, where he was awarded the Order of the Slovak Rising, first class, and he went on to Budapest, where he received the Cross and Star of the Hungarian Order of Merit.

His publications included, in addition to *Revolt on the Clyde*, *The Rolling of the Thunder*, and *The Case for Communism*.

He married, in 1913, Jean Roy.

* * *

TOM JOHNSTON

The elder statesman of Scotland, 'a man of unswerving integrity of purpose'

6 SEPTEMBER 1965

THE RT. HON. THOMAS JOHNSTON, P.C., C.H., died yesterday at the age of 83. In his day one of the ablest practical minds in the British Labour movement he was Secretary of State for Scotland in the wartime Coalition Government from 1941 until 1945, and after he had retired from Parliament for some years chairman of the North of Scotland Hydro-Electric Board and of the Scottish National Forestry Commissioners. He was Chancellor of Aberdeen University. In recent years he was widely regarded as the elder statesman of Scotland.

Possessed of a clear and orderly mind, a man of unswerving integrity of purpose, Tom Johnston commanded the wholehearted respect of his political opponents as well as of his colleagues in the Labour movement and all those associated with him in public affairs in his native Scotland. In one sense, perhaps, he disappointed expectations. There was a time when he seemed a possible leader of the Labour Party and destined for the highest office. But Johnston himself was almost too disinterested a Socialist, possibly too modest a person also, to aspire to the heights of political responsibility. Much of his energy was concentrated on his long and lively editorship of the Scottish Labour journal, *Forward*, which he founded in 1906 and edited for 27 years from 1919. In the Commons, which he entered in 1922, he was all the more impressive in debate for a marked absence of personal ambition. As early as 1937 he announced his intention of retiring from Parliament at the next election, giving as his reasons the physical strain of travelling backwards and forwards between Glasgow and Westminster and his desire to devote himself to writing and to research. Only the outbreak of war in 1939 made him continue in active politics for longer than he had intended.

It was fortunate for Scotland that he did change his mind, for he was to prove an outstandingly successful Secretary of State. It is doubtful if any of his predecessors or successors equalled him as a spokesman for his country, vigorous, forthright, but always practical. The case for Scotland never went by default while he sat in the Cabinet.

Johnston's skill in using facts and figures, which lent an engaging touch of Scots didacticism to his combative debating style, was joined to genuine moral passion. Of sincerely Puritan temperament (he was a teetotaller by principle), he was a formidable Socialist propagandist, who for many years preached the I.L.P. doctrine with seriousness and moderation; he was shrewdly and – in the 1920s – very fairly described as "a moderate extremist". In 1945 he refused the peerage that was offered him in order that he might continue a parliamentary career, and became chairman of the Scottish National Forestry Commissioners. The following April he began his major task of the postwar years when he became chairman of the North of Scotland Hydro-Electric Board. Throughout his whole tenure of office he declined to draw the salary attaching to it, just as he had declined his Cabinet Minister's salary of £5,000 a year during 1941-45. In these later years he was held in continuously growing respect in Scotland and received many marks of honour, among them the freedom of Edinburgh.

Born in Kirkintilloch, Dunbartonshire, in 1882, Thomas Johnston was educated at the Lairdsland Public School there, at the Lenzie Academy, and at the University of Glasgow, where he was the contemporary of

Walter Elliot. He had some general commercial experience, but soon went into the newspaper business and realised an ambition of his early years by founding the weekly Socialist journal, *Forward*. It promptly became one of the strongest influences for Socialism north of the Tweed. Johnston was an early associate of James Maxton and his Clydeside I.L.P. group. He served for some years on the Kirkintilloch town council and inaugurated various practical experiments in Socialism, including the foundation of the first Scottish municipal bank. When in 1931 he rose to be Lord Privy Seal Kirkintilloch made him its first freeman.

In 1914, as was to be expected, *Forward* took a strongly anti-war line, and during the subsequent troubles in the Glasgow munition factories was suspended for reporting a speech of Lloyd George's against orders. Characteristically Johnston asked to see Lloyd George, put his case, and secured the removal of the ban. *Forward* was, without question, a major factor contributing to the return of the large Labour group from Clydeside in the election of 1922. Johnston himself was returned for West Stirling and Clackmannan in that year and from the first established a reputation in the House of Commons for informed, dour and occasionally sardonic criticism. The impression of dourness, it should be said, sprang in part at least from the rather unmusical quality of his voice. He lost his seat in 1924, but came back almost immediately at a Dundee by-election caused by the death of E. D. Morel.

In 1929 he again represented West Stirlingshire and was appointed Under-Secretary for Scotland in the second Labour administration. He did first-rate work in that office, especially in connexion with housing, medical services, agricultural research and the fishing industry. In March, 1931, he succeeded Vernon Hartshorn as Lord Privy Seal, charged in particular with employment schemes, and was sworn to the Privy Council. One of the many notable Labour casualties in the "crisis" election of that year, he returned to Parliament for his old constituency in 1935.

In August, 1939, he was appointed Regional Commissioner for Civil Defence in Scotland, and in 1941 entered the Coalition Government under Mr. Churchill as Secretary of State for Scotland. Recognition of his services in wartime – and in earlier years – to his own land and people was evidenced in a variety of distinctions conferred upon him. He was made a freeman of the City of Edinburgh in 1944; a freeman of Campbeltown, Argyll, in the following year, as a tribute to his work for the Scottish herring industry; and, in the same year, an honorary Doctor of Laws of Glasgow University and an honorary Fellow of the Educational Institute of Scotland. This last honour, rarely conferred, was a mark of appreciation not only of his concern for Scottish education generally but of his distinctively unromantic views on the teaching of history, which he first elaborated in a *History of the Working Classes of Scotland* published in 1922. In his work, after the end of the Second World War, for Scottish electricity schemes and Scottish forestry he displayed the efficiency and the practical temper that were expected of him. He will be particularly remembered for the immense benefits which the Hydro-Electric Board brought to the north of Scotland during his term of office.

He resigned from the Forestry Commission in 1948 and from the Hydro-Electric Board in 1959. In 1958 he became president of the British Electrical Development Association. He had also served as a member of the board of governors of the B.B.C., National Governor for Scotland, chairman of the Broadcasting Council for Scotland, and chairman of the Scottish Tourist Board. In *Memories*, published in 1952, he gave his own account of his career in public life. He was created C.H. in 1953. Johnston was married and had two daughters.

DAVID MAXWELL FYFE, EARL OF KILMUIR

Former Lord Chancellor and Deputy Chief Prosecutor at Nuremberg

28 JANUARY 1967

THE EARL OF KILMUIR, P.C., G.C.V.O., D.C.L., LL.D., who was Lord Chancellor from 1954 to 1962, and a former Home Secretary, died yesterday at the age of 66. A careful lawyer, a lifelong Conservative, conscientious in all he undertook, he did the work by which he will be most remembered at the trial of the Nazi war criminals at Nuremberg.

As a politician he might have termed himself, as Dr. Johnson defined a lexicographer, "a useful drudge", he was perhaps the most useful maid-of-all-work the postwar Conservative Party has had, and did not mind being used as such. As a lawyer he had an extraordinary capacity for hard work, an eye for the essence of a case, and the gift as an advocate of throwing his own Scottish honesty over even the most questionable clients. He was also in two complicated professions at a complicated period, quite simply a man of good character. It was his character which gave him weight in public life.

David Patrick Maxwell Fyfe was born at Edinburgh on May 29, 1900. His father, W. T. Fyfe, was first a schoolmaster, later a schools inspector and examiner. He was also a minor writer, his most memorable book being *Edinburgh under Sir Walter Scott*. There is no doubt David Fyfe's love of literature came from him. His mother, Isabella Campbell, was a teacher before her marriage. David went to a convent school, then to George Watson's College in Edinburgh, and to Balliol. He said that at Oxford Conservatism came first, the Union second, his work third, and games fourth. Politics absorbed so much of interest that he got only a third in his Final Schools. He plunged himself into the 1921 Transport Bill, worked at the British Commonwealth Union, passed his Bar Finals, and was called in June 1922.

his Home Secretary. He was not outstanding but to the multifarious responsibilities of the post (perhaps wider than those of any other department) he brought his usual care. He showed it simultaneously by proving a Scot could be a most assiduous Minister for Welsh Affairs.

When Churchill reconstructed his Cabinet in October, 1954, Fyfe became Lord Chancellor, took the title of Viscount Kilmuir, and closed a 20 years' membership of the House of Commons. He said in his memoirs that he had no ambition to be a candidate for the Prime Ministership as a tertium quid between Eden and Butler. Perhaps strangely he might have had a chance of being the tertium quid between Butler and Macmillan in January, 1957. He was a very shrewd politician. He could often see farther and more clearly than many of his colleagues more in the limelight. Yet his real ambitions and abilities both favoured law more than politics.

As Lord Chancellor he dignified the Woolsack. Once more he was patient, courteous, indefatigable – on his first Bill in the House of Lords he made 82 speeches; it was on Town and Country Planning – giving equal attention to great things and small. No one act made his tenure of the Lord Chancellorship historic. The office has been less well served by more flamboyant but less conscientious men.

Finally, so far as his political career was concerned, came the holocaust of July, 1962, when Macmillan dismissed seven of his Ministers. Why Kilmuir was one of them has remained a mystery. Kilmuir, who was created an Earl, said frankly in *Political Adventure* that Macmillan lost both nerve and judgment. He was attacked for this frankness, but nothing became him better than his treatment of Macmillan in his autobiography. He was fair to Macmillan's Prime Ministership as a whole; he was entitled to write candidly about what seemed to many an irrational episode.

Having quit politics "at seven hours' notice" Kilmuir caused some eyebrows to be raised by becoming chairman of Plesseys. He had never been a rich man; and the days when even a Lord Chancellor's pension sufficed to meet a life of imposed idleness had gone.

When in November, 1962, Lord Thomson announced the

establishment of the Thomson Foundation to provide educational and vocational training facilities in the emergent countries Lord Kilmuir agreed to become the foundation's chairman.

Many honours came to him – D.C.L. Oxford; LL.D. from Liverpool and other universities; an honorary Fellowship of his old college; rectorship of St Andrews; honorary membership of the Canadian and American Bar Associations – and they rightly meant much to him.

Lord and Lady Kilmuir had three daughters, one of whom is dead. The title lapses.

* * *

JIM CLARK

The greatest of Grand Prix drivers, remembered for his immaculate driving style and lightning reactions

8 APRIL 1968

JIM CLARK, O.B.E., twice world champion race driver (1963 and 1965), who died when his Lotus 48 crashed in the European Formula II championship race at Hockenheim, west Germany, yesterday, will be remembered as the greatest Grand Prix driver of all time.

He had already surpassed the total of 24 world championship race victories scored by five times world champion Argentine Juan Manuel Fangio, and was leading this year's world championships following his victory in the South African Grand Prix in January – first round of the 1968 series. Clark, a 32-year-old bachelor, had driven for team Lotus regularly since 1960 and was in his ninth season with the Norfolk based team founded by his patron and personal friend Colin Chapman. Clark won the Tasman championship in New Zealand and Australia this year for the third time.

He was born on March 4, 1936, in Kilmany, Fifeshire, the only son of a prosperous farmer, and educated at Loretto School, Edinburgh, where he was not particularly happy and left at 16, working on his father's 1,300-acre farm for 18 months as a shepherd. He later took over his own 1,200-acre estate at Edington Mains, Berwick – one of the best border farms in the country. At one time he had about 1,100 feeding sheep, 500 fat cattle and flocks of Suffolk and Border Leicester sheep, and as his time became more and more occupied with racing, his father made three regular weekly visits to discuss points with Clark's resident farm manager. Clark was acknowledged as an expert on cattle and pedigree sheep.

He made his racing debut in a D.K.W. saloon at Crimond airfield, near Aberdeen, in 1956, and was later given considerable assistance by his Border farmer friends. Recognizing his natural ability, they clubbed together and sponsored him with a variety of cars with which he scored numerous victories. He had his first single-seater drive on Boxing Day, 1959, in a Gemini Formula Junior car and early in 1960 he was tested by the Aston Martin team. But he was released after failing to get a grand prix drive and signed for Colin Chapman's Team Lotus in formula junior and formula two.

Small and wiry, the Latin-looking Border Scot was ideal for the diminutive rear-engined Lotuses and after winning at Oulton Park and Goodwood, he was promoted to the Formula one team, finishing fifth in the 1960 Dutch Grand Prix. From that day on, Clark became a regular member of Team Lotus and has driven for them in Formula one cars ever since.

After giving Team Lotus its first continental race victory by winning the 1961 Pau Grand Prix, Clark shrugged aside criticism that he was running before he had learnt to walk and won the 1962 Belgian, British and United States Grands Prix. He narrowly failed to take the title, when his Lotus lost a tiny bolt while he was leading the South African G.P., allowing Graham Hill into the world championship crown. Clark showed scintillating form in 1963, however, and brilliant successive wins in the Belgian, Dutch, French and British G.P.s and went on to take his first drivers' championship. That year, he shook American racing pundits by finishing second in the Indianapolis 500 in a revolutionary Lotus-powered-by-Ford and two years later won it outright at a record average speed of 150.6 m.p.h.

Clark's other grand prix victories included 1964, Dutch, Belgian, and British; 1965, South African, Belgian, French, British, Dutch, and German; 1966, United States; 1967, Dutch, British, American, and Mexican. He can thus claim two incredible records of having won the same grand prix four years in succession, the Belgian (at Spa) and the British Grands Prix in 1962-63-64 and 1965 respectively ... Fangio won the Argentine G.P. in 1954-55- 56 and 1957.

Clark was equally at home in all types of machinery ... formula one, formula two, formula junior (joint champion in 1960), saloon car racing.

For the 1967 season, Clark was once again with Colin Chapman and the Team Lotus and had as his teammate Graham Hill in the powerful new Lotus fitted with an all-new Ford engine.

Clark found motor racing the utmost in pleasure and will be remembered for his immaculate driving style and lightning reactions. He was rarely headed from the starting grid and was definitely a driver who liked to control the race from the front of the pack and at a blistering pace. He seemed to be born with not only a "silver spoon" but also a charmed life and escaped without injury in several high-speed crashes, including Aintree, Brands Hatch, and Monaco. Clark was a non-smoker who drank in moderation and rapidly became frustrated if he was not active. He played cricket at school, learnt the violin, was an excellent dancer, hockey player, sprinter, and water-skier and enjoyed rough shooting and photography.

In 1967, Clark announced that for tax reasons he would not be resident in Great Britain and only expected to make infrequent racing appearances here. He was a hard and successful businessman and was a director of his own self-promotion company, Clarksport Ltd. He was a talented private pilot and flew his own Comanche aircraft all over Europe to and from races.

Away from the cockpit, Clark's modest – even shy – manner and quiet Scottish speaking voice belied the fact that he was a double world champion in the most dangerous and demanding of all sports. It was behind the wheel of a racing car that he started to live.

* * *

GAVIN MAXWELL

Author and adventurer, whose 'Ring of Bright Water'
remains one of the most memorable accounts of man's
relationship with wild creatures

8 SEPTEMBER 1969

MR. GAVIN MAXWELL, the writer and portrait painter, who died yesterday in his fifties is perhaps best remembered for his best-seller *Ring of Bright Water* in which he told of his life with his two otters Mijbil and Edal in the lonely cottage Camusfearna in the West Highlands which for some years was his home. The book was recently made into a successful film.

Mijbil was brought back by Maxwell from the Tigris marshes and was later tragically killed by a road mender with a pick axe. To fill the gap in his life Maxwell acquired Edal, who belonged to a doctor on leave from Nigeria. The book was informed by Maxwell's great love for his native Scotland and by his obvious gift for establishing a relationship with wild creatures.

Maxwell belonged to the school of naturalist authors in which an animal, however delinquent, is treated with tolerant affection. Even the ring-tailed lemur which tried to blind him and succeeded in cutting his tibial artery only provoked him to reflect on the "insuperable problems" of her "psychoanalysis". This year he published the last of the trilogy which started with *Ring of Bright Water*: the book *Raven Seek Thy Brothers* followed *The Rock Remains* (1963).

Maxwell spent several weeks with Wilfred Thesiger among the Marsh Arabs of Iraq – he told of the strange culture based on reeds and water-buffaloes in *A Reed Shaken by the Wind* (1957), which won the Heinemann Award of the Royal Society of Literature. In *Lord of the Atlas – The Rise and Fall of the House of Glaoua, 1893-1956*, Maxwell told of the Berbers in Morocco as tough and rebellious as the Kurds. Between 1953 and 1957 Maxwell spent several months of each year in the remote northwest corner of Sicily and in *The Ten Pains of Death* he set out, almost entirely in their own words and with the briefest of introductions, the autobiographies of a dozen Sicilians of that area, among them a pedlar, a prostitute, a nun and a doctor.

Maxwell wrote of his boyhood – running wild on a Scottish estate – in *The House of Elrig* (1966). It told the story of sunshine and shadow in the childhood and adolescence of a gifted, sensitive writer whose parents were both scions of ancient, and sometimes eccentric, Scottish and English families, the Maxwells of Monreith and the ducal house of Northumberland.

Maxwell was born in 1914 – the youngest son of Lieutenant-Colonel A. E. Maxwell and was educated at Stowe and Hertford College, Oxford. In the Second World War he served with the Scots Guards, was seconded to S.O.E. and was invalided with the rank of major in 1944. After the war he bought the island of Soay in the Hebrides and experimented with commercial shark-fishing which resulted in his book *Harpoon at a Venture*.

AIR CHIEF MARSHAL
LORD DOWDING

*Chief of Fighter Command, who laid the plans for the Battle of Britain
and was responsible for its triumphant outcome*

16 FEBRUARY 1970

AIR CHIEF MARSHAL LORD DOWDING, G.C.B., G.C.V.O., C.M.G., victor of
the Battle of Britain, died at his home in Kent yesterday at the age of 87.

As Chief of Fighter Command from 1936 to 1940, he laid the plans for
and directed the Battle of Britain when "the Few" won imperishable glory.

"Stuffy" Dowding, as he was always called – a nickname given him
in the artillery though no one quite knew why – had grown up with the
R.A.F., but that nickname "Stuffy" completely belied his gift of charm
and accessibility. One writer said of Dowding – "Never in history has a
commander won so signal a victory and been so little thanked by his
country, and even in his own service. Even the barony was belated."

Hugh Caswall Tremenheere, First Baron Dowding of Bentley Priory,
was born on April 24, 1882, the eldest child of A. J. C. Dowding. From the
successful preparatory school run by his parents at Moffat he followed
his father to Winchester, where he was not happy. A distaste for Greek
verbs led him to the army class and the Royal Military Academy at
Woolwich. Failing to qualify as a sapper he was gazetted to the Royal
Garrison Artillery. He served at Gibraltar, Colombo and Hongkong
before obtaining a transfer to the Mountain Artillery and spending six
agreeable years in India. After many unsuccessful requests to be allowed
to sit for the staff college entrance examination he was granted a year's
furlough to prepare for it.

At Camberley in 1912 and 1913, Dowding was struck by the prevailing
ignorance of aviation. Attracted by flying and believing that ability to fly
would further his career, he qualified for his pilot's certificate on the
day of his passing-out from the staff college. After a short course at the

newly-formed Central Flying School he applied for transfer to the Royal Flying Corps Reserve and rejoined the garrison artillery.

On the outbreak of war, Dowding was called from his battery to command the camp from which the first squadrons of the Royal Flying Corps left for France. In October, he went to Belgium with No. 6 Squadron, hastily dispatched on the eve of the fall of Antwerp. He served briefly at Royal Flying Corps headquarters in France and was thence posted to No. 9 (Wireless) squadron, where his technical bent stood him in good stead. On the disbandment of the squadron early in 1915 Dowding, who had succeeded to the command, was sent home to form a new unit with the same designation. Later in the year he commanded No. 16 squadron at La Gorgue. Electing to fly as observer on a particularly dangerous mission during the Battle of Loos, he narrowly escaped a forced landing behind the enemy's lines.

In 1916 he served with the administrative wing at Farnborough and afterwards as commander of the ninth wing at the Somme. In the meantime he had the congenial task of putting through its final training the first squadron of Sopwith aircraft armed with guns firing through the airscrew. Command of the ninth wing brought him directly under Trenchard, with whom he had had a disagreement. Dowding was not convinced that his chief was wise to insist on frequent patrols over the enemy's lines at the cost of heavy casualties. Characteristically, he did not hide his views. He was deprived of his command and received no further appointment in France. Employed at home in various capacities, he rose to Brigadier-General and was awarded the C.M.G. for his war services.

On the creation of the Royal Air Force, Dowding was not selected for a commission, but after representations from his commanding officer he was granted a temporary attachment, afterwards made permanent. His chance came in 1929 when he was sent to report on service requirements arising from disturbances in Palestine. His observations on the spot confirmed views already formed by Trenchard, and his report found favour.

From 1930 to 1936 Dowding served on the Air Council as air member successively for supply and research and for research and development.

No better choice was ever made. A fearless pilot, Dowding was never an outstanding one. But he had a good grasp of the practical side of airmanship and a rare understanding of the limitations of air power. Almost from the start he was keenly interested in the application of radar to night fighting, but he saw that defence against a massive onslaught in daylight must come first. Even had he not lived to win the Battle of Britain his work in the field of technical development would place him high among his country's saviours.

In 1936 Dowding was picked for the new post of Air Officer Commanding-in-Chief, Fighter Command, with overriding control of all branches of active air defence at home. He held it for more than four years. Passed over for preferment to Chief of the Air Staff in 1937, he was reserved for a more crucial role. In May, 1940, the Government contemplated sending to France a substantial part of his already-depleted force as a gesture of encouragement to the French. His advice that a sacrifice which could not save France would mean defeat for his own country was tendered with an authority no other airman could command. His squadrons were spared to fight the battle for which he had prepared them. A series of setbacks for the Luftwaffe culminated on September 15 in a hard-fought struggle over London which robbed the Germans of all colourable hope of achieving the right conditions for a landing in this country.

Towards the end of the battle Dowding was accused of allowing his squadrons to be used in smaller formations than some critics thought desirable. At the same time the bombing of Britain after dark brought demands that certain day-fighter squadrons should be relegated to night fighting. He opposed them, predicting that only fighters with airborne radar would master the night bomber. Overruled on several issues, in November he was relieved of a post already held longer than the normal term. In 1941, after a visit to the United States and Canada and the writing of a brilliant report on the Battle of Britain, his name was placed on the retired list. Within a month he was recalled to suggest economies in manpower. He retired in 1942 without attaining the rank of Marshal of the Royal Air Force, then reserved for officers who had held the post of Chief of the Air Staff. Next year he received a barony. From 1937 he was Principal Air Aide-de-Camp to King George VI.

There was controversy surrounding Dowding's removal as chief of Fighter Command. Some of his admirers said it was because he had dared to question Whitehall. In 1957, the controversy was revived by the publication of Dowding's authorised biography, *Leader of the Few*, by Basil Collier, whom Dowding had helped to write the book. "To many members of the public", Collier wrote, "Dowding's removal from his post immediately after he had won, brilliantly, a hard-fought battle, seemed an act of almost monstrous folly and ingratitude".

In recent months there had been renewed controversy over Dowding's dismissal from his command in the second week of November, 1940, just after the Battle of Britain. He should, it was suggested, have been promoted to the most senior rank of Marshal of the Royal Air Force, which would almost have doubled his income. Lord Balfour of Inchrye, wartime Under-Secretary of State for Air, last year pioneered a campaign pressing for Dowding's much-belated promotion to Marshal of the R.A.F. He denied that he connived to get rid of Dowding, and said that he "yielded second place to none" in his admiration of the Air Chief Marshal.

A passage in Robert Wright's book, *Dowding and the Battle of Britain*, suggesting that he had been dismissed from his command in the course of a brief telephone conversation by the Secretary of State for Air, Sir Archibald Sinclair (now Lord Thurso), was dismissed by Sir John Slessor in a letter to *The Times*. Slessor stated he had consulted a number of people in recent months associated with the events in 1940, and all agreed that it was incredible that Sir Archibald Sinclair could have acted in the manner described. Mr. A. J. P. Taylor later wrote revealing a document indicating that Sir Archibald Sinclair had indeed met Dowding and not dismissed him on the telephone.

Last September Dowding, confined to a wheelchair because of arthritis, received a standing ovation to a trumpet fanfare at the premiere of the film, *Battle of Britain*. He took his place in the stalls among 350 of the pilots he had once commanded.

After his retirement Dowding became keenly interested in spiritualism, a subject which had long dwelt in the background of his mind. A confident speaker and a lucid writer, he did much selfless work for the spiritualist movement and wrote many books and articles, mostly on occult subjects. He was also interested in animal welfare and advocated strict control of vivisection. A keen shot, he gave up field sports and became a vegetarian. In his prime he was a skier of international standing and an enthusiastic polo player.

His first marriage in 1918 to Clarice Maud, daughter of Captain John Williams, was cruelly cut short by her death in 1920. His second marriage in 1951 to Muriel, widow of Pilot Officer Maxwell Whiting, who shared his interests and who survives him, brought him great happiness.

* * *

SIR ARCHIBALD SINCLAIR, VISCOUNT THURSO

Liberal Party leader who became Churchill's wartime Air Minister, described by Beaverbrook as 'the best in our experience'

17 JUNE 1970

LORD THURSO, K.T., P.C., C.M.G., died at his Twickenham home on Monday night after a long illness. As Sir Archibald Sinclair he led the Liberal Party during the critical decade 1935-45; he brought to public life fine gifts of character, liveliness and endurance; as Air Minister throughout the war he carried responsibility for the critical role of Britain's air force.

Endowed with striking good looks and charm of manner, he won a distinctive position for himself both with supporters and opponents – a position which was strengthened by his integrity and his power of driving through to the heart of any problem. The position which was achieved by his small following in the House of Commons in the 1930s – the Liberals then numbered 17 – was out of all proportion to their strength and was in a measure due to the personal authority of his leadership. Some indication of this is suggested by the pressure brought to bear on him to fortify and rejuvenate Neville Chamberlain's Government at the outbreak of war in 1939; when Churchill joined that Government as First Lord he strongly urged this course both on Sinclair and on Chamberlain.

When Churchill became Prime Minister Sinclair was made Secretary of State for Air, remaining in that office for the duration of the war and until the break up of the wartime coalition.

Archibald Henry Macdonald Sinclair, the first Viscount Thurso, was born on October 22, 1890. His mother, Mabel Sands, an American lady of great beauty, died a few days after he was born, and his father, Clarence Granville Sinclair, died when he was five. Consequently Archibald Sinclair was brought up by his grandfather, Sir Tollemache Sinclair, third baronet, to whom he was heir, and by his uncle and aunt, General and Mrs. Owen Williams. Owing to the remoteness of Caithness, where the family property lay, much of Sinclair's boyhood was spent at Temple House, Berkshire, with General and Mrs. Williams. The former was a friend of King Edward and provided a background for the conventional pastimes of fashionable life which were at no time naturally congenial to Sinclair. He was somewhat reserved, underneath an expansive manner, and the ordinary pleasantries of social life did not come easily to him. He had a small impediment in speech and he often lamented that he was a poor hand at the companionship of the smoking-room in the House of Commons. Yet among friends he was delightful company, ever lively and courteous. He went to Eton, where he did not especially distinguish himself but is remembered for his pertinacity in argument, and then to Sandhurst. On passing out he joined the Life Guards (1st and 2nd).

He succeeded his grandfather when he was 22. His imagination was from the first captured by the possibilities of flight and he spent some time shortly before the First World War in experimenting with a primitive aircraft of his own, with some rather novel features, which he kept at Shoreham airfield.

During the war he served in France and he was, for some time, adjutant of the battalion of the Royal Scots Fusiliers which was commanded by Mr. Churchill. Although he knew Mr. Churchill before, this comradeship in the field helps to explain a friendship which coloured the whole of his political life. In the closing months of the war he married Marigold, daughter of Colonel and Lady Angela Forbes, by whom he had a family of two sons and two daughters.

After the war he became personal military secretary to Mr. Churchill at the War Office, following him to the Colonial Office as private secretary in 1922. In the autumn of that year he was returned to Parliament for his own constituency of Caithness and Sutherland. He was at this time a Churchillian Liberal and rather naturally gravitated towards the Lloyd George section of the party. His maiden speech in the House of Commons was, appropriately enough, devoted to air matters and in particular to the importance of an independent Air Force and to the vulnerability of Great Britain in air attack. He held his seat throughout the spate of elections between 1922 and 1924 and his reputation in the House steadily grew.

In 1930 he became Chief Liberal Whip: this was a position which greatly taxed both his diplomacy and forbearance because the party was falling apart under the vagaries of Lloyd George's leadership and the difficulties created by Sir John Simon and his following. Simon roundly told Sinclair in the summer of 1931 that the party had reached the depths of humiliation. In the autumn of that year Sinclair, with the other Liberal leaders, joined the National Government and became Secretary of State for Scotland. Like many other progressive leaders – Lord Grey at Howick, Rosebery at Dalmeny, or Gladstone at Hawarden – he was inclined to disappear and become inaccessible in his native land, but Liberal policy was often fashioned in private gatherings of his

Liberal colleagues in the summer at Thurso or on the Caithness moors, where Sinclair, in the kilt and surrounded by his attractive family, was seen at his splendid best.

When Sir Herbert Samuel lost his seat at the 1935 election, Sinclair was chosen to succeed him as leader of the Parliamentary party. In the four years which intervened between his election as leader and the outbreak of war, Sinclair enormously enhanced his reputation. He was in close alliance with his old chief, Mr. Churchill, as the indignant critics of the foreign policy of the Baldwin and Chamberlain eras. Lord Cecil said at that period that "Sir Archibald Sinclair was the only Liberal leader of recent times who has infused vigour and reality into his party".

When war began Sinclair rejected all overtures from Neville Chamberlain. When Churchill succeeded Chamberlain he immediately offered Sinclair the Air Ministry. In this post he was not automatically a member of the War Cabinet, but he remained as Secretary of State for five years and history will probably echo an observation of Lord Beaverbrook that he was the best Air Minister "in our experience". His best work was done in Cabinet and few Ministers can have fought with more tenacious loyalty for their department than he did. Certainly with a less determined Secretary of State, the manpower needed to sustain the bomber offensive could never have been kept. While the exact value of the bomber offensive is likely to be long debated, Sinclair's conviction that, in the circumstances of the time, it was our only effective means of grappling with the Germans was widely understood even by critics at the time. His role in the dismissal of Lord Dowding as chief of Fighter Command is likely to be remembered as controversial.

During the war he scarcely visited his home in Caithness, and this helps to explain his totally unexpected defeat at the General Election of 1945 by 60 votes. He failed by 269 votes to regain his old seat at the 1950 general election, and did not stand again the following year.

In the New Year Honours of 1952 he was created a Viscount, but because of the ill-health which dogged him in later years he did not take his seat in the House of Lords until the summer of 1954 – and it was not until 1956 that he made his maiden speech in the Upper Chamber.

In 1954 he was appointed to the Political Honours Scrutiny Committee, remaining a member until 1961. The viscounty now passes to his son, the Hon. Robin Sinclair.

* * *

IAIN MACLEOD

Statesman of spirit and conviction, who helped grant
independence to British colonies in Africa

22 JULY 1970

THE RIGHT HON. IAIN MACLEOD, P.C., M.P., who died on Monday night at the age of 56, had been Chancellor of the Exchequer for only a month but for nearly 20 years he had been one of the most considerable figures in British public life. He might have proved a great Chancellor. He had the imagination and the determination required to be more than the creature of the Treasury. Under him British economic policy might have been directed along more adventurous lines. But his place in British political history does not depend on what might have been.

He deserves to be remembered above all as a Colonial Secretary who pursued a historic policy with a full sense of history. He saw the need to grant independence more quickly to the British colonies in Africa and had the courage to act on this conviction. It required courage. Although Macleod had the support of Mr. Macmillan's Cabinet, or at least a majority of the Cabinet, he was defying some of the most powerful sectors in the Conservative Party. Except on the younger, liberal wing, party sentiment was not with him. Yet he achieved his purpose in ensuring that Britain's withdrawal from most parts of Africa was accomplished with more speed and goodwill than it would otherwise have been.

This was not an isolated example of his political courage. He further offended established opinion within his party when he refused to serve under Sir Alec Douglas-Home in 1963. Whether or not his judgment was right on that occasion, he had given an undertaking and he stuck to it when it could not possibly have been to his advantage to do so. Then two years ago he once again took an unpopular stand on principle when he voted against the Kenya Asians Bill, even though it was accepted by most of the Shadow Cabinet.

With this record of acting from conviction it must seem surprising that he earned a reputation for being devious. This reputation came partly from the bitter criticism of those who disagreed with him on policy. Partly it came from his own love of political tactics. There can be no doubt that he enjoyed the game. He was adroit and ingenious. He had an acute political ear. Some of those who were not such obvious political animals felt that this was inappropriate, even distasteful. But a gift for political manoeuvre ought not to be regarded as too black a mark against a politician. Allied to conviction, it is the stuff of statesmanship – and the sincerity of Macleod's conviction is to be measured by what it cost him.

He was an ambitious man, but even before ill-health made it impossible to consider him for the party leadership it was evident that he could never achieve it. He had the intellectual, administrative and oratorical capacity. As a speaker he was superb. He was probably the finest Parliamentary debater of his generation. On the public platform or at party conferences he was equally effective. That rasping voice, with scorn or passion controlled, but not too much, could thrill a large assembly with biting phrases of a quality too rarely heard in political rhetoric these days. But with all these gifts the highest post was bound to be denied to him because he had made too many enemies in his party. He was not forgiven for his liberalism on race and colonial independence, or for his act of rebellion against the leader thrown up by the customary processes of his party.

It was a political failing on his part that he took so long to appreciate that he had disqualified himself for the highest office. He retained his hopes beyond the point of realism. But he had accepted his place in the Tory team and there was a certain heroic quality in his last years as progressively crippled with arthritis, he none the less prepared for office once again with all the distinctive ardour that he brought to public life.

Iain Macleod was born on November 11, 1913, and was the son of a Scottish physician practising at Skipton, in Yorkshire. Educated at Skipton Grammar School and Fettes, he graduated in history from Gonville and Caius College, Cambridge, and spent three years in the City. He was reading for the Bar when the war broke out, and he joined the Army as a private. He was commissioned in May, 1940, and was wounded in the battle of France. He was promoted major and was on Field-Marshal Montgomery's planning staff for the Normandy Campaign. He was appointed D.A.Q.M.G., 50th Division.

Like many others to whom the war had brought the first experience of real responsibility, Macleod felt the attraction of politics, and in the General Election of 1945 he decided, on an impulse, to fight the Western Isles in the Conservative interest. Honourably defeated, he joined Mr. Butler's stable in the Conservative Research Department where, in company with several other young men of promise who were eventually to achieve political distinction, he played, as head of the Home Affairs department, a prominent part in the post-war process of redefining Conservatism.

Returned to the House of Commons as member for West Enfield in 1950, he attracted attention as a leading member of the One Nation Group, a body of young, intelligent and independent-minded backbenchers who were known to have the paternal protection of Mr. Butler.

Though generally regarded as progressives, the men of the One Nation Group were in fact firm enemies of the prevailing type of collectivism in British political thought. They demanded positive State action in economics and welfare, but held that this should be directed towards releasing private energies, increasing effective industrial and commercial competition, and ensuring that the resources of the State, when dispensed in the form of social services, should be concentrated on those who needed help.

A good mixer and a debater of outstanding skill, often in a most effective style of controlled, rational ferocity, Macleod's rise was mercurial, and in 1952 he was promoted straight from the back benches, to be Minister of Health, a post in which, over the next three years, he displayed an outstanding command of administrative ability and showed a valuable capacity for being prosaic in speech when the circumstances called for it. At the Ministry of Labour between 1955 and 1959 he acquired the reputation of a patient but immovable negotiator, who would brave a strike rather than make an uneconomic concession.

It was at the Colonial Office between 1959 and 1961, however, that Macleod made his greatest impact, and it was during this period also that, for the first time, he began to acquire bitter enemies in his own party. With that strategic clarity which always distinguished him, he appreciated that it was now necessary for the process by which self-government was achieved in British imperial territories in Africa must go on at a greatly accelerated pace. The old formula that Britain would continue to rule until the territories under her care were "fit for self-government" could no longer apply, if indeed it had ever applied; the forces of change were too strong and the resources of material strength and imperial self-confidence too weak to resist them. Macleod believed that Britain must neither try to resist the inevitable nor wash her hands of her responsibilities; by presiding over a process many aspects of which could not fail to alarm her, she might exercise at least some influence on the character of future African regimes, and she might even eventually succeed in bringing the emergent countries into free and meaningful partnership with the rest of the Commonwealth.

These aims, though practical, were not ignoble, and few honest men could reject the diagnosis on which they proceeded, but their pursuit, involving the exercise of very high diplomatic and administrative gifts with which Macleod was abundantly endowed, also involved compromises and the suspicion of deception, a suspicion at times shared equally by African extremists and imperially-minded Tories, and felt acutely and constantly by the white settlers of East and Central Africa and especially those of Kenya whose leaders proved no match for his negotiating skill.

Macleod's prowess as a bridge player (he was the author of an excellent book on the subject and a former bridge correspondent of the *Sunday Times*), once regarded as an amiable proof that he had the authentically Tory quality of living for other things than politics, was now cited by Lord Salisbury, once his firm admirer, as evidence of a Machiavellian disposition. The accusation that Macleod was "too clever by half" stuck for a long time and undoubtedly damaged his reputation with the centre as well as the right wing of the party. Mr. Macmillan, on the other hand, saluted both the courage and the ingenuity of his Colonial Secretary, and rescued him from this exposed position in October, 1961, by making him chairman of the Conservative Party and leader of the Commons, relieving him of other administrative duties by making him Chancellor of the Duchy of Lancaster.

When the disastrous Profumo scandal broke, it was Macleod's misfortune to be among the five Ministers who had accepted Profumo's word, and a chance remark made off the cuff to the press when the erring Minister's confession was reported to him led unscrupulous critics falsely to attribute to Macleod a lenient, or at best a credulous, attitude in the affair.

Nevertheless, Mr. Macmillan continued to admire him, and his brilliant speech at the Blackpool Conference of 1963, when all minds were preoccupied with the succession, was also well received by the Party. But there was really no chance of his being selected and at the end, like most of the other candidates, he threw his weight behind Mr. Butler. That was why he declined to serve under Sir Alec Douglas-Home. It was an honourable decision but a dangerous one in terms of his own career prospects. On leaving the Government Macleod had become editor of the *Spectator* and it was there that he published what was in fact a lengthy rejoinder to the version of events put forward in a book by Randolph Churchill.

A man of outstanding personal warmth and loyalty, who continued after his withdrawal from the Government to defend its policies in the country, Macleod was now accused by some of looking for his own personal future to a defeat of his colleagues at the election. It is a charge that is always likely to be made against the party rebel.

In the event, the Tories were defeated in October, 1964. Sir Alec, as Leader of the Opposition, instantly and characteristically invited Macleod to join the Shadow Cabinet. Macleod was put in charge of the Opposition's case against steel nationalisation, and this was a shrewd recognition of his remarkable forensic powers.

When, in 1965, Sir Alec resigned, Macleod, in spite of a number of effective speeches, stood no chance of being elected as his successor. Wisely he did not enter the lists. Mr. Heath succeeded, and immediately resolved to restore Macleod to prominence on the front benches. As Shadow Chancellor he occupied a position of crucial importance.

Macleod acquitted himself admirably in his new role. His attacks on Mr. Callaghan's financial policy, particularly on the selective employment tax, were almost comparable in effectiveness with those of Oliver Stanley against the budgets of Stafford Cripps. Macleod now applied himself again earnestly to the redefinition of Conservatism. His main task, however, was naturally to prepare the economic policy of the future Tory Government. He concentrated on the reform of taxation rather than on the monetary techniques for managing the economy, and managed to produce a programme that was distinctive and adventurous without being entirely clear in all particulars. If he had lived there can be little doubt that Iain Macleod would have been determined for good or ill to be the master of his own department. Whether or not the country has lost a great Chancellor, it has undoubtedly lost one of rare spirit.

Iain Macleod married in 1941 Evelyn, daughter of the Reverend Gervase and the Hon. Mrs. Blois of Fretherne, Gloucestershire. She and one son and a daughter survive him.

LORD REITH

Creator of British broadcasting, 'who had always behind
him a huge if silent reserve of national support'

17 JUNE 1971

LORD REITH, KT, GCVO, GBE, CB, who will long be remembered as
the creator of British broadcasting and the first Director General of the
British Broadcasting Corporation, died yesterday at the age of 81.

He was one of the outstanding personalities of his time, an engineer
with a turn for business management, who, by sheer force of character
and intellect, established himself as autocrat of a new realm of human
expression. He was destined and well equipped to be a pioneer. He
saw far and clearly – none the less so because at times he focused
narrowly. He had too a zest for the development of freshly discovered
possibilities. A keen sense of the practical told him how far he would be
allowed to go; but he possessed in addition the courage to force issues
and the strength frequently to secure the decisions he desired. He made
of the BBC a model for many other countries, and an ideal that could be
admired in others with different systems. It would almost seem as if, in
spite of his energy and comparative youth, fate had regarded this great
achievement as sufficient for one man. His great gifts were never given
the same scope again. None of his later achievements can compare with
his creation of the BBC.

Towering well over 6ft. 6in. in height, and with strongly marked
features accentuated by beetling eyebrows and a conspicuous scar, he was
a formidable figure. On most occasions stern, unbending, withdrawn,
he had few of the arts which charm strangers into friendship and more
often than not seemed deliberately to repel by his air of self-sufficiency.
Yet his quiet, deep voice belied these externals and on occasion his face
would light up with a smile of great beauty and warmth. He seldom
gave confidences, but when he did there was no reserve and his friends,
who knew this trait, found under his stern exterior a sensitive, if proud,

nature singularly attractive and worthy of their regard and loyalty. His first volume of autobiography, *Into the Wind*, published in 1949, reveals something of this dichotomy to a wider public. By then he had indeed "warmed both hands before the fire of life"; it no longer burned fiercely as in his youth and the period of his greatest achievement, but it still glowed warmly. He published a second look at his own life in *Wearing Spurs* (1966).

John Charles Walsham Reith was born at Stonehaven on July 20, 1889. He was the fifth son of the Very Rev George Reith, DD, a saintly man who at the time was minister of the College Church at Glasgow and later Moderator of the United Free Church of Scotland. His earliest days were therefore spent in a deeply religious household and his character developed in conformity with it. To the end he was to remain a devotional and a pious man.

He was educated at Glasgow Academy; at Gresham's School, Holt, and at the Royal Technical College at Glasgow, whence after two years' study he entered upon a long apprenticeship in locomotive works in his own city. In 1913 he obtained a post in London with Messrs. S. Pearson and Sons. Early in the war he joined the Scottish Rifles – he had had some previous military experience as a Territorial – but was shortly transferred to the Royal Engineers with the rank of lieutenant. He served in France during the winter of 1914 and was severely wounded in the following autumn. A sniper's bullet, which travelled through his face, almost ended his life. It left a conspicuous scar. At the end of 1916, unfit for further active service, he was transferred as a major to special duties. He did well and was sent on a mission to North America in charge of contracts for munitions. He liked the warmth of American friendship, the speed and directness of their working methods, and seriously considered settling there for life, but after two years there he was appointed to the Department of the Civil Engineer-in-Chief of the Admiralty. When the war ended he was put in charge of the liquidations of ordnance and engineering contracts for the Ministry of Munitions. At the end of the war he found himself a lonely young Scot in London. He would have liked to enter politics, but he had few friends and soon found himself travelling back to Scotland again to become general manager of the Coatbridge works of Messrs. Beardmore, and it was during this period that he married Miss Muriel Katherine Odhams, whose father had given his name to the well-known publishing firm. Though he was a successful engineer and got positive joy from the processes of construction he was not satisfied. "I still believe there is some great work for me to do in the world" he noted in his diary after hearing a stirring sermon.

In 1922 the newly formed British Broadcasting Company advertised for, among other officials, a general manager. Reith answered the advertisement and received the appointment. The company was small, somewhat speculative in character, and financed by a group of electrical manufacturers. Its resources were limited and its prospects doubtful. Reith threw himself none the less wholeheartedly into his new duties, organizing, experimenting and innovating. In early 1923 progress permitted the business to move from its first home in Magnet House to Savoy Hill. By the end of the first year it had surmounted a number of initial difficulties and was growing to considerable dimensions.

As a result of the report of the Sykes Committee of 1923 its licence, originally limited to two years, was extended by two more. Reith, conscious by this time of the almost unlimited possibilities of the instrument he controlled, believed that broadcasting must eventually become a public service. Consequently he began to shape his organisation with a view to such a development. In 1925 the Government appointed a committee under the chairmanship of Lord Crawford to consider the future of British broadcasting. On their invitation Reith prepared and placed before them a plan for a public broadcasting service. In doing so he deliberately jeopardised both the future of his company and his own position. He had thought deeply and seen far, for the ideas which he presented were those which were subsequently to govern British broadcasting. Some of his recommendations, such as that of Sunday observance, on which he always insisted, were calculated to provoke criticism. He was, however, concerned solely with the public welfare as he conceived it.

At this time Reith published *Broadcast over Britain*, a book which summarised his views. It was in the nature of an apologia for a monopoly; but he argued convincingly that any practical alternative presented still greater objections. Characteristically, he presented broadcasting as a means to social betterment rather than as an end in itself. While the committee were deliberating the General Strike broke out, and the value of broadcasting as a governmental and political instrument became apparent both to Parliament and the country, but Reith stood out against those in the Government, including the late Sir Winston Churchill, who wanted to commandeer the organisation. On January 1, 1927, the British Broadcasting Corporation came into being with Reith, to whom its establishment and form were so largely due, as Director-General.

His aim achieved, he found himself in a new and in some ways difficult relationship both to the state and to his listeners. Within the broad limits of its Charter the BBC was autonomous. For all practical purposes of administration and selection of programmes he was a dictator, though it is true that as time went on he increasingly delegated responsibility. His task was to develop a system of broadcasting which should be attuned to the peculiar temperament of the British people. He was a pioneer of what was truly a new form of statecraft, the government of a huge field of national education and diversion with the consent of the governed. The magnitude of his achievement is not to be discounted because of the criticism which indeed he sometimes seemed to court. It is to be measured rather by the fact that he had always behind him a huge if silent reserve of national support. His judgment was such that he never aroused that slumbering force of British opinion which could when roused have swept him and his system away.

A man of Reith's forcefulness and even uncouthness of personality was bound to make enemies. As an administrator he was often open to criticism for he trusted to precept and discipline rather than in more human arts of leadership. Possibly to his own sorrow he made friends with difficulty and must often have been conscious of the loneliness of the austere. Like many formidable men he was deeply sensitive. He was, however, able to inspire affectionate respect among those of his staff who learned to understand him. Experimenting as he did – he could do no other – he made some mistakes; at times he appeared obtuse; but on the whole it is surprising how little to his discredit those who attacked him were able to disclose. He was, no doubt, ambitious; but in the outcome it was his country which gained.

In 1938, his difficulties largely overcome and his ideals established as traditions, he left the BBC to become chairman of Imperial Airways. It was his second venture in developing a new application of science to human uses. Unlike the BBC however, it offered scope only to some of his many powers. The outbreak of war in 1939 not only robbed him of any chance to do much, it also meant that at a time of national crisis the all-important instrument of broadcasting lacked the hand which had formed it and knew it best. In 1940 to the general surprise Mr. Chamberlain appointed him to the Ministry of Information. A safe seat was found at Southampton and he was returned for it unopposed. His prestige was high, and no one should have understood publicity on the home front better. He had, however, only time to achieve the internal reorganisation essential in a huge and top-heavy improvisation.

Meanwhile, Chamberlain had been succeeded by Churchill and Reith was transferred to the Ministry of Transport, again deprived of the variety of stimuli he needed to achieve his best. His stay was brief, and in 1941 he moved on to the Ministry of Works and Buildings, where he was charged with the preparations for physical reconstruction after the war. He said of his task: "I have to prepare now, as it were, a physical framework within which the great postwar national policies can be fitted." During the period the centres of Coventry, Plymouth, and Portsmouth were destroyed and Reith urged the local authorities to make bold and ambitious plans for their postwar rebuilding. In early February, 1942, all the Town and Country planning functions formerly exercised by the Minister of Health were transferred to him, and the title of his office was changed to that of Minister of Works and Planning. Only a fortnight later to the concern of many who regarded him as both a dynamic and stabilizing element in the Government, he ceased to be a member of it for reasons hardly adequately explained by Churchill's curt remark that he found Reith "difficult to work with".

Shortly afterwards he joined the RNVR as a lieutenant-commander, on the staff of the Rear-Admiral Coastal Services, and in 1943 was promoted Captain, RNVR, and appointed Director of the Combined Operations Material Department at the Admiralty, a post he held until early in 1945. His strange relegation to these comparatively minor positions was the subject of a question in the House of Commons, but no satisfactory explanation was ever vouchsafed. That at this time he felt that his talents were buried in the ground was no secret to his friends.

Later he was chairman of the Commonwealth Telecommunications Board, the Hemel Hempstead Development Corporation, and the National Film Finance Corporation, where he held office until 1951. That he felt his talents had been ill-used is reflected in a letter of disconcerting candour which he wrote to Churchill: "Even in office I was nothing like fully stretched; and I was completely out of touch with you. You could have used me in a way and to an extent you never realised. Instead of that there has been the sterility, humiliation and distress of all those years – 'eyeless in Gaza' – without even the consolation Samson had in knowing it was his own fault." This was the protest of a proud man conscious of his worth and intent only to have the opportunity to serve his fellow men to the best of his great abilities. From 1950 to 1959 he was chairman of the Colonial Development Corporation. He held a number of commercial directorships, and in 1967 he was appointed Lord High Commissioner to the General Assembly of the Church of Scotland. In February 1969 he was made a Knight of the Thistle.

In establishing the Reith Lectures in 1947 the BBC expressed a sentiment, warmly applauded by the great majority of listeners – in practice the great majority of the men and women of this country – which did signal and deserved honour to the man who had cast the finely wrought mould in which a great new medium of communication had its being and its life.

LORD BOYD ORR

Scientist and crusader for better nutrition, who averted post-war
famine, and won the Nobel Peace Prize

26 JUNE 1971

LORD BOYD ORR, C.H., F.R.S., internationally known for his work
on nutrition, and first Director-General of the United Nations Food
and Agriculture Organisation, died at his home near Brechin, Angus,
yesterday, in his 91st year. The man who was a doctor for a month
became a pioneer in the movement to relate health and agriculture, and
to raise the food standards of the world. He was made a Companion of
Honour in 1968 for services to human and animal nutrition.

John Boyd Orr was born at Kilmaurs, Ayrshire, on September 23,
1880. He was the son of R. C. Orr and Annie Boyd. His father was a
"bonnet laird", a small property owner and quarrymaster. His mother
was a woman of strong intellect and determination, qualities which
were as pronounced in her son as the "Boyd" which he put in his
title.

John was bred for the church (two of his brothers were ordained as
ministers) but while studying for his MA degree at Glasgow University,
on his way to a divinity course, he strayed into the zoology classes where
the teaching of Darwinism diverted him from the fundamentalism of
his parents' sect. He gave up the idea of becoming a minister and, with
his MA degree, became a school-teacher for four years. He returned
to Glasgow University to study for his medical degree. Following his
graduation in medicine, he gained the Barbour Scholarship and, for
his MD thesis, the coveted Bellahouston Gold Medal and the invitation
of the great surgeon, Sir William McEwen, to become his assistant.

His career as a doctor lasted a month. As a medical student "walking
the wards" of the Glasgow hospitals, he had been distressed by the
diseases of poverty, the malnutrition and rickets of the slum-children,
for which the doctors had no physic; and his brief experience of practice

confirmed a resolve. He returned to the university to do post-graduate research on metabolic disease and became a DSc.

He was offered the post of Director of Animal Nutrition Research at Edinburgh University. His laboratory was a cellar. He had scarcely taken up his new appointment when the First World War broke out and he joined the RAMC. On the battlefields he won the MC (with Bar) and the DSO as regimental medical officer with the Sherwood Foresters, in a comradeship with miners which influenced his subsequent research. He transferred to the Navy, in an inter-service inquiry into the physical requirements of servicemen, and was at sea in the "Q-ships".

At the end of the war he returned to his £380-a-year post and his cellar-laboratory. From this grew the Rowett Research Institute for Animal Nutrition, the Reid Library, the Duthie Experimental Stock Farm, the Imperial Bureau of Animal Nutrition, and Strathcona House, a "club" for the world's nutritionists. His persuasiveness and his capacity for fund-raising were responsible for all of those.

His later career as a scientist-statesman overshadowed the substantial research record which made him a Fellow of the Royal Society. One of his earliest contributions (with Professor E. P. Cathcart) was *Energy Expenditure of the Infantry Recruit in Training*. Even more significant, in terms of modern agriculture were the studies of the mineral requirements of animals. In the 1920s his most impressive field-work was the investigation of the pastures of East Africa. It was primarily concerned with mineral deficiencies and soil-exhaustion but, typically, he added a clinical unit to investigate the effects on the human population, the Masai and Kikuyu. This report, apart from pioneering the regeneration of pastures, is a classic in social-medicine.

By reference, his professional concern was with farm animals. He protested that he had no difficulty in persuading farmers of the virtues of nutrition – because they could prove in terms of their stocks that it paid dividends – but that he could not convince anyone that the same was true of children, Stretching his research mandate during the economic crisis, he carried out a feeding experiment among 1,500 children of unemployed Lanarkshire miners. He fed them, at school, with the skimmed milk which was being thrown away by the farmers who could not sell it. The results were convincing, and school milk and school meals have consistently reaffirmed them since, but no one listened then.

As a critic of the marketing boards (because they were "organizing shortage") he was allowed to undertake, with Government financial help, the survey which became *Food, Health and Income.* Short memories have forgotten the political impact of that scientific measurement of poverty and hunger. It was embarrassing to the Government. Economists were engaged to re-examine his figures, with results which were even more embarrassing because he had shrewdly modified them so that when they were "corrected" they came out worse. He was made a Knight Bachelor, and appointed to the food commissions.

Food Health and Income had world-wide repercussions. Similar inquiries were carried out in 19 countries, including the United States, and the analysis of *Hunger in the midst of Plenty* led to the setting up of the Mixed Commission of the League of Nations, under Lord Astor. This "marriage of health and agriculture", as Mr Stanley (later Viscount) Bruce called it, was the forerunner of the UN Food and Agriculture Organisation. The news reached Sir John Boyd Orr in Aberdeen as a telegram from Mr Frank MacDougall, economic adviser to the Australian delegation. It read: "Be of good cheer, Brother Orr, for we have this day lighted in Geneva such a candle as, by God's grace, shall never be put out".

The report, and the popular discussions and "committees against malnutrition" which were set up, created a public awareness which simplified the introduction of rationing at the outbreak of war. Sir John Boyd Orr, combining Directorship of the Rowett with the Professorship of Agriculture at Aberdeen, served on the Ministry of Food commissions and made an eventful journey to the United States. He was nominally delivering lectures, but his self-appointed mission was to see President Roosevelt and Vice-President Henry Wallace. He was successful and was, in part, responsible for what became the Hot Springs Conference, which was given effect by the Quebec Conference of 1945, bringing the UN Food and Agriculture Organisation (FAO) into being.

By this time Sir John Boyd Orr was in the House of Commons as Independent MP for the Scottish Universities. By unanimous vote, he was acclaimed the first Director-General of the FAO. In almost his first speech, he reproached the statesmen for the organisation they had created: "The hungry are crying out for bread and we are going to give them pamphlets."

Before he had properly established his headquarters in Washington, he took action by summoning in May 1946 a conference of producer and consumer nations to deal with the famine which threatened 75m people. Contrary to all expectations, that conference agreed on self-denying ordinances to share supplies with the more desperate countries. Britain accepted the bread-rationing which it had not had even in the worst days of the war. Other countries did similar things. The famine of 1946 did not happen. The conference called for a scheme which would ensure that food would be available at prices fair to the farmers and consumers. It might have been the ventriloquial voice of Boyd Orr giving himself instructions. He produced a scheme for a World Food Board and fought for it with untypical heat. After one impassioned intervention at Geneva, an awe-struck delegate declared "He had the fire of God in his belly and he belched."

The subsequent attrition of his scheme discouraged him. Governments were nervous of this Old Testament prophet in modern idiom and hedged him round with officialdom; he resigned. Attlee made him a peer as Baron Boyd Orr of Brechin Mearns (1949). His own university honoured him. He found himself simultaneously elected Lord Rector by vote of the students and Chancellor by vote of the graduates. He became Chancellor. He was awarded the Nobel Peace Prize in 1949, and disbursed the prize among the organisations working for peace. When reminded that he would want the money to travel, he said he could always sell a cow.

In 1915, he married Elizabeth Pearson Callum, of West Kilbride, whose warm and winsome personality charmed people wherever the couple went in six continents. She was engrossed in all his work and devoted to all his enterprises. In his years of retirement, without a secretary at his farm in the foothills in the Grampians, she typed his world-wide correspondence, with two fingers. It was an ideally happy marriage, tragically marred by the death of "Billy", their only son, on a Coastal Command mission during the war. She was his inseparable companion abroad and whenever he was from home in Britain he telephoned her ("The Boss") every evening. They had two daughters and seven grandchildren, who knew as "Popeye" the man who was revered by millions.

This lean, long-jawed Scot, with eyebrows like eaves above deceptively mild blue eyes, was a spellbinder. He had no tricks of oratory and an uncompromising Scots accent yet he could bring conferences of government officials to their feet cheering his forthrightness and obvious sincerity. He was by instinct a doctor who wanted to do something for his patient without waiting for the laboratory reports. In research, he was a cautious scientist, but in nutrition he insisted that scientific facts should "work for their living". He was a practical farmer but his acres extended round the whole world. The preacher who rejected the pulpit became the evangelist of peace through plenty.

JOHN GRIERSON

Founder of the documentary film movement, for whom "the motion picture can open for us a window on the world"

21 FEBRUARY 1972

MR JOHN GRIERSON, CBE, the film producer, died on Saturday in Bath. He was 73. Grierson as founder of the documentary film movement, had a profound and world-wide influence not only on developments in the realm of film but also on the whole conception of the use of mass-media in the public service.

A small, wiry man with piercing eyes and an aggressive stance, Grierson pushed forward his plans with an energy which often left his colleagues far behind. He had a reputation for ruthlessness; but he was in fact only ruthless when all other courses failed. His bristling exterior camouflaged an affectionate and sympathetic nature, as those comparatively few who came close to him very soon discovered. He was regarded by film-makers as a hard taskmaster, but he rewarded hard work with a complete loyalty. As a producer he was brilliant. He never imposed his own ideas, but compelled each director to extract from his own inner resources the solutions to his problems.

He was born at Kilmadock, in Stirlingshire, in 1898, the son of Robert Morrison Grierson, a schoolmaster. From 1915 to 1919 he served with the RNVR. In 1923 he took his MA degree at Glasgow University with distinctions in English and moral philosophy. In the following year he won a Rockefeller Research Fellowship in social science and spent the next three years in the United States studying what later came to be called the mass-media of communication.

During his stay in America he was particularly influenced by two events – the premiere in New York of Eisenstein's *Battlecruiser Potemkin* (a film which he analysed in minute detail), and his meeting with Robert Flaherty, in writing of whose films he first coined the word "documentary". Both *Nanook* and *Moana* had a strong effect on Grierson, and although he subsequently differed from Flaherty's somewhat romantic conception of documentary, he never ceased to respect what he once called "the finest eyes in cinema".

His experiences in America led Grierson to the conclusion that the film was the most powerful as well as the most universal medium of public persuasion and information the world had ever known. It was, he felt, of vital importance that it should be used as such.

On his return to England in 1927 he succeeded in getting an introduction to Sir Stephen Tallents, head of the Empire Marketing Board. Tallents, a public servant of rare vision, realised the importance of Grierson's ideas and arranged for him to be appointed Films Officer of the Board. In this capacity he bombarded the members of the EMB with memoranda on the use of films in other countries and with specially arranged showings of films from many parts of the world, including the Soviet Union. Eventually the point was reached when it was felt the EMB might embark on the production of a film of its own. The board, however, was split between two propositions. One, based on an idea by Rudyard Kipling, concerned a small boy's dream about the dominions and colonies bringing to Buckingham Palace the ingredients for the King's Christmas pudding. The other was to be a wholly realistic film about the North Sea herring fleets. In the event both films were made, but only *Drifters* (by far the less costly of the two) was a success. In this film Grierson put to good use his intensive studies of film techniques – and especially those newly developed in Russia – and by imaginative cutting, no less than by fine photography, created something which, in the context of the uninspired and over-conventional British films of the day, was nothing less than sensational.

The success of *Drifters* gave Grierson and Tallents the chance to expand the EMB's film activities. At this point Grierson took the most important and far-reaching decision of his career. He decided to give up film-directing and to devote all his energies to producing. Thus in the last two months of 1929 there appeared the nucleus of a film unit; and within a couple of years this unit had become a force to reckon with.

With the demise of the EMB in 1933 Tallents took the Unit with him to the GPO to which he had been appointed public relations officer. Here the unit continued to flourish and expand. This period produced such works as *Coalface, Song of Ceylon, Weather Forecast, Night Mail* and *We Live in Two Worlds*. To these young artists from other fields made their own contributions – W. H. Auden, Benjamin Britten, William Coldstream, Walter Leigh – to name but a few.

By this time Grierson's influence was reaching far beyond the confines of government departments. Various practitioners in the comparatively new profession of public relations began to sense the potentialities of the documentary idea. Grierson therefore encouraged some of his colleagues to move out of the GPO Film Unit and set up their own production companies to serve the film needs of sponsors like the oil and gas industries and similar organisations. In 1937 Grierson was invited to Canada to prepare plans for the development of government film production. The report he wrote resulted in his being asked to draft a Bill to be placed before the Dominion Parliament; and in 1939 the National Film Act became law. It provided for the creation of a National Film Board through which all Government production and distribution should be channelled.

While Grierson was visiting Australia and New Zealand for the Imperial Relations Trust, and in fact laying the foundations for new government film organisations there, the Second World War began. The Canadian Government immediately invited him to become the first Film Commissioner under the new Act. This post he accepted, for a trial period of six months. In the event he remained in Canada until the end of the war, by which time he was effectively in charge of all Canadian Information Services, while the National Film Board had become one of the most influential film-making centres in the world.

At the end of the war Grierson resigned from the Film Board and with Legg and Raymond Spottiswoode, went to New York. Here they formed International Film Associates, a body designed to produce on a world basis, and with allied companies in Europe and elsewhere, a series of films of international interest and validity on scientific, technological, and artistic developments as well as on human skills and excellencies in general, wherever they might be found. Unfortunately the distribution negotiations with United Artists could not be brought to a satisfactory conclusion. Moreover the beginnings of the anti-Red panic which ended in McCarthyism did not leave Grierson unscathed. An ex-secretary at the Film Board was involved in the Canadian spy trial and on both sides of the border Grierson found himself (quite unjustifiably) smeared.

In 1947 he was back in Europe at the headquarters of the newly formed Unesco in Paris where, at the invitation of its first Director General, Julian Huxley, he became Director of Mass Communications and Public Information. He flung himself into this new job with his usual intensity. The trouble was, however, that there was money for planning but not for production.

In 1948 he returned to Britain to become Film Controller at the Central Office of Information. Faced by interdepartmental skirmishes on the one hand and a certain post-war lassitude on the part of the film-makers on the other. Grierson experienced a period of frustration, but with the setting up of the National Film Finance Corporation in 1949, came the creation of a production company named Group Three designed as a training ground where young feature film directors could be tried out on low-budget productions. There could be no doubt that a number of these would be documentary in style, if only for purposes of economy, and the direction of the new company was entrusted jointly to Grierson and to John Baxter, an established feature director who had made *Love on the Dole*.

Although for a number of reasons, mostly relating to government and film trade politics, the Group Three project was not a financial success, Grierson's invigorating approach to the experiment was of no small value. It brought to the fore young film-makers like Philip Leacock, Pennington Richards, Cyril Frankel and John Eldridge; and actors such as Peter Finch, Kenneth More, Peter Sellers and Tony Hancock had their first chances at Group Three.

With the demise of Group Three in 1955 Grierson found himself, for the first time in his life, in the doldrums. In 1957 he met Roy (now Lord) Thomson and put forward a plan to put out on Scottish Television a programme entitled *This Wonderful World*. This was agreed. The programme was an immediate success and was soon networked through the British Isles. In *This Wonderful World* Grierson personally introduced, with comments of his own, films, or extracts of films from all over the world.

It was a programme which, towards the end of his career, vindicated the saying with which he began his documentary work – "The motion picture can open for us a window on the world." The series continued until 1968 when a severe illness caused him to give up the programme. Subsequently, however, he accepted a professorship of mass communication at McGill University, Montreal; and from here in 1970 he made a sabbatical visit to India where he combined his advice to the Government on the use of the mass media with a penetrating aesthetic study of the relations between Indian dance movements to those of the motion picture.

He married Margaret Taylor in 1930.

* * *

SIR COMPTON MACKENZIE

Novelist, sometime spy, creator of 'Monarch of the Glen'
and 'Whisky Galore'

1 DECEMBER 1972

SIR COMPTON MACKENZIE, OBE, who died yesterday in Edinburgh at the age of 89 began as an infant prodigy and ended as an octogenarian with the gaiety and undimmed zest for life of a teenager.

The ups and downs of fortune in his long pilgrimage were dramatic. By 1914 he had established himself in the first flight of daring young novelists; Henry James hailed him, as a rising hope of English fiction. American publishers bowdlerised him (cutting out such wicked words as "tart" and "bitch") and he was attacked for corrupting youth. By 1924 he had been dropped by the highbrows, but continued to be a best-seller. By 1934 his position was unchanged, except that his output of novels and other work had flowed on unceasingly in a Balzacian spate of words. By 1954, thanks to broadcasting and the cinema, as well as to his unflagging output, he had become a popular figure on a national scale and he remained one to the last. As he grew aged – though never venerable – the critics began to scrutinise him again, first with curiosity and then with growing respect.

Through all these fluctuations "Monty" Mackenzie remained his cheerful, egotistic, ebullient, pugnacious self. The incense of the pundits in his youth did not go to his head. Critical neglect between the wars left him unsoured. At the nadir of his reputation, when he was often dismissed as a pot-boiling hack, he said that the theatre was in his blood, and he asked nothing better than to succeed as an entertainer. A microscopic memory served him well as novelist and autobiographer. He retained a practically continuous recollection of his life from before he was two, and not merely of incidents but of what he thought about them at the time. He taught himself to read at 22 months.

His hundred books were far from absorbing all his energies. He threw himself with zest into Scottish nationalism and the championing of Greece. His connoisseurship embraced music (he edited *The Gramophone*), gardening, the collecting of islands and the cultivation by day and night of the art of good talk; to have heard him, Max Beerbohm and Ronald Knox reminiscing together was a delight never to be forgotten. His friends of both sexes were drawn from all classes and many countries.

Edward Montague Compton Mackenzie was born on January 17, 1883, at West Hartlepool (where his parents were on tour), the eldest son of Edward Compton, the actor/manager, and his American wife,

Virginia Bateman, daughter of another stalwart Victorian man of the theatre, Hezekiah Linthicum Bateman, who launched Irving at the Lyceum. His paternal grandfather, Charles Mackenzie, had taken the stage name of Henry Compton. This family background brought him into contact, while still a preparatory school boy, with many stage and literary celebrities. Educated at St Paul's, he disappointed his High Master, the great Dr Walker, who saw in him a Balliol classical scholar, by preferring to go up to Magdalen as a commoner and reading History. The atmosphere of late Victorian and Edwardian London and Oxford was exquisitely caught in his early novels *Carnival* and *Sinister Street*; in them he showed himself a master of Cockney idiom and humour. They had been preceded by some pleasant conventional poetry and a first novel *The Passionate Elopement*, a graceful eighteenth-century pastiche for which he had much difficulty in finding a publisher, until Martin Secker came to the rescue.

During the 1914-18 War he served on Ian Hamilton's staff in the Royal Marines at Gallipoli, and then as an intelligence officer in the Aegean. These experiences were used in a series of novels and memoirs, including *Greek Memories*, which led him to be prosecuted under the Official Secrets Act. He hit back at what he regarded as a frivolous and spiteful action in *Water on the Brain*, satirizing the Secret Service. The offending *Greek Memories* was accident prone in encounters with the law; having sold the copyright of his first twenty books for £10,000 in 1943, believing this would be a capital transaction, he had to pay income tax in the year of sale.

His output of novels never stopped, *Guy and Pauline* (1915), *Sylvia Scarlett* (1918), and *Sylvia and Michael* (1919) were linked with those of his school and Oxford days. During the twenties and thirties he poured out light comedy, including *Poor Relations and Rich Relatives* and *Vestal Fire* and *Extraordinary Women* in which he revealed a humorous, sympathetic understanding of male homosexuals and Lesbians, which was considerably in advance of the times. His absorption in questions of faith and ritual, dating from school days, went into a trilogy on clerical life beginning with *The Altar Steps*. As in so much of his work, these were partly autobiographical, and helped to show how he followed the path to conversion, in the spring of 1914, to the Roman Catholic Church. Between 1937 and 1945 he produced *The Four Winds of Love* in which he spread himself, again to some extent autobiographically. By then, he was deeply committed to Scottish nationalism, and had found a home in the Hebridean island of Barra, where he commanded the war-time Home Guard. Scotland gave him material for exploiting his genius for high spirited fun in, among others, *Whisky Galore* and *Monarch of the Glen*.

Novels did not exhaust his powers. The Abdication brought him into the ring with *The Windsor Tapestry*. He did biographical sketches of Roosevelt, Benes, Pericles and Prince Charlie. At the end of the war he visited the battlefields in India as a guest of the Indian Government, and described it in *Eastern Epic*. In 1963 be brought out "Octave I" of *My Life and Times* and thereafter new volumes appeared each year until 1971 which saw the publication of Octave Ten. Here that microscopic memory, helped by the hoarding of letters, served to make this a unique tour de force; no detail, no small change had got through the net from earliest childhood. The tabby cat which, at two, impressed him as "large as a lion" was by no means his first memory.

Passionately though he identified himself with places, he had a restless temperament and would turn his back without regret from a beloved spot where he had grown roots. For years the London he had known so well and with such deep affection scarcely saw him except in brief visits to the Savile Club. He divided his time in old age between Edinburgh and Pradelles, Les Arques, Lot, the French house which he found so conducive to recollecting times past.

Many honours and distinctions came his way. He was Rector of Glasgow University in the 1930s; Governor-General of the Royal Stuart Society; an honorary LLD of Glasgow; a C.Lit of the Royal Society of Literature; and a former president of the Croquet Association.

He married three times, first in 1905 Faith, younger daughter of the Reverend E. D. Stone, of Eton, and sister of Christopher Stone; she died in 1960. His second wife, Christina, whom he married in 1962, was the daughter of Malcolm MacSween, of Tarbert, Harris. She died in the next year, and in 1965 he married her sister Lilian.

* * *

THE DUKE OF HAMILTON

Pioneer of aviation, who was the object of Rudolf Hess's mysterious flight to Britain in the Second World War

2 APRIL 1973

GROUP CAPTAIN THE DUKE OF HAMILTON AND BRANDON, KT, PC, GCVO, AFC, died on Friday in Edinburgh at the age of 70. His death recalls the extraordinary flight to Scotland of Rudolf Hess, Hitler's Deputy, in 1941. Believing he might arrange a peace settlement between Britain and Germany, Hess sought to get in touch with the Duke of Hamilton through whom he thought he might arrange a link with Winston Churchill. The Duke had never met Hess, though he had been at the Olympic Games in Berlin in 1936, which was also attended by Hess.

He was Hereditary Keeper of Holyroodhouse and also hereditary bearer of the Crown of Scotland (which the kilted duke carried before the Queen to St Giles' Cathedral in Coronation Year). He was ceremonial head "Below Stairs" of the royal palaces as Lord Steward of the Household 1940-1964, being awarded by the Queen the Royal Victorian Chain. From 1948 he was Chancellor of St Andrews University.

He was an active elder of the Church of Scotland and was Lord High Commissioner to the General Assembly in 1953, 1954, 1955 and 1958.

The duke was kind and gentle in nature, with immense stamina. His sometimes apparently vague manner usually meant that he was keeping his own counsel until he had thought things over and discussed them with his talented duchess, who unobtrusively helped him in directing the driving-force behind the wise and good influence that emanated from them in the home they acquired and established in the old Scottish castle of Lennoxlove.

After a formal sitting of Lyon Court (in which the Duke sat as one of Lyon's two hereditary Lords Assessors), a foreign prince observed of the duke: "only a true *grand seigneur* could look so naturally distinguished while wearing a soft collar under his state robes".

But he overcame his inborn modesty only to help other people and to carry out the many duties – both ceremonial and in business, but more particularly in social welfare and in setting a public example – that his historic role and personal aptitude properly fulfilled in contemporary Scotland. He cared very much about everything to do with Scotland: both in the preservation of her past traditions and continuing identity, but more especially in the building of her future as a meaningful country in the modern world.

He was born on February 3, 1903, eldest son of the thirteenth Duke, and was educated at Eton and Balliol College, Oxford. Styled Marquess of Douglas & Clydesdale, he became a national figure as "the boxing Marquess", winning many amateur contests. After Oxford, where he captained the university boxing team, he went round the world with Eddy Egan, an American friend, challenging all comers: and had an alarming bout with a gigantic stoker whom he managed to knock out just in time.

But his chief interest was already in social welfare, youth clubs (he was for many years treasurer of the Boy's Brigade in Scotland and was later made honorary president) and housing in the Glasgow and Lanarkshire areas; and he worked incognito as "Mr Hamilton" at the coal-face down one of the family mines, where he learnt working-class problems at first hand and got his trade union card.

From 1930 until his succession to the dukedoms in 1940, he was MP for East Renfrew, greatly increasing the Unionist majority. But, filled with the zest for daring and adventure of his forefathers, the mighty Red Douglases, he had become one of the earliest private owners of an aeroplane, had made himself an exceptionally expert pilot, and rose to command 602 Squadron of the Auxiliary Air Force. In 1932 a meeting of his constituents unanimously gave him leave of absence to act as chief pilot in the Houston Mount Everest Expedition, which he called "the only one original flight worth while". The flight story is told fully in *First Over Everest* (1933), to which the Duke and his second-in-command added their individual experiences in *The Pilots' Book of Everest* (1936). Overcoming great difficulties and hazards, he was the first man to fly over Everest, clearing the summit by a narrow margin. On his return, he received the Freedom of the Burgh of Hamilton, and was later awarded the AFC.

He played a large part in the foundation of Scottish Aviation Limited at Prestwick Airport, which now employs several thousand people in the West of Scotland. It was mainly due to his vision that Prestwick airport was established at a site which is practically fog-free. During the war he was a controller with 11 group Fighter Command, and was mentioned in dispatches for his services in France. During the Battle of Britain he commanded the Turnhouse Air Sector, and afterwards he commanded the Air Training Corps in Scotland.

In 1964 he chaired a government committee on pilot training and he was for many years president of the Air League. He was associated with the Air Cadet Council, the Air Training Corps, the Guild of Air Pilots and Air Navigators, and was president of the British Air Line Pilots Association.

In 1941, Hitler's Deputy, Rudolf Hess, parachuted into Scotland with the idea of personally negotiating peace between Britain and Germany using Hamilton as an intermediary. He landed near to the Duke's home but was at once arrested. He asked to see Hamilton, who had never seen him before; Hamilton encountered him at Maryhill Barracks. The Duke's account of what followed, which he gave to Prime Minister Churchill, was published in *Motive for a Mission* by his son James Douglas-Hamilton which was serialised in *The Times* in 1971. The Duke flew in a Hurricane to Northolt and was then driven to Ditchley Park in Oxfordshire where he was seen by the Prime Minister and by

Sir Archibald Sinclair, Secretary of State for Air. Churchill found the tale improbable saying: "Well, Hess or no Hess, I am going to see the Marx Brothers." Later that night, however, he had a long and detailed talk with the duke going over again every detail of what the duke had told him earlier.

He married in 1937 Lady Elizabeth Percy, elder daughter of the eighth Duke of Northumberland, KG. They had five sons of whom the eldest, the Marquess of Clydesdale, succeeds.

* * *

SIR BASIL SPENCE

Architect of Coventry Cathedral, whose modernist buildings sparked hostility as well as praise

20 NOVEMBER 1976

SIR BASIL SPENCE, OM, RA, who died yesterday at the age of 69, was one of the best known architects of his day. He possessed unusual fluency as a designer and draughtsman and, during the three decades that followed his victory in the competition for a new Coventry cathedral in 1951, was responsible for a number of buildings prominently in the public eye. Some of these, however, brought him blame as well as praise; for his name was, especially in the early 1970s, perhaps somewhat unfairly identified with the developments in London against which much public criticism was at that time being levelled.

He had an engaging personality and great persuasive powers, which he enjoyed using to get his own way with committees and clients; and when the design, for example, for Knightsbridge Barracks on the southern edge of Hyde Park was first made, rather than responding to public and professional dislike of a tower in this position, where it would obtrude on the leafy skyline of the park, he chose passionately to defend it and used his persuasiveness to carry the design past all objections.

Similarly with the building that replaced the Victorian Queen Anne's Mansions near St James's Park: although he was only the consultant architect called in to improve another architect's design, Spence made a personal issue out of defending the design against attacks on its bulk and ungainliness and was at the centre of a long controversy about it.

These and some other widely disliked buildings must however be set against a number of far more successful ones, and the criticism some of his work met with – which caused him much distress in the 1970s – must not be allowed to obscure his very real merits. He had the ability to solve difficult problems quickly and a subtle sense of space and of the relation of buildings to the landscape. His design for the first buildings for Sussex University, made in 1959, which determined the layout and character of the whole subsequent complex, showed a sensitive exploitation of their beautiful Downland setting.

Basil Urwin Spence was born in India (of an Orkney family) on August 13, 1907, the son of Urwin Spence, Indian Civil Service, and Daisy Crisp. He was educated at George Watson's College, Edinburgh, and at the Bartlett and Edinburgh schools of architecture. As a student he won three RIBA prizes. He worked in the office of Sir Edwin Lutyens (on the drawings for the Viceroy's House, New Delhi) and himself designed some country houses, but it was not until after the 1939 war (during which he served in the Royal Artillery, rose to the rank of major and was twice mentioned in dispatches) that he began to make his mark in architecture.

He first emerged as an inventive designer of exhibitions, being successively chief architect for the "Britain Can Make It" exhibition of 1947 and for the Scottish Industries exhibition of 1949 and designer of the "Sea and Ships" pavilion at the South Bank (Festival of Britain) exhibition, 1951. In fact he was in danger of becoming labelled as a designer only of such ephemeral things as exhibitions and exhibition-stands when, in 1951, he won the first prize in the Coventry Cathedral competition.

This changed both Spence and his fortunes. He became a celebrity, his public personality developed and he showed himself fully able to deal with the complex problems and situations that building a cathedral entailed. He threw himself enthusiastically into many activities connected with the cathedral, making for example a lecture tour of Canada to raise money for the project and working hard at arousing the interest of artists and craftsmen whose collaboration he sought.

His Coventry design showed one masterly stroke of imagination: the notion of preserving the ruins of the burnt-out, medieval cathedral as an approach to the new one. The building itself was orthodox in conception and structure, and so cannot be said to have made a permanent contribution to the art of architecture; it was considered by some to be too frankly theatrical. It is chiefly to be admired as a skilfully planned repository for the many works of art commissioned to embellish it: the tapestry by Graham Sutherland, the glass by John Piper, the sculpture by Jacob Epstein to mention only a few.

Coventry Cathedral, being widely regarded as a symbol of the reconstruction of Britain after the war, received a vast amount of public attention, and he became one of the most sought-after architects in the country. He had large offices in London and Edinburgh, with partners in each who for the most part remained in the background, and the flow of work from them was prodigious.

Besides the initial buildings for Sussex University, where he first employed that idiom based on repeated segmental arches which appeared frequently in his later work (they were, in fact, not arches but shaped concrete lintels), he designed a number of buildings for Southampton University, science buildings for Liverpool, Durham and Exeter Universities, the civic centre at Swiss Cottage, London, Kensington town-hall, housing at Glasgow, the British Embassy at Rome (a building with some distinguished qualities, whose faults arose more from the brief Spence was given than for his own decisions), as well as a number of churches and agreeable small houses for his own occupation in the New Forest, Majorca and Malta.

Some of his most successful buildings came from his Edinburgh office, notably the Glasgow air terminal at Abbotsinch and Edinburgh University library. He also worked in Greece and Amsterdam, was architect of the British pavilion at the Montreal international exhibition of 1967 – not one of his happiest designs – and was consultant for the extension to the Palais des Nations at Geneva and for the international airport at Baghdad.

Spence was appoined OBE in 1948 and elected ARA in 1953 and RA in 1960. He was a conscientious member of the Royal Academy, serving as treasurer in 1962-64 and professor of architecture in 1961-68. He was also an associate of the Royal Scottish Academy, a Royal Designer for Industry and a member for 15 years of the Royal Fine Art Commission. He was made an Hon DLitt by Leicester and Southampton universities and an Hon LID by the University of Manitoba. He was knighted in 1960. The climax of official recognition came to him in 1962 when, in the wake of all the attention Coventry Cathedral had aroused, he was awarded the OM.

Spence had a number of other interests which he pursued with vigour; sketching (the many drawings of his own work that he showed at the Royal Academy were invariably by his own hand) and sailing small boats. On occasions he sailed with something less than prudence and was at least once lucky to escape disaster. He lived his life fully, enjoyed good food and wine and could be excellent company. He worked hard and was always confident of the validity of his own ideas, with which he became emotionally involved, causing him to feel persecuted when subjected to criticism of a kind that other architects might have accepted as all in the day's work.

He had, however, courage and resolution which were both needed and forthcoming during his terminal illness; then the courage of his wife Joan was – as it always had been – equal to the occasion. She was Mary Joan Ferris and they were married in 1934. They had a son and a daughter.

JOHN MACKINTOSH

Influential and independent backbencher, who was the father of devolution

31 JULY 1978

MR JOHN MACKINTOSH, MP for Berwick and East Lothian, and Professor of Politics at the University of Edinburgh, died yesterday at the age of 48. He achieved distinction in two separate careers, as an active politician and as an academic student of politics. Indeed, one might add a third because he was also a compulsive and compelling communicator – on television and radio and in newspapers, as readers of his column in *The Times* will recall.

There were two surprising features about his career in active politics: that he was never given office and that he managed to win such a reputation for his performance as a backbencher. Both his success and his failure may be ascribed to the same quality: his independence of mind combined with his readiness to speak his thoughts on all occasions. His brilliance and eloquence were acknowledged on all sides. They provoked, however, not only admiration but also doubts about his judgment among those who require men in high office to be, above everything else, "safe".

John Mackintosh was never a safe man in that sense. He pursued his ideas wherever they led him with an almost foolhardy courage – and because he had a gift for memorable expression, and an intense manner of delivery that etched his words upon the mind, others were readily aware of the course he took. He was combative and witty, totally without malice but no respecter of persons in his wit. On occasions, however, his sense of assurance, which made him so invigorating as a speaker, did jar on his parliamentary colleagues and on others. It may have been one reason for his failure to gain preferment. One may also doubt whether his roots were sufficiently deep in the Labour movement.

Over the years he became more and more disenchanted with his party, moving progressively farther to the right. He was caustic about the leadership of Harold Wilson and was an enthusiastic supporter of Mr Roy Jenkins's claims to the succession. He had for many years been an ardent advocate of British membership of the EEC and in November, 1976 he and Mr Brian Walden, the former Labour MP for Birmingham, Ladywood, effectively wrecked the Dock Work Regulation Bill for that session by abstaining from the vote on two critical Lords' amendments. Nor was that the only occasion on which he was to prove a trial for the party Whips.

One of the subjects on which he felt most intensely in recent years was the need for parliamentary devolution within the United Kingdom. He favoured this for two essentially different reasons. As a keenly patriotic Scotsman he believed that country required greater control over its own affairs. From time to time there was speculation that his heart was really with the Scottish Nationalists, speculation that was indeed on occasion fanned by his own words. Certainly he felt a degree of rapport with them, but what he sought was not independence for Scotland but an assembly with very wide responsibilities within the United Kingdom.

The other reason why he advocated devolution was that he believed in the general dispersal of power within Britain, to Wales and the regions of England as well as to Scotland. As long ago as 1968 he had set out his ideas on this theme in a Penguin Special: *The Devolution of Power*, and the substance of his views remained consistent.

But John Mackintosh is likely to be remembered equally for his achievements as an academic student of politics. He was the author of the most authoritative work on the British Cabinet. To this role he brought not only the perception of the practising politician but also the erudition of the professional historian and an immense capacity for hard work.

If in his politics he always retained something of the dogmatism of the stimulating teacher so to his teaching he brought the vitality of the active politician. He was an inspiring teacher, lively and challenging with the gift of establishing easy human relationships. To any gathering, whether the lecture hall, an international conference – where he tended to be more highly regarded than in British political circles – or an informal social occasion, he brought sparkle, controversy and a sense of fun. No man could have been more clubbable and few could have lived their lives with greater zest.

John Pitcairn Mackintosh was born on August 24, 1929, the son of Colin M. Mackintosh and Mary Victoria (nee Pitcairn). He was educated at Melville College, Edinburgh; and at the universities of Edinburgh, Oxford and Princeton. He became an assistant lecturer at Glasgow University in 1953 and the following year was appointed to a lectureship in history at Edinburgh. He continued at Edinburgh until 1961 when he went to Nigeria as Senior Lecturer in Government at the University of Ibadan. Returning to Britain in 1963 he was Senior Lecturer in Politics at Glasgow University for two years and from 1965 to 1966 he was Professor of Politics at Strathclyde University. He decided to return to academic life while remaining in active politics, when he was appointed, early in 1977, to the chair of Politics at Edinburgh. It was a tribute to his standing, that the university was prepared to make such an appointment on a part-time basis.

In 1966 he gained the seat at Berwick and East Lothian for Labour and entered Parliament at his third attempt, his two previous sorties having been at Edinburgh Pentlands in 1959 and Berwick and East Lothian in 1964. This seat he briefly lost when he was beaten by the Earl of Ancrum at the General Election of February, 1974, but in the election of October of that year he regained it.

This was the only seat that Labour won from another party in that election and the success had much to do with Mackintosh's personal popularity. At a time when few MPs could justifiably claim that they were able to add more than a few hundred votes to their party's total – if that – Mackintosh really did have a strong, personal following. He was an assiduous constituency member. Although a city-dweller himself in his life-style and interests, he commanded the respect of a largely rural constituency by the thoroughness with which he mastered their concerns. As a right-wing Labour member of conspicuously independent views he was able to command an unusual degree of support across party boundaries.

As an MP he was a member of several Select Committees; Agriculture, 1967-69; Scottish Affairs, 1968-70; and Procedure, 1966-73. He was Vice-Chairman of the British Council GB/East Europe Centre; a member of the Executive Committee of the British Council from 1968 to 1973 and was Chairman of the Hansard Society until the Spring of this year. He had been Joint Editor of *The Political Quarterly* since 1975.

The first edition of *The British Cabinet* appeared in 1962; other publications were: *Nigerian Politics and Government* (1966); and *British Government and Politics* (1970). More recently he had been the editor of *British Prime Ministers in the Twentieth Century*, Volume I.

He married first, in 1957, Janette M. Robinson, by whom he had one son and one daughter. This marriage ended in divorce in 1963. He married in that year Catherine Margaret Una Maclean. There was a son and daughter of this marriage also.

* * *

HUGH MacDIARMID

Creator of the Scottish Renaissance, 'the most explosive force in Scottish literature'

11 SEPTEMBER 1978

HUGH MACDIARMID, the Scottish poet and nationalist – the pseudonym is known and used far more widely than his real name of Dr Christopher Murray Grieve – died in hospital in Edinburgh on Saturday at the age of 86.

He was for over forty years the most explosive force in Scottish literature. He set himself against the debased Burns tradition in Scots vernacular poetry – a tradition of "pawkie" and "couthis" verses of a stereotyped sentimentality – to reconstruct a bolder and richer

Scottish language, drawing both on a diversity of modern regional dialects and on the dazzlingly rich language of the medieval Scottish poets, especially William Dunbar. His omnivorous reading in modern European literature made him from the start responsive to every genuinely creative new movement in the use of language (both in poetry and prose), so that his work both looks back to the past and is excitingly, sometimes devastatingly, contemporary. As a diagnostician of Scotland's ills and a prophet and preacher against the Establishment, Grieve was at the same time a militant Scottish nationalist and exultant anglophobe, a passionate communist, a devoted internationalist who was in love with every small nation and minority culture in the world, and a sworn fighter against what he called "the whole gang of high mucky-mucks, famous fatheads, old wives of both sexes, stuffed shirts, hollow men with headpieces stuffed with straw".

The inconsistencies and violences of his thought were bound up with his drive towards realizing his almost mystical vision of a people redeemed from fakery and perpetual second-handness. His poetry, which ranges from his wonderfully articulated early Scots lyrics (where reality is penetrated to its inexpressible core with an amazing combination of tenderness and violence) to his later long discursive pieces in English, with their long Whitman-like catalogues covering the whole world of modern knowledge, defies classification. There is nothing like those wonderful lyrics that make up the sequence *Au Clair de la Lune* from his volume *Sangschaw*, or like the magnificently phrased mixture of natural observation, grotesquerie, and mysticism in *Ex Vermibus*, from the same volume. He can move from the cosmic to the intimate, from religious to domestic imagery, from eternity (a favourite word) to the kitchen sink or the farmyard dunghill or the slum streets of Glasgow.

His Scots poems seem to grow out of the language ("not an idea gradually shaping itself in words, but deriving entirely from words", he once explained) but yet at the same time to be the compelled utterance of an intense personal vision. Some of his later poems, wholly different in style from his early lyrics in Scots, read in parts like doggerel; but put them in their context and they can be seen as part of the whole sweep of his response to experience.

Christopher Murray Grieve was born on August 11, 1892 at Langholm, Dumfriesshire, "the wonderful little Border burgh" as he once called it, a town that haunted his imagination. His father was a rural postman. Young Grieve broke away from his parents' religion, but without bitterness, retaining a respect and affection for his father (whose death he refers to in his poem "The Watergaw"). Grieve later attributed his deeply ingrained left-wing political feeling to the "old Radicalism" of the borders and insisted that from his earliest days he had hated the gentry "for what they, by their very existence, prevented other people from being and doing ".

He attended Langholm Academy, where he was taught by the composer Francis George Scott, who became a warm friend and discerning critic. Under family pressure he agreed to train as a teacher but his father's death released him from the obligation. For some years he worked as a journalist for newspapers in Scotland and Wales. He was already active in left-wing politics, and did some research for a Fabian Committee on Land Problems and Rural Development which was duly acknowledged in *The Rural Problem*, a Fabian Research Department publication of 1913. In the same year he wrote his first contribution for Orage's *New Age*.

In 1915 Grieve joined the RAMC and served in Salonika, Italy and France. Invalided home with cerebral malaria, he married Margaret Skinner in June 1918. They settled in Montrose, and had a son and daughter; he worked on the *Montrose Review* and began to work out his programme for Scottish poetry.

Between 1920 and 1922 Grieve edited three volumes of *Northern Numbers*, whose aim was to do for Scottish poetry what *Georgian Poetry* was doing for English. Grieve's own contributions were in English, and while they show little distinction in idiom or rhythms some of them possess a combination of sensuous precision and mysticism which critical hindsight can at once identify as pointing forward to some characteristic qualities.

In August 1922 Grieve founded his periodical *Scottish Chapbook*, a much more ambitious project than *Northern Numbers*, dedicated to the furthering of a Scottish Renaissance. In working for this, Grieve exploited the possibilities of Scots as a serious medium of poetic expression (not merely as a vehicle for whimsy or low comic verse or pseudo-Burnsian sentimentality or regional nostalgia); the result was his remarkable poetry in Scots, which first began to appear in the *Chapbook*. This coincided with his adoption of the pseudonym, Hugh MacDiarmid, which he used consistently for the rest of his life. Much later, he wrote: "It was an immediate realisation of this ultimate reach of the implications of my experiment which made me adopt, when I began writing Scots poetry, the Gaelic pseudonym of Hugh MacDiarmid (Hugh has a traditional association and essential rightness in conjunction with MacDiarmid)." This is the only explanation he ever offered, and it leaves many points in obscurity.

The Scottish Renaissance, which is now a reputable term in Scottish literary history, was Grieve's own creation. His first collection of mostly Scots poems was *Sangschaw* (1925) which was followed by *Penny Wheep* (1926). In these poems he brilliantly justified his use of "synthetic Scots" (ie a Scots whose vocabulary was drawn from a variety of different regions as well as from Middle Scots writers and from Jamieson's *Dictionary of the Scottish Language*) by producing lyrics of combined delicacy and toughness, of tenderness and violence, which seemed to penetrate reality to the core by sheer verbal virtuosity. But his great masterpiece in this idiom was *A Drunk Man Looks at the Thistle* (1926), a poem-sequence in which the most Goliardic satire and the most delicate lyricism combine to explore and interpret the state of Scottish civilisation. It is a sort of latter-day *Inferno*, yet done with humour as well as sorrow, with wild gaiety as well as with bitter wit, a work absolutely *sui generis* whether one considers Scottish literature only, or the whole literature of the English-speaking world.

Grieve remained in Montrose until 1929; served as a Labour councillor, and he was appointed a JP. And he established himself as the dominant literary figure in Scotland. His position was, however, far from being universally accepted. His polemical habit, his Anglo-Scottish "Establishment", the savage gaiety of his controversial manner (in the old Scottish "flyting" tradition), appalled the more conservative and the more respectable, who tended to regard him as a purely destructive force. His individualism was incorrigible. He founded the Scottish Centre of PEN in 1927 and helped to found the National Party of Scotland in 1928, but his subsequent relations with these bodies (as with other organised bodies) were stormy. He did not formally proclaim himself a communist until 1932, and joined the party in 1934. (He was expelled from the party in 1938, and only rejoined in 1957, when so many others were leaving because of the Hungarian affair.) His position here as elsewhere is best put in his own words:

"... I am like Zamyatin. I must be a Bolshevik before the Revolution, but I'll cease to be one quick when Communism comes to rule the roost."

The following year Compton Mackenzie invited him to London to work on his magazine, *Vox*, but the enterprise proved abortive. A period in Liverpool as public relations officer for the Organisation for Advancing the Interests of Merseyside followed in 1930, and then he was in London again for a short time working for the Unicorn Press. In 1932 he divorced his first wife and soon afterwards married a Cornish girl, Valda Trevlyn, in keeping with his belief in the essential unity of the Celtic peoples. In 1933 the Grieves moved to Whalsay, "the little north Isle of the Shetland Group", and lived there under Spartan conditions until 1941, when he took a war job as a manual labourer in a Clydeside factory. They had one son. He joined the Merchant Service and, until the end of the war, he worked on ships engaged in estuarial duties. In 1951 he moved to a little cottage near Biggar, where he spent the rest of his life.

Meanwhile his literary career had been developing in an unexpected direction. An ambitious long poem, largely in English but often tinged with Scots, *To Circumjack Cencrastus*, appeared in 1930; it is a discursive metaphysical work concerned, as so much of his later work was to be, with finding a way of including all significant reality in language, and it does not wholly come off. *First Hymn to Lenin and Other Poems* (1931) and *Second Hymn to Lenin and Other Poems* (1935) were hailed as first bringing communist ideas into English poetry, but in fact their significance was literary rather than political: the *Second Hymn to Lenin* is really a poem about the difficulty of adjusting consciousness to true reality.

His later style is best represented by the long *In Memoriam James Joyce* (1955). His *Collected Poems* were first published in New York in 1962. He wrote two characteristically digressive and pugnacious autobiographical volumes, *Lucky Poet* (1943) and *The Company I've Kept* (1966). A representative selection of his prose appeared in 1968 as *The Uncanny Scot* (ed K. Buthlay); *Selected Essays* (ed D. Glen, 1969) contains his most pungent literary criticism.

In the 1970s there were reissues of some works, notably *Lucky Poet* for his eightieth birthday and the *Hugh MacDiarmid Anthology* (both in 1972), and in 1976 a reissue of his 1926 *Contemporary Scottish Studies*.

In 1974 he became Professor of Literature to the Royal Scottish Academy, and in 1976 president of the Poetry Society.

He had been awarded a Civil List pension in 1950, and in 1957 he received an honorary LLD from Edinburgh University. For, in spite of his unremitting war against anglophobia he had by now become a Scottish institution, and no matter how many people were irritated, angered, or outraged by him, his remarkable original genius was widely recognised. He received this new turn in his fortunes with complacency: he had never doubted his genius.

SIR FRANK FRASER DARLING

Prophet of concern over ecology, and pioneer of conservation

19 NOVEMBER 1979

SIR FRANK FRASER DARLING, one of the most influential and internationally famed figures in the modem advance and public acceptance of ecology and nature conservation, died on October 22 at the age of 76.

Although a fertile and continuous expositor of an ecological approach, and author of more than two dozen published works, Frank Darling, as he was named at his birth on June 23, 1903, remains a somewhat mysterious and obscure figure. His antecedents were apparently English, but while employed by the Buckinghamshire County Council in an agricultural capacity (for which he had qualified at the Midland Agricultural College) he made his first marriage to Marian Fraser, and not long afterwards moved to Edinburgh. Here he quickly rose to be Chief Officer of the young Imperial Bureau of Animal Genetics and in 1932 launched his first publication, on the biology of the fleece of the Scottish mountain blackface breed of sheep – a topic giving little hint of his future breadth of interest.

In 1934, however, he published a first work on wild life conservation, and by means of successive research fellowships was enabled, with his wife, to spend a number of years in north-west Scottish wildernesses, partly in the Dundonnel deer forest in Wester Ross and partly on the islands of North Rona and Tanera. Here he devoted his strong empathy and his background knowledge of population genetics and nutrition to working out the life patterns of red deer and seals, and paying also some attention to social behaviour in seabirds.

The Second World War found him badly out of touch and out of sympathy with the main currents of national life, and only towards its close did he find a bridging activity as Director of the West Highland Survey on behalf of the Government. However, by 1952, when his first report appeared, political and administrative circles gave it a chilly reception, despite or perhaps because of the the fact that it foreshadowed the more integrated human and ecological approach which slowly gained official acceptance. During this period his divorce from his first wife was followed by remarriage to a gifted and imaginative young ornithologist, Averil Morley of the Edward Grey Institute at Oxford University.

Having been appointed Senior Lecturer in Ecology and Conservation at Edinburgh University in 1953 he found himself unable to live up to its demands from his southern English home, and a painful parting with the university ensued in 1958, although he had deeply influenced students.

In 1952 the Nature Conservancy had given him a contract for a red deer survey in the Scottish Highlands which, although extended over six years, never led to a publication; the results however were of great practical value to the conservancy in the framing of what became the Deer (Scotland) Act 1959 and in creating a successful advisory and research organisation on this subject. Meanwhile Darling had been invited to become a member of the Nature Conservancy, to which he contributed his unique blend of philosophic and ethical approach and down-to-earth appraisal of conditions of plant and animal life in a rugged semi-natural state.

In 1957 his wife Averil died at an early age, leaving him with three young children, one still a baby, and in 1960 he married his third wife Christina, who had successfully stepped into the breach with the upbringing of the family. During this period he had accepted Fairfield Osborn's invitation to serve as Vice-President of the Conservation Foundation in New York, and he also made ecological survey journeys in Alaska with Starker Leopold (whose father Aldo had perhaps been Darling's nearest prototype as a philosophic ecologist) and to various African territories, ending up with a reassessment in depth of the United States National Parks system.

With Fairfield Osborn's powerful backing he enjoyed substantial success in America, but his encounters with the authorities in Africa, for example, were no happier than with the Scottish administration earlier. During the 1960s however, the loyal following which he had gradually been building up among educated laymen helped him at last to be taken seriously both in governmental and scientific circles.

With his highly successful Reith lectures published as *Wilderness and Plenty*, in anticipation of European Conservation Year 1970 he shook off his status as a prophet without honour in his own country, and his new public eminence was confirmed, to his great surprise, by his knighthood in 1970. The world had sufficiently caught up with his cosmic and reflective ecological approach to begin to understand its debt to him.

His manner was deliberate, even hesitant; profoundly, although rarely aggressively, emotional; arriving at conclusions as much through feeling as intellectually. He saw himself and others as unique individuals in the round to an extent which now seems old-fashioned, and he tried hard to resist the erosion of values of living by too great a hurry or by attending to too much business at a time. Even in scientific work he declined to become a slave of record-keeping. He often failed in achieving his ends through not thoroughly dealing with the means, so that much of his life passed under a shadow of disappointment and denial of recognition. While this cannot be said to have embittered him, his acute sensibility to the savour of life made it harder for him to bear.

BERNARD FERGUSSON,
LORD BALLANTRAE

*Distinguished author and soldier, who saw action in Burma and
Palestine, and became Governor-General of New Zealand*

29 NOVEMBER 1980

BERNARD FERGUSSON, LORD BALLANTRAE, KT, GCMG, GCVO, DSO,
OBE, who died in London yesterday was a figure who escapes exact
classification. Dedicated to the profession of arms from youth he
distinguished himself in irregular warfare in Burma in the Second
World War yet thereafter never commanded a formation larger than
a brigade; he was the author of some admired books on military
matters, idiosyncratic, witty and marked by a true love of soldiers and
soldiering; and long after his military career had ended he confounded
his critics by shining brightly in several different spheres of public life,
as Governor-General of New Zealand from 1962 to 1967; as Lord High
Commissioner of the General Assembly of the Church of Scotland in
1973-74 and from 1972 to 1976 as chairman of the British Council.

It could be said that Fergusson once seen was never forgotten. He
was tall and powerfully made, built one might say, to ceremonial scale.
His moustache was crisp and behind his eyeglass lay an eye that even on
fairly serious occasions it was risky to meet if one wished to keep one's
composure for his humour was highly catching and his charm hard to
resist. As our grandfathers might have said, Fergusson was a tonic.

An Elder of the Church of Scotland, his appointment as Lord High
Commissioner in no way cramped his style; he was a clear and pungent
speaker, qualities he believed were not always to be found in church
assemblies – and said so in an article in the Kirk's magazine in February,
1975, in which he called for the "elimination of waffle".

Descended from an ancient Ayrshire family the Fergussons of
Kilkerran, he was a younger son of General Sir Charles Fergusson,

7th Baronet, who commanded a corps in the First World War. His mother was Lady Alice Boyle second daughter of the 7th Earl of Glasgow. Bernard Fergusson was born on May 6, 1911; from Eton and Sandhurst he joined the Black Watch in 1931. Four years later he became ADC to Major-General A. P. Wavell, an old Black Watch officer then commanding the 2nd Division at Aldershot. Thus began a warm personal friendship, which only ended with Field-Marshal Earl Wavell's death 15 years later. Despite their disparity in age they were mutually devoted; under Wavell's guidance Fergusson acquired not only a sound military apprenticeship, but also a love of literature and especially of poetry. Fergusson himself wielded the pen skilfully both in prose and verse. In 1961 he wrote a short, but very readable biography of his chief, *Wavell: Portrait of a Soldier.*

After two years as Wavell's ADC, Fergusson rejoined the Black Watch and embarked with his battalion for Palestine, where serious trouble had broken out between the Jews and the Arabs. Fergusson was soon in the thick of it as he was appointed Brigade Intelligence Officer, a role in which he came in close contact with the Palestine Police and their problems. When the Second World War broke out Fergusson was an instructor at the Royal Military College, Sandhurst but he was soon selected to undergo a shortened course at the Staff College, Camberley.

In July, 1941, Wavell was transferred from Cairo to New Delhi on being relieved by Auchinleck: Fergusson accompanied him as his Private Secretary, and then joined the planning staff at GHQ, India. In October, 1942 he was given command of a column in Burma under that eccentric exponent of irregular warfare, Orde Wingate. Infiltrating beyond the Chindwin River behind the Japanese lines, Wingate's columns blew up railway bridges and disrupted the enemy's communications throughout 1943. In the following year Wingate carried out a second and larger incursion across the Irrawaddy with the aid of gliders and parachute drops. On this occasion he employed six brigades, one of which was commanded by Fergusson, but these raiding forces were withdrawn after Wingate's death in an air crash. Fergusson has vividly described these hazardous forays in *Beyond the Chindwin* (1945) and *The Wild Green Earth* (1946).

During the next two years (1945-1946) Fergusson directed the military wing at Combined Operations Headquarters, and told the story of that organisation in *The Watery Maze* (1961). In 1946 he made an unsuccessful attempt to stand for Parliament. Towards the end of that year he was offered command of the 2nd Battalion of his regiment, then in India, but he chose instead, rather unfortunately, to take command of the Police Mobile Force in Palestine. This assignment was not a happy one. By that time, the Jews, not the Arabs, had become the principal trouble makers, and the Palestine Police had to contend with two ruthless insurgent bodies, the Irgun Zvai Leumi and the Stern Gang, to which was added the problem of illegal immigration. Fergusson did not hit it off with all his associates in the Palestine Police, and got involved in the notorious Roy Farran case and was forced to resign.

After being commissioned by Lord Wavell to write the War History of the Black Watch, (published in 1950 with the title *The Black Watch and The King's Enemies*) in March, 1948 Fergusson was given command of the 1st Battalion of his regiment, then stationed at Duisburg on the Rhine. Three years later he was appointed Colonel, General Staff (Intelligence) at Supreme Headquarters Allied Powers Europe under Eisenhower's command. In 1954 he was a student at the Imperial Defence College, and was then given command of an infantry brigade of the 51st (Highland) Division, but was taken away to act as Director of Psychological Warfare in the abortive Suez Expedition of 1956. After that episode he was transferred to command a Regular infantry brigade at Dover, but when that was disbanded in 1958 he retired from the Army. In his variegated military career one can give him the credit of *proxime accessit.*

This was by no means the end of his public service, for in 1962 he was appointed Governor-General of New Zealand a post which had been held by both his father and his grandfather. In the five years that followed he and Lady Fergusson won the hearts of all in that distant

Dominion. In 1969 he was appointed Colonel of the Black Watch, a fitting recognition of his deep devotion to his regiment.

In 1968-69 he was head of the British element of the international Observer Team in the Nigerian civil war. He was made a life peer in 1972 and created a Knight of the Thistle in 1974. From 1973 he was Chancellor of the University of St Andrews and from 1968 chairman of the London board of the Bank of New Zealand.

Besides the literary works mentioned above, Fergusson wrote *Eton Portrait* (1937); *Lowland Soldier* (1945) a book of verse; *Rupert of the Rhine* (1952), a short biography; *The Rare Adventure* (1954), a novel; *Return to Burma* (1962), a travelogue, and *The Trumpet in the Hall* (1970), an autobiography. Harold Nicolson paid a tribute to his literary merit with the words: "He can write sensitive as well as muscular prose."

Fergusson cherished, and exalted, the traditions of his regiment, of his Service of his clan and of his country. But he saw all tradition not as a totem-pole but as a springboard: as a small, often precarious bridgehead on the long coastline of history which could have no purpose unless some advance was made from it. He did not strive officiously to keep alive the honourable legends he held dear; he imparted a new, idiosyncratic vitality to them. As a commander he may have been little feared but he will be long remembered.

In 1950 Fergusson married Laura, daughter of Lieut-Col A. M. Grenfell, DSO, and they had one son. His wife, whose sister was the actress Joyce Grenfell, died in an accident in December, 1979.

BILL SHANKLY

Manager of the greatest of all Liverpool football teams

1 OCTOBER 1981

MR BILL SHANKLY, OBE, who as manager of Liverpool Football Club from 1959 to 1974, created a team which became a byword both for its successes in competitions and the tough, uncompromising manner in which it achieved those successes, died on September 29 at the age of 67. Shankly found Liverpool a Second Division club and piloted them to the First Division and a remarkable run there of three League championships, two FA Cups and a Uefa Cup. During this period Anfield became the graveyard of many reputations in the Football League and its chanting, roaring Kop, fanatical in its faithfulness to the home team, struck terror into the hearts of many visiting sides. During Shankly's reign the club seemed to come to symbolise more than just footballing success for Liverpool; overshadowing rival Everton it seemed like the Beatles and the Mersey Sound, to be a part of the city's folk culture.

Shankly was always the first to admit that good footballers do not always make good and successful managers. But Shankly who forged one of the greatest Liverpool teams is, with Matt Busby, an example of a Scot whose managerial skill transcended outstanding ability on the field. He was a tougher player than Busby. In 1932 he left his village of Glenbuck in South Ayrshire to move to Carlisle. Then he went to Preston where he played in more than 300 matches, including the 1937 and 1938 Cup Finals. He also won five full caps for Scotland.

Shankly became a manager at 34, first with Carlisle, then Grimsby, Workington and Huddersfield. He took over Liverpool in 1959. They were then in the Second Division and Shankly shoved and guided them into the First. He then came into his inheritance. Fit, tough, demanding and demonstrative, the most aggressively Scottish of all Scots who have managed an English club, he fulfilled himself with his dedication to Liverpool and made them one of the most successful sides in Europe.

Had there been a football manager's *Who's Who* his recreation would have been Football, and his address Anfield. These were his consuming passion.

Yet the family man lurking inside the football fanatic emerged surprisingly in July 1974 when he announced his resignation in order to spend more time with his family. An OBE followed together with a slight decline in the fortunes of the club – but significantly only that slackening of tension and effort when a great director leaves the stage. He would have been the first to agree that some decline was inevitable had he stayed on himself.

The profile of the player gives the key to the man. This old-fashioned half-back was said to have run with his palms turned out like a sailing ship striving for extra help from the wind. "I played on me toes all the time like a ballet dancer. That gave me strength in me calves, and ah've still got it." He was light on his feet, fierce in the tackle, sharp but not bitter with his tongue, generous in spirit but a bit on the mean side when it came to the details of playing the game.

About the great masters he was never wrong. On Tom Finney his Preston team-mate, Shankly said: "He had everything, good with both feet, good in the air, a deadly shot, precise in his passing. Many skills have improved but he had one that is a lost art today – the accurate cross when running at speed."

Shankly became a hero on Merseyside. Everton, hardly a block away, never produced the spirit there to match his drive and enthusiasm. It might be argued that he created a winning side which was not attractive to watch. One doubts that Tom Finney would have fitted in with Shankly's heavy mob. His strength of character, based always on the techniques and reading of the game and backed by the roar of the Kop forged a sledgehammer rather than a rapier. Some rush into the limelight, others back into it. Shankly tramped into it and showed little surprise, when he was treated like a god. But he was always more human than divine and amid the euphoria and fantasy of the football game he always kept his feet on the ground.

JAMES CAMERON

Journalist and war correspondent 'who wrote the
grim, hard truth from the heart'

28 JANUARY 1985

JAMES CAMERON, CBE, journalist, author, and broadcaster, who died
on January 26 in London, aged 73, was one of the most widely travelled
foreign correspondents of his day.

In the days when he worked for the *Daily Express* he was once
praised by Lord Beaverbrook as one who wrote the grim, hard truth
from the heart. He claimed to have spent more time in aeroplanes, and
to be familiar with worse hotels and more abominable food than any
of his colleagues. As a freelance he specialised in the Middle East and
Asia.

He was one of very few journalists who, having achieved success
with the written word, made the transition to radio speech, and
finally to visual appearances on television, which he called "this eerie
medium". To do this demanded a wide range of talents, all of which
were supported and linked together by Cameron's integrity, dry wit and
capacity for summing up a situation.

As an international reporter he probably won more awards than
anyone in history. In 1984 his television series *Once Upon A Time* set the
seal with a new form of autobiography on what was by now a legendary
career.

James Mark Cameron was born in Battersea in 1911 of Scottish
parents. His father was an unsuccessful barrister who took to writing
serials for popular magazines. His mother died while he was still
a child, and his memories of childhood were of poverty treated with
offhand gaiety "... my father and mother uproariously dressing for
dinner of boiled eggs".

Coming from an unconventional home, this least conventional of
journalists had a conventional journalistic start in life – 15s a week as

office-boy in the Salford office of the *Weekly News*. After some years on journals in Dundee and Glasgow, he came in 1940 to Fleet Street.

By then both his father and his first wife had died tragically within a few months, and he had been left with a baby daughter. Rejected for military service, Cameron worked as a sub-editor on the *Daily Express* until, as war ended, he got back to the reporting he loved and understood.

Almost his first assignment was the 1946 atom bomb "experiment" at Bikini. The horrific nature of this, combined with the bizarre publicity surrounding it, had, Cameron wrote, "a stunning and lasting impact on my attitudes to almost everything". This took two forms: a distrust of soothing utterances from authority, whether political, military or scientific; and a concern for the ordinary man everywhere – since he passionately refused to accept that human beings living on one side of the world are in any basic way different from those living on the other.

In 1950 Cameron – by now a highly successful newspaperman – resigned from the *Daily Express* over what he considered an unjust attack on John Strachey, Minister of War in the Labour Government, made by the *Evening Standard*, sister paper to the *Daily Express*. Invited to join *Picture Post*, he was in trouble again within the year for an exposure of the treatment of prisoners in South Korea.

From there he moved to the *News Chronicle* which he felt to be his spiritual home, and after the paper's undignified demise in 1960, he resolved never to be a staff man again. During this period Cameron's obsession with the bomb and mankind's imminent destruction – though expressed with bitter wit and memorable phrases – became at times strident and repetitive.

In 1965, however, he realised an ambition, that of visiting North Vietnam at the height of American bombing. He was obliged to travel home across Siberia in mid-winter with only tropical clothing, and no one wished to show the impressive film which he and his Italian cameraman had made. "It took me years", he said, "to repay the money I raised to finance it".

The first of several long spells in hospital after a car crash in India in 1971 provided the theme for his play *The Pump* which was a success on radio, winning the Prix Italia for 1973, and later on television.

There was hardly a country he had not visited from Taiwan to Tibet, from the Seychelles to Albania – the latter the only place in the world, he said, where he had found wine "undrinkable even by me". He had also met most of the notable figures of our age, from Albert Schweitzer to Ho Chi Minh, on their own ground.

In recent years Cameron had contended against prolonged ill-health with the same fortitude he showed as a journalist in opposing officialdom and exposing cant. He produced a number of books, of which his auto-biography *Point of Departure* (1967) and *Witness in Viet Nam.* (1966), are probably the best-known. He was appointed CBE in 1979.

He leaves a widow, Moneesha, a daughter and a son by earlier marriages; and several stepchildren.

* * *

JOCK STEIN

Powerful force in Scottish football, and manager when Celtic won the European Cup

12 SEPTEMBER 1985

MR JOCK STEIN, CBE, who died after an international match between Scotland and Wales at Ninian Park, Cardiff on September 10, aged 62, had been the Scotland Football Team Manager since 1978.

A former miner, he had had a successful career as a player, but it was as manager of Celtic that he became internationally known, and his creation of one of the most formidable powers in British football resulted in Celtic's winning the European Cup in 1967, the first success in that competition by a British club.

As Scotland's manager Stein always tried to avoid the parochial view, which, it is sometimes argued, afflicts Scottish football and its managers and, though no-one was more delighted than he when Scotland beat England, he maintained that if Scottish supporters became mesmerised by this goal, progress on the international stage would be impeded.

His ambition was to see Scotland's team recognised internationally for its strength and skill and to that end he travelled extensively abroad to study foreign styles of play and potential future opposition.

John Stein was born in Blantyre, the son of a miner. He worked in the mines himself until at the comparatively late age of 27 he became a professional footballer. Until then he had played for his local junior club as a centre half.

His introduction to senior football came with Albion Rovers but he moved to South Wales to play non-League football for Llanelli. When Celtic were in need of a strong centre half they sent for him. He became captain and was on the verge of international honours. An ankle injury ended his career.

Although Celtic gave him charge of their reserve team, his first experience of management came at Dunfermline. Despite limited financial backing, he raised a team good enough to win the Scottish Cup and enter European competition. The excitement and challenge of European cup football stayed with him and in the 1960s he became one of Britain's first real experts on the continental game.

After a period with Hibernian, he returned to Celtic in 1964 to become the club's first Protestant manager. A tough and persuasive leader, he produced teams to dominate Scottish football. Celtic won the League championship on nine successive occasions between 1966 and 1974. They won the Scottish Cup eight times and the League Cup six times.

However, the highlight of those remarkable years was 1967 when Celtic became the first British club to win the European Cup, beating Inter-Milan 2-1 in Lisbon.

Jock Stein took Celtic to a second European Cup final in 1970 when they lost 2-1 to Feyenoord after extra time. In that year he was appointed CBE. He was later severely injured in a car crash and after several years' ill-health he turned his back on Scottish football.

However, that was for less than two months as manager of Leeds United. He returned to Scotland to take up the position as national team manager, a post the Scottish football public felt he should have held many years before. He was 56 when he started his international career and under his guidance Scotland qualified for the 1982 World Cup finals.

However, he always maintained that success was of less importance than sportsmanship and entertainment. And though his nickname "the big man" implied toughness, he was popular both with players and supporters.

He leaves a widow and two children, both married.

* * *

MANNY, LORD SHINWELL

Veteran of the socialist cause

9 MAY 1986

LORD SHINWELL, CH, PC, the elder statesman of the Labour Party who was held in great affection by political foe and friend alike, died yesterday, aged 101.

An apprenticeship in the tough Clydeside politics of the early years of the century instilled in Shinwell the staunch socialist principles which were to remain with him during more than half a century in both Houses of Parliament. He held Cabinet posts under Attlee as Minister of Fuel and Power, a controversial stewardship which resulted in his being moved subsequently to the War Office and the Ministry of Defence. But the public will remember him as the politician of fiery temperament and sharp wit who never shrinked from speaking his mind. They saw in him both the spirit of individuality and of Labour orthodoxy which the passage of time and an elevation to the peerage did nothing to quench.

Emanuel "Manny" Shinwell was born in Spitalfields, east London, on October 18, 1884, the son of Samuel Shinwell, an East End clothing manufacturer. He left school at the age of 11 to be apprenticed to the tailoring trade. He soon went to Scotland where, as a young man, his interest was caught by Clydeside politics. At the same time he read widely, particularly books on English grammar. The subject fascinated him, and he got into the habit of noting unusual words in a little book. Thus he acquired his discriminating taste in English usage.

When he was only 22 he was elected to the Glasgow Trades Council, of which he was twice president, and five years later he took a hand in trade union organisation among the seamen in the Clyde ports. Here, he learnt revolutionary politics, and on "Red Friday", January 31, 1919, the authorities' panicky handling of a strike led to a clash with the police in the Glasgow streets. For his part in this Shinwell spent several months in jail.

Seven years as a Glasgow councillor gave him excellent training in a robust school of dialectic, but when he entered the Commons in 1922 as member for Linlithgow he shrewdly tempered his style to the parliamentary tradition. He was defeated in 1924 after a few months as Parliamentary Secretary to the Department of Mines, but was returned again for Linlithgow in 1928. He was Financial Secretary to the War Office in 1929-30, and then returned to his post at the Mines Department until he lost his seat in 1931.

Shinwell thought he had been betrayed by his leaders and his sense of injustice, nourished during four years of political exile, flared up in the astonishing onslaught on Ramsay MacDonald at Seaham Harbour in 1935. In one of the most savage elections in modern times, he drove his old chief out of politics. Three years later occurred the extraordinary incident when Shinwell, provoked by a remark from Commander Robert Bower, a Conservative member and former naval boxing champion, crossed the floor of the House and struck him in the face. Shinwell then turned on his heels and stalked out of the chamber, muttering angrily to himself.

During the Second World War, Shinwell, like Lord Winterton, and largely in consort with him ("Arsenic and Old Lace" they were called), took upon himself the role of constructive critic believing the country needed a "win the war" Government. Churchill paid him the compliment of always listening with interest to his speeches.

It was commonly believed that Shinwell stayed out of the wartime Coalition because he had refused a junior post. Nevertheless, he would certainly have liked the Ministry of Fuel and Power, and Attlee gave it to him when Labour won the 1945 election. Shinwell at once addressed himself to the task of getting the mines fully under state control. The Bill introduced that December was the Government's first measure for the nationalisation of a basic industry. Hope was high in Labour ranks that the transference of ownership would give a fillip to production, but vesting date, January 1, 1947, found Britain at the point of crisis.

Although Shinwell had often warned of the possibility of shortages, he had denied emphatically that there would be any dislocation of industry or closing of factories. So when, unexpectedly and perfunctorily, on Friday, Feburary 10, 1947, he told the Commons that much of the nation's industry would have to close because of coal shortages, he encountered a storm of criticism.

In subsequent debates and questionings he was not convincing and there was some surprise that he remained at his post. He bore the brunt of the charge of having failed to plan ahead, but first the miners, to whom he had given the five-day week, and then the Prime Minister publicly expressed confidence in him. Shinwell was moved to the War Office in October of that year and ceased to be a member of the Labour Cabinet.

He was bitter at what he regarded as enforced removal from an office of which he had been proud, and in which he had hoped to integrate the three power industries; but he soon found himself more at home with the problems of military organisation than he had been with those of industry, and he got on well with his Army colleagues.

He returned to the Cabinet in March, 1950, when he became Minister of Defence. He was soon confronted with the military implications of the Korean situation, mounting tension in Berlin, and terrorism in Malaya, while Russia was busy testing nuclear bombs. He was largely responsible for carrying out the "phased defence programme", and did his utmost to modernise the armed forces. For him, the Western Alliance was vital and he was a strong supporter of Nato.

His views on the issue of the nuclear deterrent underwent a change. He had been one of the "fathers of the British contribution to the deterrent", but in Labour's years of opposition after 1951, he argued for contracting out of it. By 1958, he was speaking strongly against the "onward march of that detestable apparatus", and in 1960 he warned Gaitskell, who had pledged himself to reverse the party conference vote against retention of the nuclear deterrent, that he was endangering the future of the whole party.

However, Shinwell's political influence within the party waned during these opposition years; he had been unseated from its national executive as early as 1941, and failed to gain re-election in 1952 and 1953. In 1955, he left the Shadow Cabinet and moved to the back benches. In the same year, he published his autobiography, *Conflict Without Malice*. His mettlesome qualities brought him into conflict with ministers and backbenchers in 1967 when he expressed bitter opposition to the Government's decision to apply for membership of the EEC, a stance many thought incompatible with his position as chairman.

At a party meeting he lost his temper and became heatedly embroiled with the Foreign Secretary and Leader of the House and on another occasion he differed strongly with the Leader of the House and the Chief Whip on the matter of party discipline which he wished to see enforced more strictly. Murmurings against him led eventually to his resignation and he retired once more to the back benches where he continued to oppose the principle of British membership of the EEC.

He was made a Life Peer in 1970, and he continued well into his 90s to be a vigorous and outspoken member of the House of Lords, alive to all the main issues of the day.

For several years he had chaired the influential all-party House of Lords Defence Study Group, but no single action of his caused so much surprise as his resigning the Labour Whip in March, 1982, as a protest against what he saw as left-wing militancy. Though he remained a Labour Party member, he sat thereafter with the Independents in the Lords. He published several memoirs. Lord Shinwell was three times married; his first wife, Fay, to whom he was married for 52 years, died in 1954; in 1956 he married Dinah Meyer, of Denmark, who died in 1971; and in 1972 he married Mrs Sarah Hurst, who also predeceased him.

* * *

JENNIE, BARONESS LEE

Britain's first Minister for the Arts, founder of the Open University

18 NOVEMBER 1988

BARONESS LEE OF ASHERIDGE – Jennie Lee, widow of Aneurin Bevan – died on November 16. She was 84. Once the youngest member of the House of Commons, she exercised political influence through a large part of the 20th century. Her ardour for left wing solutions to social ills never flagged. It was a fitting climax when, in 1967, she was elected chairman of the Labour Party – an organisation which over the years had often seemed not big enough to contain the ambitions of either her or her husband. She was Britain's first Minister for the Arts; her term of office saw the founding of the Open University.

Jennie Lee was born on November 3, 1904, in Lochgelly, Fife, daughter of a miner. It was an environment where it was natural, in the words of one commentator, that she should be "swept into socialism long before the age of consent". And although it was a warm-hearted socialism, of the heart rather than the head, there was, then and later, an element of bitterness in it. "I am learning," she wrote to a girlhood friend, "how guillotines find favour in a revolutionary period."

The family tradition in revolution was that of the then lively Independent Labour Party. ILP activists were frequent guests at James Lee's home. With a succession of scholarships Jennie Lee graduated in arts and then in law at Edinburgh University, and worked for a time as a teacher. Meanwhile the ILP identified her as a propagandist with powers beyond her years. She was witty as well as fervent. They put her up, at the age of 24, as their candidate at a by-election at North Lanark. She won the seat from the Tories with a majority of nearly 7,000.

At Westminster she quickly achieved something of a national reputation (faster indeed than that other firebrand from a mining background who was to become her husband). Her youth, her sex, an attractive "Salvation Army lassie" image (and an accent more engaging than some Scottish voices Westminster was accustomed to) – all that, combined with her revolutionary ardour, caught the fancy of the media of the time. When the Tory Government was replaced by Ramsay MacDonald's minority Labour administration, there was still no shortage of targets for her political ammunition.

But her Westminster career was interrupted. She lost the North Lanark seat in the socialist debacle of 1931 and did not return to the House until 1945, when (now an official Labour candidate) she won the Midlands constituency of Cannock. The intervening years she spent as a journalist and lecturer. Her platform skills were in demand in the United States, the Soviet Union and various European countries. For a time, after the war, she was joint editor of *Tribune*.

In 1934 she had married Bevan. They were both Left-wingers and romantics who saw politics as much more than an exercise in economics. With no children to distract her, they established themselves as a formidable partnership of equals.

But during the war (part of which Jennie Lee spent with the Ministry of Aircraft Production, and part as a political correspondent) it became clear that her husband's career had to be measured on a different scale of magnitude. Churchill could dismiss Bevan as a "squalid nuisance", but in fact he was evolving into something much more important in Labour's destinies: as a major custodian of the mantle of the Left. When Labour came to power after the war it was he, not his wife, who was given high office.

Thus in 1945, in the words of Bevan's biographer (Michael Foot), "Jennie found herself moving towards a far-reaching personal decision to subdue her own strong and never-abandoned feminist instincts. It was not made in a moment, and with her temperament it was far from easy." The public image of Nye Bevan was aggressive; but there was a vulnerable innocence to him which could have been his destruction. His wife could stop him laying himself unnecessarily open to attack from his many enemies, outside and inside the Labour movement. At other times she probably hardened his heart when he might have compromised.

There were practical ways she helped him with his writing: Bevan, brilliantly self-educated, lacked the discipline formal schooling would have given. Above all, she provided private support. Their homes, in London plus a farm in Buckinghamshire, were always places with the intellectual glamour of what would in a different stratum of society would have been called a *salon*. Part of the secret of the success of the domestic arrangement was that they had brought in the Lee parents to run the practical side of things.

To his friends, Bevan's death in 1960, at the height of his powers, came at a particularly cruel time, when he seemed to be losing the fight for his kind of socialism. Yet in a sense, "Bevanism" – source of so much internecine conflict in the party in his lifetime – was to come into its own a couple of decades later. The shade of Nye was visibly hovering in the air when Michael Foot was chosen as party leader: the party's heart was thought by some to rule its head. Jennie Lee, by her nurturing of Bevan's memory, which she guarded with sometimes fierce loyalty, must accept part of the credit (or blame) for the way the Labour Party chose to go.

Meanwhile, at the age of 60, she herself saw Ministerial office when Harold Wilson gave her responsibility for "the arts". In the following four years, Government spending on the arts doubled, a fact that owed something to the special respect shown to her by the Prime Minister. But part of her achievement was to disarm the inevitable criticism of the very idea of an "Arts Minister". She proved commendably more interested in encouraging imaginative schemes of artistic endeavour than in bureaucratic planning. The heart was still more important than the head.

She saw the job, as her husband would have done, as proving that socialism was concerned with eliminating spiritual as well as material poverty. The same doctrine inspired her in putting into effect the plan for a "University of the Air", a name she abolished in favour of the "Open University". Her particular pride was to insist that it must not compromise on academic standards. Party controversy still threatened while she was in office. She was tempted to resign (as Nye once did) when cuts on social security were mooted, but compromised on the ground that defence expenditure was to be trimmed too. In 1966 she was made a Privy Counsellor. In 1970 (having lost her seat in the General Election) she became a life peer. She was an honorary Fellow of the Royal Academy and an honorary LLD of Cambridge.

She published an early autobiography, *Tomorrow is a New Day*, in 1939 and during the war wrote *Our Ally, Russia*. Her major book was *My Life with Nye* (1980).

R. D. LAING

*Controversial psychiatrist and social philosopher, who believed
the family was the source of all trouble in society*

24 AUGUST 1989

DR R. D. LAING, THE CONTROVERSIAL PSYCHIATRIST, psychoanalyst,
polemicist, social philosopher and writer, died yesterday in St Tropez,
south of France. He was 61.

His ideas were not generally accepted by the majority of practising
psychiatrists, but he had a very widespread – and international –
influence on many of those concerned – at a nursing level – with the
care of the mentally ill, and on lay attitudes to mental disorder. He also
influenced some quite well-known writers, including the playwright,
the late David Mercer.

Ronald David Laing was born in Glasgow in a three-room tenement
in 1927. He attended school in his native city, and graduated as a
doctor from Glasgow University in 1951. He then spent two years in the
British Army. From 1953 until 1956 he trained as a psychiatrist, again in
Glasgow. In 1957 he joined the Tavistock Clinic; he was Director of the
Langham Clinic from 1962 until 1967.

As a Fellow of the Foundation Fund for Research in Psychiatry,
he spent six years (1961-7) in research into psychiatric familial disturbance; this work conducted under the auspices of the Tavistock Institute
of Human Relations, reinforced his earlier theories, which had attracted
as much opposition from the medical establishment as they did support
from victims of mental disturbance, social workers, and others.

In 1964 he had founded the Philadelphia Association, a registered
charity whose aim was to establish a network of households where
those in mental distress could live without undergoing orthodox
treatment, which Laing opposed on the grounds both that it did not
work and that it treated distressed patients as if they were insane.
According to him, they were not: it was society that was sick, and it used

the "schizophrenic" as a scapegoat.

Laing first came to wide attention in 1960 with his book *The Divided Self: An Existential Study in Sanity and Madness*. From that time onwards he became a hero of the New Left: his view that the ego-disintegration of the schizophrenic was a Marxist-style revolution against the exploitative forces of the Super-ego, and that the family – with its emphasis on morality and its incest taboo – was the basis of all the troubles of society, became widely accepted, although by very few of his medical colleagues.

Later, with the decline of the New Left, and with his missions to India and Sri Lanka to meditate upon Buddhism and Hinduism, he became one of the acknowledged leaders of the sub-culture which has developed out of, first, hippiedom, and then "psychedelic bliss". He was well known to be interested in the allegedly therapeutic affects of LSD.

The Divided Self, Laing's most influential book, set out to redefine the meaning of madness (which for Laing often seemed to consist only of schizophrenia or schizophreniform states): the schizophrenic was according to him, a rebel, an "outsider", estranged from society by both its insufficiencies and, in particular, by the "schizophrenogenic parent", usually the mother.

Laing's most famous practical experiment in treatment of schizophrenia was the setting up of the regressive therapeutic community at Kingsley Hall in the 1960s. Here patients were encouraged to behave as they wished, to the extent of nudity and smearing of faeces.

But the regressive techniques were in no way new, and the results fell into a familiar pattern: no conclusion could be reached on the validity of Laing's theory of schizophrenia because the emphasis in treatment had been on the old-fashioned regressive techniques rather than on his theory.

One criticism frequently levelled at Laing, who was not and never claimed to be a real clinician, was that many of his allegedly schizophrenic patients were in fact gross hysterics "trained" by him, rather as Charcot trained his "hysterical women" in Paris in the last century.

In *The Politics of Experience/The Bird of Paradise* (1967) Laing turned his attention from mental illness to the illness of society. Here the insane, the outcast, the criminal and the revolutionary were presented as mystical explorers in a vicious and mechanised world.

Laing was in private practice as a psychoanalyst during the latter part of his life. He was prominent in the movement to legalise cannabis and to encourage the clinical use of hallucinatory substances. He will be remembered less for his originality than for his ability to synthesise the mood of the rebellious young and the revolutionary elements in society; less as a psychiatrist than as a self-styled "anti-psychiatrist"; and for his timely concentration upon what it is actually like to be mad as distinct from the various forms which madness takes.

* * *

COLONEL SIR DAVID STIRLING

*'The Phantom major' who created the SAS and destroyed
Rommel's armoury behind the lines in the desert*

6 NOVEMBER 1990

THROUGH THE EXPLOITS of the regiment he created, David Stirling became an almost legendary figure, not only in the British forces but also among the Germans and Italians in the desert. From insignificant beginnings – a handful of officers and a few score men – Stirling triumphed over early disaster to forge a weapon whose annoyance value and elusive character led Rommel to create a unit with the sole function of tracking Stirling's movements and bringing this desert fox to bay. The Germans, almost as mesmerised by the aura the 6ft 6in colonel created around him as his own men, dubbed him "the Phantom major".

The son of Brigadier-General Archibald Stirling, Archibald David

Stirling was brought up in the Highlands and educated at Ampleforth. He then went to Trinity College, Cambridge, but, more interested in racing and gambling than in learning, he soon left. He next wanted to be the first man to climb Everest, but a five year training plan had to be abandoned on the outbreak of war and he returned home to join the Scots Guards.

Army routine did not suit him and from the bar of Whites he was recruited into the Commandos. Posted with them to the Middle East he found they were to be disbanded to provide urgent reinforcements for divisions which had been badly mauled in the Western Desert. Believing that there was great scope for a raiding force to work behind enemy lines in the desert, building on the experiences of the Long Range Desert Group, in July 1941 he presented to General Auchinleck plans for a light, mobile unit.

In spite of the fact that Auchinleck was suffering from acute manpower shortages he allowed Stirling to raise a detachment of 60 men and six officers. Their first operation, a parachute drop in conjunction with a general offensive, was unsatisfactory. None of its objectives was achieved. Stirling refused to be discouraged. For his next attempt he asked the Long Range Desert Group, vastly experienced in the ways and moods of the desert, to carry his men in their jeeps. This enabled him to work deep behind enemy lines. In two weeks in December 1941 SAS units destroyed 90 aircraft on the ground.

Auchinleck was satisfied. Stirling was given permission to recruit more men and in 1942 his force was officially designated a regiment, thus initiating a famous tradition which has endured undimmed to this day. Over the next 14 months the SAS destroyed over 250 aircraft, cratered vehicle parks, derailed trains, blew up ammunition and petrol dumps and mined roads, forcing the enemy to withdraw troops from the battlefield to protect lines of communication. In all these forays Stirling provided the ideas, the planning and the leadership; his cool courage beneath a deceptively vague casualness of manner became a byword. His apparently charmed life repeatedly brought him back from his desert raids full of new ideas and enthusiasm for further adventures.

But after 14 months Stirling's luck failed him. On January 10, 1943, he was captured by Rommel's special unit after being given away by Arabs in Tunisia, where he was reconnoitring behind enemy lines far ahead of the advancing Eighth Army. Rommel recorded his capture in his diary with this comment: "Thus the British lost the very able and adaptable commander of the desert group which had caused us more damage than any other British unit of equal strength."

Stirling must have been an endless worry to the guards at his prison camp in Italy. He escaped four times until eventually he was taken away and shut up in Castle Colditz for the rest of the war.

After 1945 Stirling settled in Southern Rhodesia. Believing that the future policy for Africa must come from within, in 1949 he formed the Capricorn African Society, which expanded to include the six Commonwealth countries of East and Central Africa. Stirling worked to lay the foundations of a non-political society based on common citizenship without racial discrimination and a qualitative franchise. But he was viewed with suspicion and scepticism by blacks and whites alike and his efforts were in the end overtaken by political events.

Returning to Britain, in 1961 he formed Television International Enterprises, a consortium to provide capital loans for building and equipping television stations in emerging countries of Africa. A more controversial idea was a company called Watchguard, offering bodyguards and other security services to foreign heads of state. In 1970 it was involved in an abortive plot to free political prisoners from a Libyan jail.

Then in 1974, in the wake of the miners' strike which brought down the Conservative government of Edward Heath, Stirling secretly set about forming GB 75, which he described as "an organisation of apprehensive patriots." Its aim was to take over and run essential services, such as power stations, in the event of a general strike. This and other similar organisations which sprang covertly into existence at that time were publicly condemned by the defence secretary of the day, Roy Mason. Feeling that it had gone off at half cock, Stirling disbanded GB 75 in 1975, the year in which its existence was to have been made public. Stirling was next invited to lend his backing to the Movement for True Industrial Democracy (Truemid), a group of moderate trade unionists committed to fighting left wing extremism in the unions. He wrote the foreword to Truemid's inaugural pamphlet, *The Day of the Ostrich.*

Stirling's belated knighthood, awarded only in this year's new year's honours, perhaps reflected official hesitancy in the face of his unorthodox activities in the 1970s. Nevertheless, "Who Dares Wins", the motto he chose for his SAS Regiment, is a fitting epitaph for a man who not only has his niche in the history of the desert war, but who also created a unit whose advice and services have, at times to this day, been much sought after by governments at home and abroad in the resolution of terrorist crises.

* * *

LORD MacLEOD OF FUINARY

Founder of the Iona Community, who had 'the magnificent presence of a Highland chieftain'

28 JUNE 1991

GEORGE FIELDEN MACLEOD was a Church of Scotland minister who was known internationally, chiefly as founder of the Iona Community, and he was the first such minister to be made a life peer. He remained the sole minister of the Church of Scotland in the House of Lords. Decorated for his bravery in the first world war he became a pacifist in the second and a prominent campaigner for nuclear disarmament after that.

The Iona Community is a Christian fellowship of ministers and laymen who live and work together on the island where St Columba landed in the sixth century, bringing Christianity to western Scotland. The community began in 1938, when MacLeod resigned from his ministry at Govan Parish Church, Glasgow, and set off with a dozen men, half unemployed craftsmen, half young ministers, to restore the Benedictine ruins.

MacLeod was a grandson of one of Queen Victoria's favourite Scottish clerics, Norman MacLeod of the Barony Church, Glasgow. His own father was a successful man of business and became a baronet. George MacLeod, therefore, was born into a world of wealth and privilege. His own education was at Winchester and Oriel College, Oxford (which later made him an honorary fellow). But, as for many of his generation, a far harsher education was given in the trenches. He served in the Argyll and Sutherland Highlanders, winning both the MC and the Croix de Guerre. His theological education was gained at Edinburgh University and Union Theological Seminary, New York. At the early age of 31 he was called to be collegiate minister of St Cuthbert's, one of Edinburgh's most wealthy, famous and influential churches.

He seemed set, at this point, for a conventional career of ecclesiastical eminence on the Scottish pattern. Then, after only four years at St Cuthbert's, he did the unpredictable and accepted a call to Govan at the heart of Glasgow, populated largely by unemployed shipyard workers and their families. He had begun the career of paradoxes that was to mark the rest of his life – the decorated first world war combatant who became the vehement pacifist, nuclear disarmer, and president of the International Fellowship of Reconciliation; the baronet (he succeeded his nephew – but did not use the title – in 1944) who became a convinced Christian socialist whose best known book had the deliberately ambiguous title *Only One Way Left*; and the apostle to industrial Scotland who founded a religious community on Scotland's most romantic island.

MacLeod's ministry in Govan did for Scotland much of what Dick Sheppard had done for England at St Martin-in-the-Fields. Like Sheppard he had great gifts as a broadcaster (the gifts did not later prevent him being among those pacifist preachers denied the microphone by government decree during the war). He was passionately concerned about the social and political implications of the gospel. The lessons he learned in Govan reinforced the experience he had had in the trenches.

This led him to his most creative act, the foundation of a religious community – something unknown in the Scottish church since the Reformation – on the improbable site of Iona, improbable in the sense that it seemed so unrelated to the urban industrial scene about which MacLeod was so concerned. But there was a deliberate rhythm built into the community of ministers and industrial workers. They shared in the summer months in the reconstruction of the community buildings of the abbey, but in the winter they were on the mainland at work in the industrial centres and the great housing estates. Lessons learned in common manual work, and in the remarkably fresh worshipping life of the community (for which MacLeod had a genius), were applied at some of the toughest points for the Christian mission in Scotland.

"Iona Men" became some of the most effective church extension ministers of the Kirk. And MacLeod's many journeys seeking the necessary financial resources in the USA and elsewhere, and the coming of world church leaders to conferences on the little island, ensured a world-wide influence for the experiment. MacLeod remained leader of the community that he had founded until 1967. As the result of a world-wide campaign by the community, £1.2 million was raised to build an international centre for reconciliation on Iona named after MacLeod and opened in 1988. The community was not without its critics among more traditional members of the Church of Scotland, but MacLeod's election as Moderator of the General Assembly in 1957 marked recognition of its immense contribution to the life of the Kirk. Two years ago he was awarded the Templeton Prize for religion by the Templeton Foundation, an American body, for his peace-related activities. Only last month, he was made a freeman of the city of Glasgow.

MacLeod had the magnificent presence of a Highland chieftan, and a certain aristocratic confidence that could sustain the ardours of founding a large and controversial enterprise. Most of all he had a charismatic personality expressed in thrilling oratory. The size of the achievement expressed the size of the man.

In 1948 he married a cousin, Lorna MacLeod, who predeceased him. There were two sons and a daughter of the marriage, who survive him. The elder son, the Hon Maxwell MacLeod, born in 1952, succeeds to the baronetcy.

* * *

WILLIE WADDELL

*Gifted Rangers footballer and Scottish international who
rebuilt his club after the Ibrox disaster*

16 OCTOBER 1992

WILLIE WADDELL WAS A RARITY amongst footballers, a gifted player who went on to establish a distinctive career as a journalist before returning to the game with equal success as a manager and administrator. His contribution to the development of Rangers at every level over a period of fifty years is unsurpassed and he steered the club through the most traumatic passage of its history following the Ibrox disaster of January 2, 1971, when 66 spectators were crushed to death and 145 injured in an accident on Stairway 13 at the end of an otherwise tranquil derby game between Rangers and Celtic.

It was Waddell, then the manager of Rangers, who took the initiative when the club's board of directors were seemingly paralysed into inaction by the magnitude of the calamity. He insisted that there should be Rangers players in attendance at the funeral of every victim and two days after the disaster Rangers volunteered £50,000 to the Lord Provost of Glasgow's appeal fund for their relatives.

Waddell was deeply disturbed at the prospect of another such accident occurring at Ibrox and quickly came to the conclusion that the stadium would require to be reconstructed rather than overhauled. He travelled extensively in Europe, seeking a model for his vision. Finally he found it in Dortmund, where Scotland played in the 1974 World Cup finals, and by this time he was general manager of Rangers.

He persuaded his directors to begin a £10 million project which turned Ibrox into a modern stadium with a seated capacity of more than 40,000. So successfully did he oversee the project that the ground has become a prototype for others, such as the newly-opened Parken Stadium in Copenhagen, which incorporates many features pioneered in Glasgow.

If Ibrox is an extraordinary monument to Waddell's abilities as a football administrator it has not eclipsed the memory of his achievements on the field, which remain vivid to those who saw him perform. He was born in the mining village of Forth in Lanarkshire, a county which has produced a disproportionate number of Scottish footballers, and Waddell was very much part of the tradition.

He made his debut for Rangers at the age of 15 in a reserve game against Partick Thistle in 1936. He signed as a professional two years later and made his first team debut against Arsenal on August 9, 1938, scoring the only goal of the game.

A winger in the dashing Scottish mould, he was an imposing figure with a powerful build, strong torso and broad shoulders, although he had a tendency to sustain thigh injuries caused by the strain of his exceptional acceleration. His comparatively meagre total of 17 caps for Scotland would undoubtedly have been greater but for the war, although he did also make five wartime appearances for his country.

He specialised in tormenting opposing left backs before directing looping crosses into the penalty area, usually bound for the head of his attacking colleague and friend, Willie Thornton. The Rangers pair together made marvellous entertainment and created great excitement amongst the massive postwar football crowds. He won four championship and two Scottish Cup medals with Rangers, for whom he played a total of 558 matches, 296 of them in the first team, and scored 143 goals.

Waddell retired as a player in 1956 and began his career in journalism as a sportswriter for the *Glasgow Evening Citizen*. But Kilmarnock invited him to be their manager a year later and under his guidance the unfashionable Ayrshire club won the Scottish championship in 1965. With this achievement behind him Waddell returned to newspaper work with the *Scottish Daily Express*.

In 1969, increasingly eclipsed by Celtic's exploits under Jock Stein, Rangers turned to Waddell for salvation. He did not win the title for Rangers but his impact was impressive nevertheless and in the Scottish League Cup final of 1970 he dropped Colin Stein, a forward who had cost Rangers £100,000, in favour of a 16 year old teenager, Derek Johnstone.

Johnstone repaid Waddell's confidence by striking the only goal of the game against Celtic to become the youngest scorer in a major Scottish cup final. Two years later Rangers won the European Cup Winners' Cup but a brawl involving Scottish fans afterwards caused the club to be banned from European competition for two years.

Waddell flew to Switzerland to plead with Uefa for a reduction in the punishment which was duly granted, Rangers being excluded for a year. He retired as manager in 1972, appointing Jock Wallace in his place, and had the satisfaction of seeing his protégé win a clean sweep of domestic honours twice, in 1976 and 1978.

Willie Waddell went on to become managing director and vice-chairman of Rangers and after his retirement he was appointed an honorary director in recognition of his outstanding service.

He is survived by his wife Hilda and three children, Ronnie, Peter and Ailsa.

JO, LORD GRIMOND

Charismatic leader of the Liberals who "marched his party towards the sound of gunfire," but never quite reached the front line

26 OCTOBER 1993

JO GRIMOND'S CAREER IN POLITICS lacked fulfilment. A man of great talent and charm who, at one period, was a dominating figure in the House of Commons, he led his party when it never really gathered strength. There was constant promise but no results. And, in consequence, he never obtained office so that his ideas were not sharpened by the need to put them into practice. Grimond's great potential was never utilised and even his effort to hold the Liberals together and to "march them towards the sound of gunfire", was eclipsed by the later upsurge in Liberal votes (if not in seats) which occurred after he retired.

Yet it would be wrong to let subsequent disappointments dim the memory of his great resolution in the Liberal cause and his real stature in the politics of the 1960s. His principal achievement, after becoming leader within six years of entering the Commons, was to give his party a youthful idealism.

Nothing in his career was more striking than his development as a parliamentary performer. In his earlier years his interventions were shy, diffident, hesitant. But increasingly, with experience, his command of the House mounted. He always had something fresh and original to say and he had a knack of recalling members to the obvious which they had overlooked. He was a year ahead of Hugh Gaitskell in advocating Britain's leadership of a non-nuclear club and he was the first party leader to come out positively for entering Europe.

He held his small parliamentary party together with easy skill and shouldered an immense burden of work for the Liberal cause. He was passionately serious in pursuing his cherished, if elusive, concept of a non-socialist radical party as an alternative to Conservatism but at the same time he never became obsessive and retained an excellent and slightly self-deprecating sense of humour.

Joseph Grimond, or "Jo" as he liked to be called, was the son of Joseph Bowman Grimond, a Dundee jute manufacturer and his wife, formerly Helen Lydia Richardson. From this Scottish background he went to Eton and Balliol. He was a Brackenbury Scholar and got a first in PPE. In 1937 he was called to the Bar by the Middle Temple, and in the next year married Laura Miranda, daughter of the late Sir Maurice Bonham Carter, and through her distinguished mother, Baroness Asquith of Yarnbury, a grand-daughter of Herbert Henry Asquith.

Grimond joined the Army just before the outbreak of war, served with the Fife and Forfar Yeomanry and became a staff major with the 53rd Division. Meanwhile he had accepted an invitation to stand as Liberal candidate for Orkney and Shetland. He lost in 1945 by only 329 votes to a well-established Conservative. He spent two years as director of personnel in the European office of UNRRA and a further two as secretary of the National Trust for Scotland. This latter experience confirmed his enthusiasm for Scottish affairs. In spite of his Asquithian connections by marriage – which opened many political doors to him – he remained at heart a Scottish radical.

He won the constituency of Orkney and Shetland in 1950 by more than 2,000 votes and was promptly appointed whip of the nine Liberal members. The tall, handsome, young MP soon showed that he had an intellect as clearcut as his profile. When the Liberal membership in the Commons slumped to six in 1951, Grimond more than doubled his own majority and increased it again in 1955.

He was only 43 when he was elected on November 5, 1956, to succeed Clement Davies as leader of the party. Having committed his party within a few days to opposing the government's Suez policy and to support of the Common Market, he threw himself into making Liberalism a political force to be reckoned with. Under his impetus the attention paid to his party improved and its victory at the Torrington by-election in 1958 was hailed as setting the seal on his endeavours to project a vigorous, youthful image of Liberalism, especially among the newer generation of voters.

As leader of the party he set up the Liberal Research Department and collected a very able team of young research workers who drew together a large number of outside advisers and academics to help the party prepare a modern programme. Grimond did much to take the Liberal party away from the old, rather negative laissez-faire type of Liberalism which still hung on under Clement Davies's leadership. He put his own views together in his books, *The Liberal Future* (1959) and *The Liberal Challenge* (1963) and, though few of these policy departures affected national thinking, they certainly increased the relevance of the Liberal party.

He was sworn a member of the Privy Council in October 1961 – a belated recognition by the Conservative government of his widely acknowledged position as a public figure. Five months later, in March 1962, the Liberals astonished everybody, including themselves, by capturing the safe seat of Orpington from the Conservatives at a by-election which came to be hailed as a political portent of high significance for Grimond and his party. A sharp upward swing of Liberal votes at other by-elections followed.

Grimond aroused the party assembly in September 1963 to its highest pitch of fervour and he realised that the forthcoming general election would be crucial. He was convinced that a Labour party committed to doctrinaire socialism had a poor future. Given a Labour defeat in the coming election, he foresaw the possibility of a realignment of the left, the socialist element splitting off and leaving room for the emergence of a radical party relieved of socialist dogma. In such a party Liberals could play a major part.

In the event, the outcome of the election – a Labour overall majority of four – was about the worst possible result for Grimond. Had Harold Wilson been prepared to make an arrangement with the Liberals, his majority would have been much more secure. But to attempt to form a broad social democratic and radical front was not in Wilson's make-up. Nor was there anything Grimond could do to bring it about. The

1964 general election was a terrible blow to Grimond's ambitions for his party, as he recognised. Between 1964 and 1966 he saw no tactical or strategic role for the Liberals. His resignation as party leader in 1967, to be succeeded by Jeremy Thorpe, could, therefore, be seen as a resignation in the face of failure. It was fortunate that he lived to witness the launch of the Alliance in 1981, a consequence of the process he had foreseen. If Roy Jenkins founded the Alliance, Jo Grimond was its prophet.

He had a very successful and happy period as Rector of Edinburgh University and in 1971 was appointed chairman of the review body to report on the role, constitution and functioning of Birmingham University. He also enjoyed and worked very hard at his long-held position as Chancellor of the University of Kent. But whenever the rumours of other occupations surfaced he could say: "I enjoy politics, I enjoy the House of Commons, I enjoy my constituency."

Grimond continued his work inside and outside the House but he was ageing a little. Colleagues noticed his increased isolation (partly through deafness) though he could, and did, still make effective speeches and remained persuasive on television. Then, when public speculation about Jeremy Thorpe drove him to resign in 1976, it was clearly necessary for the Liberals to restore confidence.

There was heavy pressure on Grimond to return to the leadership but he refused to act for more than a limited number of months until the new machinery devised by the Liberal party to involve active members was able to produce a leader. Grimond's seniority and the great respect in which he was held helped to tide over the few months until David Steel was elected and he resumed the life of a private MP.

At the Llandudno Liberal assembly in 1981, together with Shirley Williams, Roy Jenkins and David Steel, he addressed a meeting of some 2,000 people and it was at this point that the Alliance took off. His gifts as a popular orator were seldom better displayed than at the Hillhead by-election of 1982 when, in support of the victorious Roy Jenkins, he addressed a succession of huge meetings in Glasgow. His abilities to persuade and to "play" a large audience were brilliantly exhibited.

In many ways, the 1980s saw the political mainstream catch up with Grimond's long-held political ideas. In the 1950s and 1960s his call for the Liberal party to become a radical, non-socialist alternative to the Tories was a cry in the wilderness (collectivism and state intervention then still retained their ascendancy in Britain). But the collapse of communism, the internal turmoil of the Labour party and the rise of "new right" thinkers such as Milton Friedman gave his views new force. For a time he even joined with Thatcherites like Lord Tebbit in founding the Radical Society. He was a fierce critic of the state socialism nurtured, he felt, by both Tory and Labour governments. He was, therefore, a supporter of Margaret Thatcher's early years in office from 1979, carrying – as they intitially seemed to – the promise of some sort of return to 19th-century liberal and, indeed, Liberal values. He soon, however, became disillusioned with Mrs Thatcher. The rapid increase in inflation during the early part of Sir Geoffrey Howe's period as Chancellor tarnished her government's image as a battler against inflation, an evil which Grimond saw as public enemy number one.

Equally serious in his eyes was her failure to tackle bureaucracy, her centralising tendencies and, perhaps worst of all, the tawdriness and what he saw as the unfairness of the society that was being created. For, like the 19th-century Liberals, Grimond had a strong sense of morality. For him Liberalism and morality went hand in hand. Writing in 1980, he gave warning of the threats to decent liberal society: "Tolerance, respect, care for other things than power, all that goes to make civilisation, are under attack."

His move in 1983 to the House of Lords kept him on the sidelines of politics. He described the Lords as "the old folks home," but he enjoyed his time there. Freed of the frustrations of having to deal with constituents, he was able to devote more time to other interests. A feature of Grimond's life was his civilised style and his affection for what had started as his constituency home, the Old Manse of Firth in Orkney. He had a remarkable eye for paintings, was a keen gardener and in Orkney, where he continued to live part of the year after ceasing to be its MP, was much concerned with local affairs as well as with Scottish and national questions.

He continued to attend the House of Lords (in which he spoke only last week) but in the past year was much taken up with looking after his wife Laura, following the severe stroke she suffered in 1992. She survives him together with two sons and one daughter, one son having predeceased him.

* * *

SIR MATT BUSBY

The best manager British football ever produced, who rebuilt
Manchester United after the Munich air crash

21 JANUARY 1994

SIR MATTHEW BUSBY WAS often described as the best manager British football has ever produced. During his reign Manchester United was more than a household name; it was a world-wide name.

Much of his fame derived, rightly, from the team's skill and success but a great deal was due, it was sometimes said, to Busby's great talent for public relations. It is true that no club's image had ever been more carefully and deliberately nurtured than that of Manchester United, that no players had their claims more persistently or persuasively put forward than those of Manchester United.

Busby's genius for making friends in the media, and for not making enemies within the game, also protected those around him when things went badly – 'slow to chide and quick to bless' was a line from a famous hymn that well described the popular attitude to Busby's club.

He was a fine player for his club and his country. But a few have been better. As a tactician he was unexceptional; other men carried through the revolution in styles of the 1960s. Busby contented himself with largely playing to the old theories, and merely sought better players to carry them out. Other managers proved themselves better at buying players; yet others showed themselves his equal in developing young prospects, and a few managed to win nearly as many trophies. It was never his success that stood out, but his style; not his competence, but his warmth.

His secret as a manager resided in his relationships with his players. It stretches no truth to suggest that Busby created with his teams the sort of relationship men would wish to have with their sons. Calmly protective and understanding towards them, he was repaid with a fierce loyalty.

His refusal to deal with players' transgressions in a public way earned him, from time to time, accusations of being "soft". Critics who leapt to this too-easy conclusion did not know of the confrontations in Busby's office. Then his tongue could be sharp and his warnings could never be ignored. The final sentence was usually: "Right, son, the fine is £200 – and it's double that if a word about this ever appears in a newspaper."

Busby's love for football, and especially of good footballers, was his life. It was with no trace of embarrassment that in a speech, when awarded the freedom of Manchester, he spoke of the "wonder, romance and mystery of a game ... that on great occasions is larger than life." Football shaped his character just as much as it made his name.

It was, to begin with, his escape from the constricting and deprived life of a miner. Matthew Busby was born into the colliery community of Bellshill, Scotland. He was only six when his father was killed by a sniper's bullet at Arras and as a teenager Busby was to join his kin down the mine. "There were only two ways for boys to go in those days," he later recalled, "down, working in the pits, or up if you happened to be good at football." Busby was good at football, like two other Bellshill boys Alex James and Hughie Gallagher, and the well-organised system of Scottish junior football reached out to start him moving up.

From Scottish junior football he graduated to Manchester City, becoming a distinguished right-half of the City team of the early 1930s

— distinguished, that is, by a habit of creative football that he was never to abandon. But he was determined as well as artistic, and having played in the 1933 side that lost a Cup Final to Everton he was a powerful influence on the City team that returned to Wembley a year later and gained the trophy by beating Portsmouth. That year, too, he won his only "full" international cap.

The honours were accumulating only slowly at his door, although after joining Liverpool in 1936 he remained a model player and during the curious hiatus of the war years he was to be a regular member of the Scottish team that fought many splendid battles with England in a series that the record books ignore. Matt Busby got his chance to gain the honours that the world could scarcely fail to recognise in 1946 when, upon his demobilisation, he was appointed manager of Manchester United. Little about the circumstances surrounding his appointment suggested what was to follow: Old Trafford, the club ground, had been badly damaged by enemy action, and "home" matches had to be played elsewhere. The club was £15,000 in debt, and most of United's better players were still scattered in the forces.

He was soon into his stride, adding to a nucleus of prewar players with finds of his own to create a team that finished runners-up in the three postwar championships, and winning the FA Cup in 1948. Busby's United won the league title in 1952, did so again in 1956 and thereupon made history by ignoring official disapproval and entering themselves for the European Cup.

That decision to play where no other English team had played before was a fateful move in every sense. It led to United becoming Britain's best-known, best-loved club, it led eventually to supreme honour in becoming champions of Europe in 1968. But it led via a tragic route. In February 1958, the aeroplane carrying Manchester United back from a European Cup match in Belgrade crashed on take-off at Munich. Eight of his players, famous youngsters such as Edwards, an England player at 18, and Whelan and Coleman, together with senior players like Taylor and Byrne, died in the crash.

Busby himself was severely injured. It took the breeding of a miner and the constitution of a professional athlete to pull him through a crisis. During the weeks of recovery his deputy, Jimmy Murphy, assembled a scratch side of survivors and replacements and carried on to the FA Cup final at Wembley. And there, with Busby, hobbling to the touchline, United lost. Munich had ended the lifespan of the two great United teams created by Busby. Simply, he began again and built a third. It meant buying talented players like Law and Crerand, searching out others like Best and Stiles. It meant a patient wait, but only until 1963 for victory in the FA Cup and until 1965 and then 1967 for the League Championship. There were setbacks in failures to snatch the European trophy that Busby felt he owed to himself – and to his dead team. But that finally came in 1968 when, in extra time at Wembley, Busby rallied a tired team to beat Benfica. Twenty years to get there, the one thing that mattered most. His knighthood later that year was the icing on the cake and after one more year he began to relinquish control. He was succeeded by Frank O'Farrell in 1971.

Yet he stayed on at Old Trafford as a director from 1971, a genial welcoming figure, deliberately not becoming involved in the everyday problems, successes and crises. "Manchester United is now O'Farrell's job" he would say. Yet it was still, somehow, Busby's club. He never quite succeeded in becoming a mere figurehead.

His wife Jean, whom he married in 1931, died in 1988. One son and one daughter survive him, four sons having predeceased him.

JOHN SMITH

Labour's lost Prime Minister who was a formidable shadow
Chancellor and helped make his party electable

13 MAY 1994

LIKE HUGH GAITSKELL 30 YEARS AGO, John Smith seems destined to go down in his own party's folklore as Labour's lost Prime Minister. He died at a time when his party was leading the Government by 20 points and more in the opinion polls, when his own standing easily out-ranked that of John Major and after Labour had just inflicted on the Conservative Party its most crushing defeat in local government elections since the Second World War.

He himself was quietly convinced that after the next general election he would enter No 10 and had already started laying his plans for the formation of his government. He may never have possessed the more colourful political gifts but in terms of positioning his party for office – and of persuading the electorate that Labour no longer posed any dangerous threat – he had built upon and consolidated the work achieved by his predecessor, Neil Kinnock, in his nine years as party leader.

Yet from the moment, just short of two years ago, that John Smith was massively elected to the Labour leadership, he had not had an entirely easy ride. By deliberately choosing to play a long game, he disappointed not only the media but some of his own supporters. Only perhaps last September when he staked his leadership on winning his victory at the party conference on the issue of "one member, one vote" did his critics begin to reconsider their initial estimate of him as an Edinburgh lawyer with altogether too narrow a background to appeal to the whole country. He was certainly every inch a product of the Scottish Labour Party establishment and this tended to give his leadership of the party less of a radical cutting edge even than some of his closer associates would have liked.

Ironically, however, it was his own essentially redistributive tax proposals that played at least some part in blunting Labour's appeal to middle-class voters at the last election. The lesson was not lost on Smith – and one aspect of his leadership that attracted hostile comment was the almost total lack of economic content in Labour's policy proposals. But that fitted his cautious nature. He was not just a Scot, he prided himself on being a canny one, too.

John Smith was a West Highlander, and his background could stand as a model of Scottish self-improvement. He was the only son – there were two younger sisters – of the village schoolmaster at Ardrishaig, at the Loch Fyne end of the Crinan Canal. It was a cultured home, where strict rules and high moral standards, including assumptions about social morality, were taken for granted.

As with many children brought up in the Highlands, secondary schooling meant leaving home to go into lodgings in the nearest town of any size. Smith went to Dunoon Grammar School where he lodged in the town with a landlady, going home only during the holidays. Then came Glasgow University, where he was recognised as an outstanding student, even in a period which in retrospect came to assume something of the appearance of a golden age. His generation produced a rich crop of graduates on their way to the top in politics and elsewhere, and talent rubbed off on talent (at least one of his contemporaries, Donald Dewar, was later to sit with him in the shadow Cabinet). It was a fruitful period for debating as well – in 1962 Smith, with another Glasgow student, won *The Observer* mace awarded every year to the best student debaters in the United Kingdom.

His political ambition was obvious early on – he stood as an unsuccessful parliamentary Labour candidate at a by-election in East Fife while he was still a student – but first he had to earn a living. Having trained and indeed practised (for a year) as a solicitor he determined to be called to the Scottish Bar. It was perhaps the first sign that he saw his future as being a public, rather than a private, figure. But it was still a high-risk gamble; the Edinburgh Bar was regarded then as even more of a closed shop than its English counterpart. He also acquired a job, during his unpaid period of "devilling," as a newspaper libel lawyer, reading for both the *Daily Record* and its sister paper, the *Sunday Mail*.

But Smith's real aspirations still remained for politics. After an abortive effort to gain the Labour nomination for a by-election in the Glasgow seat of Rutherglen in 1963, he fought East Fife again in the general election of 1964, once more easily being defeated by the sitting Tory. But at the 1970 general election he was elected MP for North Lanarkshire. When Labour returned to office in 1974, Harold Wilson at once offered him the post of Solicitor-General for Scotland – an unexpected mark of recognition as Smith had never been a member of the Opposition front bench. Smith, however, refused the Prime Minister's invitation on the ground that he did not want to be "parked in a legal byway". It was perhaps the first overt indication that in politics he would always believe in playing the game long. In any event, despite his own premonition that it would wreck his ministerial prospects, the refusal did him no harm. A few months later he started his front bench career in a job which took him much nearer the centre of the political stage, as Under-Secretary at the Department of Energy. He took up the appointment at a crucial period when North Sea oil was becoming a reality and Smith was effectively in charge of the award of North Sea concessions.

American oil tycoons soon discovered that they were up against an extremely tough negotiator in Smith. He may not have had the in-built automatic hostility of the far left to big business, but he saw oil as a national asset that should yield tangible rewards to be shared equitably. In 1976 he was appointed deputy to Michael Foot at the Privy Council Office. Foot had been given responsibility for the Labour Government's proposals on Scottish and Welsh devolution which, after two attempts to get an unamended Bill through Parliament, eventually ran into the ground on the joint Scottish and Welsh referendums of March 1979. The issue, however, was one of the liveliest and most contentious of the 1970s. It was Smith's handling from the Treasury bench of the complexities of the devolution legislation that really made his name as a formidable parliamentary performer.

In 1978 James Callaghan, who in April 1976 had succeeded Wilson as Prime Minister, promoted Smith to a full department of his own as Secretary of State for Trade. At 40, two months younger than David Owen, he was the youngest member of the Cabinet. Presiding over his largely technical department, his command of detail was legendary. "You know," he would say dryly, "I have actually *read* the General Agreement on Tariffs and Trade." But the Labour Government had not long to run. When the Conservatives returned to power in 1979 under Margaret Thatcher, Smith went first a little into the shadows. He could not, however, entirely avoid being drawn into the internal struggle then going on – and he was a leading organiser for Denis Healey in his successful effort to repulse Tony Benn's bid for the deputy leadership in 1981. Two years later he was Roy Hattersley's campaign manager in his leadership contest against Neil Kinnock of 1983. This formed a bond between the two men which was shortly to pay a substantial political dividend. Although Hattersley heavily lost the leadership battle, he did become deputy leader and shadow Chancellor – enabling him in 1987, when he gave up the shadow chancellorship and reverted to being shadow Home Secretary, to insist that his successor as shadow Chancellor must be John Smith. This was really Smith's moment of breakthrough into the big political league.

Once he became shadow Chancellor, he was immediately recognised by Nigel Lawson (his opposite number until October 1989) as the most formidable of any of the successive opponents he had faced from the Opposition front bench. A measure of the impact he had made was the sense of despair that seized the whole of the Labour Party when, in the weekend after the party conference of 1988, he suffered his first heart attack. If he had not fallen victim to it when already attending an Edinburgh hospital for a check-up, it is more than possible that he might not have survived.

As it was, he considered his options – freely admitting that the thought of abandoning politics had gone through his mind – but decided instead to throw himself back into the Westminster fray. He knew, of course, that he was a pivotal figure in Labour's effort, after its disappointing 1987 election result, to climb the hill of recovery. As if to symbolise that, he himself immediately started climbing mountains. By the time of his death the Leader of the Opposition had succeeded in climbing 108 "Munros" (mountains higher than 3,000 feet).

The years of his shadow chancellorship were not always comfortable ones for Smith. Correctly loyal to Neil Kinnock, there was never any real rapport between them – something that publicly surfaced over the famous affair of the Luigi's Restaurant dinner party for journalists given by Kinnock just three months before the 1992 general election. Here Labour's then leader insisted that his party's proposals for increases in national insurance charges would not neccesarily take immediate effect once Labour came to power but might well be "phased in". Smith, who was determined that Labour should give an impression of total fiscal rectitude, was appalled – and a serious fissure seemed to have opened up between the party Leader and his chief economic spokesman. Revealingly or not, it was resolved wholly in Smith's favour.

If there was criticism of Smith from within the Kinnock camp, it tended to concentrate on his being too "laid back," of not being around when there was real work to be done. This was almost certainly unfair, and was never taken very seriously even by the PLP, as was shown by his triumphant victory in the leadership election. Smith cleaned up in all three sections of the electoral college but nowhere more decisively than among Labour MPs. The truth was that he was a parliamentarian par excellence – a master of wit, mockery and, when required, sheer invective. But, barrister that he was, his speeches were carefully crafted performances and he never really found the instant tennis match of Prime Minister's Questions to his taste – though he had latterly got better even at that.

In his own way, he was an old-fashioned figure, never wholly at home in the modern world of the sound-bite and the papier-mâché politics of the television studio. But what no one doubted he possessed was gravitas – and that might well have proved his greatest asset in the general election he was never to be permitted to fight as Labour's Leader. With his firm belief in morality in politics and the need for total integrity in public life he himself might well have found some wry consolation in the fact that, like W. E. Gladstone 96 years before him, he should have died on Ascension Day – for there was always a firm basis of Christianity to both his political and his economic outlook.

John Smith is survived by his wife Elizabeth, whom he married in 1967, and by three daughters.

* * *

LORD LOVAT

Landowner, Highland chief and soldier, who founded the commandos

17 MARCH 1995

LORD LOVAT, WHO HAS DIED a year after the death of his estranged eldest son, was the most romantic of all the Highland lairds. A legendary figure in the Second World War, he played a key role in the development of the commandos and was actively involved in both the Dieppe Raid of 1942 and the D-Day landings of June 1944. Greatly admired by Winston Churchill, he appeared at the end of the war to have a political career at his feet; but he preferred to return to his native land to resume charge of his Scottish estates, which prospered under his direction before he disastrously made them over to his eldest son in 1965. The last year of Lovat's life was clouded by tragedy – his youngest son Andrew being gored to death by a buffalo on a safari in Tanzania ten days before the death of his eldest brother in March 1994.

Simon Christopher Joseph Fraser was himself the elder son of the 16th Lord Lovat, KT. As a Roman Catholic he was educated at Ampleforth, going on to Magdalen College, Oxford. His father died in 1933 while attending, as a spectator, the New College and Magdalen point-to-point, in which he had just seen his son win the Old Members' Challenge Cup for the second time.

Thus as a young man, only recently of age, the young Lovat found himself facing the responsiblity of administering a large landed estate, then about 190,000 acres. Fortunately his father's two major interests, agriculture and soldiering, were also his and he carried on the dual tradition for the remainder of his life. For a time he was a regular officer in the Scots Guards but later, feeling the need to remain nearer his land, he served in the territorial cavalry regiment originally raised by his family, the Lovat Scouts.

He was with the regiment when war broke out in 1939, commanding a squadron with the rank of captain. Even then it was clear that he had inherited the gifts which had made his father a distinguished soldier. The drastic overhaul of organisation and training, which was undertaken after Dunkirk, resulted in, among other things, the formation of the Special Service Brigade, out of which sprang the commandos. Lovat was an obvious choice for command in this new type of unit – as also was his friend, the late Duke of Wellington, who was killed while leading his men at the landing at Salerno in 1943.

As 1941 wore on, the raids increased in scale and scope; Bruneval and St Nazaire were attacked and by the spring of 1942 it was felt that a raid on an altogether larger scale ought to be executed with a view to getting a great deal of information, not only concerning the state of the German coastal defences but also about the state of battle training of our own troops.

Thus came about the Dieppe Raid in which, despite the overall disaster of the enterprise, Lovat and his commandos signally distinguished themselves. It was for his part in the action that he was awarded the DSO. His foot was now well on the ladder of promotion and by 1943 he had attained the rank of brigadier. He led his commando brigade ashore on the coast of Normandy soon after dawn on D-Day, having told them before they sailed: "We have been given a proud task and I expect this brigade to fight in such a manner that your children and your children's children will say, 'They were men; they were giants in those days'." They went into battle led by a piper, but their gallant commander, who moved his headquarters with his own forward troops often within 100 yards of the enemy, was so seriously wounded that he had to be evacuated to England.

When he recovered Churchill sent him as one of a parliamentary delegation to the Kremlin. Quoting Byron, Churchill wrote to Stalin that he was sending him in Lord Lovat "the mildest-mannered man that ever scuttled ship or cut a throat". Churchill also offered him the post of Captain of the Gentlemen-at-Arms – or Chief Whip in the House of Lords – as the prelude to a political career; but Lovat declined the offer and, although he later accepted office as Under-Secretary of State for Foreign Affairs, he resigned on the defeat of the Caretaker Government in July 1945, preferring to leave national politics to his younger brother, the late Sir Hugh Fraser, MP.

After the end of hostilities Lovat, a DL and JP, returned to his farming interests and served for a record 42 years as an elected member of Inverness County Council. He was a lively pioneer of farming developments in the Highlands, using New World cattle ranching methods. He transformed the Lovat estates and at one stage had 35,000 acres in hand: the largest single farming unit of the kind in Britain.

Lovat was especially interested in the Shorthorn breed and was one of the best-known judges at the national shows here and overseas. As chairman of the Anglo-Scottish Cattle Company his aim was to encourage the improvement of stock at home and abroad by using better bulls for grading up less good cattle and producing more early maturing quality steers to feed the hungry people of the world.

A traditional Catholic and a Knight of Malta, he was made a Knight Commander of St Gregory with Star by the Pope in 1982. "Shimi" Lovat – the name was traditional for the chief of the clan Fraser – was also a renowned big-game hunter, and was chairman of the Shikar Club, which holds an annual dinner for those who have sought adventure in lonely places. In 1978 he published his memoirs in a book entitled *March Past*, of which Bernard Fergusson (Lord Ballantrae) wrote: "It combines a rugged and honourable refusal to accept the low standards of a changing world with passages of great beauty and sensitivity." He never forgot for a moment his duties as *Mac Shimidh*, hereditary chief of Clan Fraser of Lovat, well aware that "Frasers far afield in Toronto or Brisbane, Chicago or Wellington, can find in their history those roots that give them identity and distinguish them from being merely numbered ants in some enormous, urban anthill".

Lovat was, above all, a *grand seigneur* in the finest sense; as well as being what a perceptive commentator called "by far the best looking of all the Highland chiefs".

He married in 1938 Rosamond, the only daughter of Sir John Delves Broughton, Bt, who survives him together with two of his four sons and two daughters.

* * *

ALEC DOUGLAS-HOME, LORD HOME OF THE HIRSEL

Prime Minister and Foreign Secretary, who claimed he used matchsticks to aid his economic calculations

10 OCTOBER 1995

OCCUPYING NO 10 FOR A SHORTER TIME than any other Prime Minister this century, save for Bonar Law, Alec Douglas-Home may well be remembered as the unlucky Prime Minister. He had the misfortune to come to the highest office after the Conservatives had been in Government for a dozen years, using up three previous Prime Ministers in the process. Not surprisingly, there was a widespread feeling that it was time for a change. On a more personal level, he had immediately to make the adjustment, which he did not find easy, from the quieter, more courteous atmosphere of the House of Lords to the bear-pit of the Commons – something which he had not experienced since his involuntary recruitment to the Upper House 12 years earlier.

His selection as Prime Minister had been engineered by his predecessor. The role that Harold Macmillan played in October 1963 effectively destroyed the royal prerogative of the monarch choosing the nation's First Minister, at least from within a single party, and saw to it that Lord Home was the last Tory leader to emerge by what used to be known as "the customary processes of consultation".

Many Conservatives maintained that the party would have done better under R. A. Butler's leadership. Yet it should not be overlooked that in October 1963 Home took over a Government whose morale was shattered and whose standing in the opinion polls was abysmal. A year later Labour won the general election, with an overall majority of only four seats. That the new Prime Minister recovered so much ground in so short a time was in itself an achievement.

Home had two weaknesses as Prime Minister. He had no expertise in economic matters: indeed, he had joked in a newspaper interview, before any thought of the premiership occurred to him, that he did his sums with matchsticks (a confession Harold Wilson never allowed him to forget). He was also not at ease, and did not look his best, on television. As a TV make-up lady once brutally told him, he had the misfortune to possess a head that came across on the screen looking like a skull.

Throughout his career, though, he possessed the enviable gift of inspiring trust in those who served under him: it was Margaret Thatcher who in June this year called him "the best Prime Minister to work with that I have ever known". He knew how to run a government. He did not try to perform the work of his departmental ministers. He had courage in the big things, and the judgment to know which things were big. In his two spells as Foreign Secretary, he displayed a firm grasp of large issues and a conspicuous independence of mind. The fear that he might simply, in that office, be a yes-man to Macmillan proved to be totally unfounded – on African policy in particular Home was far to the right of Macmillan; and somewhat surprisingly he emerged as the darling of the party conference. After standing down as Prime Minister he was, for almost five years, Edward Heath's Shadow Foreign Secretary before returning to the Foreign Office in June 1970 where he remained throughout the Heath administration until March 1974.

He brought to the office once again his capacity for straight talking, for toughness towards the Soviet Union and for firmness (sometimes interpreted as a lack of sympathy) towards the countries of Africa and Asia. But he brought something else as well: an unusual degree of international respect. Harold Wilson had mocked him as "the 14th Earl" (though Home got his own back by modestly murmuring on television: "I suppose Mr Wilson is really, when you come to think of it, the 14th Mr Wilson"), but in the event Home's unmistakable patrician air strengthened the impression of a disinterested detachment.

Alexander Frederick Douglas-Home, Baron Home of the Hirsel, former 14th Earl of Home in the peerage of Scotland and Baron Douglas in the peerage of the United Kingdom, was born at 28 South Street, Mayfair, the eldest son of Lord Dunglass who in 1918 became the 13th Earl of Home. He spent his childhood among a family of five brothers – one of whom was the playwright, William Douglas-Home – and two sisters at Coldstream in the Scottish Border country, where he developed a love of country pursuits, particularly fishing and shooting, which he was never to lose.

At Eton, where Cyril Connolly famously recalled him as being "honourably ineligible for the struggles of life" he was one of those apparently effortlessly successful boys who combine popularity with more tangible achievements. He became president of Pop and played cricket for the XI, scoring 66 against Harrow at Lord's in 1922. At Oxford, where he was up at Christ Church, he got only a third in history but played for the university on a number of occasions, though without getting his Blue.

His political career began in 1929 when he stood unsuccessfully in the safe Labour constituency of Coatbridge in Lanarkshire. Two years later he was elected as Unionist MP for South Lanark, the constituency he was to represent for the next 14 years as Lord Dunglass. Almost immediately he became Parliamentary Private Secretary to the Under-Secretary of State for Scotland, and in 1935 he was switched to be PPS to the Parliamentary Under-Secretary at the Ministry of Labour.

His first big step forward came the following year when Neville Chamberlain, then Chancellor of the Exchequer and due to become Prime Minister within a matter of months, chose Dunglass as his PPS. He stayed with Chamberlain until the latter's retirement from office, went with him to the final meeting with Hitler in Munich and was an active supporter of the appeasement policy – a fact which, however unpopular in later years, he never attempted to obscure. While criticising Chamberlain for the naivety of his claim that the agreement with Hitler meant "peace for our time", Home maintained in later years that it had, nonetheless, brought a breathing space that was essential for Britain.

After Chamberlain's retirement he went on active service as a major with the Lanarkshire Yeomanry in which he had been commissioned in 1924. Soon, however, he fell ill with tuberculosis of the spine and after a delicate operation had to spend two years on his back in plaster.

It was not until 1943 that he was able to return to the House of Commons and subsequently attracted notice again with a vigorous attack on the Yalta Agreement. In May 1945 he was appointed Joint Parliamentary Under-Secretary of State for Foreign Affairs in Churchill's short-lived "caretaker" administration. He was defeated at the general election that summer and spent the next five years concentrating mostly on local and Scottish affairs. In 1950 he won back his seat in South Lanark, but the following year had to move up to the House of Lords on the death of his father. Following the 1951 general election he was, for the next four years, Minister of State for Scotland.

When Anthony Eden succeeded to the premiership in April 1955 Home became Secretary of State for Commonwealth Relations during a period which saw the Suez crisis and Macmillan's declaration of the "wind of change". Home remained to the general public a shadowy figure, whose personality had made little impact. As Foreign Secretary in 1960 he created quite a different impression, speaking on numerous occasions of the need for a firm and realistic attitude towards the Soviet Union. In the Cuban crisis he showed that his strength of purpose was not confined to his rhetoric. Yet in his negotiations on the future of Berlin and disarmament he demonstrated his capacity for diplomatic flexibility. On the most critical foreign policy initiative of those years, however – the application to join the European Economic Community – Home's role was limited to that of the loyal team player.

On October 10, 1963, Macmillan was forced by ill-health to get Home to read a letter to the Conservative Party conference at Blackpool intimating his intention to resign. It seemed at first that there were just three possible successors: Butler, Lord Hailsham and Reginald Maudling.

Hailsham's excitable manner, however, made many people question his judgment. The Tory Right strongly resisted the choice of Butler, and Maudling was considered too young. Home impressed the conference, and there was an understandable appeal in a possible successor whose instinctive dignity was beyond question. At the eleventh hour, in an attempt to stop Home, the other two main contenders agreed to unite behind Butler.

It was because of these manoeuvres and uncertainties that Home, whose nerve almost entirely failed him early on the Friday morning, at first did not accept the Queen's commission but informed her only that he would see if he could form a government. Had the other contenders, especially Butler, declined to serve under him it is unlikely that he could, or would, have tried to go ahead. But they all eventually agreed to come in and on the next day – Saturday, October 19 – the 14th Earl of Home became the first peer to be Prime Minister since the days of the 3rd Marquess of Salisbury at the beginning of the century.

Macmillan and his friends always maintained that Home was unquestionably the choice of the party. But the episode left behind a residue of bitterness. Home had put himself forward, alongside the Lord Chancellor, Lord Dilhorne, as one of the two colleagues who could be consulted freely by the others as they were not themselves candidates. This was seen by some as a commitment from which Home should have sought to be released before agreeing to be a candidate.

Iain Macleod subsequently wrote a famous article in *The Spectator*, of which he had become Editor, alleging that the choice had been made by a small social elite within the party. It was a damaging, divisive charge which convinced Home that no succeeding Conservative leader should ever be put in the position where his claim to office was questioned by his own party.

There then began what may be regarded in many respects as the climax of his career. He was the elder statesman, once more in charge of foreign affairs for the Conservatives, but more honoured than ever before. He had a claim now upon the affections of his party and the country which no office could bestow. His term in the highest office, however, lasted less than a year before the Conservatives faced a general election that they narrowly lost.

Home's second spell as Foreign Secretary was from 1970 to 1974. He became the first British Foreign Secretary to visit China since Palmerston. He attempted to negotiate a Rhodesian settlement, which might have avoided guerrilla warfare in that country, though it came to nothing when a commission under the chairmanship of Lord Pearce found that it was unacceptable to African opinion. Perhaps, though, the most characteristic episode of this second stewardship was the expulsion of 105 named individuals from the Soviet Embassy for spying: a firm and typical action taken with deliberation.

His weaknesses as well as his strengths were evident in his attitude towards Scottish devolution down the years. As a Scotsman who sat for a Scottish constituency and whose home was in Scotland, he was peculiarly well placed to sense the mood of the Scottish people. He judged that some greater decentralisation of power from Westminster to Edinburgh was needed.

This made him a supporter in principle of a measure of parliamentary devolution within the United Kingdom. But his attempts to put that principle into practice were never happy. In 1968 Heath made what became known as his "Declaration of Perth" in which he called for an elected Scottish assembly. Home was then invited to chair a committee of distinguished men and women to put flesh on the bones of this proposal. The committee suggested that there should be a directly elected Scottish Convention in Edinburgh that would take the second reading, committee and report stages of those Scottish Bills referred to it by Parliament. No solutions were provided to the problems that would occur if the majority in the House of Commons were of a different political persuasion from the majority in the convention. Subsequently Home supported the Labour Government's devolution proposals, but then retracted, saying that a future Conservative government would offer a better scheme – which it never did. It was not an impressive episode in his career, though he later assured *The Times* that it had always been his intention to deliver for Scotland.

After the defeat of the Heath Government in the February 1974 election Home announced his retirement from the Conservative front bench and he did not stand for the House of Commons again in the second (October) election of that year. On becoming Prime Minister in 1963 he had disclaimed his peerages, taken the title of Sir Alec Douglas-Home and stood for election in the by-election that was pending in Kinross and West Perthshire. He won the seat with a substantially increased majority and held it comfortably until his retirement from the Commons.

A life peerage, as Lord Home of the Hirsel, was then conferred upon him. Although his active political life was over, he continued to make characteristically trenchant contributions to public debate, especially on international affairs, in the House of Lords and elsewhere. In 1976 he published his autobiography, *The Way The Wind Blows* (which Rab Butler dismissed as "a book about fishing"). His other publications included *Border Reflections* (1979) and *Letters to a Grandson* (1983).

Home was sworn of the Privy Council in 1951 and was created a Knight of the Thistle in 1962. He became Chancellor of that Order in 1973, only retiring from the office in 1992 after suffering a stroke. From 1966 until 1977 he served as the first Chancellor of Heriot-Watt University, in 1966-67 he was president of the MCC, and in his later years many other honours were bestowed upon him.

In 1936 he married Elizabeth Hester, daughter of the Very Rev Cyril Alington, sometime Dean of Durham and Head Master of Eton. She died in 1990. They had one son and three daughters. The earldom, which Home had renounced for his lifetime, now passes to his son, David Alexander Cospatrick Douglas-Home, chairman of Morgan Grenfell International, who in 1963 discontinued the use of his courtesy title of Lord Dunglass.

* * *

NORMAN MacCAIG

Poet whose whimsical work belied the depth of feeling of a 'real' poet

24 JANUARY 1996

NORMAN MacCAIG WAS ONE OF THE most important Scottish poets of this century. Unlike his compatriot, Sorley MacLean, he was never tempted to experiment in Gaelic. Nor was he particularly avant-garde in his use of rhyme or metre. During certain parts of his writing career, indeed, he wrote in quite a conventional manner. But mostly, he worked a creative middle ground between the traditional and the experimental.

Like John Donne, his formative influence, he was essentially a love poet, but not just in the romantic or erotic sense. He also wrote about the environment he knew and loved best: Edinburgh, and the Scottish countryside around Assynt, in southwest Sutherland, where he spent every summer. He dug deep in search not just of his own roots but of common human roots. His poems evoked a world of water and stone, small lochs, city streets at night, and among other enthusiasms – "grasshoppers, fishes, snails and me".

Norman Alexander MacCaig was born in Edinburgh and educated at the Royal High School and at Edinburgh University. His first book of poems was *Far Cry*, published by Routledge (as were all his earlier works) in 1943. Before that, his only substantial appearance in print had been in the anthology *The White Horseman*, edited by his fellow Celts J. F. Hendry and Henry Treece. His nine poems were no better or worse than most of the other contributions. He continued his apprenticeship in the clotted verse of *The Inward Eye*, published in 1946.

If the story had ended there, it would have been forgotten. MacCaig was, after all, 36 years old at the time of the publishing of *The Inward Eye*, and one could have assumed that his ways were set. A critical verdict then might have set him down as an incurable rhapsodist, a writer of incantatory rubbish. Times change, though, and poets grow up and recover from their first few bouts of language. After the Second World War – during which he was a conscientious objector – MacCaig was employed as a teacher in primary schools in Edinburgh. At the same time he worked away, refining the richness of his early outpourings, simplifying an almost irritable alertness of the senses in the interests of clearer communication. The poems in *Riding Lights* (1955) marked the emergence of a new poet. He was, as one critic remarked, the man who put the *me* in metaphysics. But the early verbal surface, as thick as glue and only slightly less gelatinous, was gone for ever. *Riding Lights* and *The Sinai Sort* (published by Hogarth in 1957, as were all his subsequent publications) showed a tougher intellectual manner. These were confident, clever, rhetorical poems, committed to the thoroughly Donneish notion that "hard feeling is true exercise for wit", and finding far-fetched ways to break straws with the best of them.

The poems in these books, however intricately fashioned, never give a sense of insincerity, but they do tend to talk to themselves somewhat exclusively, posing a number of questions that are elegant rather than urgent. *Poem for a Goodbye* and *Gifts* stand as MacCaig's best work from this time. They were poems with a pressure of lived experience behind them, carefully patterned shapes of sound and image where the very care seemed to test the gravity of what is being said. It was work like this that Edwin Muir was thinking of when he announced of MacCaig: "He is a *real* poet."

Six books followed during the 1960s: *A Common Grace* (1960), *A Round of Applause* (1962), *Measures* (1965), *Surroundings* (1966), *Rings on a Tree* (1968) and *A Man in My Position* (1969). Each book saw the poet growing less complicated, less ceremonious, less tense. The process looked like a gradual maturing, although it was not to everyone's taste. It was possible to suspect, for instance, that a poem like *The Men from Assynt*, originally commissioned by the BBC, represented a dilution of thoughts and feelings about landscape which would have been more stringently expressed in the days when the poet's musings were at least given backbone by the demands of end-stopping rhyme.

In other poems – for example *Numismatist, God in the Grass*, and the title poem of *A Man in My Position* – even musing dwindled to a single thread, and one extended image was asked to do all the work. Norman Cameron used to manage this kind of thing excellently, but in MacCaig's hands it sometimes had less of a concentric clarity than a slightly factitious air, as of fancy circumscribed in an attempt to make it mean something extra. The last five lines of *Numismatist* could even be taken as a metaphorical description of the activity:

> *But see me now*
> *blackjawed medieval smalltime crook*
> *shaking gold coins in a bag*
> *for the pinch of rich dust*
> *left in the bottom.*

MacCaig's "gold coins" – the counters and concepts of this poetry – had not lost their value. However, they did grow a bit smooth and he had to shake them harder and harder in the bag to get the required pinch.

In 1967 he gave up his schoolteaching to become the first holder of the Writing Fellowship at the University of Edinburgh. MacCaig proved immensely popular and successful in this capacity, and it was followed by another academic appointment in the University of Stirling. His

Selected Poems appeared in 1971. It showed the poet's own view of his work to be in accord with the commonly held critical opinion that his progress had been a sort of gradual paring down.

Sometimes, as in a slender piece of whimsy such as *Flooded Mind,* a single metaphor is turned inside out or upside down and then made to do the work of a poem, wandering down the page with a look of discovery which the actual language never quite reports.

This, though, is to criticise from the highest standards a genuine poet who threatened briefly to be a 20th-century Donne in lines like these, from *Poem for a Goodbye:*

> *When you go through*
> *My absence, which is all of you,*
> *And clouds, or suns, no more can be my sky,*
> *My one dissembling will be all*
> *The inclusive lie*
> *Of being this voice, this look, these few feet tall.*

In his later years MacCaig published less, particularly after the death in 1990 of his wife, Isabel, whom he had married in 1940. His *Collected Poems* (1985), republished in 1990 to mark his 80th birthday, was all the same a substantial volume, and several critics hailed him then as the greatest living Scottish poet, the natural successor to his old friend Hugh MacDiarmid.

MacCaig himself, while knowing his own worth, tended to be indifferent to praise and blame alike. It was typical of the man that on the eve of his 80th birthday he described on television his method of writing as just sitting down with a blank sheet of paper and letting his mind wander freely down the page, as he thought about places and friends. He liked to claim that it took him about as long to write a poem as to smoke a cigarette.

MacCaig was appointed OBE in 1979 and among other honours he was perhaps most pleased by having being made a Fellow of the Royal Society of Edinburgh in 1983. He spent all his adult life in Edinburgh, with the exception of the period at Stirling. He was always his own man, and once declared in a poem called *Patriot:*

> *my only country*
> *is six feet high*
> *and whether I love it or not*
> *I'll die for its independence.*

In his person, MacCaig was tall, thin, graceful, quizzical, gentle. He could be sarcastically witty in conversation but his epigrams seemed like the prickles of a hedgehog – something useful to protect an essentially shy nature. Some of them, delivered in a snapping voice at a poetry reading or just as likely on a windy Edinburgh street corner on a chance meeting with a friend, deserve to be remembered as much as anything he wrote: "Whenever I hear the word gun I reach for my culture."

He is survived by a son and a daughter.

* * *

GEORGE MACKAY BROWN

Scottish poet and story-writer, who reflected the rhythms of Orkney life

15 APRIL 1996

A WRITER WHOSE WORK was rooted utterly in the Orkney in which his life was spent, George Mackay Brown drew his inspiration from the harsh, unadorned lives of the people of that gale-lashed and sea-beaten northern outpost. Paradoxically, his earlier work sometimes showed the lush influence of Dylan Thomas, an influence which was at odds with his natural instincts and proclivities. But he soon learnt to pare away the adjectives to produce poems of a muscular gait which reflected the rhythms of Orcadian life, with its fishing and its tilling of an unyielding soil.

The Bible, the Norse sagas and his Roman Catholicism (he converted in 1961) were powerful impulses in his work. As the years went by, it was sometimes said of him that the simplified saga-like style he adopted in his later verse, tended to militate against its poetic charge. If this be true then it was fortunate for Brown – as he himself appears to have recognised – that he developed a second string to his bow as a prose writer. If his novels had their critics, he was particularly admired as a writer of short stories which are strong in a sense of the timeless preoccupations of the people among whom he lived.

He was an enemy of the 20th century and looked on almost all its works with a sense of barely disguised horror. Some felt that as a result his poetry was not contemporary enough in its inspiration. But the fact was that to Brown historical and contemporary Orkney were one, so totally were the islands a part of his life and his mental outlook. The fishing town of Stromness, on the Hoy Sound, where he spent virtually his entire life until his final illness compelled his removal to hospital in Orkney's capital, was enough for him. In his work it was always "Hamnavoe", its ancient name. It was his Laugharne, and the doings of its people provided a rich tapestry for his creativity to work on. Indeed, the composer Sir Peter Maxwell Davies bought a cottage on Hoy after reading Brown's book *An Orkney Tapestry*, and later set some of his work to music.

George Mackay Brown was the youngest of five children of a postman and part-time tailor in Stromness. His mother, a Gaelic speaker, was from the Highlands of Scotland. He always attributed the mystical element in his work, which observers felt to be the least Orcadian feature of it, to her. At Stromness Academy, where he went to school, Brown wrote poems from an early age (his first being an ode to Stromness). His health was never good; he contracted tuberculosis which left him with chronic bronchitis, and he did not at that time go on to higher education. For a period he was Orkney correspondent for a number of mainland papers.

He continued writing and was lucky enough to strike up an acquaintance with the older Orkney poet Edwin Muir, whom he met when he resumed his education at the age of 30, attending Newbattle Abbey College, in mainland Scotland, in 1951. Muir happened to be Warden there, and took a great interest in the work of his fellow Orcadian.

Brown's first volume, *The Storm*, which was published in Kirkwall in 1954, showed him to be a poet of talent. But it was the influence of Muir that brought him to the notice of the wider world. Without telling Brown, Muir sent a selection of his verse to the Hogarth Press in London and this led to the publication of his first major collection, *Loaves and Fishes*, in 1959. Though some of the poems in *Loaves and Fishes* showed lingering traces of Dylan Thomas, the best of them established him as a fresh, new voice, seen at its most characteristic in the unforced simplicity of:

> *Go sad or sweet or riotous with beer*
> *Past the old women gossiping by the hour*
> *They'll fix on you from every close and pier*
> *An acid look to make your veins run sour*

Brown next went as a mature student to Edinburgh University where he took a degree in English in 1960. He went on to do postgraduate work on Gerard Manley Hopkins.

By the time of his third volume *The Year of the Whale* (1965) Brown had already become a convert to Roman Catholicism, and a deepening vein of religious seriousness is evident in the collection. Brown's feeling for, and natural delight in, the beauty of the natural world is frequently reined in by his taste for austerity. The biblical temper of his mind continued to be indicated by the title of his next collection, *Fishermen with Ploughs*, a poem cycle set on the island of Hoy and describing the colonisation of Orkney by the Vikings, which was published in 1971. The title also expressed Brown's conviction of the abiding importance of the twin pillars of Orkney life – husbandry and fishing.

Some critics found it bare of ideas, rather than merely spare in its mode of expression. Yet a collection, *Poems New and Selected*, published the same year in London (and two years later in New York) gave the lie to the idea that Brown's creative vein had already been worked out, and enabled readers to savour the full range of his gifts. The opening lines of "Horsemen and Seals" are an example of the undemonstrative yet deep love with which Brown views his fellow islanders.

> *On the green holm they built their church.*
> *There were three arches.*
> *They walked to the village across the ebb.*
> *From this house they got milk.*
> *A farmer cut and carted their peats.*
> *On their rock Fishermen left a basket of mouthing silver.*

In the meantime Brown had already begun to write prose. The stories in *A Calendar of Love* (1967) were admired for the simple beauty of the language in which they celebrated the power of earth, sky and sea, and the elemental island lives heroically battling down the centuries against that uncompromising backdrop. *A Time to Keep*, a second collection of stories, published in 1969, was praised for similar qualities and reviewers murmured of a new Turgenev. But Brown's first novel, *Greenvoe* (1972) suggested that the longer form was not really his metier. It seemed palpably, merely a series of short stories stitched together. More puzzlingly, it abandoned the austere tone and structure of his finest writing, seeming instead to suggest a relapse into the rolling Dylan Thomas style prose poetry of his earliest work. There were further novels, among them *Magnus* (1973), the story of the 12th-century Earl of Orkney who became St Magnus the Martyr.

Brown also wrote a number of plays of which *Witch* and *A Spell for Green Corn* were produced at the Edinburgh Festival in 1969 and 1970. His opera libretto *The Martyrdom of St Magnus* was set by Sir Peter Maxwell Davies and produced in Kirkwall, London and Santa Fe. Brown also produced a son et lumière text, *A Celebration for Magnus* (1987), for

Sir Peter Maxwell Davies, and a further opera libretto for the composer was *The Two Fiddlers* (1978), an adaptation of the story by Brown.

Brown continued to publish poetry and short stories. His poetry and prose tended to converge in his later work. He was never a great creator of character in the tradition of mainstream novel and story writing, but rather an observer, a setter of scene, and a purveyor of bardic utterance. As civilisation marched on past him, its technical trappings eroding the empire of the imagination, he lamented a vanishing world with redoubled force. "We cannot live fully without the treasury our ancestors have left to us. Without the story – in which everyone living, unborn and dead, participates – men are no more than bits of paper blown on the cold wind."

Brown was appointed OBE in 1974 and had honorary degrees from Dundee, Glasgow and the Open University. He never married.

* * *

SIR FITZROY MACLEAN, BART.

Soldier, author, diplomat, adventurer, who fought
with the Long Range Desert Group and forged links
with Tito in Yugoslavia

18 JUNE 1996

IN AN ERA SHORT OF HEROES, Fitzroy Maclean came closer than most to filling the role. His life was full of adventure, high drama, danger and diversity. As a diplomat, he witnessed the show trials of Stalin's Russia; as a soldier he fought with David Stirling in the fledgeling SAS; as a traveller, he explored parts of Soviet Central Asia never visited before by a Westerner; and as an author and historian he wrote with passion and authority about his native Scotland.

Above all he was a central figure in one of the crucial episodes of the Second World War when he parachuted into Yugoslavia as Churchill's personal envoy; his favourable assessment of Tito meant that the Allies backed the Communist partisans rather than the Cetniks of General Mihajlovi, a decision that undoubtedly altered the course of postwar European history. In the light of subsequent events in that troubled country, it remains a matter of controversy. But neither Maclean nor Churchill was ever in doubt that it was the right decision, and that Tito's independence of mind made him not only a valuable resistance leader in combating the German occupation of his country, but acted as a buffer against Moscow domination after the war.

Fitzroy Hew Maclean was the son of a distinguished soldier, Major Charles Maclean, of the Queen's Own Cameron Highlanders who had won a DSO in the First World War and had, during an earlier adventure, been shot through the mouth during hostilities in Sierra Leone in the 1890s. The bullet was irretrievable by surgery, but eventually dropped out during a polo match. The Maclean connections in Argyll could be traced back to the 13th century and a forebear called Gillean of the Battle-Axe, as well as the 15th-century Lachainn Bronnach, or big-bellied Lachlan of Dowart, a cousin of the Lord of the Isles. Those clan links were always to remain important to him.

Conceived in Inverness, Maclean was born in Cairo and spent his first two years in Scotland. Long spells in India and Italy followed. His mother, who instilled in him a love of languages, taught him French and German (later he was fluent, too, in Russian and Serbo-Croat). She guided him away from Walter Scott to more intellectually challenging works by Thomas Mann and Anatole France.

He was educated first at Heatherdown preparatory school, Ascot, then Eton, where he was described by the *Eton Chronicle* as having won "all the prizes for which he was allowed to compete". He won a scholarship in 1928 to study Modern Languages at King's College, Cambridge, but spent a year in between in Germany where he studied Latin and Greek, thus enabling him to switch to Classics and to win a first in his Classical Tripos. He read History in his third year and got a second in Part Two.

After Cambridge, he joined the Diplomatic Service and was sent, as third secretary in 1934, to the Paris Embassy, where he found himself caught up in the volatile atmosphere of French politics, the riots of 1934, the sit-down strikes of 1936, and the massed demonstrations on the Champs-Elysées, where he listened to the crowds chanting the *Internationale.*

From the outset he was fascinated by the Soviet Union, and in 1937, at his own request, he was posted to Moscow. The next two years, up to the outbreak of war, were, he believed, "the most horrendous in the whole of Russia's blood stained history," and few episodes horrified him more than the trial of Nikolai Bukharin, one of Lenin's closest associates, which he attended throughout, and which opened his eyes to the full terror of Stalin's regime.

Returning to London in 1939, he listened to Neville Chamberlain's announcement on September 3 that Britain was at war, and decided that he must leave the Diplomatic Service and join the Army. The only way of doing so was to pursue a political career – that being the swiftest way out of the Diplomatic Service – which he did by standing successfully for election as Conservative MP for Lancaster. More importantly for him, it allowed him to join the Cameron Highlanders as a private.

Promoted to lieutenant in August 1941, he fell in with David Stirling who had formed the SAS, a fighting force which consisted of no more than half a dozen officers, and was employing guerrilla tactics against Rommel's Afrika Korps in the Western Desert. This involved him in several hair-raising commando raids behind enemy lines, none more so than a raid on Benghazi with the Long Range Desert Group, wearing Arab headdress, and fooling German sentries with a stream of schoolboy Italian.

But it was a subsequent adventure, no less dramatic, that was to plunge Maclean, by now promoted to brigadier, into the mission for which he will always be remembered. On the strength of his experience of irregular warfare, he was chosen by Winston Churchill, in the summer of 1943, to be dropped into German-occupied Yugoslavia as his personal representative with Tito. Churchill described him as "a daring ambassador-leader to these hardy and hunted guerrillas". His role was to pass on his assessment about whether Tito or Mihajlovi was most effective in fighting the Germans. He was in no doubt that Tito was the right man, and during his time with the partisans, the two formed a strong personal attachment.

After the war, Maclean resumed his political career, first as MP for Lancaster. But then, to the surprise of some, in 1959 he gave up this seat for Argyll and North Bute, for which he sat until February 1974. In 1946 he married Veronica Phipps, second daughter of the 16th Lord Lovat, and widow of Lieutenant Alan Phipps, RN. It was a marriage of two equally strong characters, close but volatile, in which no assertion would be left unchallenged, no opinion unquestioned, but where in the end mutual love and respect underpinned the strongest of unions. They made their home at the Maclean seat of Strachur in Argyll, from where, to the end of his days, and despite growing lameness, Maclean would set off on endless travels, often undertaken in conditions of extreme discomfort.

In 1954 he was made Parliamentary Under-Secretary of State for War and Financial Secretary at the War Office. But his postwar life will be remembered more for two great passions: the Soviet Union and Scotland. Throughout the Cold War he returned regularly to the USSR, where he retained close contacts and where he was allowed access to places that most Westerners never saw. Georgia was a favourite destination.

A travel writer of great fluency, his most vivid work was *Eastern Approaches* which documented his colourful life as traveler and adventurer. He was also a talented photographer. He and his wife were welcome guests in Yugoslavia, where Tito had given them a house on the island of Korčula, and where they continued to go even after civil war had broken out in Bosnia. Both were indomitable. At the age of 80, when crippling arthritis meant that he could walk only with the aid of a stick, he was planning a trip to Afghanistan to write about the Mujahidin.

A Highlander and a Jacobite, he relished the title of 15th Hereditary Keeper and Captain of Dunconnel. He wrote several books about Scotland, including his invaluable *Concise History of Scotland*, a biography of Charles Edward Stuart and a history of the Highlanders. He and his wife ran a restaurant and hotel at Strachur called the Creggans Inn, where he was always the most entertaining of companions – his recollections accompanied by liberal drams of his own whisky, the MacPhunn.

Created a baronet in 1957, Maclean was appointed CBE (Military) in 1944, the French *Croix de Guerre*, the Partisan Star (First Class) and the Order of the Yugoslav Star. In 1993 he was created a Knight of the Thistle, Scotland's highest order.

Tall, stooped, with craggy good looks, Maclean had enormous charm. He enjoyed good food, good wine, good conversation, and especially the company of women. It was always believed that Ian Fleming had based his hero James Bond on Maclean, and the idea is certainly more convincing than some which have been suggested. In terms of romance, intrigue and dangerous action, Maclean's career was at least as varied as that of 007, but as a man of rather greater modesty than his fictional counterpart, he himself would never have accepted the comparison.

He leaves his widow Veronica, two sons, a stepson and stepdaughter.

SORLEY MacLEAN

*The greatest Gaelic poet of his time, who 'confronted the
great issues of the 20th century'*

25 NOVEMBER 1996

SORLEY MacLEAN WAS REGARDED as the greatest Gaelic poet of the
century. He gave new literary standing to a language which seemed close
to extinction. His work was musical, resonant of a rich oral tradition; it
mourned the Highland Clearances but also confronted the great issues
of the 20th century.

MacLean was born on the small island of Raasay, over the sound
from Skye. Three influences shaped his art and animated him until his
death. The first was musical: he grew up in a world of Gaelic song and
poetry; his father was a fine singer and an accomplished piper.

The second was historical. He heard the old Gaelic songs at his
grandmother's knee and acquired a powerful "folk" memory. He told
the stories of both Culloden and the Battles of the Braes of 1882 (when
Skye crofters resisted eviction) as if he himself had been present.

The third influence was religious; he was brought up in the Free
Presbyterian Church, which broke away from the Free Church in 1893
in protest against liberalised doctrine. Raasay was one of the secession's
centres but MacLean was always at pains to kill the myth of a closed
and narrow Calvinist society; he drew a distinction between the
communicants, a small minority, and the "adherents", who observed
the sabbath dutifully enough but retained all the convivial habits of
their ancestors.

He was educated at Portree High School and Edinburgh University,
where he graduated in 1933 with an honours degree in English. He
embraced socialism and denounced fascism; he would have fought in
the Spanish Civil War had not his salary as a teacher been the chief
support of the extended family dependent on his help to complete their
education.

This always preyed a little on his mind. In later life he was at pains to correct an impression, given by one of his poems, that the love of a woman had kept him at home. The reasons were, he said, entirely economic; but he still had to suffer some snide barbs from the close-knit world of academic Celtic studies. When Edinburgh City Corporation agreed to make up the salaries to teachers who went off to the war – he was by now head of English at Boroughmuir – he joined up and fought with the 8th Army in North Africa, where he was wounded at El Alamein.

He began to write poetry while at university, choosing to do so in Gaelic not only because he felt comfortable with its literary tradition but also as part of a specific effort to halt its decline. His first published work, produced with Robert Garioch, was *Seventeen Poems for Sixpence*. In 1943 came *Dain do Eimhir agus Dain Eile* (Poems to Eimhir and Other Poems), mostly written in the Thirties. Some were addressed as love poems to the legendary Eimhir of the early Irish sagas but they dwelt also on political themes, contemplated the rise of fascism, and were unsparingly hostile to Christianity.

MacLean's fellow poet, Iain Crichton Smith, an early translator of his work, has called this the greatest book of Scottish poetry this century, with the possible exception of Hugh MacDiarmid's *A Drunk Man Looks at the Thistle*, noting that the poems were unusual in the Gaelic tradition because of their European sensibility.

After the war MacLean returned to teaching. He became headmaster of Plockton High School, Wester Ross, in 1956, retiring to Braes in Skye in 1972. He was writer-in-residence at Edinburgh University, 1973-75.

His *Poems to Eimhir* were published in a translation by Crichton Smith in 1971. A major volume, *Reothairt is Contraigh* (Spring Tide and Neap Tide) appeared in 1977. His collected poems, *O Choille gu Bearradh* (From Wood to Ridge), were published by Carcanet in 1989 and won the MacVitie Prize. He brought out new work intermittently until his death.

Unlike MacDiarmid, whose early poetry he admired but whose political judgment he found wanting, MacLean was not a satirist nor a polemicist. His poems are incantatory, using repetition and the cadences of the Gaelic language to reinforce their strong emotional content. The poet is a witness and not confessional, though the themes are often autobiographical.

The poems crystallise and celebrate the historical experience of the Scottish Gael. Many are laments for Highlanders brutally evicted in the Clearances. Others are love poems, or lyrical evocations of nature. The link between land and people is a drumbeat through the verses: *Great Raasay of the MacLeods ...*

Some critics felt that something was lost when the work was translated into English, a view MacLean shared, though he published his own translations. Yet he was also influenced by the metaphysical poets, whom he had studied at Edinburgh, and he reinvigorated the Gaelic literary tradition by enlarging it into a medium which could confront contemporary themes.

The Spanish Civil War continued as a painful memory, and his lament for three poets who lost their lives in the International Brigade – John Cornford, Julian Bell and Garcia Lorca – is one of his most moving works:

> *What to us is the empire of Germany*
> *or the empire of Britain*
> *or the empire of France, and every one of them loathsome?*
> *Bruth the frief is ours in the sore frailty of mankind ...*

Sorley MacLean was a man of great kindness, keeping up the traditions of Highland hospitality in Skye. His moustache and tweeds gave him an Orwellian air and he told his stories in a slow, lilting cadence. He poured the island malt with liberality and liked nothing better than to show visitors the magical beauties of the islands and recount their intimate history.

He is survived by his wife Renee and two daughters.

SIR ALEC CAIRNCROSS

Economist who was determined to maintain the parity of sterling,
but who finally urged devaluation on James Callaghan

26 OCTOBER 1998

MORE THAN ANY OTHER official in Whitehall, Alec Cairncross had the
decisive role in influencing James Callaghan, the then Chancellor, to
go for devaluation in November 1967. Yet nothing in his background
suggested this course of action. In his own memoirs the future
Labour Prime Minister specifically recalls Cairncross as being "one
of the staunchest of the Praetorian Guard determined to maintain
sterling's parity". It, therefore, came as all the more of a shock when at
the beginning of November 1967 he found himself the recipient of "a
personal and pessimistic typed memorandum together with a covering
handwritten letter", both urging him that the game was up and that
there was no alternative but to devalue. (The letter, Callaghan ruefully
wrote, "burnt a hole in my pocket for the rest of the day".) When the two
of them eventually met alone on November 2, it was an understandably
painful encounter.

For Alec Cairncross that was, however, a thoroughly uncharacteristic
initiative. He was one of those old-fashioned government servants
always anxious never to step beyond his own proper role. Yet that
did not stop him from qualifying as one of the leading managerial
economists and government mandarins of the postwar period, a paid-
up member of the great and the good and an inevitable ingredient of
innumerable committees on matters ranging from police pay and the
running of Lloyd's to the feasibility of a Channel Tunnel (he advised
against it as late as 1982, prophetically fearing that it would generate
insufficient revenue).

Alexander Kirkland Cairncross was born in Lanarkshire and
educated at Hamilton Academy, winning a scholarship to Glasgow
University, where he specialised in economics. He then went to Trinity

College, Cambridge, where in 1934-35 he shared rooms with his younger brother John (the alleged Fifth Man, to whose posthumous memoirs Cairncross contributed a moving but candid preface only last year). There is no doubt that as with the former Eton art master Wilfrid Blunt, the revelation – about which he first heard in 1964 – that his brother had been for more than 15 years until 1952 a Soviet agent came as a profound shock to so meticulous and dedicated a public servant.

He took a first in the Economic Tripos, and became a lecturer in economics, under the considerable influence of John Maynard Keynes, but soon after the outbreak of war in 1939 he followed many of his academic colleagues and became a temporary civil servant. Although he was for a short time in the economic section of the Cabinet Office, most of his work was with the Ministry of Aircraft Production, where he rose to become director of programmes.

After a brief period on the staff of *The Economist* in 1946, he was recalled to the Civil Service and became economic adviser to the Board of Trade, at the instigation of Sir Stafford Cripps, who had known him during his wartime period at the Ministry of Aircraft Production. He was seconded to be economic adviser to the Organisation for European Economic Co-operation in Paris in 1949 and left to become Professor of Applied Economics at his old university, Glasgow, in 1951.

He became a well-known and trusted figure nationally and internationally among those concerned with practical affairs, and he was borrowed by the World Bank in 1955 to go to Washington to start the Economic Development Institute then being established to train economic administrators from underdeveloped countries. For many years he advocated the removal of tariffs and trading quotas, and the freeing of world trade.

When in 1961 Sir Robert Hall resigned as Economic Adviser to the Government, Cairncross was invited to succeed him and for the next year he worked closely with the Permanent Secretary to the Treasury, Sir Frank Lee, of whom he was an old and trusted friend. Their collaboration with Selwyn Lloyd led to the experiment of running the economy under rather less strain than had been customary, and this policy was followed by Reginald Maudling (who succeeded the sacked Lloyd in July 1962) until, as might have been expected, it broke down in 1964 under the shadow of the forthcoming general election. This period also saw the introduction of various forms of incomes policy, which were to cause a severe deterioration of relations between government and unions.

The advent of Harold Wilson's first Labour administration in October, 1964 put Cairncross in an embarrassing position, since the new Government divided economic responsibility between the Treasury and George Brown's new Department of Economic Affairs. He felt that the Prime Minister – himself an economist – took very little notice of the wealth of advice available, and he gradually became disillusioned by the amount of support afforded by the enigmatic, Buddha-like figure of Sir William Armstrong, the Permanent Secretary to the Treasury.

Cairncross thus welcomed the invitation in 1967 from St Peter's College, Oxford, to become its Master. He took up the post at the beginning of 1969, and was noted for his encouragement of young scholars. He retained, however, a significant influence on government policy. In 1970 he expressed some scepticism about the State's ability to foster industrial success directly, but the following year he chaired a review body which recommended the establishment in Northern Ireland of an Industrial Finance Corporation with £50 million of public money to help companies suffering liquidity problems.

In 1973 he published an article calling for a new kind of incomes policy with centralised bargaining, and in 1974 he was among the authors of *Economic Policy for the EEC*, which advocated a redistributive land tax, and an economic and monetary union run with the help of an "exchange equalisation account".

Cairncross was seen as the sort of "good mind" needed to devise policy in all kinds of fields, and he sat on working parties advising on crofting, the wool trade and anthrax. An empirical economist, he was wedded to the postwar belief that people like himself should be steering the economy with their "gentle touches on the tiller" and occasional "shots in the arm". So in the 1980s he was shocked by the extent to which Margaret Thatcher put her faith in the free market, and he repeatedly expressed his disgust at her monetarist policy.

He was appointed CMG in 1950 and advanced to KCMG in 1967. In 1961 he was elected a Fellow of the British Academy, and was President of the Royal Economic Society 1968-70. He published a number of books, of which his substantial *Introduction to Economics* (1944, 6th ed 1982) was long a standard text for students. After his retirement from Oxford he wrote various accounts of the work of government economic advisers, and in 1997 published an interesting, if slightly elliptical, diary account of his final period in Whitehall, *The Wilson Years: A Treasury Diary 1964-69.* Pragmatically rather than dogmatically minded, he remained a strong advocate of the importance of economic history, which had absorbed him since Cambridge.

Among his many academic honours, he probably got most pleasure from his election as Chancellor of his first university, Glasgow, in 1972; and from being chosen as President of the British Association for 1970-71. He also valued his association as a supernumary fellow with St Antony's College, Oxford, where he became a frequent and familiar presence on high days and guest nights.

He married in 1942 Mary Frances Glynn and had five children, who formed an obviously happy and close-knit family. His wife died earlier this year, but he is survived by their three sons and two daughters.

LORD MACKENZIE-STUART

Scottish lawyer and passionate Europhile who became
President of the European Court of Justice in Luxembourg

5 APRIL 2000

JACK MACKENZIE STUART was the first British judge to sit in the European Court of Justice. If his appointment, which was within the gift of the Government, was the cause of political infighting, his election by his peers as President of the court was a reflection of the regard his fellow judges had for him. He had been a Europhile before his appointment and continued to beat the drum for Community law after his retirement.

When Britain nominated judges to the court after Edward Heath signed the Treaty of Accession in 1972, there were fears that the Scottish legal system would not be given its due place and that there would be only English nominees. Lord Wylie, then Lord Advocate, insisted – some say to the point of threatening resignation – that a Scottish judge should be nominated. His candidate was already in place – Mackenzie Stuart having been appointed to the Scottish bench only a few months previously, evidently on the understanding that he was en route to Luxembourg. Wylie's stance had an historical resonance since Scots law owes much of its distinctive nature to its pre-1707 European provenance.

Alexander John Mackenzie Stuart was born to the law. His father, Professor A. Mackenzie Stuart, had in 1932 published the standard work on the Scots law of trusts. Born in Aberdeen, he was educated at Fettes in Edinburgh. After Sydney Sussex, Cambridge, and Edinburgh University, he served in the Royal Engineers from 1942 to 1947, attaining the rank of temporary captain. He was admitted to the Faculty of Advocates in 1951 and took silk in 1963, building up an extensive practice largely in civil work, defending insurance companies against claims for reparation and representing the Coal Board.

By this time his interest in Europe was clear and he was an active member of the Scottish European movement. Lord Wylie, who became Lord Advocate in 1970, marked him down as a candidate for Luxembourg. He served as Sheriff Principal of Aberdeen, Kincardine and Banff, 1971-72, before his translation first as a Senator of the College of Justice and then as a member of the European Court.

At that time the quality of the court in Luxembourg was somewhat uneven. Not every country sent its best talent there. Governments were also slow to increase funding, though the caseload had grown fourfold in a decade.

When Mackenzie Stuart became Resident 12 years later the 11 judges, assisted by five advocates-general, were delivering well over 100 decisions a year, but the backlog meant it was taking an average of 13 months for a judgment to be read. Part of the solution was the establishment of a Court of First Instance to sift preliminary material before cases went to the full court.

Upon his retirement in 1988, Mackenzie Stuart returned to live in Edinburgh, while continuing to pay frequent visits to the house he had acquired in the Ardèche, entering enthusiastically into the local life of Le Vans. He remained a Francophile, fond of claret and pétanque.

Created a life peer (as Lord Mackenzie-Stuart), in retirement at his house in Edinburgh's New Town he carried on his hobbies of collecting 18th-century pictures and drawing. He also enjoyed researching the Auld Alliance: in 1995 he published a work of history, *A French King at Holyrood*.

He continued to argue for the community-wide rule of law and was hostile to the notion of "subsidiarity" embodied in the Maastricht treaty. The principle that decisions should be taken as locally as possible was a means of placating those who feared the loss of sovereignty. Mackenzie Stuart wrote in *The Times* in 1992 that the idea would make the court's task "impossible", adding that the formula was "gobbledegook".

He remained active, as president of the British Academy of Experts from 1989 to 1992, in the European movement in Scotland, and as a lecturer on Community law and other matters. He received honorary doctorates from the universities of Aberdeen, Edinburgh, Glasgow, Stirling, Exeter, Cambridge and Birmingham. He was also awarded the Prix Bech for services to Europe.

He is survived by his wife, Anne Burtholme Millar, and four daughters.

Lord Mackenzie-Stuart; Scottish and European lawyer, was born on November 18, 1924. He died on April 1, aged 75.

* * *

DONALD DEWAR

First Minister of the new Scottish Parliament, who presided over devolution, and earned the title 'Father of the Nation'

11 OCTOBER 2000

FEW STATESMEN CAN CLAIM genuinely to have changed the course of constitutional history. Donald Dewar did, by steering through the complex process of Scottish devolution, with the minimum disruption to the smooth governance of the United Kingdom, in the teeth of much scepticism and often hostility.

At the same time he won the affection of the Scottish people through a combination of modesty and self-deprecation which set him apart as that rarest of creatures – a trusted politician.

The title "Father of the Nation" was ironically accorded him by some commentators, and was brushed aside with embarrassment by Dewar himself, but he earned it, despite the setbacks he encountered during the Scottish Parliament's first year. He was unwavering in his conviction that the parliament's creation was, in John Smith's phrase, "the settled will of the Scottish People". He accepted that it was his responsibility to ensure that it worked efficiently, that its relationship with Westminster was clearly understood, that it never pretended to offer more than it could deliver, but that it was sufficiently sturdy to keep at bay the insistent demands of the Scottish Nationalists.

Whether, with its faltering start, the parliament has done enough to keep independence at bay remains to be seen, but if devolution becomes a settled constitutional arrangement, it will justifiably be recognised as Dewar's legacy.

History may also judge, however, that when it came to the exercise of power, Dewar lacked the sure touch and iron will that are the hallmarks of a true leader. Too often he seemed to be thrown off course by events instead of controlling them. His assumption that others would see the sense of his arguments and share his views took too little account of a determined opposition with tactics less scrupulous than his own. He managed government rather than led it from the front. His inclination for sensible compromise rather than rock-like intransigence meant that he was sometimes judged to be a ditherer.

By contrast, his performances as a speaker, both in the House of Commons and in the Scottish Parliament were stylish and assured. He had a feel for parliamentary language that was almost Disraelian, and a sharpness of response that left opponents reeling. In Scotland, where he took on the Scottish Nationalist leader, Alex Salmond, one of the quickest-thinkers on the political scene, he scored regular victories through a combination of killer instinct and elaborate courtesy. "I sense that the gentleman is attempting to lure me into an indiscretion," he might observe, "but I fear that he may be disappointed. Indiscretions are not my stock in trade."

In his private life he came across as a lone, and sometimes a lonely, figure. One of the great tragedies of his life was the loss of his wife, Alison McNair, whom he met at university, but who left him for his friend, Derry Irvine, later Lord Chancellor, taking their two children with her. He never remarried, and though he had a wide circle of friends, when it came to Christmas or summer holidays, he preferred to be on his own. Rejecting self-pity, he simply commented that "if you haven't got anyone particularly to go on holiday with, what's the point of going?"

This meant that to outsiders he presented a somewhat dour exterior, "always looking to find the cloud behind the silver lining," as one political journalist put it. In reality, he was excellent company, dry of wit, scathing in opinion, relishing, as he said, "a good old-fashioned gossip".

He was born the only son of elderly parents, both of whom were ill. His father, a Glasgow dermatologist, suffered from tuberculosis, his mother developed a brain tumour. So at the age of two, he was sent away to a boarding school, first in Perthshire, then near Hawick in the Scottish Borders. "I suppose, in a funny sort of way, I was in care – organised by my parents," he said later.

This was his life until the age of nine, when he came home to Glasgow to go to Moss Park primary school, where he was teased for his Borders accent. After that, he went to Glasgow Academy, which was still in those days run on traditional, authoritarian Scotch lines. Being neither athletic nor particularly bookish, he formed few friendships. "I left the school alone, and they left me alone," was his bleak comment.

At Glasgow University, he read history and there came into contact with a group of would-be politicians who were to remain his friends for life, including John Smith, the future Labour leader, and Menzies Campbell, Foreign Affairs spokesman for the Liberal Democrats. It was there that he discovered his debating skills and a love of left-wing politics, more Fabian Society than Socialist. He left with a second-class degree and a determination to make a career in politics.

He was adopted as a Labour candidate for Aberdeen South in 1962, and won the seat in 1966 against the redoubtable Lady Tweedsmuir, a Tory junior minister. A year later he became PPS to Anthony Crosland at the Board of Trade. His conversion to the cause of devolution can be dated back to Winnie Ewing's sensational victory for the SNP at the Hamilton by-election of 1967, when a small group of Scottish party members who included Dewar, Smith, the late John Mackintosh, and Robert It was not until the second election of 1974, when the SNP won

11 seats, that the Wilson Government began to explore devolution as a serious policy.

In 1970, Dewar lost his seat, and was out of the Commons for eight years. He became a partner in a firm of solicitors run by Ross Harper, a friend from university days and a leading Scottish Tory. Three years later his marriage came to an end. However, he stood again as a candidate at Glasgow Garscadden in 1978 and successfully held off the Nationalist challenge to win.

The following year he campaigned for a Yes vote in the unsuccessful 1979 devolution referendum, in a group that included the Conservative Alick Buchanan-Smith. As a passionate Scot, Dewar never hesitated to form cross-party alliances in support of a cause in which he believed, and though deeply hostile to the Nationalists, he was prepared, nearly 20 years later, to join forces with the SNP, to canvas support for the 1997 referendum which finally delivered devolution.

As Shadow Scottish Secretary from 1983 to 1992, Dewar had the thankless task of promoting a vision of Scotland's political future that was actively derided by the Labour leader Neil Kinnock, who found it hard to take devolution seriously.

In 1988 the Scottish Constitutional Convention, a cross-party affair, was established, and Dewar supported it, throwing his weight not only behind the notion of a Scottish Parliament, but, critically, endorsing proportional representation. Since this undermined Labour's guaranteed majority in Scotland, it was, as he put it, a "spectacular act of charitable giving". It was also, however, a shrewd calculation, since a parliament permanently dominated by Labour could never have held the country together.

Against expectations, Labour lost the 1992 general election and Dewar was made, first, shadow spokesman on social security, and then Chief Whip, a job he performed exceptionally well, gaining the confidence of MPs from left to right of the party. Being single, he was able to devote long hours to managing parliamentary tactics, and it was his competence and patent integrity which won the respect of Tony

Blair, who succeeded to the leadership following the death of Dewar's friend John Smith in 1994.

After Labour's sweeping victory of 1997, he was entrusted with mounting the referendum campaign which asked voters to support a Scottish Parliament with limited tax-raising powers. The triumphant result – a high turnout, with a two-thirds majority in favour – was a vindication of his disputed decision to include the tax issue as a separate question. At least as important, however, was the meticulous drafting of the Scotland Bill which followed the referendum and gave the parliament its shape. The Bill's simple but telling first sentence: "There shall be a Scottish Parliament" was a classic Dewar touch, as was his speech at the opening of the Parliament in the presence of the Queen on July 1, 1999, which he described, eloquently, as "a moment anchored in our history".

His suits were baggy, his ties unfashionable, he famously never had an overcoat on the grounds that his old one had simply become unwearable. His Glasgow home groaned with the books he had collected which had yet to be put on a shelf. He had a fine collection of Scottish Colourist paintings, but typically protested that it was only a modest one and that people shouldn't assume he was a latter-day Guggenheim.

He enjoyed music and the theatre, but he shunned social gatherings, making his dislike of small-talk almost painfully obvious. When asked how he liked spending his free time, he answered: "Sloth is a great companion, just lying on the floor with a novel." In all of this he was the antithesis of the glad-handing populist.

None of this lost him support. On the contrary, it confirmed him in the nation's affections. He shrugged off party minders and made regular gaffes, without incurring any noticeable hostility. Walking into an old people's home, he took one look at the elderly inmates and asked: "Was anyone here in the Titanic?"

His more than healthy appetite, which had led to his being nicknamed "The Gannet", did nothing to fill out his gaunt frame and gloomy features. "I'm not dour and horrid," he protested, "but people do say that I am the most melancholic man in British politics. I can usually find some reason to take a very dim view of the prospects."

It was perhaps for this reason that the Chancellor of the Exchequer, Gordon Brown, was drafted in to run the party's campaign headquarters in the first Scottish elections in 1999 rather than leaving the task to Dewar. The result was a coalition government, the almost inevitable outcome of the PR voting system, and Labour found itself in uneasy partnership with the Liberal Democrats, facing a truculent SNP as the main opposition party.

From the beginning Dewar, as First Minister in the new administration, was beset by difficulties which chipped away at the image he had projected of paternal competence or "everyone's favourite bank manager", as he was once described. In an uncharacteristic display of meanness, he refused to sanction a knighthood for Scotland's favourite son, the actor Sean Connery, an avowed Nationalist. The loss of two special advisers in controversial circumstances revealed a fatal air of indecision in dealing with the affairs of his own office, and the escalating costs of the new parliament building, of which he had taken personal charge, gave the distinct impression that he had suppressed the true figures to begin with, then found costs spiralling out of control later on. The perception remained that Dewar was not wholly in control of events, and setbacks in two by-elections suggested that the public was less than impressed by the early performance of the Parliament and the Scottish Executive under his leadership. It was, however, a measure of his stature, that no single figure in Scotland emerged to qualify as a replacement when heart trouble was first diagnosed in April 2000. His death robs Scotland of one of its very few substantial political figures, and reveals a distinct absence of comparable talent. He is survived by a son and a daughter.

HAMISH HENDERSON

Folklorist who rescued an oral tradition from seeming oblivion, served
as an intelligence officer, and translated Gramsci's prison letters

11 MARCH 2002

THE FOLKLORIST, POET AND SINGER Hamish Henderson will be remembered by his friends for his charm and conviviality, by his students for his enthusiasm and erudition, by Marxists as the first translator into English of Gramsci, but by history as a key figure in the folk revival of the 1950s and for his part in creating the rich archive of Scotland's oral traditions in the School of Scottish Studies at Edinburgh University.

In his hands the work of the folklorist became dynamic or, in his own word, "proselytising". He not only helped to rescue an oral culture from apparently inevitable oblivion but wrote "folk songs" of his own, along with a substantial body of poetry, much of it highly regarded. He mined the rich oral heritage of Scotland's travelling folk and brought to prominence such singers as the majestic Jeannie Robertson, of whose talents the country had been completely unaware. His work also persuaded young musicians to explore ancestral styles.

Throughout his life he was inspired by the songs of the travellers, who were often looked down upon as "tinkers", but whose cheerful exuberance he remembered from when they came to pick berries in the fields around his birthplace of Blairgowrie in Perthshire. A collaborator said of him: "Hamish loved the company of travellers: the rain on the bow-tent, the whisky, the old songs, the rant of the pipes." And near his home in Edinburgh, at Sandy Bell's pub in Forrest Row, he would meet up with pipers and folk musicians, avidly collecting new tunes.

It was the absence of travellers' songs from Gavin Greig's classic collection of Scottish balladry in the library of King's College, Aberdeen (some of which he would perform during "bothy nichts" at the Imperial

Hotel) which first gave Henderson the desire to explore traditional music.

His life was changed by the arrival in Europe in 1950 of the American musicologist Alan Lomax, who was working on his great collection of world folk song, which was later issued in 18 volumes by Columbia Records. He came to Scotland with a tape-recorder which, though unwieldy, was far superior to anything Henderson had seen before.

Henderson agreed to help Lomax with his work in the north-east of Scotland, home of the bothy ballads. Meanwhile the poet Sorley MacLean and his brother, the Celtic scholar Calum, agreed to do the same in the Gaelic-speaking west. Lomax's recordings were among the first deposits in the archive of the School of Scottish Studies, of which Henderson and Calum MacLean became founding fellows in 1952. They thus began years of fieldwork which was to produce a bulging collection which, 40 years on, amounted to 8,000 hours of recordings, together with photographs and written material. Henderson later described his time collecting songs from travellers in the berryfields of Blairgowrie as "like sitting under Niagara with a tin can".

For three years from 1951 Henderson also organised the People's Festival Ceilidhs which brought the best of Scotland's native musical traditions to an urban audience during the Edinburgh Festival, and is regarded as the forerunner of the Fringe.

Hamish Scott Henderson was the son of a soldier who died soon after the First World War. His musical mother, who competed at the Mod (the annual festival of Gaelic music), brought him up to be fluent in French and Gaelic. He was educated at Blairgowrie High School and, after his mother moved to a job in Somerset, at Dulwich College.

By the time he went to study modern languages at Cambridge, where he developed a particular love of Italian, war was looming and he had formed a profound hatred of Nazism. Spending the summer of 1939 in Germany, he joined a clandestine Quaker group which helped people to flee the country. He himself left Germany just before the outbreak of war. He served as an intelligence officer, with the rank of captain, in the 51st Highland Division and other infantry divisions in Egypt, Libya, Tunisia, Sicily and Italy, being mentioned in dispatches in 1945.

His knowledge of Germany, his love of its literature, and the distinction he drew between the soldiers and the Nazis, combined with his gentlemanly charm to make him an extremely effective interrogator of captured officers. But the war, particularly the Battle of Alamein, had a profound impact on him. He later recalled: "In many ways I enjoyed the desert war. It sounds ridiculous to say that, but looking back, I felt we had to win this war, and I felt my anti-Fascist feelings rising to the top." His *Elegies for the Dead in Çyrenaica*, written from the point of view of the ordinary soldier, were published in 1948 and won the Somerset Maugham poetry award the following year.

He used the prize money to travel to Italy to work on his translation of Antonio Gramsci's Prison Letters, the posthumous work in which the founder of the Italian Communist Party elaborated his ideas. Because Henderson's work brought him into contact with many Marxists at a sensitive time, immediately after the war, he was asked to leave the country. His translation was eventually published in 1996.

His passionate concerns for justice, equality and the common man, and his mixture of a nationalism which took pride in Scotland's heritage and an internationalism which rejected racism and xenophobia, were recurring themes in many songs and poems. *The Freedom Come All Ye* was often proposed as a Scottish national anthem, and he was visibly moved when it was sung by a crowd of 25,000 which gathered for the so-called "Democracy Demonstration" in Edinburgh during the European Summit in 1992.

His *March for John McLean*, written, like several of his other works to a pipe tune, celebrated the Clydeside Marxist whose popularity troubled Lloyd George's Government during the First World War. *Seven Men of Knoydart*, describing a postwar confrontation between squatters and the landowner Lord Brocket, became the anthem of hill-walkers claiming free access to Scotland's hills. Characteristically, in his poem *The Flytin o Life and Daith* ("The Argument between Life and Death"), it is Life that emerges triumphant.

In 1963 Henderson had a real "flyting", with his mentor, the poet Hugh MacDiarmid, whose contempt for popular song Henderson regarded as "spiritual apartheid". He published a collection of essays, *Alias MacAlias*, in 1992 and a selection of his letters, which he entitled *The Armstrong Nose*, in 1996. To his MA were added various honorary degrees, and after his retirement in 1988 he remained an honorary fellow of the school, retaining his room there.

In 1983 Henderson turned down an OBE offered by Margaret Thatcher's Government, complaining about its "suicidal defence policy, organised in collusion with the Americans and their crazy, trigger-happy President".

Tall, with a shambling gait, and accompanied everywhere by his faithful dog Sandy, he was held in exceptional affection and regard.

He is survived by his wife, Felicity Schmidt, and their two daughters.

* * *

EUGENIE FRASER

*Refugee from Revolutionary Russia who formed a living link
back to the days of Napoleon*

7 NOVEMBER 2002

NINETY-SIX YEARS AGO, a baby girl, half Scottish, half Russian, wrapped in furs against the bitter cold of an Archangel winter, was taken by sledge across the River Dvina to the house of a very old lady. Nanny Shalovchika was 105 and had lived long enough to remember seeing Napoleon's troops fleeing down the roads of Smolensk and to have had a son killed in the Crimean War. The baby, christened Yevgheniya Ghermanovna Scholts, was placed on her knee, and the nanny smiled proudly. "I am content," she said. "I have now nursed four generations."

The child who sat on that knee – and years later recalled and wrote about her link with history – was herself a truly remarkable woman. The life of Eugenie Fraser, as she became, reads like something out of a novel by Turgenev. When, at the age of 80, she published her story, *The House by the Dvina*, it was greeted with amazement, not only in Britain, but in Russia, where people found it hard to believe that there could be someone alive in the 20th century who could so vividly recall a place and a period that had so completely vanished.

To meet her, in her later years, was to encounter a respectable Morningside lady, who took tea in the afternoon, and whose husband wore the kilt. But when she spoke, the refined Scottish accent was heavily laced with Russian. It was, after all, her native language.

Eugenie's father, Gherman Scholts, was the son of a well-to-do family in Archangel, Russia's most northerly port. He had travelled to Dundee in 1903 to learn about the timber trade. On his first day there he spotted in the street a beautiful girl, Nelly Cameron, the daughter of a wealthy Dundee flax merchant from Broughty Ferry. He determined to meet her, and succeeded in doing so. After courting her secretly, he married her. Although she had never set foot out of Scotland, she made the hazardous journey to Russia, by train and by sledge, arriving in Archangel to find the Scottish flag fluttering in welcome over the house by the River Dvina, where she was to live.

Her child, Eugenie, who was born soon afterwards, was brought up as part of a large and colourful family that lived in the old Russian style, in a house with many servants, at least one Uncle Vanya, and a babushka – her grandmother. It was she who instilled in Eugenie her love of family history.

She told of a dramatic journey that she had made as a young and pregnant wife across Russia in the depths of winter by horse-drawn troika, pursued occasionally by wolves, to plead with Tsar Nicholas II for the release of her officer husband from prison in Siberia. She had succeeded in her mission, returning just in time for her baby to be born in Archangel. This and many other stories became part of Eugenie's folk memory.

Her Russian idyll came to an end with the Revolution in 1917. Although to begin with Archangel was untouched by events in St Petersburg, the port later became the centre for the ill-fated intervention by British and American forces on behalf of the White Russian army. Finally, in 1920, Eugenie, her brother and her mother were forced to leave, escaping with only the clothes they stood up in. Her father stayed behind, and she never saw him again. Other members of the family were imprisoned or executed by the Bolsheviks.

The house by the Dvina, with its lake and gardens, was abandoned and bulldozed. Eugenie never forgave the regime. "Bitter would be too small a word," she said later. "I loathed communism. It destroyed the country, it can never be the same again."

She went on to marry a senior administrator in the jute industry, Ronald Fraser, and spent many years in India and Thailand. It was only at the age of 80, after attending classes on creative writing at Edinburgh University, that she began composing her memoirs. Her book was a huge success, and was made into a television documentary. She was invited back to Archangel, where she feasted and was entertained by a population thrilled to meet this throwback to a previous era. She was not much impressed by the featureless high-rise town that had grown up in her absence, but she was not depressed. "I was glad to go back," she said. "I had to go back." She visited the grave of her father, and paddled in the now heavily polluted river where her beloved babushka and she had spent many happy days.

Fraser wrote two other books, *The House by the Hooghly* (1989), about her time in India, and *The Dvina Remains* (1996). She was awarded an honorary doctorate by the University of Abertay, Dundee, a scroll of achievement by the City of Edinburgh and a Scottish Arts Council award for literary merit. In 2000, Transworld Publishers issued its 13th reprint of *The House by the Dvina.*

Fraser died in Edinburgh after a long illness, and her Russian Orthodox Church funeral service was attended by a senior dignitary from Archangel.

Her husband predeceased her. She is survived by two sons.

RIKKI FULTON

Scottish comedian and actor whose hapless homilies as the
Rev I. M. Jolly became a regular part of the Hogmanay festivities

29 JANUARY 2004

RIKKI FULTON, ONE OF SCOTLAND'S most gifted comedians, was something of a national institution. At Hogmanay the televised fireside homilies of his lugubrious creation the Rev I. M. Jolly, a parody of a well-meaning minister, were as much part of the new year festivities as whisky and black bun.

As a performer, Fulton was most at home in the sketch, having honed his technique and his timing in the variety theatre that once dominated Scottish popular entertainment. But he was also an accomplished stage and screen actor, and adapted with great success to the television age, although he remained less familiar to audiences south of the border.

His art, based on a close observation of Scottish manners, depended to some extent on his long but mobile face, which he used to wrap his comedy in a mantle of melancholy. His lampoons, whether of ministers, motorcycle policemen or Old Firm football managers, punctured their pretensions but remained affectionate and somehow respectful, for Fulton was of a conservative bent, both socially and politically.

Robert Kerr Fulton was born in Dennistoun, Glasgow, the son of a master locksmith who had turned to running a newsagent and stationery business. He was educated at Whitehill Secondary School, where he showed a certain talent as a pianist. During the war he was lucky to escape with his life when his ship, HMS *Ibis*, was torpedoed in the Mediterranean in 1942. She sank with the loss of her captain and two thirds of her company. An exhausted Fulton was rescued after five hours in the water.

Afterwards he was commissioned and served in an ML boat, one of an army of small armed craft that carried out escort and protection duties during the Normandy landings. After D-Day and subsequent operations, the strain told on his health, and he began to suffer blackouts. He was invalided out with the rank of sub-lieutenant.

On demobilisation he took to commerce while flirting with the amateur stage, and in 1948 made his first professional appearance with Dundee Rep in the comedy *Bunty Pulls the Strings*, a play forgotten now but then a staple of the repertory theatres' festive season. His broadcasting career began around the same time with the BBC in Glasgow when he took part in the popular Scottish radio soap opera, *The McFlannels*.

In 1951 he moved to London, where he presented the BBC Showband radio programmes, featuring artists such as Frank Sinatra and winning an enormous following. He did the job for four years but never took to the capital.

He returned to Scotland as a result of appearing in a late-night revue at the Edinburgh Palladium in 1954. The powerful producer Stewart Cruikshank of Howard and Wyndham had been unconvinced until then of Fulton's ability to relate to Scottish audiences, but now he changed his mind. In the next decades Fulton appeared in numerous pantomimes in winter and in a musical review called *The Five Past Eight Show* in summer. This mix also nurtured comics such as Stanley Baxter and Jimmy Logan.

The Five Past Eight Show brought Fulton into contact with the comedian Jack Milroy, and in 1960 they began a collaboration based upon the characters of Francie and Josie, teddy boys more daft than dangerous. The success of the duo was established by a television series on BBC Scotland and they became favourites with audiences throughout Scotland (though Fulton and the citizens of Aberdeen never warmed to each other), and the two comedians formed a lifelong friendship. The act won the Light Entertainment Award in 1989. Milroy died in 2001.

From 1978 Fulton had become established as one of BBC Scotland's major assets. The series *Scotch and Wry*, which ran for 15 years, brought forth the Rev I. M. Jolly and other characters, such as Supercop, a kind of glum Clouseau on a motorbike. In one sketch lampooning the bigotry of the Old Firm, Fulton played a Rangers manager aghast on discovering that a brilliant player, unaccountably absent in the second half of a trial game after scoring seven goals in the first, had departed to attend Mass.

Fulton also turned to the serious theatre, appearing in productions of *The Miser* and *A Winter's Tale.* In 1981 he took the leading role in *Let Wives Tak Tent,* Robert Kemp's free translation of Molière's *École des femmes.* This was the first production to be staged by the Scottish Theatre Company, an embryonic national theatre which eventually foundered on regional jealousies and financial constraints. He was happier in *A Touch of Class,* Frank Dunlop's adaptation of *Le Bourgeois gentilhomme* in 1985.

He returned to television in 1994 with Gregor Fisher in a new version of *The Tales of Para Handy,* Neil Munro's classic stories about the adventures of the *Vital Spark,* a coal-powered "puffer" that hauled cargoes between the Clyde and the Western Isles. He played the engineer McPhail.

His films included *The Dollar Bottom, Gorky Park, The Girl in the Picture* and two films directed by Bill Forsyth, *Local Hero* and *Comfort and Joy.*

Fulton was Scottish television personality of the year in 1963 and 1979, and won the president's award of the Television and Radio Industries Club in 1987. He received a lifetime achievement award from Bafta in 1993. St Andrews University conferred an honorary degree on him, and he was appointed OBE in 1991.

He published an entertaining autobiography, *Is It That Time Already?* Music, chess and bridge were among the hobbies he enjoyed in his home in Glasgow's West End. Although not politically active, he made it clear during the Thatcher years that he did not share Scotland's general dislike of her policies. He is survived by his wife, Kate Matheson (Craig-Brown), who in 2002 announced that he was suffering from Alzheimer's disease. His first marriage, to Ethel Scott, was dissolved in 1968.

ROBIN COOK

*Labour politician and foreign secretary, who resigned from
the Cabinet over the decision to wage war on Iraq*

8 AUGUST 2005

IN OPPOSITION AND IN GOVERNMENT alike, Robin Cook showed himself to be one of the finest parliamentary performers of his generation.

Certainly he was one of the Labour Party's most skilful politicians.
In Opposition, he destroyed the career of one Conservative Cabinet
Minister and attacked others to the point of persecution. He spoke with
wit, elegance, occasional cruelty and not seldom with arrogance.

Yet in parliamentary performances as different as his demolition
of the Government position over the Scott report on arms to Iraq
in 1996 and the speech he delivered on his resignation as Leader of
the Commons over the invasion of Iraq in 2003, he commanded
respect and admiration even from those who disagreed profoundly
with him.

But his career seesawed between extremes, and the public perception
of him did so likewise. At one time it had been possible to think of him
as a future Prime Minister. Even after Tony Blair became Labour leader
– in a contest which Cook decided not to enter, though afterwards he
regretted this – he retained hopes of succeeding. But events in the
first period of the Blair Government, in which he served as Foreign
Secretary, went a long way to putting paid to these.

The public and painful breakup of his marriage in 1997, involving
the revelation of a double life, considerably lowered his personal stock.
While travelling to Heathrow Airport with his wife, Margaret, to start a
holiday, he was alerted to the fact that a Sunday newspaper was about
to expose his affair with his personal secretary, Gaynor Regan. He
commandeered a VIP lounge at the airport in which to tell his wife that
their marriage was over. The marriage was dissolved with expedition,
and Ms Regan swiftly became his second wife.

Robin Cook

The weakness of his position as Foreign Secretary was that he had never wanted the post. He would much preferred to have been Chancellor of the Exchequer, and the fact that this did not happen was one reason for his dislike of Gordon Brown. Yet their rivalry went back to their early days in Scottish politics. So bitter was the dislike that on the morning of April 2, 1997, at the moment of their party's greatest election victory since the Labour landslide of 1945, they took separate aircraft from Edinburgh to the celebrations in London.

Shortly afterwards, having been given the overseas portfolio, Cook served notice that he was going to make waves. He implied that he was not going to be the creature of his civil servants. On the Queen's visit to the Indian subcontinent he infuriated the Indians. On his visit to the Middle East he infuriated the Israelis.

Certainly he had his successes. Discarding his earlier views on Europe, he made a good impression in Brussels. He worked doggedly on the various crises in the former Yugoslavia. There was trouble, though, with his party colleagues in the Commons Foreign Affairs Select Committee when he brushed aside their criticism of the Foreign Office over the arms-to-Sierra Leone furore and backed his officials all the way. He may not have been the creature of his civil servants but he was certainly their ally.

All this was in contrast with his years in Opposition, when he had been so much the iconoclast, the conscience of the party, and a leftwinger who might yet be seen as a possible challenger to the New Labour philosophies of Tony Blair.

Arresting though his parliamentary debating style was, he had an irritating and self-righteous manner of speaking. When asked an awkward question he would sound affronted and swallow half of his words in an effort to emphasise only those that he considered positive. Despite holding the respect of many of the party members he decided not to stand against Blair after John Smith's death. He admitted: "I didn't have the votes." And he was equally realistic about his chief handicap when he said on another occasion: "I have never been under any illusion that I got elected to anything because of my classical good looks."

Robert Finlayson Cook was born in 1946, in Belshill near Glasgow. An only child, he was brought up in his early years in extremely modest circumstances. His father was a headmaster, and this made him determined to succeed as a pupil. He was educated at Aberdeen Grammar School and the Royal High School in Edinburgh and once summed himself up: "I have always had the character of the school swot. I was not massively popular at school."

Things were easier for him, as they often are for intelligent children, at university. He went to Edinburgh University with the aim of becoming a Presbyterian minister, and read English literature, since an arts degree was a useful asset in the Church of Scotland. However, he soon lost his faith and he later he admitted that the Labour Party was a substitute for his original religion.

Cook became a comprehensive school teacher and then a lecturer for the Workers' Educational Association, but all the time he was thinking of Westminster. He fought Tory Edinburgh North in 1970 and then, after serving as chairman of Edinburgh City Council's housing committee, he was chosen as the candidate for marginal Edinburgh Central. He won it by fewer than 1,000 votes in the first election of 1974, which was held on February 28. It was his 28th birthday.

He started to emerge as the brightest of the 1974 intake. He duly served his apprenticeship on various party committees before gaining his reward in 1980, being appointed deputy spokesman on Treasury and economic affairs. But just as his stock rose in the House, his hopes of holding Edinburgh Central fell. He realised he would be extremely lucky to win there again. Relief came in the form of Livingston, the new overspill town between Edinburgh and Glasgow. Cook held it easily for the rest of his career. Proof of his growing reputation came when Neil Kinnock chose him as his campaign manager in the leadership contest after the disastrous 1983 election. He was elected to the Shadow Cabinet and given the post of European spokesman. Later he became deputy trade and industry spokesman.

His majority at the 1987 election was up by 6,000 and he was appointed Shadow Social Services spokesman. This was the start of a series of memorable shadow posts – health, trade and industry and foreign affairs – in which he delivered the coruscating speeches which made him Labour's most menacing front bench performer.

His attacks on two successive Health Secretaries, Kenneth Clarke and William Waldegrave, gained him *The Spectator's* Parliamentarian of the Year award in 1991. But it was his controlled fury and apparent contempt when dealing with John Moore, the hapless Secretary of State for the Department of Health and Social Security, that virtually ended Moore's political career.

Cook's towering performance in Opposition was at the presentation of the Scott report on arms to Iraq in the House of Commons in February 1996. He was given only three hours to take in its 1,800 pages. For the Government, Ian Lang, with the advantage of foreknowledge, appeared to be winning the argument until Cook rose and demolished the government case in a series of witheringly destructive points, which showed he had somehow managed to beat the clock and master all he needed.

His reward from the party leader after the Labour victory at the general election of 1997, was one of the highest offices of state in his appointment as Foreign Secretary. But Cook did not see it as such. He had always regarded the channelling of his energies into foreign affairs, while Labour had been in opposition, as an attempt to keep him out of policy making at the centre of the party. His insistence on an "ethical" dimension at the very heart of British foreign policy became a high-risk strategy, well meant but unsustainable in the face of Britain's long-standing commercial alliances.

After the general election of 2001 Cook was relieved of his ministerial responsibilities and offered the leadership of the House of Commons. It was an obvious demotion, and one designed to keep him even further removed from any influence in the counsels of the party.

When it became clear from 2002 onwards that Blair intended to commit Britain to war on Iraq alongside the US, Cook made his unease clear to the Cabinet. He said with some force that he did not believe that the intelligence proved that Saddam Hussein could possibly pose a strategic threat to a country such as Britain, and that it was preposterous to claim that this menace could be launched in the short time that was being posited. His objections were ignored, and his career in the senior ranks of Labour government finally came to an end when in March 2003 he resigned from the Cabinet over the impending war, in a speech that was given a standing ovation in some parts of the House.

That was the effective end of his career. Though he altered over the years, notably in his attitude to Gordon Brown, towards whom he had latterly mellowed, at bottom there was an undeniable whiff of Old Labour about Robin Cook. He was a closet Keynesian, and still believed in public spending and taxing to find the money. What remained basic to him was his feeling for the party which turned him from a potential theologian into a practical politician.

He published *Point of Departure*, an insider's account of the build-up to the invasion of Iraq, in 2003. He also enjoyed horse-riding and racing, deer-watching, and was a keen mountain walker. It was while he was enjoying this favourite pastime that he apparently suffered a heart attack that led to his death.

Robin Cook married in 1969, Margaret Whitmore, whom he had met at university. The marriage was dissolved in 1998. He married in that year Gaynor Regan. She survives him with the two sons of his first marriage.

JIMMY JOHNSTONE

*Mesmerising winger who, with charm and determination,
endeared himself to the Parkhead faithful*

14 MARCH 2006

WIDELY REGARDED AS one of the finest players to put on a Celtic shirt, Jimmy Johnstone was one of Scottish football's best-loved characters of the 1960s. He was a legend at the Glasgow club, for which he scored more than 100 goals, helping the side to win nine consecutive titles and lift the European Cup in 1967 – the first British team to do so.

He endeared himself not only to the Parkhead faithful, but to the whole Scottish – and British – nation. In many ways he was a mirror image of his contemporary, Jim Baxter of Rangers; like Baxter, Johnstone was ebullient, skilful, crafty and prolific, and became much loved by Catholic and Protestant alike. Some have also drawn comparisons to Alan Ball, for Johnstone was also a diminutive, tenacious redhead renowned for his cheeky disposition. Others have likened him to George Best: a hard-living maverick who should have shone at international level, yet was adored by his fans. Comparisons aside, in the opinion of his team-mate Tommy Gemmell "he had the heart of a lion and the ability of a maestro".

Jimmy Johnstone was born in Viewpark, Lanarkshire, in 1944. He was spotted by Manchester United at the age of 13 while playing for the Viewpark team Boys' Guild, but a Celtic scout soon afterwards spotted his talents, and persuaded him to come to Glasgow instead. He signed for Celtic and after a few years on loan with Celtic Blantyre, where his talents manifested themselves with abundance, he made his debut for Celtic in 1963 (in an inauspicious 6-0 defeat by Kilmarnock).

The Parkhead faithful swiftly took him to their hearts, impressed by this winger's mesmerising dribbles, his aggression and his audacious capacity to take opposing defences apart – dubbing him "Jinky". Celtic came into their element in the late 1960s, breaking Rangers' domination of the game by winning the Scottish title consecutively from 1966 to 1974. It is often said that if Jock Stein was the architect of this success, then Jimmy Johnstone was Celtic's magician in chief.

After such success at domestic level, Celtic embarked on a continental adventure that would eventually make them champions of Europe, and Johnstone was one of the "Lisbon Lions" who overcame Inter Milan in the 1967 European Cup final.

Their Italian rivals were much derided for their defensive, if effective, tactics, and it was feared that a buoyant Celtic, having won the league, Scottish FA Cup and League Cup, would be naive to employ again their typically flamboyant, attacking game. Indeed, having conceded a penalty after eight minutes, Celtic looked to be out of their depth, but the Bhoys took the game to their opponents, with right-winger Johnstone proving a particular nuisance. Goals by Gemmell and Steve Chalmers eventually made Celtic "Kings of Europe".

Johnstone's most notorious appearance came in the ensuing World Club Championship against Racing Club of Argentina. Alongside the battles of the Berne and Santiago, this tie is considered to be one of the most violent matches in soccer history. Even the police were brought in to stop players fighting on the pitch.

After the two-legged affair had ended in stalemate, a decider was held in Montevideo, during which six players were sent off – including Johnstone, who after being remorselessly hacked and spat upon, retaliated by elbowing one of the Argentinians.

Memorable for rather more positive reasons was Johnstone's outstanding performance against Leeds United in the 1970 European Cup semi-final. He ran circles around the Yorkshiremen in both legs, tormenting in particular Terry Cooper, and set up the final goal to land Celtic a 3-1 aggregate victory. In the final, however, Feyenoord's mean defence proved too resilient, and Celtic, perhaps a little overconfident, were defeated 2-1.

Johnstone's relative paucity of Scotland caps – 23 – has been attributed to many factors. Some thought that the national selectors merely failed to recognise his talent, while it is also said that he was the victim of anti-Celtic feeling, but the most likely explanation is that he simply had a morbid fear of flying – thus preventing him from travelling with Scotland abroad. Indeed, Jock Stein promised Johnstone that he would not have to travel to Yugoslavia if he helped Celtic to beat Red Star Belgrade handsomely in the home leg: Johnstone scored and Celtic won 5-1. His team-mates, unaware of the arrangement, were bemused when Johnstone celebrated the result by dancing on the pitch and singing "I'm no' going!"

At international level he scored four times and with Celtic he netted on 129 occasions, in 515 appearances. Johnstone left Celtic in 1975 and went on to play for San Jose Earthquakes, Sheffield United, Dundee, Shelbourne and Elgin City. He later worked as a lorry driver and construction worker. Motor neuron disease was diagnosed in 2001 and Johnstone subsequently worked to raise awareness of the disease.

He is survived by his wife, Agnes, two daughters and a son.

Jimmy Johnstone, footballer, was born on September 30, 1944. He died on March 13, 2006, aged 61.

* * *

DAME MURIEL SPARK

Writer whose conversion to Catholicism inspired her to works of wit and variety, not least 'The Prime of Miss Jean Brodie'

17 APRIL 2006

THE SPARKLET WAS HER NICKNAME, and anyone who met her could tell why. Perhaps Scotland's most important modern novelist, Muriel Spark was a small, striking woman, with a coruscating mind. She brought a vivacious imagination to her writing, backed by pitiless powers of observation. "You may not call Spark's novels lifelike," her fellow Scottish author Allan Massie once wrote, "but it is probable, even certain, that you will some day, sometimes, find life to be Sparklike."

She wrote more than 20 novels, as well as stories, plays and children's books, and was a master of taut, quirky plots, often focusing on a small group of people whose lives are altered by a strange twist of fate. She admired what she called a literature of ridicule – "the only honourable weapon we have left" – and even in her own social life, she said, she picked up the craft of being polite while people were present and leaving the laughter until later.

She made her name with the character of Miss Jean Brodie, the unconventional and incorrigibly romantic Edinburgh schoolmistress with an admiration for Mussolini and dedication to the *crème de la crème* of her pupils. A restrained comedy of manners, mocking the old Edinburgh politesse, *The Prime of Miss Jean Brodie* (1961) sold hundreds of thousands of copies. It was adapted for the Broadway stage and made into a film in which Maggie Smith took the schoolmistress's starring role.

Spark wrote rapidly, rarely revising what she scribbled in the spiral-bound notebooks, which she had sent to her in consignments from the Edinburgh stationer's James Thin. She claimed to have dreamt up *The Public Image* (1968) – about a film star's struggle with the scandal industry – while asleep: "When I woke up every detail was in my head. I just wrote it all down." In *A Far Cry from Kensington* (1988), she dispenses authorial advice. Write as if you are writing to a friend, she suggests. "Write privately, not publicly; without fear or timidity, right to the end of the letter ... Remember not to think of the reading public. It will put you off."

In 1992 Spark published her autobiography, *Curriculum Vitae*, a series of vignettes and flashbacks of a life full of intriguing characters and peculiar subplots. But she detested intrusion into her private life, and the book tells very little about Spark herself. She could be prickly and had a reputation for falling out with friends and associates. A former editor fell from grace when he described her in an interview as "really quite batty".

Muriel Spark was born Muriel Sarah Camberg in the genteel Edinburgh suburb of Morningside. Her father, Bernard Camberg, an engineer in a rubber factory, was a Jew whose family had settled in Scotland. Her mother, Sarah Uezzell, was an English Presbyterian from Watford, who was later to take to drink.

The religious divide in her parents' marriage was to influence Spark's imagination considerably. In her only long novel, *The Mandelbaum Gate*, set in Jerusalem during the trial of Eichmann, a Roman Catholic woman finds herself in peril because of her part-Jewish ancestry. In later life Spark was to become involved in a bitter feud with her son Robin (a painter) about her Jewishness, and the quarrel snowballed in a blizzard of birth and marriage certificates, claims and counterclaims.

Spark's native city remained very important to her. Wherever she went in her long life, its puritanical ethos remained with her, and her religious faith came to be symbolised by Edinburgh's Castle Rock. "To have a great, primitive black crag rising up in the middle of populated streets of commerce, stately squares and winding closes," she said, "is like a statement preceded by 'nevertheless'. In the middle of worldly enterprises there is, nevertheless, the inescapable fact of God."

At James Gillespie's School for Girls, a merchant foundation where pupils started classical languages at seven, Spark encountered Miss Christina Kay, the inspirational teacher who was the model for Miss Jean Brodie. "She entered my imagination immediately. I started to write about her even then. Her accounts of her travels were gripping, fantastic," Spark later wrote in her autobiography. "Her dazzling non-sequiturs filled my heart with joy."

And Miss Kay encouraged Spark to write. She had written her first poem at nine, and, being reared on the *Border Ballads*, she had a taste for a good yarn. By adolescence she was composing torrid love letters that she signed with fictitious men's names and hid under the sofa cushions in the hope of shocking her mother.

On leaving school, she went briefly to a technical college, but in 1936 ran away on a romantic impulse to Salisbury in Southern Rhodesia to marry Sidney Oswald Spark, a schoolteacher more than 12 years her senior. "I don't quite know why I married SOS," she later said. "I suppose I was attracted to a man who brought me bunches of flowers when I had 'flu. But my husband was very much a nut." He became increasingly quarrelsome and violent, often shooting his revolver at the walls.

Spark separated from him shortly after her son was born in 1938, and the marriage was later dissolved, although Spark kept the name because "it possessed some ingredient of life and fun". She was never to marry again, and although there were several subsequent love affairs she was always "a very bad picker of men", she said. In 1944 she returned to Britain and, depositing her seven-year-old son with her parents, took a room at a London club for "ladies of good families" – later to serve as a model for the boarding house in *The Girls of Slender Means* – and found work in the Political Intelligence Department at Woburn Abbey, where her creative talents were put to use inventing bogus news items for "black" propaganda broadcasts.

Once the war was over she found employment with a jewellery trade paper and then as a press agent for businessmen before, in 1947, joining the Poetry Society.

In 1951 Spark won a short story competition in *The Observer* with *The Seraph and the Zambesi*, in which a tawdry troupe of travelling actors, staging a Christmas pageant on the banks of an African river, are interrupted by an argumentative angel. Encouraged by this small success, she continued to write, scribbling through the nights, while working part-time during the day as an editor in the offices of Peter Owen Publishers. She also reviewed occasionally under the *nom de plume* Evelyn Cavallo.

In 1952 she published a collection of poems, *The Fanfarlo and Other Verse*. She also worked in collaboration with Derek Stanford, who had co-edited the second edition of *Forum* and was to remain her literary partner until 1957 on a number of publications. It was when she came to edit the *Letters of John Henry Newman* (1957) that she found her life changed. Newman's writings inspired her, and she decided in 1954 to be received into the Roman Catholic Church, in a process which she later described as "both too easy and too difficult to explain".

With conversion came her freedom to write. "Everyone said that I would be so restricted, but in fact the very opposite happened," Spark said. "I didn't get my style until I was a Catholic," she explained, "because you haven't got to care and you need security for that. That's the whole secret of style in a way."

Her first novel, written at the suggestion of her publishers, Macmillan, was intended simply as a way of working out the technique of what she considered at the time an inferior literary form. Aided by a stipend from Graham Greene – given on condition that she didn't say thank you or pray for him – and by a loan of a cottage in the country, she completed and published *The Comforters* in 1957.

It was a daring piece of metafiction, before the term had been coined. Hailed by Evelyn Waugh as a masterpiece, *The Comforters* made her literary reputation. She followed it in 1958 with *Robinson*, in which another convert, a young widow, finds herself marooned with three men on a desert island. Spark had honed her humour to a sharp, unsparing edge by 1959 when she published *Memento Mori*, in which a group of octogenarians are plagued by an anonymous caller who tells them "remember you must die" and produces ever more absurd reactions. The novel was adapted for the London stage in 1964 and later televised by the BBC in 1978.

The biting verbal humour of *The Ballad of Peckham Rye* (1960) – in which the Devil is sent to one of the tattier boroughs of South London – lent itself to a prizewinning radio adaptation, and *The Bachelors* followed in the same year, about a phoney spiritualist medium. But it was for her 1961 *The Prime of Miss Jean Brodie* that Spark was to be most remembered.

It was shortly after that success that Spark, now slavishly courted by the London literati, left Britain. "If people know you are famous," she said, "they quiver in a different way. You don't get the same natural response." She was also fed up with her alcoholic mother, who kept falling down and breaking her bones. She left for New York City, procuring an office overlooking Times Square. "I had lots of fun," she later said, "I bought pretty clothes, went to the hairdresser and travelled a great deal – I think I felt free for the first time." Being an expatriate helped her writing, she thought.

In 1967 she was appointed OBE. But by then she was ready for another move. She changed her wardrobe, recoiffed her hair, and set off for Rome where, taken up by a succession of English-speaking monsignors and expats such as Anthony Burgess, Gore Vidal and William Weaver, she indulged in a dramatic *dolce vita*, hosting glamorous parties in a palazzo drawing room that had once been the library of Cardinal Orsini. When she wanted to write she would withdraw, persuading a doctor friend to sign her into a private hospital room where nobody could contact her.

Novels from this period included *The Driver's Seat* (1970), *Not to Disturb* (1971), and *The Abbess of Crewe* (1974), most commonly described as Watergate in a nunnery.

By the 1980s, however, Spark had begun to retreat more frequently to the Tuscan countryside, where she eventually moved to a converted 14th-century monastery house set in a garden of olive trees and vines on precipitous slopes above a village. Here, protected from the press by her long-standing companion, Penelope Jardine, a painter and sculptress, she would relax watching the interminable South American soap operas whose tortuous and protracted plots she so enjoyed.

In later years she was a familiar figure to locals, speeding through the Tuscan lanes in an Alfa Romeo brought from part of the proceeds of the David Cohen Literature Prize, awarded for a lifetime achievement in literature. Part of this prize money she also presented to her old school, the place where Miss Jean Brodie was born.

Spark's later novels include *Symposium* (1990), *Reality and Dreams* (1996), and *Aiding and Abetting* (2000), which was based on a real London murder case. Her last book, *The Finishing School*, a tense and comic portrayal of a creative writing teacher's consuming jealousy of his teenage pupil's talent, was published in 2004.

Spark was appointed DBE in 1993. She is survived by her son.

GEORGE DAVIE

Philosopher, who explored the intellectual legacy and
continuity of the Scottish Enlightenment

18 APRIL 2007

OF GEORGE DAVIE'S CELEBRATED BOOK *The Democratic Intellect* one
commentator remarked that it should be read by the vice-chancellors
of the English provincial universities. Another commentator said that
it should be read by every member of the Scottish Parliament and by
everyone interested in education or in Scotland.

The book appeared at a time when the Robbins Committee was
rethinking the role of the university in society, and Davie's defence of
the generalist tradition of Scottish teaching, against what he saw as the
overspecialised English universities, was quickly recognised as a key
contribution.

With elections now on the near horizon and with restructuring of
universities taking place on both sides of the Border, these comments
are no less valid today than when they were first made in the early 1960s.

George Elder Davie was born in Dundee in 1912. His mother was a
teacher and his father a pharmacist. From Dundee High School, where
he excelled, he went to Edinburgh University, graduating with a first
in classics in 1935. He stayed on at Edinburgh as a junior lecturer until
1941 when he joined the Signals Corps. During the war he served in
North Africa and Italy. On demobilisation he took a post as lecturer in
philosophy at Queen's University Belfast.

There he caught the eye of the librarian, Philip Larkin. "Try Davie in
Philosophy," Larkin advised a visiting Routledge scout on the prowl for
manuscripts that might suit its lists.

Routledge agreed to publish Davie's DLitt dissertation provided
it was supplemented by a historical introduction. The historical
introduction grew into *The Democratic Intellect*, first published by
Edinburgh University Press in 1961.

Nothing less than poetic justice was being done therefore when Routledge stood by its conditional acceptance of the dissertation and in 2001 brought out *The Scotch Metaphysics*, a book from which it is evident that the epistemological investigations of the philosophers of the Scottish Enlightenment treated in it were every bit as subtle as the philosophical analyses being produced in the 1950s on the banks of the Isis and the Cam.

Davie's arguments did not prevent his taking very seriously the teaching of Gilbert Ryle at Oxford. He expressed the opinion that aspects of the latter's *The Concept of Mind* had been anticipated by John Macmurray, who had included Davie among his possible successors at London. Macmurray retired from the Chair of Moral Philosophy at Edinburgh in 1958, a year before Davie returned to the department there where he had studied and then worked as an assistant to Norman Kemp Smith.

Davie was not an uncritical admirer of Macmurray – or indeed of Macmurray's most publicised recent admirer, the Prime Minister. There is a dash of vitriol in a dictated text named *The Tony Blair Tapes*. Davie liked in Macmurray what he found to his liking in the phenomenological investigations of Edmund Husserl and Maurice Merleau-Ponty, philosophers whom Ryle too found attractive. All of them are preoccupied by the question of how to describe intersubjectivity. Davie raised this question in citing Robert Burns's words about seeing ourselves as others see us, words that revive an idea of an Adam Smith somewhat different from Margaret Thatcher's.

Reflection on this idea led Davie to focus on the philosophy of James Frederick Ferrier, which without any qualms he called phenomenology.

Ferrier's remark "Sight pays back every fraction of its debt to its brother sense", namely touch, which is inseparable from the experience of movement, resounds with poignant irony, given the serious problems Davie had with his own sight. These might to some extent have motivated his interest in Ferrier's descriptions of perceptual experience and contributed to the authenticity of his own.

Davie never retreated into the a priorism he regretted in Ferrier's later writings. Nor did he ever shirk the labour of combating what he saw as a tendency among Scots intellectuals generally to neglect the riches of their own tradition.

When at departmental and faculty meetings he explained to his colleagues: "This is how it used to be done," it was not his intention to imply "so this is how it ought to be done". His aim was to register historical facts of which some of them may have been ignorant in order that resolutions would be more fully informed.

His own knowledge of historical background and his insight into how it might be brought to bear on the future are manifest in the Dow Lecture of 1974 entitled *The Social Significance of the Scottish Philosophy of Common Sense*, in *The Crisis of the Democratic Intellect* (1986), in two collections of essays published by Polygon under the titles *The Scottish Enlightenment and Other Essays* (1991) and *A Passion for Ideas* (1994), and in a monograph published by the *Edinburgh Review* in 2003 entitled *Ferrier and the Blackout of the Scottish Enlightenment.*

After Davie's retirement in 1982 the importance of his contribution to learning in Scotland was marked by the conferring of an emeritus readership at Edinburgh, honorary doctorates at Dundee and at Edinburgh, a fellowship of the Royal Society of Edinburgh, the Saltire Society's Andrew Fletcher Award, and a fellowship of the Educational Institute of Scotland.

Davie was an endearingly idiosyncratic teacher. On one occasion, wishing to dramatise to his class an argument Kant used against Leibniz's relational theory of space, Davie – whose interest in topology had been roused by one of his teachers as early as his years as a pupil at Dundee High School – turned inside out one of a pair of gloves he had brought with him only to find to his dismay that in doing so he was emptying coal dust over himself and the students in the front row.

Something that is reported by all his former students is his practice of inviting them to his flat at the end of the academic year to take tea and cake (Dundee cake, of course, in honour of his native city) with his wife Elspeth (née Dryer) whom he had married in 1944. Her short stories and novels were among the texts he asked to be read to him in his last years.

Although posterity will remember Davie chiefly as the author of *The Democratic Intellect*, he was a man with many friendships, such as that initiated when, in 1935, he introduced the Gaelic poet Sorley MacLean and the Scots poet Hugh MacDiarmid.

Davie's wife, Elspeth, died in 1995, and he is survived by their daughter.

* * *

SIR BERNARD CRICK

'Public intellectual in the mould of the great socialist sages'

22 December 2008

Sir Bernard Crick belonged to an endangered species. He was a public intellectual in the mould of the great socialist sages of the first half of the last century – Graham Wallas, G. D. H. Cole, R. H. Tawney and Harold Laski. He was a distinguished political theorist, with three important scholarly works to his credit, as well as one great one.

He also intervened incessantly in public debate, on matters ranging from parliamentary reform to the politics of divided societies. But his academic works and his essays and journalism dealt with the same themes, and were written in the same accessible, slightly quirky and occasionally waspish style.

Not for him the gnarled prose of the self-consciously professional scholar or the windy exaggerations of the media columnist. He wrote for another endangered species – the educated and thoughtful general reader.

His best-known book is probably his *George Orwell: A Life*, a biography commissioned by Orwell's second wife, Sonia, and published in 1980. The biography won Crick great public *réclame* but led to a breach with

Sonia, who thought it had not done justice to the subject.

In truth, Crick was too much the political theorist, and perhaps too lacking in human empathy, to be a natural biographer. His treatment of Orwell the novelist, polemicist and (not least) prose stylist was scrupulously thorough, but Orwell the man never quite came to life.

Of much greater long-term significance than Crick's *Orwell* was his glittering masterpiece, *In Defence of Politics*, first published in 1962, when he was only 33. It was a young man's book, written with exhilarating *panache*. It was translated into four languages, and went through five editions.

It set out an essentially republican vision of politics – of politics as freedom and of freedom as politics – heavily influenced by the great German Jewish political philosopher, Hannah Arendt, and ultimately derived from Aristotle.

Thanks partly to Crick, that vision is now quite common; indeed a whole academic industry is now devoted to the republican themes that Crick brought back into public consciousness. But in 1962 he swam against the current. Parliamentary politics were dominated by the twin paternalisms of Fabian centralism on the left and *noblesse oblige* Conservatism on the right. In the academy, political scientists had retreated from civic engagement into pseudo-scientific number-crunching or a weary quietism.

Against these orthodoxies Crick raised a flag of revolt. He sought to return to a much older tradition of political thinking, centred on active and participatory citizenship in a pluralistic political community.

Politics, he insisted, was not universal. It had been absent from many, perhaps most, societies known to history. It was not an ideology: ideology was one of its most dangerous enemies. It was not to be equated with democracy. Unrestrained democracy – democracy as a euphemism for mob rule or as camouflage for the tyranny of the majority – was another enemy. Politics was about conciliation, compromise, argument and debate between diverse groups. It was grubby and unheroic; negotiation and deal-making were of its essence. Yet only by and through it could free men and women live together in society. But there was nothing inevitable about it. It depended on "deliberate and continuous individual activity".

"Activity" was the key word. Crick was not content to theorise. He wanted to do what he could to realise his vision of politics in the real world of practice. In that spirit he published *The Reform of Parliament* in 1964, and helped to set up the Study of Parliament Group in the same year.

The Reform of Parliament was a rather decorous manifesto, setting out the case for more effective parliamentary scrutiny of the executive, while preserving the essentials of the British parliamentary monarchy.

Forty years later it reads tamely, but it did not seem tame to the young MPs who swept into the Commons on Harold Wilson's coat-tails in 1964 and 1966. It became the bible of would-be reformers in the 1966 Labour intake, in particular. Only later did it become clear that Crick had dodged the fundamental question: what would happen when gradualist parliamentary reform ran up against the buffers of executive power?

By then, however, Crick was getting itchy feet. Born in 1929, he had grown up in a middle-class family in the Surrey suburbs. He had been educated at Whitgift School in Croydon; at University College London, where he was awarded a First; and at the London School of Economics, where he was a research student.

Between 1952 and 1956 he studied and taught at Harvard, McGill and Berkeley, California. In 1957 he was appointed assistant lecturer at LSE, where he stayed as lecturer, and later senior lecturer, for eight years. But the LSE Government Department was headed by the high priest of conservative quietism, the political philosopher Michael Oakeshott; and Crick's restless spirit ran against the Oakeshottian grain.

In 1965 Crick emigrated from London to a Chair in Political Theory and Institutions at the University of Sheffield. At Sheffield Crick laid the foundations of what would become one of the leading politics departments in the country; he also won the abiding admiration of some of his junior staff. He was awarded four honorary doctorates altogether, but Sheffield's, awarded in 1990, gave him most pleasure.

He also taught the young David Blunkett, who became a lifelong friend. But the lure of the metropolis continued to beckon. Crick still made his home in London; and, until he was discovered by the cleaners, he camped out, in some squalor, in his office in the University Arts Tower.

When an indignant Vice-Chancellor asked what would happen if the rest of the teaching staff behaved like that, Crick replied airily that he supposed extra floors would have to be added to the building.

Another move was inevitable; and in 1971 Crick was appointed Professor of Politics at Birkbeck College, London. The Orwell biography was the most obvious literary fruit of his time at Birkbeck, but, ever restless, he accumulated many other roles as well. He was joint editor of *The Political Quarterly* from 1966 to 1980, and later chairman of the editorial board, in which capacity he played the part of the absent-minded professor to outrageous perfection, and waged unremitting war against unnecessary footnotes.

Later still he set up the Orwell Prize to encourage good political writing in journalism and books, in the spirit of Orwell's hope that it could become an art. He was the first president of the Politics Association, designed to foster politics teaching in schools. Not surprisingly, the Thatcher-induced chill winds that blew through British universities in the early 1980s led him to take early retirement in 1984. He even spurned the metropolitan lure and settled in Edinburgh, the home of his then partner, Una Maclean. He wrote as voluminously as ever, but hopes that retirement would give him the time to produce another big book were disappointed. He was active in the movement for Scottish devolution, and helped, behind the scenes, to broker discussions between the nationalist and loyalist communities in Northern Ireland.

His big moment came in 1997, when Blunkett became Education Secretary in Tony Blair's first Government. Blunkett appointed him as chairman of a high-powered advisory group on citizenship education. The resulting report resounded with the themes that Crick had made his own for more than 30 years. It cited Aristotle and the Roman Republic, and declared uncompromisingly that the group's aim was "no less than a change in the political culture of this country", enabling people "to think of themselves as active citizens, willing, able and equipped to have an influence in public life".

From it flowed an order making citizenship teaching part of the core curriculum. Later, Crick was charged with devising the naturalisation ceremonies for new British citizens. In 2002, in the teeth of official opposition, Blunkett secured him a knighthood in explicit recognition for his services to citizenship.

Crick's quirkiness concealed an inner insecurity, which was reflected in his rather chaotic private life. He wanted to be an outsider and an insider – a radical and a Whig – at the same time. He wanted to poke the establishment in the midriff, but he also craved its recognition. He was not the first or the last British socialist of whom that could be said.

Crick's three marriages ended in divorce and he is survived by his partner, Una Maclean, and the two sons of his first marriage.

* * *

SIR LUDOVIC KENNEDY

Writer and broadcaster, who fought injustice and
exposed wrongful convictions

20 OCTOBER 2009

SIR LUDOVIC KENNEDY was a writer and broadcaster who, with his life-long friend and colleague Sir Robin Day, set new standards in television journalism. He was a rigorous and charismatic interviewer and reporter, later employing these talents to expose legal injustices and articulate his powerful and provocative views on religion, morality and euthanasia.

With his trademark look of wry bemusement, Kennedy laced his incisive questioning with an idiosyncratic charm that became the blueprint for a generation of journalists and a huge hit with viewers. His poise as a performer was matched by his ability to see through to the truth of a story and take a full grasp of all the issues at play, and it quickly took him to the top of his profession. After rising to early success as a newscaster for the fledgling *Independent Television News*, where he worked alongside Day, he blazed a trail with investigative reporting programmes such as *Panorama* and *Tonight*.

A strong moral rectitude brought Kennedy into contact not only with current affairs but also with the past. He launched campaigns to reconsider convictions in several high-profile cases, including the hanging of Derek Bentley and the jailing of the Birmingham Six and the Guildford Four. His *exposés* of corruption and incompetence in the police and legal systems were damningly effective, and he was ubiquitous in debates on the need for judicial reform.

He was an ardent and often outspoken campaigner, also prominent in calls for the legalisation of euthanasia, castigating the Roman Catholic Church's pro-life stance as "medieval in its thinking and barbaric in its lack of compassion". Kennedy was already a committed atheist who saw religion as undeserving of any moral high-ground, and he first become involved in the Voluntary Euthanasia Society when his mother, Rosalind, suffering from painful rheumatoid arthritis, told him that she did not want to live any longer. He went on to become president of the Voluntary Euthanasia Society.

A perennially active thinker, Kennedy published a critique of religious doctrine and history of atheistic thought, *All in the Mind: A Farewell to God* (1999), aged 79. Without any sense of world-weariness, he attacked what he saw as the hijacking of altruism by Christianity, and made a cogent, lively case for the abstract nature of human moral value.

The book also allowed him to chart a much more personal journey. He wrote movingly of his father, a Christian, who died when the ship that he was captaining was sunk off Iceland in the Second World War. Describing the shattering effect of this loss, Kennedy concluded that it aptly illustrated "the uselessness of prayer". "[My father] had a very simple faith," he wrote. "He prayed every night and morning of his life, and I know he would have done that on the morning of the battle, and look what happened to him."

Yet he did not dismiss the potential for spiritual satisfaction in life and was angered at the suggestion that a life without religion might be less moral. He recalled two experiences particular resonant of such spirituality in his life: as a child hearing a piper on the moors in his native Scotland; and seeing hundreds of stars, like "a watchful presence", while standing on board a fleet destroyer at night during the war.

Ludovic Henry Coverley Kennedy was born in Edinburgh in 1919, the son of Captain E. C. Kennedy and Rosalind, daughter of Sir Ludovic Grant, the 11th Baronet of Dalvey. The family was prosperous, and Kennedy was sent to Eton, where he was a member of Pop. He then went up to Christ Church, Oxford, where he read English. He played a full part in university life, becoming literary editor of *Isis* and a member of the Bullingdon, the qualifications for which, he later recalled, were to be "rich, well born and addicted to blood sports".

When war broke out Kennedy volunteered for the Navy. His father, by then in command of the armed merchant cruiser *Rawalpindi*, asked his son's captain if he could take Kennedy on his next patrol. The captain refused, saying that Kennedy was too inexperienced. It was on that patrol that the *Rawalpindi* was sunk by the German battle cruisers *Scharnhorst* and *Gneisenau*.

But Kennedy would get his chance, and always said that the most memorable and exciting period of his life was in May 1941, when he was a 21-year-old sub-lieutenant in one of the Navy's destroyers, *Tartar*, which helped to pursue and sink Germany's biggest battleship, the *Bismarck*.

After the war Kennedy began to edge his way into broadcasting, becoming an editor of the BBC Third Programme's *First Reading* in 1953 and then, in 1955, the presenter of ATV's *Profile*. He reached a wider audience when, in 1956, he joined Robin Day as a presenter with ITN. Kennedy's authoritative yet relaxed television style made him immensely popular with the viewers while his intelligence and independence commended him to his superiors at ITN, who were consciously trying to break away from the established BBC format of simply reading the news. ITN newscasters were encouraged to be more individualistic, to put more of themselves into the programme.

The stint at ITN firmly established Kennedy's reputation as a radio and television journalist, and for the rest of his life he was in constant demand, presenting or appearing on such programmes as *Your Witness, Panorama, 24 Hours, Tonight* and *Did You See?*

He will be remembered by television viewers for his characteristic pose – looking at his interviewees over the top of his glasses, often with a slightly quizzical, almost disbelieving, smile on his lips; sometimes with a stern, schoolmasterly gaze. As an interviewer he was polite but always his own man; he believed that the interviewer should be courteous but incisive.

Kennedy did not devote himself exclusively to radio and television. He was a playwright and a prolific author. The books for which he will be best remembered are those in which he exposed miscarriages of justice. The first of three major books in this field was *10 Rillington Place*, published in 1961, which ultimately led to a posthumous pardon for Timothy Evans, a lodger in the house of the mass murderer John Reginald Christie. Evans had been hanged for the murder of his baby. Kennedy's book showed that Christie was almost certainly the real killer.

Fourteen years later another book, *A Presumption of Innocence,* examined the case of Patrick Meehan who had been jailed in 1969 for the killing of an elderly woman in Ayr. Shortly afterwards the real killer died in a fight, and his solicitor, to whom he had confessed, cleared Meehan. Meehan received the Queen's pardon and financial compensation.

The third book, *Wicked Beyond Belief,* concerned the cases of David Cooper and Michael McMahon, who had been convicted of the murder of a Luton sub-postmaster in 1969. Shortly after the book was published in 1980, the Home Secretary remitted the sentences of both men and released them.

Time and again Kennedy's nose for injustice led to the re-examinations of convictions – notably the execution of Richard Hauptmann for the kidnapping and murder of the baby son of the aviator Charles Linbergh in *The Airman and the Carpenter.*

His passion for righting injustices was jolted into action when Derek Bentley, whose 16-year-old companion had shot a policeman, was sentenced to death. Kennedy and his wife, Moira, thought the sentence so monstrous that they sent a telegram to the Home Secretary at the time, Sir David Maxwell Fyfe, urging clemency. The execution of Bentley so shocked Kennedy that he wrote a play about it, *Murder Story*, which was produced at the Cambridge Theatre in 1954.

Kennedy's naval background and the manner of his father's death also gave him an abiding interest in naval history, and he published several well-received books on the subject, including *Pursuit: the Chase and Sinking of the Bismarck* and *Menace: the Life and Death of the Tirpitz.*

At one time, Kennedy hoped to pursue an active political career. He stood, unsuccessfully, for the Liberals in Rochdale in the 1958 by-election and the general election in 1959 but left the Scottish Liberal Party in 1967 when it refused to allow him to support Winifred Ewing, the Scottish National Party candidate, in the Hamilton by-election. He believed that nationalism and internationalism were complementary, not contradictory.

Kennedy married the ballerina Moira Shearer, star of Powell and Pressburger's *The Red Shoes* (1948), in 1950. Despite his public profile he remained highly protective of his family, mentioning them in detail only once in his engaging autobiography, *On the Way to the Club* (1989). In 2001 he resigned from the Liberal Democrats party after more than four decades following the refusal of the party leader Charles Kennedy to place the legalisation of voluntary euthanasia in his party's manifesto for the general election, despite a conference vote by eight to one in favour of the policy. In the general election of that year Kennedy stood in the constituency of Devizes, where he had lived for many years, on the platform of legalising voluntary euthanasia. He took on Michael

Ancram, a Catholic and the chairman of the Conservative Party, but secured only 1,078 votes, while Ancram increased his majority to almost 12,000.

Kennedy was knighted in 1994 for services to politics, broadcasting and journalism. His wife, Moira Shearer, died in 2006. He is survived by their son and three daughters.

* * *

BILL McLAREN

'The voice of rugby' who became the best-loved sports broadcaster of his time

20 JANUARY 2010

BILL McLAREN SPENT 50 years commentating on rugby union matches for BBC radio and television. In this role his powerful Scottish tones, memorable turns of phrase, dedication to research and rigid impartiality proved an awesome combination, enhancing the broadcast experience for millions of listeners and viewers throughout club and international seasons.

His intelligence and warmth also made him one of the best-liked figures among the distinguished set of sports commentators working for the BBC over the latter half of the 20th century, and earned him the sobriquet the "Voice of Rugby".

William McLaren was born in 1923 at Hawick, Roxburghshire. His father was the factory manager of a knitwear company. As a young boy he played games of rugby by himself at home with a paper ball he had made, keeping a list of scores in a ledger given to him by his parents. His love of the game continued into adolescence, and he first represented Hawick as a flanker at the age of 17.

During the Second World War he served with the artillery in Italy and North Africa. On returning to Scotland he resumed his commitments to Hawick – eventually captaining the side – at the same time as studying for a diploma in physical education in Aberdeen.

In 1948 he was selected for the final trial to represent the Scottish national team but was unable to compete, having been given a diagnosis of tuberculosis. He spent the following 19 months at the East Fortune sanatorium. He was lucky in one respect, however, being prescribed a new drug called streptomycin. Its effects were deemed miraculous, and X-rays of McLaren's healed lungs were sent around Europe as proof of the medicine's worth.

During his isolation McLaren began to forge his broadcasting career, having set up a putting green in the hospital grounds so that he could commentate on golfing competitions between patients for the hospital radio service. When he recovered he worked for three years as a reporter on the *Hawick Express*, all the while maintaining his strong interest in rugby. Unbeknown to him, a colleague with BBC connections wrote to a friend in London recommending McLaren's services as a rugby commentator.

On the strength of this McLaren was offered a commentary test. He was characteristically reluctant to accept the challenge but eventually agreed, making his debut on the Scottish Home Service in January 1952 for the South of Scotland versus South Africa game. BBC producers were impressed and hired him immediately, initially paying him £3 a game.

From the off McLaren devoted himself to pre-match preparation. Dressed in his sheepskin coat or brown macintosh, he was a familiar, though unobtrusive, figure on the touchlines of practice grounds as he observed each team training for the following day's game in order to familiarise himself with the players.

Everyone's name, position and number would then be committed to a pack of cards which he memorised. During matches he also had two "big sheets" in front of him in the commentary box. In appearance these were described by his fellow BBC commentator Nigel Starmer-

Smith as "a work of art in multi-coloured Biros with detail that might well include what each player had for breakfast".

McLaren also jotted down phrases he had been working on to further enhance his impressive baritone. He once described the Wales scrum-half Robert Howley as "wiggling his way upfield like a baggy in a border burn". During another match, in the early 1990s, he said that the England backs passed the ball with a fluency that was "like chocolate bar service from a slot machine". Scott Hastings and Sean Lineen were described as "the Scottish centres, bobbing up and down like demented prairie dogs". A "sniping run" was assumed to refer to the sniper's bullet, but was in fact a description of the side-to-side flight of the snipe. He coined the word "Garryowen" – an up-and-under kick – named after the Limerick club which used it to great effect. He would often chortle: "They'll be dancing in the streets of . . . . . tonight," – the missing word being the home ground of whoever had scored the vital try.

McLaren's day job was to supervise sport and teach PE in Hawick's five primary schools. He filled this role from the early 1950s until 1987, and was proud to have taught several of Scotland's future international players in their youth. One was the wing, Tony Stanger, who scored the winning try in the epic Calcutta Cup match of 1990 at Murrayfield. He also coached the Scottish greats Jim Renwick and Colin Deans as juniors.

His favourite rugby moment was Scotland's 1976 triumph over England in which his son-in-law, Alan Lawson, scored twice. He later admitted he almost fell out of the commentary box on that occasion.

McLaren was sceptical of rugby union as it developed into a professional sport. He found the players to be increasingly remote, as what he knew as a game turned into a business. It was perhaps fitting that his final Six Nations commentary for the BBC, in Cardiff in April 2002, resulted in a win for his country against Wales. He was given a standing ovation that day, as the crowd sang "For He's a Jolly Good Fellow".

McLaren's loyalty was never in question. He was approached by ITV to work for them during coverage of the World Cups of 1991 and 1995 but refused, despite the large sums of money on offer, saying that he would prefer to stay with the BBC.

He was a keen Scottish country dancer, golfer and family man who lived in Hawick all his life, and used to quote the saying – "A day out of Hawick is a day wasted." In 2001 he was the first non-international to be inducted into the Rugby Hall of Fame. He was appointed CBE in 2003.

* * *

SIR JAMES BLACK

Nobel Prize winner, who discovered beta-blockers

24 MARCH 2010

SIR JAMES BLACK, DOCTOR and pharmacologist, revolutionised the treatment of heart disease, saving the lives of millions of people worldwide by discovering beta-blockers. This landmark in medical science was recognised with the award of the Nobel Prize in Physiology or Medicine in 1988. Black also developed cimetidine, now one of the most widely used drugs in the world, for the treatment of heartburn and ulcers.

A first-rate experimentalist, he was also a dedicated and inspiring teacher but he remained a modest and shy man who avoided publicity. Nevertheless, he had a dry sense of humour and when told that he had won a Nobel prize, he joked "I wish I had my beta-blockers handy." He shared the prize with Gertrude Elion and George Hitchings.

It was in 1962, while working for ICI Pharmaceuticals, that Black discovered the drug netherlide, the first beta-blocker, which led to new treatments for certain types of heart disease. From it, he was able to develop safer, more effective drugs, particularly propranolol.

Propranolol, a beta adrenergic receptor antagonist, or beta-blocker, is used for the treatment and prevention of heart attack and angina pectoris and for the treatment of hypertension and migraines. Beta receptors – protein molecules that process messages carried by the central nervous system and various hormones – in the heart muscle, when stimulated by the hormones epinephrine and norepinephrine, cause the heartbeat to speed up, increasing the strength of the heart's contractions and, therefore, increasing its requirement for oxygen. Beta-blockers such as netherlide and propranolol block the beta receptor sites, preventing epinephrine and norepinephrine from attaching to them.

The development of propranolol was a milestone in the treatment of heart disease and hypertension and revolutionised the medical management of angina. It was one of the 20th century's most important contributions to medicine and pharmacology.

It was while working for the Smith Kline & French Laboratories that he developed cimetidine. The drug inhibits the production of acid in the stomach and is used for the treatment of gastric and duodenal ulcers, acid reflux and other types of acid-peptic disease. Cimetidine blocks the histamine receptors that stimulate the secretion of gastric acid in the stomach.

To develop cimetidine he employed an approach similar to the one he used to design propranolol. Instead of making random searches for a chemical having a physiological effect, Black tried to understand the biological processes involved. This rational approach accounted for his success in designing new drugs.

Explaining his methods, he said his greatest passion was "making tools". "I call myself a pharmacological toolmaker," he said.

James Whyte Black was born in 1924 in Uddingston, Strathclyde. The fourth of five boys, he was born into a staunch Baptist home. His father was a mining engineer and colliery manager whose love of singing gave music a central place in his son's life.

Black was educated at Beath High School, Cowdenbeath. Between the ages of 12 and 14 he intensely studied music and between 14 and 16 he concentrated on mathematics. When he was 15 he sat for the entrance examination for the University of St Andrews and was awarded the

Patrick Hamilton Residential Scholarship. His success was fortunate because the family budget would not have supported another child at the university.

Under the influence of an elder brother, a graduate in medicine at St Andrews, Black chose to study medicine. Although he did not take his studies at school very seriously, he worked hard enough at St Andrews to win a number of undergraduate prizes. He had, he wrote, "learnt, for the first time, the joys of substituting hard, disciplined study for the indulgence of day-dreaming".

Black received his medical degree from St Andrews in 1946 and then became an assistant lecturer in physiology there. The following year he took the post of lecturer at the University of Malaya in Singapore but returned to the UK as a senior lecturer at Glasgow Veterinary School in 1950. Between 1958 and 1964 he worked for ICI Pharmaceuticals as a senior pharmacologist.

He then became head of biological research and deputy research director at Smith Kline & French Laboratories. In 1973 he was appointed Professor of Pharmacology at University College London. Between 1978 and 1984 he was director of therapeutic research at Wellcome Research Laboratories. He was then appointed Professor of Analytical Pharmacology at King's College Medical School in London where he stayed until 1993, when he retired as Professor Emeritus.

Between 1992 and 2006 he served as Chancellor of the University of Dundee and the university built the Sir James Black Centre, a research facility for the investigation of cancer, tropical diseases and diabetes, in honour of his achievements.

He was elected a Fellow of the Royal Society in 1976 and in 2004 was awarded the society's Royal Medal. Black was knighted in 1981 and appointed to the Order of Merit in 2000.

He married first Hilary Vaughan, who predeceased him. He married Rona MacKie in 1994. He is survived by his second wife, a daughter from his first marriage and a stepdaughter and stepson.

JIMMY REID

Trade union convenor, whose leadership of the memorable 'work-in'
at Upper Clyde Shipbuilders outfaced the Government

12 AUGUST 2010

FOR MANY YEARS A LEADING FIGURE in the Communist Party in Scotland, Jimmy Reid came dramatically to public notice for his inspiring
leadership of the celebrated "work-in" at Upper Clyde Shipbuilders
which began in July 1971 after the company had gone into liquidation,
and which ultimately compelled the Conservative Government of the
day to rethink its plan to close the yard.

Upper Clyde Shipbuilders was a publicly owned consortium which
had been created in 1968 from four ailing Clyde shipyards: Clydebank,
Yarrow, Scotstoun and Govan. But from the outset it was a struggling
concern and by early 1971 was on the verge of collapse. UCS appealed
to the Government for £28 million to bail it out, but the Conservative
Government of Edward Heath decided that such a "lame duck" industry
could not be a recipient of further funding. On July 29 the Secretary of
State for Trade and Industry, John Davies, announced to Parliament
that UCS was to go into liquidation.

At Clydebank, Reid, the Communist trade union convener, called
a meeting and in language incongruously Churchillian, given
his antecedents (though he always was something of a romantic),
announced that the workforce would run the yards themselves in "a
new era in British history". Coining a new and optimistic name for the
firm, Upper Clyde Shipyard Workers Unlimited, Reid told his men: "It
will be up to us to conduct ourselves with responsibility and maturity.
The eyes of the world are upon us."

It was all highly quixotic. Yet to a public all too used to seeing
union workers resorting to strike action as a way of confronting (or
avoiding) harsh industrial realities, it seemed, cheeringly, to speak of a
regeneration of good faith. Reid, a charismatic, silver-tongued character

with an eye to publicity, was able to make sure that the UCS case never disappeared from the news agenda.

In October 1971 his being elected the first Communist Rector of Glasgow University added an intriguing dimension to the situation. In marked contrast as a character, his fellow Communist and shipyard worker James Airlie, convener at the Govan yard, worked hard on the tactics of keeping the workforce together, and the management and Government continually on the back foot.

The workers' action obliged the Heath Government to step back from its "lame duck" industrial policy, and agree to the injection of further cash to the tune of £35 million. In the meantime donations from members of the public to help the company's cash flow problem had included a cheque for £5,000 from John Lennon.

When the work-in ended 15 months later the prospects for the Upper Clyde yards appeared to have been transformed, with at least half the 8,500 jobs at risk having been saved in the short term. The purchase of Clydebank by Marathon, an American company entering the profitable new industry of oil rig construction, promised the saving of many more and the creation of further employment for the future.

Jimmy Reid was born in 1932 in the Govan district of Glasgow. In 1948 at the age of 16 he joined the Scottish Communist Party, which had at that point largely abandoned the goal of international 100 per cent revolutionary Marxism for a road to socialism via home rule for Scotland. This policy was included in *The British Road to Socialism*, published under the aegis of the Communist Party of the Soviet Union in 1951. In 1952 Reid was elected chairman of the Young Communists.

The Soviet suppression of workers' uprisings in East Germany and Poland did not shake his equanimity, nor did the 1956 Hungarian uprising. By 1959 he had been elected to the national executive and the political committee of the Communist Party of Great Britain, alongside such veteran luminaries as Harry Pollitt and R. Palme Dutt.

This involved him in several years based in London. But in 1964 he returned to Glasgow where he became secretary general of the Communist Party in Scotland. He continued to proselytise for self-determination for Scotland, telling the CPGB's 30th Congress in 1969: "We reiterate our demand that the national aspirations of the Scottish and Welsh people for self-government must be met."

In the meantime Reid had become leader of the Clydebank shop stewards, in 1968 to become part of the ill-fated UCS. After the October 1972 victory of the workforce on the Upper Clyde, during the skirmishing for which Reid had recommended the acceptance of the Marathon offer to buy Clydebank, he felt that his job as a convener was done.

Though he stayed on at Clydebank for a short time under Marathon, Reid's thoughts were turning more towards politics of the conventional sort. After the UCS victory he looked like being the Communist Party's most promising parliamentary prospect for more than 20 years. In 1970 he had stood for Dunbartonshire East, gaining only 2.3 per cent of the votes cast. Switching to Dunbartonshire Central for the first of the general elections of 1974, in which Edward Heath sought an endorsement from the electorate for his confrontation with the coalminers, Reid scored a much improved 14.6 per cent of the poll, an increase of heady proportions, which put him third in the poll, ahead of the SNP candidate. But by October 1974, when Harold Wilson, now Prime Minister, was hoping to improve his parliamentary representation and free himself from dependency on the Liberal vote in the House, Reid suffered disappointment, slipping back to 8.7 per cent of the votes cast.

In 1976 he resigned from the Communist Party, disillusioned with its increasing centralisation and its slavish adherence to dogma laid down by full-time party workers who were unrepresentative of the people.

He joined the Labour Party and in an attempt to return to the heart of the industrial trade union scene, ran for office as Scottish representative on the national executive of the Amalgamated Union of Engineering Workers. But Reid's opponent for the Scottish post, paradoxically, benefited from right-wing support, and the former Clydeside convener was narrowly defeated.

He then stood as Labour Party candidate for Dundee East in the general election of 1979, but was beaten into second place by the SNP candidate. It was effectively the end of his chance of re-establishing any practical influence, though he continued to support Labour for some years.

Thereafter Reid enjoyed life as a newspaper and television pundit, moving increasingly towards the centre in his attacks on the unrepresentative Militant Tendency within the Labour Party, and in his criticism of the leadership of Arthur Scargill during the miners' strike of 1984. In 1994 he attempted to launch a political magazine himself but the project was abortive, and he continued to wield most influence through his column in *The Herald*. In 2000 he helped to establish the Scottish Left Review. Disillusioned by the tenor of new Labour politics after 1997, he began to urge support for the SNP, and in April 2005 announced he had joined the party.

Reid published his autobiography, *Reflections of a Clyde-built Man,* and, in 1976, *Power Without Principles*, a collection of his newspaper columns. Latterly he had been in poor health, and had recently suffered a brain haemorrhage. He is survived by his wife, Joan, and their three daughters.

* * *

EDWIN MORGAN

Last of the 'Big Seven' Scottish poets, who was fascinated by space and explored many forms of verse

20 AUGUST 2010

THE FIRST SCOTS "MAKAR", or national poet, of recent times, Edwin Morgan was associated throughout his life with the city of Glasgow, though his reputation and intellectual interests stretched much further, as the title of his 1973 volume *From Glasgow to Saturn* implied. He was the last survivor of the "Big Seven" of 20th-century Scottish poets, the others being Hugh MacDiarmid, Robert Garioch, Norman MacCaig, Iain Crichton Smith, George Mackay Brown, and Sorley MacLean.

An optimistic, "futurist" writer who maintained an enthusiasm for the political and scientific changes of the 20th century beyond that century's end, Morgan was also a learned and vital translator from Anglo-Saxon, Russian, Hungarian, Portuguese and French (among other languages).

An innovator in concrete and sound poetry with an international avant-garde following, he also wrote formally precise and tightly argued sonnets on Scottish social and political issues.

His delicate love lyrics, part of the Scottish school curriculum for a number of decades, took on new significance when he declared himself a homosexual around his 70th birthday. He contracted cancer in 1999 but continued to develop as a writer, pursuing a late-flowering career as a dramatist as well as courting public controversy with a play on the life of Christ and a public poem on sperm donation at the time he received the Queen's Gold Medal for Poetry in 2000.

Edwin George Morgan was born in Hyndland in the West End of Glasgow in 1920, moving to Rutherglen soon after. The only child of a lower middle-class family – his father was a clerk in the shipyards – Morgan was a precocious pupil at primary school, the Rutherglen Academy, and then at Glasgow High School, which he left in 1937 to attend Glasgow University.

At school he had begun to teach himself Russian – as he would later teach himself Hungarian – in his spare time from dictionaries and literary texts. Around this time he met, and later corresponded with, the slightly older Greenock poet, W. S. Graham.

In 1940, having earlier registered as a conscientious objector, he joined the Royal Army Medical Corps, serving in the Middle East. He returned to his studies in 1946, graduating in 1947 with a First in English literature and taking up a post as a lecturer at the university. This was to be a lifetime's association; Morgan became Professor of English in 1975 and, although he took early retirement in 1980, the university has continued to honour him, appointing him professor emeritus and setting up the Edwin Morgan Centre for Creative Writing in 1998.

Morgan began to publish poetry with small presses in 1952, producing a verse translation of *Beowulf* and two original collections, *Dies Irae* and *The Vision of Cathkin Braes*, in that year. While this suggests an already prolific energy, Morgan was not to get into his stride as a poet until the next decade. He wrote later, "I would almost date my life from 1960 instead of 1920. I was productive in poetry; I was in love; I was fascinated by space exploration."

Excitement at technological progress led him to formal innovations in concrete, computer, science fiction and sound poetry. Anthology pieces in this experimental vein, such as *Message Clear* (56 variations on the line "i am the resurrection and the life") and *The First Men on Mercury* (where the languages of the coloniser from Earth and a suspiciously Glaswegian-sounding alien mutate into one another) combined a mordant wit with a serious interrogation of the nature of language.

Together with Ian Hamilton Finlay, Morgan made an important Scottish contribution to an international avant-garde. *Starryveldt* (1965) was published in Switzerland, and Morgan translated and worked closely with the Brazilian innovators of concrete poetry such as Haraldo de Campos. Typically his contribution to concrete poetry was a humanist one, bringing to the new form an individualist humour and exploration of feeling which linked with the lyric tradition.

Edwin Morgan met John Scott in 1963 and, though they never lived together, this was to be the defining relationship in Morgan's life until Scott's death in 1978. Homosexuality was a criminal offence in Scotland until 1980, and Morgan's public position called for discretion, but the love poems collected in *The Second Life* (1968) – Morgan's first collection from a major publisher, dedicated to Scott – were hauntingly direct statements of passion, as for example in *The Unspoken*:

when your hair grazed mine accidentally as we talked in a café, yet not quite accidentally, when I stole a glance at your face as we stood in a doorway and found I was afraid of what might happen if I should never see it again ...

O then it was a story as old as war or man ...
and although we have not vowed it we keep it, without a name to the end.

His famous poem *Strawberries:*

> *There were never strawberries*
> *like the ones we had*
> *that sultry afternoon ...*

written in January 1965, is another lyric which addresses a loved one whose gender is not made explicit.

Wi the Haill Voice (1972), Morgan's translation into Scots of the revolutionary Soviet poet Mayakovsky again emphasised the local focus of Morgan's internationalism while beginning a long relationship with Manchester-based Carcanet Press.

In *Glasgow Sonnets*, William Carlos Williams's New Jersey epic *Paterson* and the equally innovatory urban poetry of Sándor Weöres (which Morgan had translated from the Hungarian in 1970), were starting points for a new kind of literary exploration of Morgan's home city, a "rapid flickering scan" characteristic of an environment where "to look long at anyone is dangerous":

> *A shilpit dog fucks grimly by the close*
> *Late shadows lengthen slowly, slogans fade.*

Morgan was to be a role model to a new generation of Glasgow writers (Liz Lochhead, Tom Leonard, James Kelman, Alasdair Gray), whose Scottishness was forward-thinking and vernacular. His longer sequence *Sonnets from Scotland* fused geology, history, aesthetics and knock-knock jokes in an exploration of national issues.

He used the last line in the sequence *"A far horn grew to break that people's sleep"* in the design he made in 2001 for the stamps of an imaginary Scottish republic.

To begin with, Morgan's natural reserve ("Eddie doesn't take a drink") made him a rather unclubbable figure in the close-knit Scottish literary world but with retirement from the university he became used to an increasingly public role as a poet.

As well as considerable public honours (OBE, 1982; the Hungarian Order of Merit, 1997; Poet Laureate of the City of Glasgow, 1999; the Queen's Gold Medal for Poetry, 2000; National Poet of Scotland, 2003), he grew more used to public performance, collaborating with, for example, the jazz saxophonist Tommy Smith on works like *Planet Wave*, and increasingly writing for the stage.

His work as a dramatist included adaptations of *Cyrano and Phaedra* as well as his controversial trilogy of plays *A.D.* – a humanist presentation of the story of Christ for the new millennium which was boycotted by Catholics and Calvinists alike.

Illness and age led Morgan to move to a nursing home in his early eighties, but his literary energies remained undiminished. His poem *Open the Doors*, specially written for the occasion, was read out by the poet Liz Lochhead at the opening of the Scottish Parliament building in Edinburgh on October 9, 2004. In *Cathures* (2002) and *Love and a Life* (2003) he showed himself still capable of the tenderness, imagination and daring that made him a unique figure in Scottish literature and the international poetry of the English language.

JOHN BELLANY

Artist whose vibrant canvases expressed his intensely
personal response to life and landscape

30 AUGUST 2013

ONE OF SCOTLAND'S MOST PROMINENT contemporary painters, John Bellany had thoroughly absorbed the landscape and the religious beliefs of the Calvinist milieu in which he grew up, infusing his own rebellious spirit with a transfiguring nervous energy.

His work was often described as Surrealist or perhaps Expressionist in manner, yet he always insisted that it was rooted in the stark realities of human life as he saw it around him, especially among the struggles of the fisherfolk who clawed a living from the storm-tossed coastal waters of the North Sea.

From his student days in Edinburgh his work was quite distinctive, absorbing and yet modifying the austere tones both of Scottish terrain and modes of religious thinking, instead creating brightly coloured dream-like compositions, informed by an often quirky symbolism that confronted viewers with disturbing glances aimed at them from figures in the canvas.

Although he would have shrunk from the notion that he was in any literal sense a religious painter, as time went on he rejoiced in critiques of his work that detected a strong spiritual dimension. An acquaintanceship with Italy and the establishment of a studio in Tuscany, after he had almost died from liver failure induced by his alcohol consumption in the mid-1980s, greatly enriched his palette, infusing his canvases with greater vibrancy.

John Bellany was born in 1942. His family was part of the fishing community of the Forth coast village of Port Seton, a strongly religious, specifically Calvinist, community. The fishing life was a hard and dangerous one and Bellany grew up with an awareness of the tenuous, brittle nature of life. Boats and their crews did not always return to harbour.

John Bellany

He was educated at Cockenzie Primary School and Preston Lodge in Prestonpans. In 1960 he went to study painting at Edinburgh College of Art under Sir Robin Philipson. From there scholarships took him to Paris and then the Netherlands and Belgium. Further studies followed at the Royal College of Art, and in 1968 he then took up a lecturing post at Goldsmiths College and became artist-in-residence at Victoria College of the Arts in Melbourne.

In the late 1960s he had the first of many solo exhibitions: in the Netherlands; at Edinburgh College of Art; and at Winchester College of Art. In 1986 he became the first artist to have a one-man show at the National Portrait Gallery (the show included his portrait of the cricketer Ian Botham), and in 1994 he had an equivalent show at the Scottish National Portrait Gallery, this time centring on his portrait of the composer Peter Maxwell Davies.

Bellany visited East Germany in 1967 and was greatly affected by a trip he made to Buchenwald and its museum dedicated to the concentration camp. A new darkness entered his work. The horrific deeds done in the name of a self-deluding "elect" struck a strong chord with a young artist still coming to terms with his Calvinist upbringing. His highly dramatic painting *Pourquoi?* (1967), showing a triple crucifixion of figures clad in the striped prison uniform of the camps, was a disturbing image in the tradition of Goya's *Disasters of War* etchings. Such figures were to reappear in his works.

By the 1980s Bellany was well established as an exhibitor, popular with critics and gallery goers. One celebrity admirer was David Bowie, whom he painted and who bought his works. He also became one of his generation's leading portrait painters, again popular with the critics and – unusually – with his sitters: his 1980s portrait of Sean Connery, for example, is both touching and dignified.

Bellany suffered a heart attack in June 2005, on the way to a Glasgow exhibition of his work and was apparently clinically dead for around ten minutes, during which he had an out-of-body experience. He was fond of observing that he had several chances at life, apart from the heart attack. From the mid-1980s he had begun to suffer from liver failure, but he gave up alcohol and had a liver transplant in 1988. He formed a close friendship with Sir Roy Yorke Calne, the surgeon in charge of the operation, and in 1992 paid tribute to him in a diptych which was commissioned for the National Portrait Gallery. *The Addenbrooke's Hospital Series* – self-portraits charting the experience of his transplant – is said to have greatly contributed to the speed of his recovery.

He had homes in Edinburgh, Cambridge and near Barga, Tuscany. The town adopted him enthusiastically and he had his own gallery there. Bellany described the environs as "enchanted", and the town's mayor wrote a glowing introduction to the 2005 catalogue of a Glasgow exhibition of Bellany's work.

Bellany visited China several times at the beginning of the 21st century, and found the experience of being in a fresh environment highly stimulating: "I saw with the eyes of a child again ... I felt like Gauguin in Tahiti. My whole philosophy was rocked. All of a sudden, religion didn't enter into the picture. Christianity was never mentioned and the crucifixion, the most powerful symbol in Western art and something that has been with me since my youth, didn't make sense."

The visits to China were followed by a 2005-06 exhibition (with fellow Academy members) selected from portraits and cityscapes created in Shanghai with what he called his new "non-stop, complete visual over-excitement" at the Royal Academy.

The poet Hugh MacDiarmid and other 20th-century Scottish nationalists had called for a distinctive Scottish art that would also be universal. Bellany's work, firmly rooted in a Scottish cultural past that was disappearing as he grew up, was yet fully at home in the wider worlds of London and Tuscany, and alive to the dark side of European history.

Yet the temptation to see Bellany's works as primarily a commentary, whether on his life, on his nation or on his time, was best resisted. As the critic Duncan Macmillan said that, although Bellany's art was always intensely personal, "you cannot simply 'explain' it by reference to his biography. It has its own logic."

Election to the Royal Academy came in 1991 and three years later he was appointed CBE. An exhibition of his paintings, *John Bellany: A Passion for Life*, at the Scottish National Gallery between November 2012 and January 2013, was the largest and most comprehensive display of his work.

He continued to suffer from ill-health, particularly macular degeneration, which badly affected his sight.

In 1964 he married Helen Percy with whom he had two sons and a daughter. Their marriage was dissolved in 1974, and in 1980 he married Juliet Gray. She died in 1985, and he remarried Helen in 1986.

* * *

MARGO MacDONALD

The 'blonde bombshell' who won Govan for the SNP, but had a turbulent relationship with the party

5 APRIL 2014

MARGO MACDONALD WAS ONE OF the most independent-minded Scottish politicians of her generation and an inspirational figure renowned for the courage with which she faced Parkinson's disease.

Winning the working-class seat of Govan, Glasgow, for the Scottish National Party in 1973, she immediately attracted attention not just for the significant victory – it was the fourth parliamentary gain for the SNP since 1945 – but for her striking looks.

The expression "blonde bombshell" was widely employed to the annoyance of some commentators – she herself was amused. Aged 29, she was a former PE teacher, the wife of a publican ("wee wifey" was another nickname) and mother of two. Arriving in Westminster in a purple blouse and clogs, she recalled guides pointing her out to tourists – "There's the new Scottish lady" – and remarked that she found the canteen pricey, the

Commons freezing and the upholstery uncomfortable.

However, she had been a vocal campaigner for Scottish independence since her student days and declared with her typically sharp humour: "I'm the MP for Govan – can we get that straight first of all." She marched around her constituency, knocking on doors and winkling out problems over fish and chips. "She even flew up from London to attend a tenants' protest meeting," one admirer said.

Although she lost the seat the following year she carved out a remarkable career within and outside the SNP – with whom she enjoyed a turbulent relationship. To the left of centre, she was variously quoted as calling the party "tartan Tories" and saying that "only a fool" would vote SNP – a remark that was long remembered by her SNP rivals. She was later a tough critic of Alex Salmond's leadership and backing of devolution but was held in affection by activists. "She talks to people in a language they understand," said one.

She struck out alone as a hugely popular independent candidate, recognisable just by her first name. A natural on television, she was a successful broadcaster and journalist.

An admiring journalist described Margo MacDonald as moving through Holyrood "like Lulu in *To Sir, With Love*," joshing with allies and admirers, and scorning her enemies within the SNP. Philip Larkin famously said he did not choose to become a poet ("poetry chose me"), and Margo felt exactly the same way about her enemies: "I don't choose my enemies; they choose me." Alex Salmond once remarked: "Margo likes nothing more than a camera stuck in her face – not that that's a bad thing for a politician."

MacDonald believed: "If you put your head above the parapet you get shot at." Despite all the feuding, she was a conscientious attender in Holyrood's often sparsely attended debating chamber, making her points forcefully.

She was a resolute critic of the cost and delays associated with the parliament building and helped to lead the search for the "smoking trowel". She campaigned on medical issues and for a tolerance zone for Edinburgh prostitutes. She also mentored others in their political careers, most notably the Scottish Socialist Party's Tommy Sheridan – who described himself as one of "Margo's boys" – and the Labour First Minister, Jack McConnell.

MacDonald also became a prominent spokesperson for the principle of "physician assisted dying", saying: "I feel strongly that, in the event of losing my dignity or being faced with the prospect of a painful or protracted death, I should have the right to choose to curtail my own, and my family's, suffering."

Her second marriage, in 1981, had been to fellow socialist and nationalist Jim Sillars and was a happy one. They met when he was leader of the two-MP Scottish Labour Party and she was separated from her first husband and childhood sweetheart Peter MacDonald, a former licensee of the Hoolet's Nest at Blantyre, with whom she had two daughters: Zoe, now a camerawoman for the BBC, and Petra, who married Craig Reid of the group The Proclaimers and works for Citizens Advice. Sillars and MacDonald lived in Edinburgh's Grange suburb where she indulged her passion for country music ("Dwight Yoakam, Alan Jackson and Willie Nelson do it for me"), and for Hibernian FC.

Margo Aitken was born in Hamilton in 1943, and after attending Hamilton Academy trained as a teacher and taught PE from 1963-65. She supported Scottish independence from her teenage years.

She lost the famously erratic Govan seat to Labour at the 1974 general election, becoming, with 112 days' service, the 18th shortest-serving MP in Westminster. Sillars – who was to hold the seat for the SNP from 1988-92 – described the constituency as "a community of slums, poverty, degradation, and despair".

She became deputy leader of the SNP but after the failure of the SNP to make headway in the 1979 election, she joined the left-wing "79 Group", which sought to improve nationalist fortunes by pushing for a fully independent, socialist republic. The group, which included other future stars of the party such as Alex Salmond, was proscribed by the SNP in the early 1980s. She left the party soon afterwards to build a media career, contributing to Radio 4 and newspapers.

However, she returned to the SNP in the mid-1990s, and was elected in 1999 to the new Scottish Parliament as the SNP MSP for Lothians. Her independent outlook at Holyrood clashed with the centralist approach of the SNP leadership, and in the summer of 2002 the party effectively cut its ties with MacDonald by placing her in a low position on her constituency re-selection list for the 2003 election. Some party members argued that this was not an insult, just democracy in action, but MacDonald regarded the situation as a ritual humiliation directed by Salmond.

MacDonald then accused the SNP leadership of leaking to the media the fact that she suffered from Parkinson's disease. She regarded the illness as a private matter that did not affect her work.

She resigned, for the last time, from the SNP and fought and held her seat as an independent in 2003, 2007 and 2011, when she also stood for election as Holyrood's Presiding Officer, and lost to the Tory Alex Fergusson by 108 votes to 20. She made a documentary for BBC *Panorama* – "I'll Die When I Choose" – which included a debate between herself and an old friend Cardinal Keith O'Brien on the morality of "assisted dying".

* * *

ALAN DAVIE

Considered by many critics to be the greatest Scottish painter of the 20th century

7 APRIL 2014

ALAN DAVIE WAS A JAZZ MUSICIAN, a jewelry maker, a poet, a glider, a textile designer and a Zen Buddhist – but he will always be remembered for his vivid, intense and highly expressionistic abstract paintings. His many admirers would say he was the greatest Scottish painter of the 20th century. Even his detractors would admit that he was one of only a handful of genuinely important British artists to emerge in the years following the Second World War.

James Alan Davie was born in 1920 at Grangemouth, Scotland. His father was a painter and etcher and there was considerable musical talent on both sides of the family – the composer, Cedric Thorpe Davie, and the conductor, Muir Mathieson, were both related.

Davie took up painting at the age of 16 having been inspired by reproductions of Cezanne and Van Gogh. It was immediately clear he had an immense talent and entered Edinburgh College of Art the following year. There he came under the influence of John Maxwell who intensified Davie's already resonant sense of colour. He was awarded the Andrew Grant Scholarship and began making silver jewelry and exploring his interest in jazz and learning new musical instruments.

In 1941, he left Edinburgh College for war service in the Royal Artillery. Davie was stationed at various gun sites in Britain but service did not stop his creative output. Finding a copy in his barracks of Walt Whitman's *Leaves of Grass* started an intense period of reading and writing poetry – Chinese poetry had a particular fascination for him. Whenever there was an opportunity he also played alto saxophone in various jazz groups. Davie saw many art exhibitions, while on leave in London, including Picasso and the English modernists – but it was the work of Paul Klee that most deeply impressed him.

After the war, Davie returned to painting but supported himself largely through playing jazz and making jewelry. He was an accomplished jazz musician who recorded several albums and played tenor saxophone in a number of groups including Tommy Sampson's orchestra during its 1947 English tour. He had begun making and selling silver jewelry in 1947 and continued through the early 1950s. He taught in the jewelry department at the Central School of Arts and Crafts and designed the jewelry worn by Vivien Leigh in one of her films.

Davie took up a travelling scholarship awarded to him just before he joined the war and went to Paris, Zurich, Florence, Milan, Venice and many other art centres throughout southern Europe. He was inspired by early Christian art and particularly by the work of the Surrealists,

Hans Arp and Max Ernst, which he saw in a Swiss private collection.
It was his time in Venice, however, that was most influential. Davie
came in contact with the maverick art collector, Peggy Guggenheim –
a meeting that was highly important in two ways. Guggenheim gave
him tremendous encouragement and purchased his painting, *Music of
the Autumn Landscape*. Her enthusiasm greatly helped give rise to the
international acclaim Davie achieved in the late 1950s particularly in
America. The meeting also gave him the chance to see work by the then
little known young modern American painters, Mark Rothko, Robert
Motherwell and Jackson Pollock. Davie was impressed by Pollock's
working method, his sense of scale and by the sheer visceral quality of
his work.

On returning to London, he met the young art dealers Peter and
Charles Gimpel and held his first one-man exhibition at Gimpel Fils
in 1950 (where he subsequently exhibited every second year thereafter).
Success did not come immediately and, indeed, Davie was never
appreciated as much in Britain as abroad. His one-man exhibition in
New York in 1956, where several important museums including the
Museum of Modern Art made purchases, was his first real triumph.
Many major exhibitions followed: London's Whitechapel Gallery in
1958, Amsterdam's Stedelijk Museum in 1962 and Bern's Kunsthalle in
1963 to name just three. He was awarded CBE in 1972 and, by the end of
the century, had more than a dozen important retrospective exhibitions
and paintings in well over 50 public collections.

Davie's work was often thrilling. He had a gift for handling paint and
an extraordinary eye for colour. His painting was direct expression –
automatic in the true sense that the Surrealists meant it. It was a complete
letting go. There was no preparatory drawing; each brushmark inspired
the next. "My own creations are a source of wonder also to me." From
the dark, tangled canvases of the late 1940s/early 1950s the paintings
slowly became brighter, more open, more joyous. His paintings from
the mid 1950s to the early 1970s are amongst the very best of European
abstract art.

Davie's personal life also changed greatly in the ten years after the war. He returned to Edinburgh in 1946 and, the following year, married the artist-potter Janet ("Bili") Gaul. They moved to London in 1949 just months before the birth of their only child, Jane.

They took a studio apartment in the Abbey Art Centre in New Barnet but, in 1954, Davie moved away from London to a stable block at Rush Green near Hertford which he converted into a studio house. Later they also got a cottage in Cornwall, near Land's End and he formed close links with many of the St Ives painters. His friendship with Peter Lanyon led to his love of gliding. Davie also developed a strong interest in oriental mysticism – especially Zen Buddhism – an influence which filtered through to his later work.

A free-wheeling poet, jazz musician and expressionistic painter who drove a Jaguar E-type may conjure an image of a wild individual, but Davie was quiet, shy, thoughtful and steadfast. His marriage, his Herts. home and his partnership with the Gimpel family all remained solid for well over 50 years – as did his commitment to his painting.

Davie's later work became more static, more symbolic, and more in disfavour with the art intelligentsia. He had always been fascinated by primitive art and his paintings became filled with symbolic images from Coptic, Navajo, Aboriginal, Inuit, Jain and Celtic art. While still a major painter, his work only rarely reached the high peaks that it so regularly attained in the 1960s. The paintings, however, are much better than their reputation would suggest and a reappraisal of their is almost inevitable.

Davie was totally disinterested in the mainstream art world and seemed to lack much commercial ambition. He wrote: "the artist must be a prophet; that is, he must express what is full of significance in an infinite sense, and what does not proceed from reason or knowledge or the past, but from the eternal present which is always new and marvellous." Sadly, this would not be a recipe for many successful artists now.

Davie's painting was exultant, honest and direct from the heart – a positive affirmation of life – which he led to the full.

WILLIAM McILVANNEY

*Saddled with the title 'godfather of tartan noir', he
articulated the struggle for Scottish independence*

7 December 2015

In December 1992, as European leaders gathered in Edinburgh for an
EU summit, the writer William McIlvanney addressed 20,000 people,
gather-ed under the banner of the Campaign for Scottish Democracy.
What he said has stuck in the memories of many who were there, because
it spoke for the nature of Scotland in those pre-devolution days.

"We gather here like refugees in the capital of our own country. We
are almost 700 years old and we are still wondering what we want to
be when we grow up. Scotland is in an intolerable state, and we must
never acclimatise to it – never." Then, to the dismay of many present –
including Alex Salmond – he added: "Scotland is not of some pedigree
lineage. We are a mongrel nation." A cheer went up from the crowd,
with many recognising, instinctively, something of themselves.

Willie McIlvanney was not only the finest Scottish writer of his
generation, he defined for many Scots their long journey from
dependency to autonomy. He understood, from his own working-class
background, the struggle of a nation, beset by self-doubt, seeking to
find its voice. In his novel *Docherty* he drew a portrait of a Glasgow
man, small in stature but big in pride, crushed by a form of progress he
does not understand, fighting battles which are no longer relevant, but
refusing to sacrifice his own integrity. Not everyone approved. Some
thought it played to the victim mentality of the Scottish character,
others considered it had overtones of male chauvinism. Yet it struck a
chord, and became his most celebrated book, bearing comparisons to
Zola and Balzac, chroniclers of an unjust society.

Although saddled with the title "godfather of tartan noir",
McIlvanney was far more than a writer of detective fiction. Indeed,
as his fellow-novelist Allan Massie points out, the subject of his three

Glasgow novels, *Laidlaw*, *The Papers of Tony Veitch*, and *Strange Loyalties*, is not so much crime as morality, and how people should deal with each other; its literary antihero, Jack Laidlaw, is the exact opposite of the standard hard-bitten detective. The books were cited by a generation of Scottish crime writers, including Ian Rankin who recalled: "The first time I met McIlvanney, I said I was writing a crime novel, influenced by him. He signed my book: 'Good luck for the Edinburgh Laidlaw'. A few years later he signed another: 'The Edinburgh Laidlaw done good.'"

The critic Alan Taylor picked out one passage which sums up Laidlaw's philosophy. On being told by a fellow officer that the people who live in the Glasgow district of Drumchapel must be terrible, he answers: "I find the people very impressive. It's the place that's terrible ... You've got the biggest housing scheme in Europe here. And what's there? Hardly anything but houses. Just architectural dumps where they unloaded people like slurry. Penal architecture. Glasgow people have to be nice people. Otherwise, they would have burnt the place to the ground years ago."

McIlvanney once recalled having a drink in a pub in Glasgow when a rough-looking man at the bar regaled him with: "'It was Glasgow on a Friday night, city of the stare.' It took me about two minutes to realise that he was quoting the first line of one of my novels."

The prose in these early books has the taut and electric quality that the American writer Cormac McCarthy deploys in his accounts of men pitted against their destiny, or Albert Camus uses in the novels *The Stranger* or *The Plague*; indeed McIlvanney was once described as "Scotland's Camus".

A poet, essayist, and newspaper columnist, as well as novelist, his work was recognised through numerous awards. His first novel, *Remedy is None* won the Geoffrey Faber Memorial Prize in 1967, with one critic commenting: "He creates characters so strong you feel you might not put up much of a show in their company." In *The Times*, Frederick Raphael described his work as "full of the joy of writing and alert to the anguish of life." *The Big Man*, published in 1985, was adapted into a film by David Leland, starring Liam Neeson.

Because, however, McIlvanney wrote slowly, always using pen and paper, and from "my own compulsion", his books latterly became less frequent. Then, at the instigation of his agent, Jenny Brown, Canongate republished the early work, and a new generation discovered *Laidlaw, Docherty* and the rest. The result was a renaissance, both in his literary reputation and his depleted bank balance.

William Angus McIlvanney was born in 1936 and brought up in a mining family in Kilmarnock, Ayrshire, a place he turned into the industrial town of Graithnock in his novels. The youngest of four children, he described his father as "five-feet-four with a PhD in outrage", clearly a model for Docherty. His mother was a book lover, and McIlvanney remembers her reciting poetry, and stories from *The Rubáiyát of Omar Khayyám.* He studied English at Glasgow University. McIlvanney later called Glasgow, "the city of the stare" because you never quite knew when to expect the next assault on your privacy.

He started teaching at an Ayrshire secondary school, writing in his spare time. *A Gift from Nessus* was published in 1968. After the publication of *Docherty* in 1975, he became a full-time writer.

In 1978, he was asked to cover the Scottish football team's disastrous World Cup campaign in Argentina. His own seven-week sojourn was just as ill-fated; by his own admission, it led to the break-up of his marriage to Moira Watson.

By the time of the 1979 referendum on devolution, McIlvanney was a celebrated figure in Scotland. He and a group of writers and activists, which included Neal Ascherson, set off by bus to tour the country. "He was an elegant, beautiful man, with the film star looks of a Clark Gable," said Ascherson. "His effect on people was extraordinary. He seemed to have time to talk to them about their own lives. No one had written about them in that way before."

Although the referendum ended in failure for those campaigning for a Scottish parliament, Ascherson believes that McIlvanney changed peoples' perceptions of their own country. Uncertain about the benefits of independence, he nevertheless thought that Scotland deserved more control over its own affairs. Later, in the 2014 referendum he became converted to the idea of independence and supported the Yes vote, though he was never a paid-up adherent of the SNP; indeed he even wondered sometimes about the merits of his own nationality. "Being Scottish is like having an old insurance policy," he once said. "Just when you need it you can't find it."

He leaves a son, Liam, who is a writer and academic, working in New Zealand, but was also at one stage a speechwriter for Alex Salmond. His daughter Siobhán teaches French at King's College London. His brother Hugh is *The Sunday Times'* award-winning sports writer.

He became a popular speaker at literary festivals, always accompanied by his partner, Siobhán McCole Lynch, a teacher, whom he admitted driving "loopy" with his habit of leaving unfinished writing projects strewn around the house.

McIlvanney also published a book of short stories, *Walking Wounded*, and two books of poetry. An *habitué* of the Georgic Bar in Glasgow, he was a charming and genial companion. However, there was a tough streak underneath. One newspaper editor, attempting to recruit him as a columnist, made an offer McIlvanney thought beneath his dignity. Within seconds, the editor found himself up against the wall as McIlvanney hissed: "Don't ever insult me like that again."

* * *

SIR PETER MAXWELL DAVIES

Flamboyant and influential British composer, conductor and master of the Queen's music, who had a relish for making mischief

4 MARCH 2016

AN AVANT-GARDE FIREBRAND who once provoked an audience walkout at the Proms; a prolific and protean craftsman who wrote reams of music for every medium; a republican and socialist who nevertheless became master of the Queen's music and then proceeded to castigate the "philistines" at the heart of the British establishment – Peter Maxwell Davies was arguably the most influential British composer since Benjamin Britten. And "Max" – as he was universally known – had a life as flamboyant as anything in his music.

Though he spent the final 44 years of his life on the remote islands of Orkney, his opinions and his mishaps – which included being prosecuted for eating a dead swan, and being swindled out of hundreds of thousands of pounds by his own manager – regularly made headlines in the national press. As did his gay relationship with a local builder and its bitter collapse. Charming, idealistic, impish and perhaps naive in many ways, Maxwell Davies hid nothing. A born provocateur, he mellowed with age but never lost his talent or his relish for making mischief and scandalising the prudish and conservative.

In his finest music, he went way beyond shock and satire. His chamber opera *The Lighthouse* is a terrifying study of the psychoses caused by childhood abuse, repressed sexuality, religious fanaticism and establishment cover-up – even more topical today than when it was written in 1980. Much more recently, the opera *Kommilitonen!*, which was specifically written for music students in New York and London to perform, is a moving and powerful celebration of youth protest throughout the 20th century.

In the last of his ten symphonies, composed in 2013 as he underwent chemotherapy for chronic leukaemia, he set to music a suicide note written by a 17th-century architect, Francesco Borromini, who had been persecuted by contemporary critics. "Identifying with him was a huge help in overcoming any self pity that you might feel when you're told that you have six weeks to live," Maxwell Davies observed.

He knew what it was like to be stung by a hostile press. The savagely discordant and gleefully disorientating music-theatre pieces he produced in the late 1960s – often based on medieval source-material anarchically and anachronistically distorted by 20th-century foxtrots – were incomprehensible to many British music critics. His 1972 grand opera, *Taverner* (an allegory about a 16th-century composer forced to become a tool of a repressive government to save his own skin), proved far too complex, musically and philosophically, for even those performing it at the Royal Opera House to fathom. "The chorus couldn't sing it, the orchestra didn't like it, and I was treated very badly," Maxwell Davies recalled. He vowed never to be involved with "one of those posh opera houses" again. However, he liked to cause a fuss.

Much later, when he tamed his musical style and concentrated on writing in conventional forms for conventional forces, the criticism went the other way: he had "lost his boldness", he was writing too much, and his music had become dull and functional. "I've even been called a prostitute and accused of playing to the gallery," he said. That view was exacerbated during the ten years from 2004 to 2014 when he was master of the Queen's music.

A professional composer to his fingertips, Maxwell Davies claimed with justification that he was merely tailoring his music to suit his patron. "The Queen doesn't like dissonant music," he revealed. "She has stated that very plainly. I see no point in rubbing her up the wrong way about that."

In any case, he was adept at transforming his style to suit his intended audience – royal or otherwise. Having made his name with acidly atonal music, he went on to write pieces so tonal and tuneful that they almost qualified as easy listening. His most popular orchestral piece, *An Orkney Wedding with Sunrise*, which requires a Highland Piper to stride into the hall at its climax, is a case in point.

Peter Maxwell Davies was born to working-class parents in Salford in 1934, and taken to see *The Gondoliers* by Gilbert and Sullivan before he was five. The experience opened a window for him, not so much in musical terms but as a glimpse of a potential life not bound by his grandfather's shop or the factory where his father worked. As a schoolboy, he frequented the Henry Watson music library in Manchester, soaking up huge tracts of the standard repertoire, particularly the Beethoven symphonies. Although he had virtually no encouragement or musical training at school, he had his first composition broadcast on the BBC's *Children's Hour* when he was 12.

Sir Peter Maxwell Davies

Between 1952 and 1957 he was a student, first at the University of Manchester, then at the Royal Manchester College of Music. There he became friendly with the nascent composers Harrison Birtwistle and Alexander Goehr, the pianist John Ogdon and the trumpeter and conductor Elgar Howarth. Later known as the "Manchester School", they were a phenomenally gifted group, forever bouncing ideas off each other. The others thought that Maxwell Davies's interest in medieval and Renaissance music was retrogressive, but he had already discovered Bartok, Schoenberg and Stravinsky and at university he had access to the revolutionary scores of Boulez and Stockhausen. The evidence of the latter is evident in Op 1, a trumpet sonata written for Howarth in 1955; and his Op 2, the *Five Pieces for Piano* written for Ogdon.

After a period studying in Rome with Goffredo Petrassi, during which he had astonishingly complex works performed at two consecutive festivals of the International Society for Contemporary Music, his life took a new direction. He became the music teacher at Cirencester Grammar School. The need for a regular income prompted this unexpected move, but it had a beneficial impact on his compositional style as well. To write music that his pupils could manage, he had to simplify his style considerably. Even so, he later admitted that he had to "ride fairly roughshod" over the resistance of his teaching colleagues to get the school choir and orchestra to perform the acidly dissonant *O Magnum Mysterium* carol sequence, or the *Five Klee Pictures*.

Three years later, he was on the move again. A Harkness Fellowship took him to America to study with Roger Sessions at Princeton University. Here, he had time to think – in particular about the opera *Taverner*, which had been gestating since 1956. Returning to London in 1965, he reunited with Birtwistle, and the two decided to start a flexible music-theatre of avant-garde specialists for whom both could write pieces. The Pierrot Players – later renamed The Fires of London when Maxwell Davies and Birtwistle irrevocably fell out – was launched in May 1967, and for it Maxwell Davies composed some of his most powerful and disturbing early pieces, including *Eight Songs for a Mad King* and *Vesalii Icones*.

399

Even more shocking was *Worldes Blis,* the massive orchestral "motet" that prompted the noisy exit of many bewildered audience members at its 1969 Proms premiere. One person who did approve of Maxwell Davies's riotously dissonant style was Ken Russell, who engaged the young composer to work on his surreal film adaptation of Sandy Wilson's musical *The Boy Friend.* He responded with a deliciously overblown arrangement of music that was itself a parody of 1920s jazz, and then provided a suitably acerbic score for his violent and disturbing film *The Devils.*

Aware that he was "burning the candle at three ends at least", and perhaps shaken by the extreme reactions to his music, Maxwell Davies retreated to the wilderness. In 1970, he visited the Orkney island of Hoy and decided – "instantly", he said – that he would live there. The cottage he found was primitive, initially without electricity or running water, but with a breathtaking view across "the great cliff-bound bay ... where the Atlantic and the North Sea meet". He felt at home and at peace. "Every time I walk the dog along the shore the sea is different," he told *The Times.* "That's enough entertainment for me. The television went out long ago. I still have a radio, but I use it less and less."

He immersed himself in Orkney history and culture, and struck up a close friendship with the quintessential Orkney poet George Mackay Brown, whose words he set in such pieces as *From Stone to Thorn, Fiddlers at the Wedding* and *The Blind Fiddler.* In homage to Kirkwall's patron saint, Magnus, he composed the *Hymn to St Magnus* and, in 1976, the chamber opera, *The Martyrdom of St Magnus.* That work was the centrepiece of the St Magnus Festival, which he founded the following year and which he directed, with passionate commitment, until 1986 (it continues to this day, a northerly outpost of the avant-garde).

It was during his early Orkney years that Maxwell Davies started composing in more conventional musical forms. In the end, he wrote ten symphonies, initially much influenced by Sibelius; ten accessible string quartets known as the *Naxos Quartets* after the record company that commissioned them; and a sequence of concertos for the principal players of the Scottish Chamber Orchestra, whose associate composer and conductor Maxwell Davies became in 1985. Separately, he also wrote a neo-romantic violin concerto for the great American virtuoso Isaac Stern, who was lured to Kirkwall for the premiere. The music that poured out of Maxwell Davies on Orkney was not, however, confined to abstract forms. There were also three operas, two substantial ballets, music theatre works, children's pieces, songs for choirs, and protest pieces (including an anti-nuclear cabaret, *The Yellow Cake Revue*). Ecological curiosity took him to Antarctica in 1997 and the result, premiered in 2001, was the *Antarctic Symphony* jointly commissioned by the Philharmonia Orchestra and the British Antarctic Survey.

Maxwell became embroiled in Orkney life in other ways. In 2005, he was cautioned by the police for the unusual crime of being in possession of a swan corpse. The bird, a protected species, had flown into a power cable and died; Maxwell Davies recovered it and had already cooked it when the police arrived. Two years later he had another brush with authority when Orkney council refused him permission to conduct his civil-partnership ceremony on Sanday Light Railway. He had set up home six years earlier with a local builder, Colin Parkinson, who was 20 years his junior. However, the partnership ended badly. In 2011, Maxwell Davies went to court to evict Parkinson, claiming "domestic abuse". Parkinson later left the island after a financial settlement.

Further turmoil was wrought by Michael Arnold, who – with his wife, Judy – had looked after Max's business affairs for 30 years. In 2009, Arnold was sentenced to 18 months' imprisonment for stealing more than £500,000 of his employer's earnings to pay his own online gambling debts.

Knighted in 1987, he became master of the Queen's music in 2004, succeeding the troubled Australian composer Malcolm Williamson. He proved to be a huge success, using the post to champion music and particularly music education in a series of trenchant speeches and articles, and supplying the monarch with a steady stream of well-written pieces for ceremonial occasions.

Asked how he reconciled his political views with holding such an establishment position, he gave a typically candid response: "It's true that I once had republican leaning, but I've started to see that the Queen does a bloody marvellous job. She steadies things, stops them from going – dare I use the phrase? – tits up."

Max remained utterly direct and unstuffy to the end, his gimlet eyes always twinkling with mischief, his indignation forever primed by tales of injustice, inequality, hypocrisy, warmongering, ecological madness or corruption in high places. Most of all, though, he remained a composer totally dedicated to serving his community, whether by writing for a primary school in Orkney or for one of the country's great orchestras.

* * *

RONNIE CORBETT

Diminutive comedian who delighted millions with his armchair monologues, and was one half of 'The Two Ronnies'

31 MARCH 2016

RONNIE CORBETT, THE TINY COMEDIAN with the oversized spectacles, will for ever be associated with the television show that signed off with the words: "It's goodnight from me ... and it's goodnight from him."

During its 16-year run *The Two Ronnies* became an institution, often attracting audiences approaching 20 million. With his bushy eyebrows, increasingly jowly cheeks and lively wardrobe, Corbett was so distinctive that even while riding a Vespa scooter in a helmet he was stopped by passers-by, and, years later, new comedians still approached him to remark on his sketches, saying "I'll never forget the one where ..."

Although they were never a double act in the traditional sense, Corbett and his co-star, Ronnie Barker, seemed made for each other. The series was rooted in the British tradition of double entendres, wordplays and disguised bawdiness.

"All the bloodlines of comedy converged in *The Two Ronnies*," Corbett said. "Ronnie was from the southeast, Oxford, repertory theatre, and I was from Edinburgh, the music hall and cabaret. There wasn't much we hadn't done between us."

Each show began with the two reading joke news items from behind a desk with gags such as: "Comfortable in hospital tonight is the man who heeded the warning of the ministry of transport to wear something white at night. He went out dressed in a white hat, white shoes and white trousers and was run over by a snowplough."

Corbett's speciality was a meandering monologue delivered from a giant chair, which served to accentuate his diminutive size. He would start a joke, but then wander so far off the point that it seemed he would never get back to it, until finally delivering the punchline. He called his long-winded armchair style "dilatory and digressional". He joked that even his wife – who watched in the audience at every studio recording – wanted to say, "Just get on with it!"

Unlike Barker, who also wrote much of the material for *The Two Ronnies* under the pseudonym of Gerald Wiley, Corbett was strictly a performer. Barker was responsible for the pair's most famous sketch – with Corbett as an ironmonger and Barker as a customer – based on a series of misunderstandings, such as mistaking "four candles" for "fork handles".

The show may well have been one of the last to belong to an age when television comedy appealed to different generations and could be enjoyed as peak-time entertainment for all the family. Corbett and Barker took the show to the West End, appearing on stage at the London Palladium – and, in February 1978, they both collected their OBEs at Buckingham Palace.

The break-up of the partnership was instigated by Barker, who decided to retire after the Christmas special in 1987. There was no clash of egos. "I was aware, I think, that his talents were probably more varied and deeper than mine, but it didn't bother me," recalled Corbett. "I always thought I was very lucky to be in the company of someone who was so talented."

Born in Edinburgh in 1930, Ronald Balfour Corbett – known as "Ronnie" – was the son of William Corbett, a master baker. His mother, Anne, was in the same class at school as the actor Alastair Sim, and before her marriage worked in the accounts department of the bookseller John Menzies. The family lived in a semi-detached house on a new estate. Despite their modest circumstances, all three children were sent to a fee-paying school, the Royal High, in the city. Brought up in the Church of Scotland, he went to Bible classes.

His earliest memory was of almost drowning on the beach at St Andrews. He was always small for his age and his mother took him to specialists. An aunt once paid for him to follow a course called "How to Stretch Yourself". Not surprisingly, the exercises made no difference. He reached only 5ft 1in as an adult – his father was 5ft 6in – and liked to tell how he bought his size four-and-a half shoes from the boys' department at Harrods.

He left school at 17, having set his heart on a career in showbusiness after dressing up in drag and playing a wicked aunt in a pantomime put on by his youth club. "I think I saw theatre as a way to overcome my size and the problem of not being noticed," he said.

At the age of 19, he undertook National Service, joining the RAF and becoming the shortest commissioned officer in the British Forces. He enjoyed his first romantic encounter with a nurse. Afterwards, he took a civil service exam and became a clerk in the agriculture department for 18 months.

In 1951, he headed for London, vowing to give himself until the age of 40 to succeed in showbusiness. He cut his comic teeth in London revue bars and northern clubs, often having to take menial jobs – including caring for Regent's Park tennis courts – to support himself. When the audience threw bread rolls at him while performing at a club in Streatham, he quipped: "As a baker's son I naturally noticed what sort of bread rolls they were."

Corbett got his first break playing a straight man to the drag artist Danny La Rue. His television debut came in the children's programme *Crackerjack*. He also notched up a film appearance in the 1967 spoof

Bond movie *Casino Royale*.

His second break came when David Frost spotted him in Winston's, which was Danny La Rue's nightclub, and invited him to join his new BBC show, *The Frost Report*, which went on air in 1966. Ronnie Barker, who started his career as a straight actor, was also recruited to the show.

Working in his spare time as a barman, Corbett remembered that the first words Barker said to him were, "Same again please". The two men soon hit it off. "There was an immediate comfort between us," Corbett said.

One sketch on the British class system – featuring Corbett, Barker and John Cleese – became a classic. Standing next to each other, the very tall Cleese, the chubby, medium-built Barker and the tiny Corbett made a striking physical contrast that also encapsulated their positions in society. The upper class Cleese looked down on Barker; the middle-class Barker looked up to Cleese but down on Corbett, whose punchline was: "I know my place!"

At the televising of the Bafta awards in 1970, a technical breakdown blacked out the screens. Corbett and Barker did an impromtu turn to entertain the audience, which included Bill Cotton, head of light entertainment at the BBC. He was so impressed that he signed them up.

While performing cabaret Corbett had met Anne Hart, an actress and dancer, who was the daughter of a prizefighter and 5ft 8in. She was also the leading lady with the Crazy Gang team of comedians. They married in 1965.

By the time *The Two Ronnies* took off, Corbett was mature enough to savour his success without succumbing to the pressures of stardom. The show made him a rich man and he bought a sprawling Surrey house with a swimming pool, where he would live for more than 30 years. He also bought a Rolls-Royce, the first of many beautiful cars that he would own.

The Corbetts' first child, Andrew, was born with a serious heart defect and died within a few weeks of his birth. Grief-stricken, they spent time walking in the woods of Berkshire. However, they went on to have two daughters: Sophie, who became a fashion designer, and

Emma, who became a dancer.

During the final years of *The Two Ronnies*, Corbett also starred as Timothy Lumsden, the forty-something librarian trying to escape his domineering mother in *Sorry!*, which ran for seven series. Unlike his old partner, Corbett showed little sign of wanting to ease up.

In 1998, he appeared with John Cleese in *Fierce Creatures*, the sequel to *A Fish Called Wanda*, and starred in an ITV special, *An Audience with Ronnie Corbett*. He presented the oddly engaging children's quiz show *Small Talk* on BBC television and appeared in pantomime. He undertook extensive corporate entertainment, speaking at lunches and dinners.

Barker came out of retirement in 2005 to join Corbett for *The Two Ronnies Sketchbook* in which they introduced favourite items from their old shows. By this time Barker was seriously ill; his frailty showed on screen and he died just a few months later.

Away from the screen, Corbett was a keen golfer and it was no coincidence that both his Surrey house and his Scottish holiday home backed on to golf courses. A member of four golf clubs and with a handicap of 15, he often took part in celebrity and pro-am events. Corbett's friends included Michael Parkinson, Jimmy Tarbuck and Bruce Forsyth, who would all meet for a drink perhaps twice a year. His sitting room contained the armchair which he had used in his famous monologues.

From an uncle who had been a tailor, Corbett inherited a belief in the importance of looking immaculate, favouring pastels and tartan.

He was honorary president of the Five Foot Club, which was formed to fight for a better deal for little people, and twice president of the Lord's Taverners, supporting their work for disadvantaged and disabled young people.

In 2012, his OBE was advanced to CBE. At the investiture, he committed the *faux pas* of touching the Queen's arm. Did she mind? "No," he said, "I think she was quite pleased to be reassured. She said to me, 'You've been doing this a long time haven't you'. And I said, 'Over 50 years – but not as long as you'."

JOHN MOFFAT

Swordfish pilot who took part in the decisive attack on the
German battleship 'Bismarck' in 1941

14 December 2016

No one could tell the story of the day he helped to sink the *Bismarck* better than John Moffat himself. Unlike those wartime heroes who preferred to stay silent, Lieutenant Commander "Jock" Moffat enjoyed recounting every last detail of his encounter in the North Atlantic on May 26, 1941, with the mightiest battleship in the German navy – of taking off behind the controls of his fragile biplane from the deck of the aircraft carrier HMS *Ark Royal* in a force nine gale and of flying 50ft above the waves to unleash his single torpedo.

The attack by Fairey Swordfish – aircraft known as "Stringbags" – put the *Bismarck's* rudder out of action and left her helpless in the face of the encircling British warships. His abiding memory, however – and the one that stopped his account in its tracks – was of the next day when his formation was ordered out again, and he witnessed the death-throes of the *Bismarck*, the great ship heeling over, and "hundreds of heads, bobbing in the sea. We knew they had no chance of survival."

The *Bismarck*, along with the heavy cruiser Prinz Eugen, had broken out into the Atlantic Ocean in May 1941, evading all attempts to track them down. At the Battle of the Denmark Strait, the *Bismarck* engaged and destroyed the battlecruiser HMS *Hood*, pride of the Royal Navy, and forced the battleship *Prince of Wales* to retreat.

For British naval commanders, the destruction of the German ship became paramount and there followed a hunt, involving dozens of warships, after Churchill famously said: "I don't care how you do it, you must sink the *Bismarck*."

The German ship had sustained a fuel leak during the battle and was heading for the relative safety of the French coast. A brief radio signal from its commander gave the navy the chance of pinpointing

407

its position, but conditions were appalling, with gales and low cloud. By a stroke of luck, at mid-morning on May 26, a reconnaissance plane spotted the *Bismarck*. A squadron of Swordfish, briefed that there was only one ship in the area, took off from *Ark Royal* and saw the outline of what they presumed was the target. It was, in fact HMS *Sheffield*, which then came under torpedo attack until one of the aircraft identified its familiar outline at the last minute and called off the action.

Later that evening the decision was taken to launch another attack. Fifteen Swordfish took off, with the gale at its height. As Moffat later recounted, it was a hair-raising experience.

"Timing was everything, and the deck officer, or 'bats,' was crucial; he knew exactly the roll of the ship and when you could get off. The Swordfish could lift off at 60 knots."

Moffat, with his navigator, John "Dusty" Miller, and an air gunner, AJ Hayman, flew just below cloud level at 600ft until they spotted *Sheffield*, which signalled with an Aldis lamp, giving them the bearings and distance of the *Bismarck*. Their commanding officer, Tim Coode, gave a hand signal, and they climbed. At that point the *Bismarck* spotted the formation and opened fire. "That really put the wind up us," Moffat recalled. Unable to see where they were going, they dived through cloud, at a 45-degree angle, to 600ft, then broke cover at 100ft. Almost immediately they spotted the *Bismarck* to their right, about two miles away. The ship opened fire again.

They flew in a just 50 feet above the sea, with bullets passing straight through the Swordfish's canvas structure. At 2,000 yards Moffat relied entirely on his navigator, who was hanging out of the plane, trying to calculate how close they could get before releasing a torpedo. The release of the torpedo immediately made the aircraft lighter, but Moffat could not afford to allow it to gain height, so he executed what is known as a flat turn, skidding round like a skier and heading back to *Ark Royal*. None of the pilots who returned knew whether they had been successful. Next day the navy closed in, opened up with its heavy guns, and subjected the *Bismarck* to its final agony. More than 2,000 perished that morning. Only 115 survived.

John Moffat

Moffat never claimed that it was his torpedo that disabled the German battleship, and was uncomfortable when a publisher insisted on giving his biography the title *I Sank the Bismarck*.

After analysis of the attack several years afterwards, he was told that his aircraft had indeed been responsible for the damage. Others challenged this assessment, particularly after divers inspected the wreckage in the early 2000s. Among naval aviators, however, it is generally accepted that it was Moffat's torpedo that hit the battleship's rudder.

John William Charlton Moffat was brought up in the Scottish Borders and educated at Kelso High School before leaving at the age of 16 to work for a local bus company. His father, Peter, had served in the navy during the First World War, joining in 1914 to qualify as an aeronautical engineer for the Royal Naval Air Service (RNAS), which included a stint in the seaplane carrier, *Ark Royal*.

In 1938, at the age of 19, John – usually known as Jock – applied to join the fledgling Fleet Air Arm. He was sent to a flight training school at Sydenham in Belfast, where he learnt to fly a Miles Magister. By 1941 he was serving – as his father had done before him – on board *Ark Royal*, which was stationed at Gibraltar, when the ship was ordered, as part of Force H, to hunt the *Bismarck*.

By that stage he had met and fallen in love with Marjorie Cochrane after meeting her at a tea party near Glasgow. They were married in June 1944, and had two daughters, Pat and Jan, both of whom shared an interest in horseriding. They survive him with four grandchildren.

After the war Moffat studied for a business degree and a diploma in hotel management and ran a successful hotel for many years. A lifetime supporter of the Fly Navy Heritage Trust, he marked the 75th anniversary of the sinking of the *Bismarck* by raising nearly £15,000 to keep a Swordfish flying. To the end of his days he kept with him the memory of the sinking German ship. "All I know is that there is not a single day of my life when that image of those poor men struggling in the freezing, oily waters has not entered my head, and I do not expect to see a day when it doesn't."

TAM DALYELL

Tenacious Labour politician, whose 'West Lothian question'
defined the dilemma of Scottish devolution

27 JANUARY 2017

IN FIGHTING FOR THE CAUSES in which he believed, but which his critics often regarded as obsessions, Tam Dalyell was the persecutor of prime ministers, the despair of party whips and the bane of speakers. His 17th-century ancestor was "Bluidy Tam" Dalyell, who earned his title as the brutal suppressor of the Covenanters under Charles II. This description could well have been used about Dalyell himself by successive Labour and Conservative leaders.

He helped to bring down one government (his own) and fought Harold Wilson on Europe and James Callaghan on devolution. More spectacularly he harried Margaret Thatcher on the sinking by a British submarine of the Argentine cruiser *General Belgrano* during the Falklands conflict, a vendetta that brought him notoriety.

When he announced in 2004 that he would not be standing at the next election, Tony Blair praised him in the House for his "fierce independence" and said "his persistence in pursuing causes close to his heart is legendary". This was generous, because one cause known to be close to Dalyell's heart was getting rid of Blair, a politician he described as the worst prime minister he had known. When pressed by John Humphrys on the *Today* programme about whether he had changed his mind about Blair being the worst he said: "Yes, Mr Humphrys. I have changed my mind. By far the worst."

Dalyell was against the Gulf War, sanctions against Iraq and the war with Iraq. He attacked the Gibraltar shootings by the SAS and questioned Colonel Gadaffi's links with the Lockerbie bomb. He opposed New Labour articles of faith such as university top-up fees and foundation hospitals. He called himself "Old Labour, primitive Labour even". He denied being a natural rebel, saying he was merely a dissenter. His favourite maxim was that one should never be afraid to be a bore; and he never showed any fear in this respect.

Sir Thomas Dalyell of the Binns, 11th baronet, Old Etonian, and descended from a long line of empire builders, was an unlikely socialist. His grandfather and great-grandfather were governors of Bengal. His father, Gordon Loch, became governor of Kuwait. His mother, Eleanor Isabel Wilkie-Dalyell, was the daughter of Sir James Bruce Wilkie-Dalyell, 9th baronet, and herself *de jure Baronetess*. With her husband changing his surname to hers, she assumed the surname and arms of Dalyell of the Binns, and her son was to inherit the title as 11th baronet after his mother's death in 1972, although he never used it, remaining throughout his political career plain Tam Dalyell.

It was to Kuwait that Dalyell's father and mother went when he was only a few weeks old, leaving him for five years in the care of his maternal grandmother. Although this practice was not unusual in those imperial days, Dalyell never forgave them. He spent much of his childhood at The Binns, a 17th-century turreted pile with portraits of ancestors scowling down and peacocks strutting round the lawn. With his background it seemed inevitable that when he went up to King's College, Cambridge, he should join the university Conservative association.

He left Cambridge for National Service in the Royal Scots Greys, a regiment that had been raised by "Bluidy Tam" Dalyell. It was always assumed he would be commissioned, but while on officer training he managed to lose a tank on Salisbury Plain. The view was taken that if he could lose a whole tank at this stage of his military career he might even lose a battle if he proceeded farther. "That was much exaggerated," he later said. "It's easy to do on Salisbury Plain." He was reduced to the ranks and became the only Dalyell over three centuries not to be commissioned in the family regiment. "I rather enjoyed my time in the Army," he later recalled, "which was perverse of me because I was the despair of every sergeant-major."

He was married in 1963 to Kathleen Wheatley. They honeymooned in Egypt and met President Nasser, who reproached Dalyell for not knowing Arabic as his father had. They had two children, Gordon and Moira. Both are lawyers. Like Kathleen, Dalyell became a teacher and taught at Bo'ness High School where he realised that with an accent like his he had to be as tough as his pupils. He had no trouble with discipline after his first term; his Eton background making him a believer in corporal punishment.

When he heard of a vacancy in the West Lothian constituency as a result of the death of the Labour MP he fought the 1962 by-election, winning with a majority of more than 11,000.

Dalyell's first campaign as an MP was typical. It was idiosyncratic, obsessional and successful. The tiny island of Aldabra, an atoll in the Indian Ocean near Diego Garcia, was about to become a military base with its unique wildlife doomed to extinction. Dalyell wrote and broadcast tirelessly about it until the supporters of the base abandoned their plan, worn down by his doggedness.

Later publicity was not so welcome. He was found guilty of leaking the report of a select committee on the chemical warfare centre at Porton Down in Wiltshire. While a member of the committee he revealed the contents of the report to a Sunday newspaper journalist. This produced uproar in the chamber with Dalyell admitting immediately that he was the source. He was expelled from the select committee and summoned to stand at the Bar of the House to be upbraided by the Speaker wearing a black cap, in a bizarre ceremony that has not been repeated.

It was in 1982, during the Falklands War and at one of the lowest points in his party's history, that he revived a good many Labour spirits, temporarily at least, as a result of the sinking of the *Belgrano*.

The Argentine warship had been outside the exclusion zone imposed by Britain when she was torpedoed with the loss of more than 300 of her complement. Dalyell was convinced Margaret Thatcher had authorised the sinking to scupper a Peru-sponsored plan for a negotiated peace. Despite the fact that all the time the *Belgrano* was afloat she presented a danger to the British task force, Dalyell continued his questioning. "But in which direction was she sailing?" he asked repeatedly with a defiance of the Speaker that caused him to be expelled from the Chamber five times. Evidence emerged later that the *Belgrano*, while sailing away at the moment she was torpedoed, was preparing to sail back. Dalyell was never convinced and never retracted, but what he did was to instil in the national consciousness a suspicion that there was something devious about the whole affair.

But the *Belgrano* question, effective though it seemed at the time, was eclipsed by the West Lothian question, given its name by Enoch Powell after Dalyell's then constituency. As an opponent of devolution he asked why a Scottish MP at Westminster should be able to vote on English affairs when an English MP could not vote on affairs in a constituency such as West Lothian. Logically this seemed unanswerable, but politically it was dangerous, and destructive even, for the Callaghan government. A referendum failed to secure the required percentage, the devolutionary cause was rebuffed for the time being, the two nationalist parties combined with the Conservatives and Liberals and the government was brought down by one vote. As a result, many senior Labour figures blamed Dalyell's efforts for the years of Conservative government that were to follow.

It took 18 years for Dalyell to arrive on the front bench. Michael Foot appointed him opposition spokesman on science in 1980, but he was dismissed even from this post for his opposition to the Falklands conflict.

As the longest-serving member of the Commons he became Father of the House when Edward Heath retired in 2001, but this did nothing to change his style. He remained stubborn, principled and intractable and still the same person who had deliberately called Mrs Thatcher a liar (automatic expulsion from the House) and a bounder (a splendidly Etonian piece of invective).

Distinctive in looks, with thick strands of wavy hair worn in an upturned ice-cream-cone style, he was a serious-minded man who was little given to small talk, his mode of speech shifted from low and deliberate to conspiratorial and distracted. His great passions away from politics were chess – he once played Garry Kasparov – and football.

He was a devoted fan of Hearts, perhaps in keeping with his quixotic pursuit of lost causes.

In January 2004 he announced that he would not be contesting the next general election and he left the House of Commons in April 2005, having been a member of parliament for 43 years. It was the end of a parliamentary career of magnificent, unrepentant, non-conformity.

Dalyell accepted that, in terms of career advancement, the price for being a crusading politician had been high. "But, honestly, cross my heart, I never had any prime ministerial ambitions," he said. "It would be dishonest, though, to tell you I wouldn't have dearly loved to have been a minister."

Tam Dalyell, Labour MP, was born on August 9, 1932. He died on January 26, 2017, aged 84.

* * *

INDEX